Filth

Filth

Dirt, Disgust, and Modern Life

William A. Cohen and Ryan Johnson, Editors

University of Minnesota Press
Minneapolis • London

Quotations from Lucretius, *On the Nature of Things: De rerum natura,* translated by Anthony M. Escolen (Baltimore: Johns Hopkins University Press, 1995). Reprinted courtesy of Johns Hopkins University Press.

Quotations from Edward Young, *Night Thoughts,* ed. Stephen Cornford (Cambridge: Cambridge University Press, 1989) reprinted with the permission of Cambridge University Press.

A longer version of chapter 2 appeared in *Critical Quarterly* 42, no. 1 (Spring 2000); published by Blackwell. Chapter 8 is reprinted in revised form from Neil Blackadder, *Performing Opposition: Modern Theater and the Scandalized Audience* (Westport, CT: Praeger, 2003). Praeger Publishers is an imprint of Greenwood Publishing Group, Inc., Westport, Connecticut.

Published by the University of Minnesota Press
111 Third Avenue South, Suite 290
Minneapolis, MN 55401-2520
http://www.upress.umn.edu

Filth : dirt, disgust, and modern life / William A. Cohen and Ryan Johnson, editors.
   p. cm.
   Includes bibliographical references and index.
ISBN 0-8166-4299-0 (hc : alk. paper) — ISBN 0-8166-4300-8 (pb : alk. paper)
   1. English literature—England—London—History and criticism. 2. French literature—France—Paris—History and criticism. 3. English literature—19th century—History and criticism. 4. London (England)—Social life and customs—19th century. 5. French literature—19th century—History and criticism. 6. Paris (France)—Social life and customs—19th century. 7. Refuse and refuse disposal—History—19th century. 8. Refuse and refuse disposal in literature. 9. Urban health—History—19th century. 10. Sanitation—History—19th century. 11. City and town life in literature. I. Cohen, William A., 1964- II. Johnson, Ryan, 1968-
PR8477.F55 2004
820.9'32421—dc22

2004013150

The University of Minnesota is an equal-opportunity educator and employer.

Contents

Introduction

Locating Filth

William A. Cohen

At the end of the twentieth century, New York City witnessed a propitious conjunction of literal and metaphorical filth. With the imminent closing of the Fresh Kills Landfill in Staten Island—the largest garbage dump in the world—the city faced a crisis over where to send the 12,000 tons of residential municipal waste it generates daily. Garbage barges trolled the waters surrounding New York as various proposals for waste elimination floated through city and state bureaucracies. At the same time, the *Sensation* exhibition of young British artists at the Brooklyn Museum of Art lived up to its name, largely because the painter Chris Ofili had affixed elephant dung to his picture of a Black Virgin Mary. Condemned as blasphemy by Mayor Rudolph Giuliani, the exhibit occasioned a culture war over censorship and artistic expression. The same mayor had made it the hallmark of his administration to clean up New York, both materially and morally. Changes in the city's landscape during his tenure were tangible: there was less garbage on the sidewalks (including the end of the plague of dog droppings); gone too were the squeegee men, the embodiment of urban poverty, who cleaned the windows of cars stopped in traffic for spare change; befouling city streets with crimes from drunkenness to public urination was no longer tolerated; and X-rated ("dirty") movie theaters and sex shops were aggressively driven out. New York residents and visitors regarded these so-called quality-of-life issues, attached to a decline in more serious crimes, with a mixture of relief and suspicion. Giuliani himself conceived of the relation between waste and productivity, both cultural and economic, as mutually generative: discussing the prospect of exporting New York's garbage to Virginia, he said: "People in Virginia like to utilize New York because we're a cultural center, a business center. . . . What goes along with being a cultural and business center is you're very crowded. We don't have the room here to handle the garbage that's produced not just by New Yorkers but by the three million more people that come here that utilize the place every day. So this is a reciprocal relationship."[1] If the rest of the country wanted New York's art and commerce, it would have to take the city's trash as well. In any number of ways, America's biggest city would no longer be its filthiest.

The coincidence of municipal garbage, animal feces, social outcasts, and sexual dirt in the cultural and economic capital of a triumphant America is striking, for it illustrates the ways in which filth has become a point of volatile contention in contemporary culture. Yet from a wider perspective, filth has always been a fundamental part of civilization, if only as its obverse, and while its forms vary from one culture to another, it is an enduring—perhaps a foundational—feature of human existence. While anthropologists and psychoanalysts have long recognized that the designation and rejection of filthy objects serve crucial functions in social management, psychological formation, and cultural identity, historians and scholars of the arts have recently begun interpreting the representation and significance of filth within particular cultures, recognizing that our waste and our dirt demand an analysis and a history.

This is the first collection of essays devoted to the subject of filth, and several reasons explain its appearance now. One is the contemporary urgency of the subject, encapsulated in the examples from New York City. Another reason is the evolution of academic discourse itself. Filth represents a cultural location at which the human body, social hierarchy, psychological subjectivity, and material objects converge. Standing at a theoretical crossroads, filth is at once figurative and substantive: it raises questions as much about dirty words as about the disposable paper on which they are often printed; it has as much to do with segments of the population rhetorically designated unwashed as with the water supply that might enable their cleansing. Under this rubric, we bring together interests in bodily waste, cultural refuse, and figurative dirt, considering the power of culturally mandated categories to exclude and repress. This book concentrates on a specific period of encounters with, and responses to, filth, in an effort to explicitly supply a history for the present moment, and to implicitly establish a dialogue with it. The essays in this volume take up a range of filthy topics, but they are bound together by a predominant focus on nineteenth-century Europe's foremost urban and cultural centers, London and Paris. In this period, the population of cities swelled enormously; the resulting urban filth, and the efforts to clean it up, surpassed its previous dimensions. Shifting social formations and the means developed for responding to them changed the physical topography of the city—with new slums, factories, sewers, and river embankments—as well as the civic landscape, with emerging public health bureaucracies, governmental commissions, technical specialists, and advocates for those condemned as filthy. Perceiving that cities' shapes and their inhabitants' behavior were rapidly changing, writers and other cultural producers also took filth as a novel focus in their work, devoting lavish attention not only to urban poverty and human waste but to the manifold metaphorical forms that filth might take.

The essays in this book explore aspects of filth in urban history, literature, and other arts. The next chapter sketches the historical precedents for nineteenth-century filth, while the last two consider the consequences and inheritance of filth in two crucial political formations of the twentieth century, colonialism and fascism; these closing essays accordingly broaden out from the nineteenth-century metropolitan centers to colonial India and interwar Europe. This introduction presents some foundational ideas about filth, drawing on theoretical writings from a number of disciplines, both to suggest the conceptual range of the topic and to situate the chapters that follow. To propose a theory of filth is to enter into a critical discourse already populated with studies of dirt, waste, pollution, abjection, disgust, mess, garbage, rubbish, dust, and shit. Some of these terms—cognates for and reactions to perceived filth—appear in the discussion that follows.

In a general sense, *filth* is a term of condemnation, which instantly repudiates a threatening thing, person, or idea by ascribing alterity to it. Ordinarily, that which is filthy is so fundamentally alien that it must be rejected; labeling something filthy is a viscerally powerful means of excluding it. Objects are filthy—polluting, infectious, fearful—the nearer they approach the ultimate repositories of decay and death, feces and corpses. People are denounced as filthy when they are felt to be unassimilably other, whether because perceived attributes of their identities repulse the onlooker or because physical aspects of their bodies (appearance, odor, decrepitude) do. Actions, behaviors, and ideas are filthy when they partake of the immoral, the inappropriate, the obscene, or the unaccountable—assessments that, while often experienced viscerally, are culturally constrained. All of these versions of filth have one thing in common: from the point of view of the one making the judgment, they serve to establish distinctions—"*That* is not me." For this very reason, however, filth is frequently so disturbing that it endangers the subjective integrity of the one who confronts it. By the time one has encountered and repudiated filth, it is too late—the subject is already besmirched by it. In this way, filth challenges the very dichotomy between subject and object. It does so according to a psychoanalytic logic, whereby repulsion and attraction unconsciously converge, and phenomenologically as well: the filth of the object defiles the subject who, identifying it as such, has had to rub up against it.

As it breaches subject/object distinctions in these ways, filth, in both its literal and figurative senses, covers two radically different imaginary categories, which I designate *polluting* and *reusable*. The former—filth proper—is wholly unregenerate, contaminating, even toxic, and demands to be rejected and denied. But when polluting or filthy objects are thought of as trash, waste, junk, or refuse, they become conceivably *productive*, the discarded sources in which riches may lie, and therefore fecund and fertile in their potential. Between use and refuse, the generative and the degenerate—even, at the most basic level, between life and death—there is a wide gulf. Yet distinct as these two modes of conceptualizing filth are, they are not strictly opposed, for an object can easily move from one to the other: to take a basic example, human excrement instantly taints anything it touches, but it is also the subject of countless schemes and fantasies for self-sustaining agricultural cycles. Anything designated *filthy* cannot be reused, at least until it is renamed or reconceived as waste or trash, which can be recycled. The potential for this reimagining means that the regenerative fantasy hovers at the edge of the filth that excludes it. In this way too, filth seems at once to occupy one side of the subject/object divide and to undo the opposition itself.

While filthy objects initially seem utterly repulsive and alien, then, they also paradoxically bear potential value. But are there conditions under which filth might actually provide an appealing point of identification for subjects? When people who understand themselves to be degraded, dispossessed, or abjected by a dominant order adopt and appropriate (sometimes even celebrate) what is otherwise castigated as filth, there is a possibility of revaluing filth while partially preserving its aversiveness. Not merely owning up to, but taking comfort in, one's own supposed dirtiness can serve powerful purposes of self-formation and group identification. In these senses, filth is put to important use, both psychologically and politically. The following consideration of filth is structured by the dialectical notion of it as object-making and subject-unsettling, at once dystopic pollution and utopian resource. I use this overarching scheme to bring together theorizations of filth from disparate intellectual traditions and disciplinary orientations, including psychoanalysis, phenomenology, and Marxism.

The starting point for any theory of dirt is Mary Douglas's classic study in comparative anthropology, *Purity and Danger* (1966), where she works with a structural definition of dirt as "matter out of place." Douglas proposes that an awareness of dirt indicates the existence of *system*: nothing is inherently dirty; dirt is simply "matter" that, within a particular framework, appears in the wrong location, and so violates a sense of the order of the world. Such a sense of order is culturally specific—wearing outdoor shoes in a Japanese home is considered dirty, while taking them off can be dirty in an American one—but the fundamental structure of dirtiness is constant. Pollution is not simply the opposite of cleanliness; it also arises out of a *confusion* of categories. Confronting ambiguity, Douglas argues, can be frightening, but it generates both sacred and taboo objects and practices. Douglas's account of dirt here moves from pollution toward reuse, for encountering ambiguity is potentially productive: art, humor, and horror result from such borderline feelings. Indeed, she hints, since the anomalies can "enrich meaning or call attention to other levels of existence," they can seem essential to culture itself.[2]

Those building upon Douglas's foundational work have moved in a variety of directions, from a focus on human bodies and sexuality, where this discussion begins, to the broader social and economic context addressed later. In its most intimate and familiar sense, filth is the waste our bodies excrete, which belongs to us and which we seek to dispose of. A basic task of modern civilization is to provide the means of this disposal; industrial society, for example, supplies flush toilets and underground sewers, which make this function all but invisible to public consciousness. Beyond the excrement that comes out of healthy bodies is the variety of (perhaps even filthier) bodily excretions—blood, vomit, pus, and so on—from sick ones, and other corporeal liquids (menstrual blood, semen) that can seem more or less filthy according to context. Dying, dead, and rotting bodies themselves, as they putrefy, are perhaps the filthiest of all, and our proximity to this ultimate filth may help to explain some of the psychological potency of corpses. These filthiest of substances—human waste and human remains—have long been available to utopian fantasies of reuse and regeneration, however, principally in the form of agricultural fertilizer, but it is only in the relatively clean, desiccated form of ashes and dust that they are so conceivable; a direct encounter with them is almost always polluting.

A book that lays out some of these principles, William Ian Miller's *Anatomy of Disgust* (1997), challenges Douglas's cultural relativism, arguing that some objects—those rotting corpses, for example—are, if not universally disgusting, inherently available to being coded as disgusting. "Culture can override the tendencies that come with the disgust affect," Miller writes, "but it has to work harder to do so."[3] As Miller shows, the quality of disgustingness frequently attaches to objects that move into or out of the body; it thus seems to have a virtually biological basis. For Miller, it is nearly impossible to recover *truly* filthy objects for any use at all. Disgust has much more to say about pollution than reuse, for this feeling itself is a principal means by which the distinction is made. That filth often occurs in proximity to the human body means that its *intimacy* with the human can help to account for its power.

This proximity points to another set of filth associations: the sexual. In part because of the equation between women and sex that is axiomatic to a male-dominated heterosexual order, female sexuality (and femininity itself) have a particular connection to filth. The filthiness ascribed to women, which is hardly confined to Leviticus, belongs to an age-old tradition of misogyny that, as feminist theorists such as Mary Russo have argued, reveres virginity and reproduction while condemning women for their supposedly uncontained, excessive bodies.[4] Sexual activity has often been tainted with the charge of filthiness, which has in turn made the word *filth*, like its synonym *smut* (originally meaning soot or smudge), another term for pornography, obscenity, and sometimes sex itself.

The most influential discussion of filth in its fundamental corporeal and gendered forms is Julia Kristeva's *Powers of Horror: An Essay on Abjection* (1980), which brings Douglas's theory together with Freud's and Sartre's.[5] Kristeva associates a repudiated maternal figure with "the abject" and affiliated notions of disgusting, rejected objects and experiences (frequently involving bodily orifices and fluids). The abject, neither subject nor object, is the pre-oedipal basis that the symbolic order must disavow, and yet on which it depends. Like Douglas's taboo, Kristeva's abject occurs at sites of bodily and cultural boundary violations, but now in relation to maternal separation; the horror resulting from such violation testifies to the subject's unconscious remnants of feeling undifferentiated from the mother, and thus to the disruption of the symbolic ordering of the world. Supplying a psychoanalytic explanation for the many ways in which the dominant order condemns the feminine (especially the feminine-maternal) as filthy, Kristeva also strives to revalue the abject as a position from which a critique of such misogyny is possible: the abject grants the oedipally repudiated mother a certain power.[6] In this way standing outside the subject/object divide, the abject spans our notions of both pollution and reuse.

Psychoanalytic discussions of filth, even when they do not explicitly articulate a biological basis, have rightly been criticized for their transhistorical assumptions, but they have the utility of showing how contradictory ideas—about filth as both polluting and valuable—can be held at once. While feminist discussions have illuminated the misogyny, as well as the subversive potential, implicit in orthodox views of the female body's filthiness, traditional psychoanalytic discussions—as well as revisionary and recuperative queer ones—gravitate toward the anus, the locus of filth on the normative (and thus implicitly male) body.[7] In the Freudian account of the "anal stage," associations with material that comes to be culturally coded as filthy are repressed through the process of oedipalization. Yet an attachment to anality is preserved through the mechanism of *sublimation*, which we might take as a psychoanalytic term for the reuse side of the filth thesis I have proposed. As Norman O. Brown discusses in his influential explication of Freud's theory, the child holds dear his excrement because it comes from him and might be given to another, but he is forced to renounce this attachment as part of his acculturation. The attachment does not simply go away, however; it is sent into the unconscious, where it persists, and it reemerges in sublimated form, classically as a fixation with money—"filthy lucre." Money is an intrinsically useless object on which sacred value has been magically conferred; at the same time, money has an unconscious taint of filth, while feces retain a trace of its infantile value. As Freud puts it, "excrement is aliment."[8]

Many theorists have adopted Freud's association between money and filth, but it has also been resisted and criticized for the normalizing oedipal narrative upon which its structure of psychological equivalencies rests. Particularly when it is understood to be culturally constrained, however, this account importantly links bodily matters to economic ones through the connecting term *value*. Dominique Laporte's recently translated *History of Shit* (1978) extends this analysis, bringing together Marxist and psychoanalytic theories of waste and value to show how the modern limit case of the putrescent object—human feces—has itself historically been a potent source of value. Laporte's narrative conforms to Freud's in *Civilization and Its Discontents* (1930): as human beings evolved and developed social arrangements, they renounced their attachment to excrement and its attendant sensory modality, olfaction, privileging sight and distance over smell and proximity. According to this developmental model, which each individual recapitulates ontogenetically, "civilized" society and modern sexuality require that excrement be repudiated as filthy, shameful, and private. In following these dictates, however, individuals and societies preserve a fundamental attachment to filth, which retains its psychical value. This value resurfaces, like the return of the repressed, in certain specifically bourgeois traits of accumulating and hoarding capital.

In a tone of manic hilarity, Laporte suggests that conceptions of shit are at the heart of the modern institution of a public/private divide; his translator proposes that "the history of shit becomes the history of subjectivity."[9] How can this be? Laporte's analysis originates in a 1539 French edict requiring that human waste be conserved in the home, not thrown into the street; while its aim may have been to improve the cleanliness of thoroughfares, its effect was to form a basis for ideas about private property. Filth has value in its very negativity, according to Laporte: "As a 'private' thing—each subject's business, each proprietor's responsibility—shit becomes a political object through its constitution as the dialectical other of the 'public.'"[10] Shit is the source for individuation and private accumulation; like money, it is a dirty, degenerate hoard. Particularly in the nineteenth century, human excrescences get tangled up in fantasies of emergent value, and polluting substances spill into their apparent opposite, the recyclable source of hidden riches. The frequently recounted (if improbable) origin of the quintessentially British term for a toilet encapsulates this evolutionary story: the word *loo*, according to folk etymology, is a corrupted and Anglicized form of *gardez l'eau*, the warning that was supposed to precede the pitching of chamber-pot contents into French streets before the advent of the water closet. In suggesting a development from public acts of contamination to the euphemism for an emphatically private location, this story of *loo* condenses a whole history of bourgeois manners.

Laporte sees value as ordinarily inchoate in organic waste; in other economic discussions, waste, in "higher" cultural forms, is more readily understood to contain hidden worth. At the farthest extreme of the *reuse* side of the distinction—and thus at some distance from the unregenerate pollution usually associated with filth—is Michael Thompson's *Rubbish Theory: The Creation and Destruction of Value* (1979), which analyzes the economic systems under which waste objects come to be revalued. Thompson is unusual among economists, who ordinarily consider value a function of *scarcity*, and rarely take waste as anything other than purely negative. Thompson postulates that, while most commodities are either "transient" or "durable," some objects can move from the former category to the latter; a secondhand vase, for example, once thought of as junk, might suddenly be seen as a valuable antique. His "rubbish theory" establishes that, in order for an object to shift from transient (of decreasing value) to durable (of increasing value), it must first reside in the rubbish zone, where it has no value at all. The phase of devaluation is gradual, while that of revaluation is sudden, and the process is unidirectional: an object can move from transient to rubbish, and from rubbish to durable, but not in the other direction. The largest consequence of Thompson's theory is that value in general comes to be predicated on rubbish, although there is a high degree of cultural relativity: Thompson rejects the notion that there are "natural limits" on the potential for revaluation through rubbish.[11] Rather than conceiving of rubbish as the limit to economic activity—the zone that stands outside, behind, or beneath the marketplace—Thompson places rubbish back at its center. Here is the economic fascination of filth: that reserves of value might be hidden precisely in matter that seems most worthless. In this view, almost anything can be recuperated as durable, although Thompson's focus on furniture, housing stock, and collectibles—a very bourgeois universe of discarded objects—keeps the theory away from troublesome questions about more disgusting constituents of the garbage pail.[12] Even readers skeptical about the psychoanalytic view that "excrement is aliment" will admit that something nearly alchemical has happened when the clutter in the attic suddenly gets bid up in the collectible market.

Having moved from the body and sexuality to the economic and social realm, we can turn to an influential work—yet another inheritor of Douglas's anthropology of pollution—that explicitly integrates the psychological and the political. Peter Stallybrass and Allon White foreground the notion of *transgression* in applying theories of dirt and boundary violation to European culture since the Renaissance. Using a model in which the dichotomy clean/dirty is one (but not the only) manifestation of a broader opposition between high and low, they emphasize the potential creative fecundity of transgressive experiences. Retaining Douglas's structuralism, Stallybrass and White establish isomorphic continuities ("transcodings") among different realms of experience: the social order (class and urban topography), the human body, and psychical arrangements as described by Freud. For instance, they show how nineteenth-century lumpenproletariats and the slums they inhabit are represented in terms continuous with those of base animality (pigs and rats), with the "lower bodily stratum," and with castigated forms of sexuality.[13] Stallybrass and White establish that "what is *socially* peripheral is so frequently *symbolically* central,"[14] arguing that the "high"—members of the dominant class—are fascinated and threatened by the "low," as well as by a hybrid or mixed form of low and high together. In this account, the low—what is marked as dirty, disreputable, or excluded from official culture—is itself crucial to culture's self-constitution. The distinction between categories of pollution and reuse here seems highly negotiable.

This structural argument might be extended, with some modifications, from class distinctions to those of race and ethnicity. Racial thinking, particularly in the nineteenth century, relies on a language of hygiene, purity, and taint, frequently establishing distinctions through notions of mixture and hybridity. This conception of race, which has deep roots in the West, and which both draws on and contributes to ideas about sanitation, culminates in worries over degeneration at the end of the nineteenth century and in the eugenics movements of the early twentieth century, whose legacy was in part the fascist project of racial cleansing.[15] As Richard Dyer has argued, drawing on the work of Joel Kovel, the construction of the so-called white race has historically been founded on a fundamental symbolic equivalence between whiteness and purity, between blackness (or any putative nonwhiteness) and corruption, sin, and filth.[16]

The work of Georges Bataille provides the fullest elaboration of the social, economic, and psychological dimensions of devaluing people, objects, and practices marked as filthy, which we have been following. Bataille's writings on waste and excess, however, suggest ways of connecting body and mind, the discarded and the valuable, which fall outside the more or less structuralist models of nearly all the writers considered thus far, insofar as they treat human experience as riven into positive and negative categories that cannot keep from contaminating each other. In a provocative remapping of the human body and its products, Bataille assigns the anus functions usually associated with the head, seeing in it "all the potential for blossoming, all the possibilities for the liberation of energy."[17] Bataille celebrates and finds a paradoxical potential for liberation in waste products (excrement, phlegm) and practices (mutilation, sacrifice) ordinarily considered the very opposite of what civilization esteems. But this is not a simple reversal that, by a

Freudian logic, merely reaffirms established values in inverting them. Introducing a collection of Bataille's essays, Allan Stoekl writes that "The fall of one system is not stabilized, is not replaced with the elevation of another. . . . Filth does not 'replace' God; there is no new system of values, no new hierarchy. In the *Documents* articles, Bataille's attention wanders through a disseminated field, a labyrinth, of possibilities; flowers, excrement, toes, Gnosticism, freaks, mouth, sun, severed fingers."[18]

David Trotter's *Cooking with Mud*, which considers the place of "mess" in Victorian art and literature, invokes Bataille, sharing in his effort to move outside bifurcated thinking about filth.[19] Discussing European and American works from the second half of the nineteenth century, Trotter distinguishes *mess* from objects and phenomena that psychoanalytic and economic interpretations explain as overdetermined *waste* by bringing them within a rational, bisected system of order versus disorder. While a mess can be polluting, it is the chance encounter with oddly juxtaposed objects, which sparks an idea or an insight, that most interests Trotter. He suggests that attention to both material and ideational messes comes to be part of modernity: around the 1860s, he argues, mess started to interest writers and artists in a way that presaged modernism, and he locates this shift in the context of the decline of various kinds of determinism, the rise of democracy, and a new emphasis on chance and contingency. In envisioning a shifting line between ideas and things, between subjects and objects, and between human sensory experience and the phenomenal world, Trotter's argument challenges the psychoanalytic conception of filth emblematized by Stallybrass and White's and Laporte's models. The essays in this collection draw on both kinds of methodologies, placing them in dialogue with each other.

The double nature of filth, both dangerously polluting and bounteously providing, has special relevance for London and Paris at the end of the nineteenth century, for it is an important constituent in the imagination, as well as the material reality, of modernity. These cities were capitals of a new kind, in terms of their size and scope, their place in national and imperial self-conception, and their relation to the massive industrialization earlier in the century. Discussions of urban space and modern life in this era emphasize waste in new ways, even as they adapt traditional ideas about filth.

While filth of one sort or another may have always been a basis on which cultures make distinctions, the *kinds* of distinctions it permits are historically variable. Before the nineteenth century, filth often instituted discriminations based on religious doctrine and manners.[20] Stephen Greenblatt has argued, for instance, that in the period around the Re-formation, doctrinal and affective differences between Catholics and Protestants are embodied in disparate attitudes toward excrement.[21] Showing how filth concepts function in a different set of contexts in an earlier period, Georges Vigarello analyzes attitudes toward bathing and dirt in France since the Middle Ages. He vividly demonstrates how historically variable the idea of cleanliness is: not only was clean linen, rather than clean skin, the sign of hygiene and respectability (*propreté*) for much of the sixteenth and seventeenth centuries, but immersing the body in water was long thought to be dangerous rather than salubrious, because of fears of waterborne plague and contagion penetrating the body.[22] Such attitudes are revealing not only about notions of clean-liness but also about class-appropriate behavior, respectability, and the appearance of health. Vigarello's study converges with Alain Corbin's history of the sense of smell in France, helping to explain why, toward the end of the eighteenth century, washing the body became important again to an idea of cleanliness. In this period, Corbin suggests, air quality came to be the standard of cleanliness and healthfulness, while the threshold of tolerable smells was correspondingly lowered; sanitation became equivalent with eliminating newly significant bad smells, both of individuals and of places.[23] The history of bourgeois taste, to which Corbin's study largely belongs, parallels the phantasmatic evolution that Freud recounts: a story of moving from an unselfconscious attitude toward human waste and decay (sometimes even a use and enjoyment of it) to its repudiation as filthy in the age of bourgeois individuation.

While ideas about filth continued to inform conceptions of spirit, manners, and self in the nineteenth century, the predominant discourse of filth focused on urban sanitation. The process of generating a language and a set of institutions for construing locations and populations as dirty or clean did not simply eliminate traditional notions of filth; it amalgamated these ideas, putting them to new uses. Christopher Hamlin has supplied a clear example of this appropriation in an article on the links between the science of pathology and the religious discourse of salvation in Victorian Britain, demonstrating how sanitary and spiritual ideas about filth overlapped and mutually informed each other. Just as divine revelation enabled wasteful sin and corruption to be cleansed through spiritual rebirth, Hamlin shows, so pathological processes of putrefaction might materially transform waste into abundance. Hamlin suggestively makes the case for a convergence between the two accounts of filth that I have outlined, as polluting and as reusable, on one hand in the sciences of disease pathology and agricultural decomposition, and on the other in theological discourses about sin and providence.[24]

Cleanliness and filth continue to encode and structure self-conceptions in both spiritual and social-class terms during the nineteenth century. The basic form of the Augustinian spiritual autobiography persists: abasement leads to salvation, becoming filthy enables ritual cleansing. It is propounded in religious testimonials (from Hopkins's pious confessional lyrics to Rimbaud's blasphemous inversion of the tradition) and in numerous secular life stories as well. Such continuities extend into the psychological and sexual versions of dirty abasement that proliferated in the nineteenth century, reaching an apotheosis in Leopold von Sacher-Masoch's *Venus in Furs* (1869), and sponsoring a legacy in both artistic productions and the psychological theory devoted to explaining it.[25] The expanding market and taste for pornography during the nineteenth century further testifies to the lure and the horror of dirty words.

Existing vocabularies about bodily, moral, religious, and psychological dirt persisted, then, but filth in nineteenth-century Europe—for its contemporaries, as for the historical memory of them—first and foremost signifies urban squalor and disease, as well as the public, institutional treatment of these ills. The status of waste itself changed in the course of the nineteenth century, a process most readily apparent in increasingly crowded metropolises, whose exploited workers populated the factories that were the engines of industrialism. These factories, which directly polluted air, land, and water, had secondary effects in the desolate living conditions of these laborers, who, as Friedrich Engels documented in his 1845 portrait of Manchester, were kept in destitute poverty. Even worse off than the factory workers who were made to inhabit filth—and were thus identified with it by their social superiors— were the scavengers, rag- and bone-pickers, mud larks, and other denizens of the urban underworld, whom Henry Mayhew most famously documented and brought to middle-class attention in his articles for the *Morning Chronicle* (published in 1861 as the four-volume *London Labour and the London Poor*). The spread of contagious diseases— most notoriously, cholera—associated with overcrowding and poor sanitation made the filth of urban slums still more terrifying, both for their inhabitants and for middle-class observers. As an institution, public health itself arose in the nineteenth century as a proposed solution to the sanitary problems that were identified as the great evil in the works by reformers Edwin Chadwick and A.-J.-B. Parent-Duchâtelet that have come to be touchstones for students of social history. Changes in urban topography itself—from Baron Haussmann's brutal rationalization of Paris and from Joseph Bazalgette's massive scheme for an intercepting sewer system in London—were directly tied to claims for public health. As filth came to be increasingly understood as a problem for urban planning, public health, medicine, and science, it was, in short, subject to the great nineteenth-century European project of bureaucratization. Yet if such urban filth was felt by righteous enforcers of middle-class hygiene to be unimpeachably polluting, the very moral and sanitary campaigns to which it gave rise testify to its utility, for it was an endless resource, conceptually and ideologically.

The lives and living conditions of the urban poor have been richly documented by contemporaries and historians alike.[26] Institutions that managed or sought to ameliorate urban poverty—such as poor laws, the workhouse, sanitary reform, and agencies for preventing and treating diseases—have been investigated extensively, both in Whig histories that emphasize the development of governmental entities in response to public health crises and in ideological analyses, largely inspired by Foucault, that regard such institutions as sinister agencies for the regulation of subjects and populations.[27] Foucault's studies of hospitals, madhouses, prisons, and other institutions show how modern subjectivity operates on a system of hierarchical exclusions; in combination with the work of such historians as Michel de Certeau and Norbert Elias, these studies demonstrate how even the seemingly mundane micropractices of everyday life have profound social meaning, especially in the regulation of cleanliness and dirt. Foucault, Stallybrass and White, Laporte, and Corbin share a reading of the bourgeois "obsession" with filthiness and stench, embodied in public health campaigns and the miasma theory of infection, both as a justification for surveillance and control of the poor and as a means of consolidating bourgeois identity itself (by endlessly repudiating its denigrated other). Other scholars, frequently with a Marxist and feminist orientation, have reevaluated the living conditions of the urban poor through consideration of the lives and voices of those people themselves, as well as through analyses of the institutions that patronized or coerced them.[28] The great nineteenth-century campaigns to eradicate disease and cleanse the cities of their filth were at once vast improvements and often violently discriminatory; as the monumental installation of metropolitan sanitation systems, the regulation of food and water quality, and campaigns against contagious diseases dovetailed with the increasing state regulation of individuals' bodies and freedoms, the disenfranchised—the poor, women, foreigners—suffered first and worst.

If the period is broadly distinguished from earlier moments in the powerful arsenal it developed for confronting and managing the filth of urban industrialism and the disciplinary uses to which it put these weapons, however, the nineteenth century also opened up new possibilities for subjects, objects, and bodies in the fantasies of reuse that arose from these projects, as well as in the visions of modernity—in movements decadent and utopian, bohemian and modernist—that even the most abject loss of self in filth seemed to enable. The Parisian *flâneur* enshrined by Baudelaire (and by Benjamin in discussing him) provides but one example of urban refuse remade as cultural capital; his later avatar, the bohemian, might actually get lost in the dirt, as do the decadent, immoral protagonists of Huysmans's and Wilde's fiction. Although Paris is the locus classicus for discussions of such diabolically ebullient modernity, Lynda Nead has made a case for also considering late-Victorian London in relation to Benjamin's concept of how "the sites of the modern city stand on layer upon layer of an underground city, which maintains a hellish and ghostlike presence within modernity."[29] Both Nead and Judith Walkowitz have shown how men and women, people of different classes and subclasses, different races and national origins, of varied occupations and interests, might meet each other on the street and in the shops, at the waterfront or in alleys, and their encounters cannot be resolved into formulas about condescension, aspiration, exploitation, or liberation.[30]

The new form that cities took—densely populated, sharply stratified, and pestilentially filthy—gave birth to new modes of representation as well: the chronicle of urban poverty became a literary subgenre as journalists, philanthropists, reformers, and novelists supplied rich contemporary accounts of the types of urban filth as it was lived.[31] Exposés and politically motivated fiction and nonfiction alike aimed at middle-class sympathies and working-class solidarity. This may well have been a dirtier world than was previously known; it certainly was represented to its inhabitants as being so. In fiction, the most prominent chroniclers of urban poverty and its dirt, though widely different in their political orientations, were Eugène Sue, Charles Dickens, and Émile Zola, in whose work the anatomy of the slum, its abject terrors and its sometimes romantic or sentimental promise of renewal, were major themes. Throughout nineteenth-century literature, the representation of dirt—in forms ranging from slums to contagious diseases to pestiferous rivers—was mapped onto traditional themes of moral, social, economic, and spiritual decay, in ways that made these ancient literary subjects newly relevant to contemporary life.

The relative continuity, for nineteenth-century thinkers, between domains that tend to be distantly separated for us (such as sanitary science and religious faith) helps to explain the extraordinary imaginative fascination—evident in both fiction and reality—with capturing and reusing human waste. The numerous schemes for so-called sewage farms outside of Paris and London appealed to an ideal of the city's waste becoming the countryside's riches (an aspiration, it is worth noting, updated in Mayor Giuliani's claims about New York's garbage).[32] This was not exclusively a literary fantasy, but its most eloquent spokesman was Victor Hugo, whose *Les Misérables* (1862) contains passages dear to all sewage-reclaiming utopianists:

> There is no guano comparable in fertility to the detritus of capital. A great city is the most powerful of stercoraries. If our gold is filth, on the other hand, our filth is gold. . . . All the human and animal manure which the world loses, restored to the land instead of being thrown into the water, would suffice to nourish the world.
>
> These heaps of garbage at the corners of the stone blocks, these tumbrils of mire jolting through the streets at night, these horrid scavengers' carts, these fetid streams of subterranean slime, which the pavement hides from you, do you know what all this is? It is the flowering meadow . . . it is the satisfied low of huge oxen at evening . . . it is bread on your table, it is warm blood in your veins, it is health, it is joy, it is life. Thus wills that mysterious creation which is transformation upon earth and transfiguration in heaven.
>
> . . . It is the very substance of the people which is carried away, here drop by drop, there in floods, by the wretched vomiting of our sewers into the rivers, and the gigantic collection of our rivers into the ocean. Each hiccough of our cloaca costs us a thousand francs. From this two results: the land impoverished and the water infected. Hunger rising from the furrow and disease rising from the river.[33]

Hugo makes the case for recuperating waste and transforming it into value more in terms of economic utility and organic cycles than in a religious idiom, yet the stentorian, nearly evangelical rhetoric lends a sacred aspect to these organic processes: the world cannot have been designed, by God or nature, for human waste to go unused. Modern conurbations have moved so far from the natural cycles of regeneration, he suggests, that they threaten to poison themselves with their own waste, like some self-consuming monster. This reverential attitude comes down to us in the antiquarian form of the tourist attraction, such as the ultra-hygienic sewer museum at the Pont d'Alma on the Seine, and the lovingly restored neo-Gothic Victorian sewage pumping station at Abbey Mills outside London.

The lure and the fear of contamination were not only functions of industrialized urban culture, however; as European empires increasingly came to dominate other parts of the world, filth was also a powerful marker of racial and national distinctions, which were overlaid—unevenly and sometimes unpredictably—on those of sanitary policy affecting conceptions of class and gender. That dirt was a potent force, both racially and sexually, in a commodity marketplace conjoined with an imperial imagination is an argument that Anne McClintock makes in *Imperial Leather: Race, Gender, and Sexuality in the Colonial Contest*. While this work does not address the sanitary administration at large, its discussion of the individual unit of personal hygiene—soap—and the dirt it was meant to eliminate suggests a principal line of demarcation between colony and metropolis. The feminized, domestic fantasy of cleanliness depended on an empire that worked to clean up (and to keep at a hygienic distance) colonies that were by definition dirty. Discussing Victorian advertisements, McClintock writes that soap "emerged commercially during an era of impending crisis and social calamity, serving to preserve, through fetish ritual, the uncertain boundaries of class, gender, and race identity."[34] One danger of the imperial capital's undeniable filthiness was that it would fracture a fundamentally hygienic fantasy—implicitly white, bourgeois, and feminine—of civilized English nationality.

Sanitary policing, both domestically and abroad, allowed the ascription of filth to subordinated populations, as capitals such as London and Paris were becoming more ethnically and racially mixed. Domestic subjects designated filthy for their low class or status were themselves reciprocally represented in popular culture as foreign. This process is made vividly apparent in the links Erin O'Connor establishes between the urban sanitation system and racial phantasmatics in *Raw Material: Producing Pathology in Victorian Culture*. She proposes that "Asiatic cholera staged a traumatic transformation of white, working-class flesh into worthless black stuff—in medicine and popular journalism the dark, dehydrated corpse of the cholera victim is likened to tar, coal, pitch, and even feces." Race is the central term in this equation; by importing an idea of foreign infection—cholera as the corrupt wages of South Asia's imperial domination—British commentators strove to displace the sources of filth in their domestic factories and cities. O'Connor suggests the visceral materiality of the conjunctions: "In the minds of physicians and social commentators alike, the choleraic body and the city were coextensive. . . . Shooting out gallons of fluid that, like the London water supply, was clouded with foreign matter, the choleraic body in turn became a signifier for faulty sewerage."[35] Disease, foreignness, and the sanitary administration come together in this vision of wholly unregenerate pollution; yet in being contingent upon the enormous wealth derived from extracting materials from the colonies and manufacturing goods in factories, this filth is also the other face of Victorian progress.

Filth, then, is conceptually central in the very period in which it is supposed—thanks to new technologies of sanitary science and waste disposal—to have become materially less problematic. At the point of an emergent modernity, filth supplies a means of both ordering and disrupting individual and collective experience alike. Confrontations with filth justify the regulation of populations, and while occupying the filthy position only rarely serves to empower people, adapting and responding to it can often be culturally regenerative—exciting, dangerous, exotic, and rewarding—as encounters in the modern urban marketplace, or the mutually revealing colonial encounter, attest.

The essays in this volume are local in their attentions, but considered together they contribute to this larger story about filth in the West since the mid-nineteenth century. This narrative has a number of reappearing characters—including the corpse, the prostitute, the foreigner, and the bohemian—as well as certain recurring sites in the city: the sewer, the graveyard, the slum, and, perhaps paradoxically, the well-scrubbed middle-class home. While it would be artificial to impose a plot on a collection of essays, the chapters move roughly chronologically, while shifting back and forth between London and Paris. All of the chapters concern a mix of material and metaphorical filth, although the kinds of dirt they treat vary widely, reflecting the complexity and suggestiveness of the term in this period. In frequently focusing on human bodies, identities, and the form of the modern city, they tell a story about how filth, whose exclusion supplies a means for modern urban citizens to define themselves, can also serve as a resource and a rallying point for the organization of new types of community—even if it is a community bound in its abjection.

The first two chapters make further historical and methodological contributions to what we call "fundamentals of filth." In chapter 1, Christopher Hamlin provides a general historical framework for considering one primary filth question—what happens to the body once the soul has departed it?—before investigating a particular nineteenth-century dispute over the disposal of human remains. Hamlin traces a long literary tradition of taking comfort in the organic recycling of decayed corporeal matter, which erupted into public discourse in an 1870s debate over whether cremation or decomposition was preferable for completing the cycle that returns dust to dust. This chapter brings us unusually close not only to a positive valuation of filth but to a notion of "self as filth"— to that paradox of filth as a human subject, not an object. Ultimately, Hamlin shows, the paradox cannot be sustained: to value oneself as decomposing matter is to cease to envision that matter as filthy. One can perhaps happily imagine being dust, but not being putrefied. Yet in a revealing move of historical estrangement, this chapter shows how some Victorians were willing to push the identification between human subjects and filth much further than we are ordinarily willing to go today.

Moving from decay to disgust, the second chapter also insists on the historical specificity, and the unpredictability, of reactions to filth. In considering how George Eliot, Chadwick, and Mayhew portray the sensory perception of objects, David Trotter challenges a psychoanalytic understanding of disgust as masking a latent desire for its object; he proposes instead that disgust is "an overwhelmingly disintegrative and agonistic principle." In so doing, he avoids two pitfalls of reading filth (particularly in its olfactory modality) without adequate attention to the phenomenological experience of it: an insistently causal interpretation of history (for example, the claim that *fear* of laborers causes bourgeois commentators to feel disgust for them) and an overly generalizing Foucauldian view that relegates all social encounters to surveillance and discipline. Making the case for a methodologically innovative "cultural phenomenology," Trotter uses Heidegger's remarks on anxiety to contest the psychoanalytic ascription of filth-induced disgust to a nexus of fear and desire. This argument is implicitly in conversation with other chapters that draw on psychoanalytic formulations.

The chapters in part II, "Sanitation and the City," pursue the relation between the human body and social subject-formation by investigating other affective, ideological, and sensory aspects of filth specifically in an urban topography. In chapter 3, David L. Pike compares the differing attitudes in London and Paris toward the most significant nineteenth-century contribution to fantasies of the underground: the sewer. While English commentators tended to emphasize the sewer as a disposer of waste, Pike argues, the French were enchanted by the idea of its transformative capacity, suggesting that the poles of pollution and reuse proposed above might have a national variation. Pike shows how crucial *spatial* conceptions are to such distinctions, helping to move beyond the dominant "vertical," or hierarchical, account of urban organization that relegates the underground to sheer filth, both among Victorian commentators and in recent historiography. Pursuing the consequences of such a revaluation for interclass contact and for ideas about prostitution (which were frequently entangled with debates over urban waste), Pike challenges the assignment of any given bodily experience to a structurally established category, such as Douglas's pollution. Filth, under certain circumstances, might surprisingly be a good or enjoyable thing.

The spatial organization of cities is key to understanding their representation in literary writing and social science alike, as Pamela K. Gilbert argues in chapter 4. This chapter shows how a medical practice of mapping the origin and spread of disease converges with Dickens's narrative distribution of filth in carefully specified urban locations. As Gilbert demonstrates, mapping the London metropolis for sanitary purposes—identifying the sites of dirt, disease, and poverty—was sometimes hard to distinguish from the writer's project of constructing a novel. Gilbert concentrates on Dickens's last completed work, *Our Mutual Friend* (1865), the Victorian novel most famous for a relentless focus on waste, turning our attention from the novel's renowned dust heaps to the fetidness of its river. The pestilential city correlates and commingles with the individual human subject who is in both physical and psychological danger of dissolving into a liquid mass. Dickens confronts these threats by counterposing them to a thematics of both urban and bodily continence: the novel strives to embank the self.

While Gilbert considers how, for Dickens, the river allegorizes and effects a dissolution of human identity, David S. Barnes focuses in chapter 5 on the ways in which experiences of disgust, in response to filthy rivers, have the capacity to transform urban space. Focusing on two vivid historical examples of encounters with filth, Barnes compares the reactions of French and English commentators to the nauseating stenches that emanated from the Seine and the Thames. These stenches— largely the result of untreated human waste, from rapidly growing metropolises, being deposited in the rivers—provide a telling comparative case study that enables Barnes, like Trotter, to historicize disgust. Although a seemingly physiological, transcultural experience, disgust, Barnes argues, can have widely different material consequences, even in cases separated by only twenty-two years and the English Channel. This emotion spurred the English to rapid action, resulting in the construction of an intercepting sewer system, while it drove the French into bureaucratic wrangling and protracted disagreement. Reading this history in the context of developments in bacteriology, Barnes attributes the difference in part to dissimilar national attitudes toward, and understandings of, the relation between odor and disease.

The chapters in the next section, "Polluting the Bourgeois," analyze a variety of cultural products to argue that filth contributes to the normative, middle-class national identities (both individual and collective) that repudiate it and, in so doing, helps to shape modernity. A signal marker of bourgeois Englishness was good taste, whose development, as Eileen Cleere demonstrates in chapter 6, had surprisingly deep roots in the Victorian hygiene movement. Arguing that, toward the end of the nineteenth century, sanitary science converged on aesthetic discourse, Cleere shows how bourgeois commentators' increasingly fastidious concerns about domestic hygiene catalyzed a new regime of taste in interior design. While the legacy of Chadwick's sanitary idea is usually recognized in its public forms, such as slum clearances and increased regulation of the poor, this chapter shows how it also influenced private life, in the form of middle-class residential architecture and furnishings. Having opposed the Romantic aesthetic of the sublime, hygiene eventually *became* an aesthetic of "clean" modernism in the twentieth century. Reading late-nineteenth-century English art criticism, sanitary advice, and fiction, Cleere recasts both aestheticism and literary neo-Gothicism as dirt-phobic reactions to the penetration of the bourgeois home by urban filth.

Perhaps as a testimony to the equivalence between cleanliness and good taste, George Du Maurier's sensational novel *Trilby* (1894) could look back at the 1850s and express *nostalgia* for a lost bohemian world of dirt and foreignness. As Joseph Bristow argues in chapter 7, artistic brilliance in both painting and music is a "dirty pleasure" in the novel, which Du Maurier situates in an extraordinary web of filthy identities: the dirty, if arty, Latin Quarter; the working-class Irish quasi-prostitute, Trilby; and the mesmerically corrupting (and corporeally corrupted) German-Jewish Svengali. The novel both revels in all this filth and seeks to contain it, for while the dirt entertains the middle-class British characters in the story and its readers alike, the work also challenges conventional mores. The commercial success of the very novel that sought to expose the bourgeois corruption of bohemian creativity itself recapitulated the process portrayed in it. Looking back at a world since cleansed of its exotic Parisian dirt, *Trilby*, as Bristow demonstrates, finds itself in a characteristically modern predicament: it cannot decide whether to celebrate or condemn the filth it exploits, and thus whether to join in or equally to deprecate the genteel repudiation of filth.

At almost the same moment that Du Maurier was bemoaning the supposed improvements that eliminated the stimulating corruption of *ancien* Paris, the real Paris encountered some scandalously enticing filth of its own. Like Du Maurier's well-to-do revelers in squalid ateliers, the bourgeois audience for Alfred Jarry's 1896 play *Ubu Roi*, as Neil Blackadder discusses in chapter 8, got a certain thrill from the theatrical performance of dirty words. Blackadder reads the performance, in which the term "*Merdre!*" was reiterated on stage, as a reveling in human waste that is regressive, both in ontogenetic terms (as a reversion to a pre-oedipal valuation of feces) and in phylogenetic ones (as a historical return to a prebourgeois past, when human waste was not so meticulously repudiated). The character Père Ubu, who mocks the bourgeois and embodies both political anarchy and childish disruption, shows filth to adhere to the respectable public whom it so deeply offends; the audience for this performance ratified the charge of filthiness by joining in the transgressive spewing of obscenities. It was a rule-violating pleasure permitted by the theatrical setting, where the dirty word substitutes for the filthy thing.

While in this urbane Parisian context, the performance of filth onstage challenged middle-class identities, during the same period a more sinister aspect of such identity formations began to emerge in London, as Joseph W. Childers illustrates in chapter 9. Through readings of Arthur Conan Doyle's Sherlock Holmes stories, Childers demonstrates how class, race, and nationality frequently converge around notions of filth, not just to consolidate bourgeois identities, but also to establish the normative modern subject as specifically white and English. Mysterious, sometimes nefarious, dirty foreigners who emigrated to the imperial capital were increasingly a focus for crime and its detection. Like other texts considered in this book, the Holmes stories map social hierarchies onto spatial distinctions within the urban metropolis. The importation and ingestion of foreign filth (for Holmes, often in the form of drug use) was both exotic and degrading; nationality was as much a matter of hygiene as of race, and a certain ambiguity of borders meant that English identity could not be fixed, but rather was in an ongoing process of construction.

The chapters in the final section turn to modern legacies of nineteenth-century filth thinking. Fantasies about filth organize not only worries over the present and nostalgia for the past; as Natalka Freeland argues in chapter 10, they also form an important part of dreams about the future. Examining late-nineteenth-century English utopian novels, Freeland shows waste, in a variety of forms, to be a paramount feature in fictional reactions to fin-de-siècle fears about degeneration. Utopian works such as William Morris's *News from Nowhere* (1890), H. Rider Haggard's *She* (1887), and H. G. Wells's *The Time Machine* (1895) do not simply supply reveries about productively recycling industrial refuse, however; even when they turn away from the present as the future's past, they fully engage the economic concept of waste. Like Bataille in *The Accursed Share*, these utopianists understand wasteful excess— superabundance—as the very sign of civilization, whose consumption, in the form of art, then becomes a driving social purpose in itself. An emergent modernity as well as a utopian future freed from historical determination both aim to revalue waste, not as a source of filthy pollution but as a bounteous resource.

From these nineteenth-century fantasies of the future, the volume's final two chapters move into the twentieth century, to follow the consequences of filth in two of the many possible directions it could go. If the nineteenth century witnessed a lower threshold of tolerance for urban filth, then the technical solutions developed for the sanitary crisis—the clean-up of urban rivers, installation of sewers, and institution of major public-health campaigns—helped to move some associations with filth outside of urban poverty. Considering some of the same convergences as Childers, but from the point of view of subjugated identities, William Kupinse, in chapter 11, examines the legacy of British sanitary campaigns for colonial subjects in India, who absorbed the charges of filthiness that had long been associated with racial distinction and political domination. Focusing on three novels—Lal Behari Day's *Govinda Samanta, or The History of a Bengal Raiyat* (1874), Mulk Raj Anand's *Coolie* (1936), and G. V. Desani's *All About H. Hatterr* (1948)— Kupinse traces a lineage of ideas about filth in Indian fiction. Writing in conversation with popular history, social science, and anthropology, these novelists draw from an image repertoire directly linked to that of Victorian sanitary campaigns. Kupinse shows how sanitary distinctions function both to stereotype colonial subjects and to provide the opportunity for revisionary responses by the colonized themselves, expressed in part through the formal innovations in their fiction. Well into the twentieth century, Kupinse demonstrates, Indian novels—even when cast in a modernist idiom—engaged politically and aesthetically with the Victorian conceptions of filth their culture had inherited.

During the twentieth century, European powers exported many of their concerns with filth, in both literal and metaphorical terms, into the areas of the world they dominated and fought over. The political, economic, and military crises of the early twentieth century gave the lie to the vision of civilized utopias that industrial and technological advances would bring—the vision of a world washed free of its dirt. The unregenerate putrescence of soldiers' corpses in World War I, and the truncated lives they embodied, supplanted nineteenth-century dreams of reuse with a nightmare of bodies laid to waste. The attempt at the wholesale extermination of populations later in the twentieth century, on the basis of racial and national distinctions, is the most powerfully dystopian version of the uses to which filth-thinking can be put. In the Nazi Holocaust and other modern genocides, the charges of filth no longer served simply to condemn a population but to justify eliminating it.

That filth might, then, serve as a positive resource in the midst of fascist domination is all the more extraordinary, as the final chapter of this book proposes. Providing an intellectual history of three "abject academies," Benjamin Lazier discusses contemporaneous cases in which filth was put to profound use in the late 1930s: the Parisian Collège de Sociologie, in particular its central, influential figure, Georges Bataille; Gershom Scholem, the Zionist scholar of kabbalah and founding member of Hebrew University, who was in conversation with the Collège; and, in Cologne, the obscure Josef Feinhals, who dreamed up a whole academy exuberantly devoted to excrement and then transcribed its proceedings at staggering length. In the convergence of these three writers on the brink of the Second World War, Lazier discovers a resourceful and optimistic sense of community that grows directly, if paradoxically, out of their shared interest in filth. Lazier's study, which forms a coda to the other chapters, links up with them in a number of ways. In positing an abject notion of the flesh against a sublime or divine one of the spirit, it returns us to Hamlin's concerns, although where Hamlin reaches back to classical ideas of the human body as waste, Lazier looks forward to both its immediate political crisis and to the fate of *transgression*, as an idea, within poststructuralism. The writers Lazier considers position their own transgressive ideas not only against bourgeois complacency, as the Victorians so frequently did, but also against the fascism that construed them as disposable. Surprising as it is that filth—in the sense of an abject loss of the self—could serve to establish a provisional basis for community, it is an idea anticipated in Pike's account of working-class boys in the sewers and Bristow's of the British bohemians in Paris. In broadening our sense of the context in which Bataille worked, Lazier's chapter also returns us to some of the issues in this introduction, concerning the recuperation of waste itself as a value. If, as Bataille and his inheritors suggest, abjection can serve as a mode of political critique, then it seems fitting to close with an essay devoted to tracing the history—and, at the same time, to imagining the possibilities—of this theory.

Notes

1. *New York Times,* 20 January 1999, C25.

2. Mary Douglas, *Purity and Danger: An Analysis of the Concepts of Pollution and Taboo* (London: Routledge, 1966), 53.

3. William Ian Miller, *The Anatomy of Disgust* (Cambridge, MA: Harvard University Press, 1997), 62.

4. Mary Russo, *The Female Grotesque: Risk, Excess, and Modernity* (New York: Routledge, 1995).

5. Julia Kristeva, *Powers of Horror: An Essay on Abjection,* trans. Leon S. Roudiez (New York: Columbia University Press, 1982).

6. This theory has been productive for feminist analyses of culture. See, for example, Russo, *Female Grotesque*; Barbara Creed, *The Monstrous-Feminine: Film, Feminism, Psychoanalysis* (London: Routledge, 1993); *Abjection, Melancholia, and Love: The Work of Julia Kristeva,* ed. John Fletcher and Andrew Benjamin (London: Routledge, 1990). For an application of Kristeva's theory to a nineteenth-century literary text, in terms congenial to this project, see Robert E. Lougy, "Filth, Liminality, and Abjection in Charles Dickens's *Bleak House,*" *ELH* 69 (2002): 473–500.

7. See, for example, Guy Hocquenghem, *Homosexual Desire* (1972), trans. Daniella Dangoor (Durham, NC: Duke University Press, 1993), 93–102, and Leo Bersani, "Is the Rectum a Grave?" *October* 43, "AIDS: Cultural Analysis, Cultural Activism" (Winter 1987): 197–222. On the female anus, see Eve Kosofsky Sedgwick, "A Poem Is Being Written," in *Tendencies* (Durham, NC: Duke University Press, 1993), 177–214.

8. Quoted in Norman O. Brown, *Life against Death: The Psychoanalytical Meaning of History* (New York: Vintage, 1959), 293. Brown explains: "Some of the most important categories of social behavior (play, gift, property, weapon) originate in the anal stage of infantile sexuality and—what is more important—never lose their connection with it. When infantile sexuality comes to its catastrophic end, non-bodily cultural objects inherit the symbolism originally attached to the anal product, but only as second-best substitutes for the original (sublimations). Sublimations are thus symbols of symbols. The category of property is not simply transferred from feces to money; on the contrary, money is feces, because the anal eroticism continues in the unconscious. The anal eroticism has not been renounced or abandoned but repressed" (191). The relevant texts by Freud are *Three Essays on the Theory of Sexuality* (1905–24), trans. James Strachey (n.p.: Basic Books, 1962); "Character and Anal Eroticism"

(1908), in *Standard Edition of the Complete Psychological Works*, ed. James Strachey, 24 vols. (London: Hogarth Press, 1953–74), 9:168–75; "On Transformations of Instinct as Exemplified in Anal Eroticism" (1917), in *Standard Edition*, 17:126–33; *Civilization and Its Discontents* (1930), trans. James Strachey (New York: Norton, 1961). On filth and money in a specifically nineteenth-century British context, see Christopher Herbert, "Filthy Lucre: Victorian Ideas of Money," *Victorian Studies* 44, no. 2 (Winter 2002): 185–213.

9. Dominique Laporte, *History of Shit*, trans. Nadia Benabid and Rodolphe el-Khoury (Cambridge, MA: MIT Press, 2000), viii. For treatment of related topics in a more sober idiom, see David Inglis, *A Sociological History of Excretory Experience: Defecatory Manners and Toiletry Technologies* (Lewiston, NY: Mellen, 2001).

10. Laporte, *History of Shit*, 46.

11. Michael Thompson, *Rubbish Theory: The Creation and Destruction of Value* (Oxford: Oxford University Press, 1979), 25–26, 10. In economic terms, reuse—the movement of an object out of the designation "filthy"—complicates a classic model of production and consumption: "A view which holds that consumption is the only end and object of economic activity," Thompson writes, "is extraordinarily myopic, for it fails to perceive that much of economic activity, being cyclical in nature and so having no ends, cannot be described in terms of ends, and that, even within that part of economic activity that can be described in terms of ends, there are in general not one but three alternative ends: consumption, the creation of rubbish, and the creation of durability" (127). While the reasons for the change in an object's value remain obscure, Thompson is careful to show how contests over what counts as transient, durable, or rubbish stage power struggles among classes of people. In his review of the book, "Junk and Rubbish: A Semiotic Approach," *Diacritics* 15, no. 3 (Fall 1985): 2–13, Jonathan Culler emphasizes such contests as staging grounds for broader conflicts over cultural power and ascendancy: "Struggles are always being waged over rubbish: struggles whether the system of transience or of durability should prevail" (9).

12. Susan Strasser's *Waste and Want: A Social History of Trash* (New York: Metropolitan Books, 1999) places related notions of reuse, as an economic and material category, in U.S. history. Strasser charts the shift within domestic economies away from recycling at the end of the nineteenth century, when consumers began increasingly to throw out commodity byproducts. As the women who largely managed domestic economies increasingly bought rather than made food, clothing, and other essentials, the capacity and taste for reusing domestic materials gave way to an economy of consuming and discarding. This history, as Strasser shows, is related to changes in women's roles and is also variable across the class spectrum: the poor have always been recyclers, even if they are not directly involved in the secondary economy. The distinctly modern economy based on commodity consumption is, axiomatically, one in which *disposability* is paramount and whose hallmarks are "commodity fetishism" and "planned obsolescence."

13. Peter Stallybrass and Allon White, *The Politics and Poetics of Transgression* (Ithaca, NY: Cornell University Press, 1986), 45.

14. Ibid., 5 (emphasis in original).

15. On racism in post-Enlightenment Europe, especially in relation to scientific discourses, see George L. Mosse, *Toward the Final Solution: A History of European Racism* (New York: Howard Fertig, 1978), and Neil MacMaster, *Racism in Europe, 1870–2000* (Hampshire, UK: Palgrave, 2001), both of which focus primarily on anti-Black and anti-Jewish racism. In relation to colonialism, see Robert J. C. Young, *Colonial Desire: Hybridity in Theory, Culture, and Race* (London: Routledge, 1995). Gail Ching-Liang Low, *White Skins/Black Masks: Representation and Colonialism* (London: Routledge, 1996) supplies a relevant discussion in more literary terms. For a conceptually pertinent (although historically distinct) account of racial conceptions formulated in relation to public health institutions, see Nayan Shah, *Contagious Divides: Epidemics and Race in San Francisco's Chinatown* (Berkeley and Los Angeles: University of California Press, 2001). On degeneration in Europe specifically, see Daniel Pick, *Faces of Degeneration: A European Disorder, c. 1848–c. 1918* (Cambridge: Cambridge University Press, 1989).

16. Richard Dyer, *White* (London: Routledge, 1997), especially 72–81; Joel Kovel, *White Racism: A Psychohistory* (New York: Vintage, 1970). See also Douglas A. Lorimer, *Color, Class, and the Victorians: English Attitudes to the Negro in the Mid-Nineteenth Century* (New York: Holmes and Meier, 1978).

17. Georges Bataille, *Visions of Excess: Selected Writings, 1927–1939*, trans. Allan Stoekl with Carl R. Lovitt and Donald M. Leslie Jr. (Minneapolis: University of Minnesota Press, 1985), 77.

18. Ibid., xiv. As Martin Jay explains in *Downcast Eyes: The Denigration of Vision in Twentieth-Century French Thought* (Berkeley and Los Angeles: University of California Press, 1993), Bataille makes a "defense of what he called a 'general' as opposed to a 'restricted' economy, one based on *dépense* (waste or expenditure), loss, transgression, and excess, rather than production, exchange, conservation, and instrumental rationality" (222). See especially Georges Bataille, *The Accursed Share: An Essay on General Economy*, vol. 1, *Consumption* (1967), trans. Robert Hurley (New York: Zone, 1988). One example of how Bataille's "general economy" has been put to good use is *Cities of the Dead: Circum-Atlantic Performance* (New York: Columbia University Press, 1996), in which Joseph Roach uses this theory to suggest that culture itself is ultimately a waste product—that is, an effect of superabundance, what "Bataille calls 'profitless expenditure' or what I call the performance of waste" (122–23). This sort of waste may seem altogether clean by comparison with the images the word "filth" usually conjures up, but insofar as filth overlaps with that which can afford to be thrown out—the refuse that is designated filthy, and therefore discarded rather than recycled—it suggests the economic component requisite to any understanding of filth.

19. David Trotter, *Cooking with Mud: The Idea of Mess in Nineteenth-Century Art and Literature* (Oxford: Oxford University Press, 2000).

20. Likewise, when Stallybrass and White examine the "low" in earlier periods of European culture, they explore its manifestations in popular and literary

culture; when they get to the nineteenth century, it is associated specifically with urban poverty.

21. Stephen Greenblatt, "Filthy Rites," *Daedalus* 111, no. 3 (Summer 1982): 1–16: "There is, in short, a telling difference between the Catholic and Protestant semiotics of excrement. Where the excremental in Rabelais is bound up with renewal as well as decay, in Luther it is a sign of the Church's corrupt compromise with pagan idolatry and evil. . . . Where scatology in More is part of an institutional rhetoric . . . scatology in Luther is part of a personal vision, a weapon in the struggle of an isolated believer against Satan, or an expression of the inward state of the individual fleshy man. For More, the emotion principally associated with excrement is shame; for Luther, it is not shame, the social sense of disgrace in the eyes of the community, but guilt. When Luther looks into himself, that is, into his natural inwardness unaided by divine grace, what he perceives is filth" (12). Filth associations in the texts Greenblatt considers both castigate the speaker's enemies (in a classic device of othering) and inevitably taint the subject. For stimulating reflections on clean and dirty objects in the early modern period, see also Julian Yates, *Error, Misuse, Failure: Object Lessons from the English Renaissance* (Minneapolis: University of Minnesota Press, 2003).

22. Georges Vigarello, *Concepts of Cleanliness: Changing Attitudes in France since the Middle Ages*, trans. Jean Birrel (Cambridge: Cambridge University Press, 1988): "We must not think of the bath with its modern connotations, but think instead of a cleanliness which existed in the absence of washing; we must accept a bodily cleanliness which would not be recognised by that name today; we must study a series of objects whose cleanliness long served for that of the body, to the exclusion of washing it—places, linen, clothes, various accessories, etc. We must discover the body there, where it no longer resides" (37).

23. Alain Corbin, *The Foul and the Fragrant: Odor and the French Social Imagination*, trans. Miriam L. Kochan (Cambridge, MA: Harvard University Press, 1986). "From about the middle of the eighteenth century, odors simply began to be more keenly smelled. It was as if thresholds of tolerance had been abruptly lowered; and that happened well before industrial pollution accumulated in urban space. All the evidence suggests that scientific theory played a crucial role in this lowering of thresholds" (56). "Not until the nineteenth century did sanitary reformers use tactics that created a clear distinction between the deodorized bourgeoisie and the foul-smelling masses" (55).

24. Christopher Hamlin, "Providence and Putrefaction: Victorian Sanitarians and the Natural Theology of Health and Disease," *Victorian Studies* 28, no. 3 (Spring 1985): 381–411. Hamlin documents how the influential German chemist Justus von Liebig "regarded putrefaction itself as the quintessential pathological process" (383) both in the breakdown of organic matter into agricultural fertilizer and in pathogenic disease processes. Both types of putrefaction are filthy, but one is destructive, the other generative; this logic of putrefaction, Hamlin shows, extends to theological discourses about sin and providence. In

her analysis of Dickens's *Our Mutual Friend*, Catherine Gallagher extends the collapsing opposition between decay and regeneration—imported from sanitary science, and lent a thematic distinction in the novel by the contrast between wet and dry waste—to the economic realm, through a discussion of what John Ruskin calls "illth" (possessions that harm or kill) and "wealth"; "The Bio-Economics of *Our Mutual Friend*," in *Fragments for a History of the Human Body*, part 3, ed. Michel Feher (New York: Zone, 1989), 345–65.

25. That specifically late-nineteenth-century forms of cultural masochism might have a powerful political dimension as well is John Kucich's argument in "Melancholy Magic: Masochism, Stevenson, Anti-Imperialism," *Nineteenth-Century Literature* 56, no. 3 (2001): 364–400.

26. See, for instance, Gareth Stedman Jones, *Outcast London: A Study in the Relationship between Classes in Victorian Society* (Oxford: Oxford University Press, 1971); *The Victorian City: Images and Realities*, ed. H. J. Dyos and Michael Wolff, 2 vols. (London: Routledge and Kegan Paul, 1973); and Asa Briggs, *The Age of Improvement, 1783–1867*, 2nd ed. (Harlow: Longman, 2000). I am grateful to David L. Pike for references to the following works, which compare and make distinctions between London and Paris: Joachim Schlör, *Nights in the Big City: Paris, Berlin, London 1840–1930* (1991; London: Reaktion, 1998); Andrew Lees, *Cities Perceived: Urban Society in European and American Thought, 1820–1940* (New York: Columbia University Press, 1985); Elizabeth Wilson, *The Sphinx in the City: Urban Life, the Control of Disorder, and Women* (Berkeley and Los Angeles: University of California Press, 1992); Richard Maxwell, *The Mysteries of Paris and London* (Charlottesville: University Press of Virginia, 1992); Sharon Marcus, *Apartment Stories: City and Home in Nineteenth-Century Paris and London* (Berkeley and Los Angeles: University of California Press, 1999).

27. In *Public Health and Social Justice in the Age of Chadwick: Britain, 1800–1854* (Cambridge: Cambridge University Press, 1998), Hamlin criticizes Whig histories that issue in the triumph of the modern welfare state: "The vision of the inexorable progress of science and health is usually founded in an appeal to 'conditions,' the idea that public health activity is driven by public health need" (11). He proposes instead "integrat[ing] the history of public health into the rest of history" (11) and "appreciating that the early Victorians invented one public health among many" (12), for "Chadwick narrowed public health, casting out all factors that affected health save water and sewers, which were politically innocuous" (15). On the invidious moral and ideological subtexts in Chadwick, see Mary Poovey, *Making a Social Body: British Cultural Formation, 1830–1864* (Chicago: University of Chicago Press, 1995).

28. See, for example, Anthony Wohl, *Endangered Lives: Public Health in VicTorian Britain* (Cambridge, MA: Harvard University Press, 1983); Frank Mort, *Dangerous Sexualities: Medico-Moral Politics in Britain since 1830* (London: Routledge, 1987); and Judith R. Walkowitz, *Prostitution and Victorian Society: Women, Class, and the State* (Cambridge: Cambridge University Press,

1980). The latter two works, along with Poovey's *Making a Social Body* and Seth Koven's *Slumming: Sexual and Social Politics in London* (Princeton, NJ: Princeton University Press, forthcoming), link sanitary and sexual regulation, suggesting the class/gender nexus at the heart of much Victorian thinking about what constitutes dirt. For focused inquiries on practices and representations that demonstrate the convergence of class and gender categories in Victorian sanitation discourse, see Tracy C. Davis, "Filthy—Nay—Pestilential: Sanitation and Victorian Theaters," in *Exceptional Spaces: Essays in Performance and History*, ed. Della Pollock (Chapel Hill: University of North Carolina Press, 1998), 161–86, which postulates that the prevalent miasma theory of infection in the mid-nineteenth century entailed class-inflected changes in the architecture of theaters; Jonathan P. Ribner, "The Thames and Sin in the Age of the Great Stink: Some Artistic and Literary Responses to a Victorian Environmental Crisis," *British Art Journal* 1, no. 2 (Spring 2000): 38–46, which links depictions of the dirty Thames to those of sinfulness in general and prostitution in particular; and Ellen Handy, "Dust Piles and Damp Pavements: Excrement, Repression, and the Victorian City in Photography and Literature," in *Victorian Literature and the Victorian Visual Imagination*, ed. Carol T. Christ and John O. Jordan (Berkeley and Los Angeles: University of California Press, 1995), 111–33.

29. Lynda Nead, *Victorian Babylon: People, Streets, and Images in Nineteenth-Century London* (New Haven, CT: Yale University Press, 2000), 6. In linking sewer construction (the subject of part 1) to obscenity (part 3), Nead demonstrates the spatial continuities as well between filthy matter and filthy words.

30. Judith R. Walkowitz, *City of Dreadful Delight: Narratives of Sexual Danger in Late-Victorian London* (Chicago: University of Chicago Press, 1992). For one, admittedly unique, example, consider the much-discussed relationship between gentleman Arthur Munby and his maidservant Hannah Cullwick, which was centrally organized around what Anne McClintock calls a "fetishistic" valuation of dirt, depicted in Cullwick's voluminous diaries and Munby's photographs of her subjugation in racial and sometimes transgendered forms; see *Imperial Leather: Race, Gender, and Sexuality in the Colonial Contest* (New York: Routledge, 1995). While this relation across class, gender, and race lines can be read as exploitative or perverse, the case can also be made for the filthiness on which it hinged as supplying Cullwick positive resources for self-assertion and class identity, erotic satisfaction, and a leveraging of her own power. See McClintock, chapter 3, and Leonore Davidoff, "Class and Gender in Victorian England: The Diaries of Arthur J. Munby and Hannah Cullwick," *Feminist Studies* 5 (Spring 1979): 86–141.

31. The best known of the nonfiction works are those cited herein by Engels and Mayhew, as well as Edwin Chadwick, *Report on the Sanitary Condition of the Labouring Population of Great Britain* (1842), ed. M. W. Flynn (Edinburgh: Edinburgh University Press, 1965); John Hollingshead, *Underground London* (London: Groombridge and Sons, 1862); and Jack London, *The People of the Abyss* (1903; Upper Saddle River, NJ: Literature House, 1970).

32. Donald Reid, *Paris Sewers and Sewermen: Realities and Representations* (Cambridge, MA: Harvard University Press, 1991) supplies detailed information on the French situation; see also Laporte, *History of Shit*, chapters 5–6; Corbin, *Foul and the Fragrant*, chapter 7, emphasizing the anxiety over loss of, rather than infection by, sewage; and, for an English example, Nicholas Goddard, "Nineteenth-Century Recycling: The Victorians and the Agricultural Utilisation of Sewage," *History Today* 31 (June 1981): 32–36. Reid also documents the infamously unrecuperable filth at Montfaucon, which Corbin describes as "the epicenter of stench in Paris. That malodorous complex, where sewage reservoirs and slaughterhouse stood side by side, took shape northeast of Paris during the second half of the [eighteenth] century" (31).

33. Victor Hugo, *Les Misérables*, trans. Charles E. Wilbour (New York: Modern Library, 1980), part V, book 2, chapter 1, "The Intestine of Leviathan," 1054–55.

34. McClintock, *Imperial Leather*, 211. Laporte, in *History of Shit*, notes, "As early as the mid-eighteenth century, Jonathan Swift anticipated what effectively became Victorian England's official line on effluvium and lucidly demonstrated the integral link between a state's imperialist tendencies and the policies of its waste police" (59). See Warwick Anderson, "Excremental Colonialism: Public Health and the Poetics of Pollution," *Critical Inquiry* 21 (Spring 1995): 640–69, for a methodologically relevant analysis, concerned with the medical representation of human waste in the Philippines in the early twentieth century; and Vijay Prashad, "Native Dirt/Imperial Ordure: The Cholera of 1832 and the Morbid Resolutions of Modernity," *Journal of Historical Sociology* 7, no. 3 (1994): 243–60.

35. Erin O'Connor, *Raw Material: Producing Pathology in Victorian Culture* (Durham, NC: Duke University Press, 2000), 11, 40.

Part I

FUNDAMENTALS OF FILTH

Chapter 1

Good and Intimate Filth

Christopher Hamlin

*I*n remarks curiously reminiscent of the adolescent's observation that the worth of a human can be calculated by summing the market values of the chemical substances it contains, the early nineteenth-century English evangelical preacher Edward Bickersteth reminded his congregation of the "nothingness of man." They (and he) were only clay, least valuable of earthly materials, "that which is frailest and soonest dissipated." The sense that we were more was an illusion, the product of a consciousness that existed only so long as the divine spirit continued within us. "God has but to remove his hand from under us and we fall into dust. . . . Where are the bodies of all the millions that have peopled our earth? . . . Mingled with the dust on which those now living are moving and treading. Where are the myriads that have inhabited this busy and crowded metropolis from century to century; they are mouldering in the dust, and they are mingled with the earth."[1] A mid-nineteenth-century writer actually attempted to calculate the percent of London dust that had once been human.[2]

Certainly Bickersteth's vision is a sobering one, part of a larger attack on pride, achievement, and even the concept of an autonomous self. We may admit that Bickersteth wants us to invest our concern with the next life without missing the important things he says about this world. Early nineteenth-century English readers would have been familiar with these images; they would have read them in the context of a literature, mainly

3

poetic, that insisted not only on the acceptance of death, but on a good deal of gratuitous gore besides—on imagining one's future in (as) worms, dust, or yew. The ecclesiastical term "dust" might be a euphemism for many things, but his hearers would have realized that a blunter Bicker-steth might have spoken of them as "dirt" or even "earth" just as read-ily. And whether or not these ultimate products qualified as "filth," certainly the intervening dissolution—the "mouldering"—did. Bicker-steth was inviting his listeners, then, to think of themselves as filth.

Matters of cleanliness and dirtiness are of central importance to envi-ronmental historians. Not only is the discipline itself predicated (in part) on such a distinction, but the recognition or lack of recognition of these attributes is a major historical problem in its own right. In its very imprecision, "filth," like "madness," highlights the cultural work of rec-ognition. It digests together both substances and visceral reactions to them. It makes clear that the subject under discussion is not entity but attitude. And yet the performative *filth* can be many different kinds of utterance, some of them quite far from the dominant chord of revulsion. The literature on which I focus here, which is concerned not only with what becomes of the particular body that exists as us at the time of our deaths, but also with various substances we strew about us, what Vic-torians liked to call "offscourings" of life, is characterized by a concern with the fate of our material selves. Almost always, writers acknowledge that one necessary and natural step in that fate is organic decomposi-tion, which is usually conceived of as unpleasant—certainly to others, and, by the combined means of observation and/or imagination, pre-sumably to the subject itself. It is fair to say that almost always such matter undergoing such a process was conceived of as filth. It may even be argued that it was and is the archetype of filth, though this is not the place to pursue that argument. (English *filth* is defined as "foul," from the German *faul*; German *faulnis* refers to decomposition specifically.)

Victorian writers on public issues have much to say about these filth forms. Part of what needs explaining is why they have so much to say. They are simultaneously attracted and appalled; amidst their shudders they revel in the filth they are describing. Rhetorically, one can see them play the shuddering and the wallowing off against one another—each sets up the other. But it would be wrong to focus only on the gut-wrenching sensation. By no means was the discourse of filth, even in contexts where affect was sought, single-mindedly one of revulsion, or even of revulsion spiked with the frisson of the horrific.

In different ways, two of the most influential scholars of filth, Mary Douglas and Ernest Becker, have begun to help us go beyond the repelling character of what is deemed filth by pointing to its equally compelling character. If filth is so unpleasant, why, they ask, does it deserve our notice at all, other than as a straightforward technical problem? Becker's is an existential answer: much of the matter called filth is the inescapable emblem of our biologicality. Our fixation with it is part of our futile effort to exclude it from our identity. "Excreting is a curse that threatens madness because it shows man his abject finitude," Becker writes.[3] Douglas's is a social answer. We label as polluting—as filth—whatever threatens the categories we use for the normal conduct of social business. We are particularly threatened by matters that obscure important social categories, such as the border between self and nonself. These include both the materials that issue, semi-voluntarily, from our bodies during life and those bodies themselves following death.[4] (For the Victorians I discuss, both of these, as putrescible substances, came under the category of filth, and the former is probably the usual referent when Victorian writers use "filth" as a semi-specific noun. A claim could also probably be made that, on the rationales Douglas and Becker provide, putrid corpses and excrement are, more generally, the filthiest of filth.)

Yet if the perspectives of Douglas and Becker are enormously helpful, we need something more to make sense of the representation of filth in particular places and times.[5] From their writings one might assume that, because reminders of our mortality and the threats to our social identity will be with us always, so too the filth revulsion will always arise, and societies will always be taking steps to banish filth from our senses, conversation, and thoughts.

Historically, this is problematic for two reasons. The first is that what might be called the level of filth consciousness varies enormously, not only from culture to culture but within a culture from century to century or even decade to decade. As Phillippe Ariès makes clear, the putrid corpse has moved in and out of public consciousness.[6] Ariès focuses primarily on France, but the same appears true for England. Moreover, in this, France and England were out of phase: the great concern about the hygienic status of the dead so prominent in prerevolutionary France had waned by the middle of the nineteenth century, just as it was rising in England. A recognition of these cycles of awareness puts in question any view that filth consciousness was a function of filth existence—the view that sanitary reformers regularly took and that historians have often uncritically endorsed—as well as the view that a filth consciousness was the simple product of new science, greater concern with public hygiene, more exacting sensibilities, or even changed belief: the danger is always there, but we do not always dwell on it. Indeed, quite why these changes occur is not at all clear.[7]

Second, Bickersteth's sobering vision of self as dust, along with similar allusions to filth, is much more complicated than would be suggested by the simple association of filth with disgust and revulsion. Many writers grapple with the self/filth relationship (or, better, the concept of self-as-filth) with a directness that Becker would respect and an openness that suggests a more complicated set of categories than we may expect to find.

Filth was multivalent, a powerful idiom applicable in many contexts and toward many ends, equally a serious philosophical problem that could crop up in many, generally nonexclusive, contexts. Here I want to expand the set of referents, to show that filth, without losing its repulsiveness, could represent a good many virtues—for example, justice, liberation, utility, duty, fidelity, adventure.

The main locus of these significations was the decomposing human corpse, but the bits of matter that passed through the living body, whether they were assimilated into its structures for some length of time or simply sojourned briefly in its various tubes and chambers, might also carry some of the same freight. To the degree that we identified body with self, and saw self as—broadly speaking—good, this stuff of flesh, even when filthy, was good and intimate filth. Through its connection with us it acquired inherent value, and might even acquire some of the capacities associated with personhood. Even those who believed in immaterial souls, which somehow carried personhood, were rarely indifferent to the body's matter, whose onward fate was to become other things. The idiom of good and intimate filth thus focuses attention on the continued embodiment of the matter of the body, which is presumed, to a greater or lesser degree, to retain at least some components of self—the virtues noted above, but also states of consciousness: sensation, memory, reflection, evaluation, even a sense of purpose.

One may see this view of filth as making the best of a nasty business—a compromise between one's interest in oneself (and that self's persistence) and one's recognition of natural processes that cannot be escaped by wishful thinking. Imagining oneself as filth is thus part of the individual's grappling with materiality in general and with one's own materiality in particular. This essay focuses first on several of the genres in which such ideas appeared in early modern English literature, second on a particular controversy in the last quarter of the nineteenth century involving disposal of the dead, and third, briefly, on the concept of the constant flux of the body.

The chief framework that underwrote this imagining was Epicurean philosophy, mainly as expounded in the poem *De Re Natura* by the first-century-B.C. Roman poet Lucretius. Lucretius described a cosmos in which all things, including conscious human things, were produced by the coming together and separation of minute atoms. For Lucretius, thinking of oneself as a transitory amalgam of atoms was an optimistic alternative to a painful afterlife: "Death, then, is nothing to us, no concern / Once we grant that the soul will also die" (828–29). Lucretius rebukes the old man unwilling to die in terms that acknowledge our lineage with filth:

> The old, shoved out, must always cede to the new,
> One thing restores another; it must be.
> And no one's flung to the pit or the pains of Hell.
> We need those atoms for our progeny
> Who, though they live life full shall follow us.
> Before you came, men died—and they will die.
> One thing gives rise to another, incessantly;
> Life's given to no one outright; all must borrow. (961–68)[8]

Lucretius was not thinking, of course, of any Christian hell, but the same consideration would prove attractive in later periods.

Because it denied the immortality of souls, and, less centrally, because it explained things in terms of chance and saw any gods that might exist as pretty well superfluous, Epicurean philosophy tended to be unacceptable to Christians much of the time. And yet it was an easy matter for a clever seventeenth-century natural philosopher, a Pierre Gassendi or a Robert Boyle, to Christianize atomism. In many ways, it seemed more compatible with the concept of a creator and supreme governor of the universe than did the pantheism-tending mix of Stoicism and Islamic alchemy of the chemical philosophers, which invested various kinds of matter with inherent, and often occult, qualities. At least a few of the fathers of the Church had also found Lucretius to have something to offer, though less in his natural than in his moral philosophy. In seeking both to co-opt and to combat pagan philosophy, Arnobius of Sicca found in Lucretius a critique of the pagan pantheon of busybody deities, a profound sense of human humility and abjection, and an alternative to frivolous Stoic natural theology, which seemed an attempt to hold God hostage to human concepts of propriety, beauty, contrivance, and utility. Lucretius depicted human life as at the mercy of some great unity, which might as well be the Creator God as the atomist's chance.

The resurgent Lucretianism in the Renaissance had a similar focus.

Lucretius was well known, celebrated as a poet and influential as a natural philosopher, but still a dangerous atheistical author. From a natural philosophical point of view, the most troublesome problem was of getting any particular orderly product out of the Lucretian universe of haphazard collisions between the various atoms, large and small, smooth or Velcro-like. What developed were various versions of providential atomism. One could place one's faith in natural systems of attraction and repulsion that divinely governed atoms, all the more so after Newton, though this remained more a framework in which to imagine the biogeochemical changes of the world than a demonstration of any of them, or even a program of research into them. God, accordingly, could be seen as logistics expert, ensuring that every atom went to where it was needed at the proper time.[9]

Among these atoms were those previously comprising live human bodies. A substantial literary interest in the postmortem changes in dead humans was evident in England (less so, it would appear, in Scotland) by the mid-sixteenth century, and persisted to the late nineteenth.[10] Indeed, English authors were sometimes regarded by Continental observers as uniquely preoccupied with what Fairchild calls "graveyardism," with rot and worms, the transformation of one's erstwhile atoms through the stage of filth and on to some different and possibly better state.[11] This fascination predated the Lucretian revival, and few who drew on the images were philosophical Epicureans. Indeed, most would probably have repudiated the association, and yet Lucretius, and Epicureanism more broadly, did supply a framework: the fates of atoms served as an excellent ontology for a wide variety of forms of religious melancholy.[12]

While meditation on life-as-earth is most commonly associated either with Puritanism or with the pre-Romantic "graveyard" poets (Thomas Gray, but also Robert Blair, Edward Young, and Henry Moore), what is most striking is the adaptability and persistence of the motif across the confessional spectrum and in a wide range of aesthetic and literary movements. We see it in the works of the cavalier poets (such as Marvell's "To His Coy Mistress"), the metaphysical poets (Quarles, Donne, Herbert), the Tory satirists (Gay and Swift), and in Stoic Augustans like Alexander Pope. In the nineteenth century, the new chemistry brought new possibilities for prose expression, but poets, such as Shelley ("Adonais"), Wordsworth ("The Excursion"), Tennyson ("In Memoriam," "Maud"), Kingsley, and Thompson, all continued to rely on the images as well.[13]

The genres and themes are many. Images of rot and reconstitution appear in books of divinity offering consolation or admonition, in

commercial or amateur elegiac poetry, in political satire, in works advocating social and sanitary reform. The images served as a medium to
condemn vanity, assert equality, defend the utility of the world as it was
or might be, imagine the extremes of erotic consummation or vicarious
adventure, and express futility, despair, and grief. Some of this writing
doubtless expresses existential agony or hardened faith; some is cliché
cooked up at so much a line, and we cannot always tell the difference.
Death and rot were popular subjects for teenage girls learning to write
verse, and the classical elegy a popular, easy-to-learn form.[14] A good
deal of pre-1750 death poetry is surely meant to be funny—"we ripe
and ripe and rot and rot," observes Jaques in *As You Like It*. We, who
admit sex, scatology, and even violence into our humor are not good
at seeing the hilarity and irony of dissolution, but it is of course a wonderful subject for jokes that trade on the gap between pretension and
reality. The long list of parodies of Gray's "Elegy," stretching through
the serious Victorian period, makes clear that readers were not so
bowled over by its austerity that they did not play with it.[15] And it
was clearly a popular genre: well into the nineteenth century, Young's
"Night Thoughts" and Blair's "Grave" were widely reprinted in anthol-
ogies and said to be as popular as Pope's "Essay on Man."[16]

Despite the fact that much of this literature is religious, a distinguishing feature is its focus on nature—indeed, in some ways rot stands
out as the quintessentially natural process. Sometimes rot serves rhetorically as a means to highlight the different postmortem fates of body and
soul. After death, the soul may depart or sleep; the body may be recon-
stituted on judgment day, but before that the processes it undergoes are
usually seen to exemplify the natural. It is true that God's intervention
is sometimes invoked when bodies fail to rot in usual fashion (in other
cases rapid dissolution has been seen as a sign of grace),[17] but in general
the realm of dissolution, with its worms and its "dust" or "clay," tends
not to be one of divine (or demonic) activity, and hence there is reason
to regard it as simply "natural"—certainly as part of a divine plan, but
rarely as in itself divine.

In reviewing this literature one might start with Spenser for a general
treatment of the issues. In the "Mutability Cantos" appended to the
Faerie Queene, the beings of Nature demand the meaning of the universe. But the law, they are told, is mutability, the ceaseless disappearance and reappearance of forms.

Lo, mighty mother, now be iudge and say,
Whether in all thy creatures more or lesse

CHANGE doth not raign & beare the greatest sway:
For, who sees not, that *Time* on all doth pray?
But *Times* do change and moue continually.
So nothing here standeth in one stay:
Wherefore, this lower world who can deny
But to be subject still to *Mutabilitie?*

Included in this patter are death and rebirth in new forms:

For, all that from her springs, and is ybredde,
How-euer fayre it flourish for a time,
Yet see we soon decay; and, being dead,
To turne again vnto their earthly slime:
Yet, out of their decay and mortall crime,
We daily see new creatures to arize;
And of their Winter spring another Prime,
Vnlike in forme, and chang'd by strange disguise:
So Turne they still about, and change in restlesse wise.[18]

In *Hamlet*, the focus is the utilitarian and egalitarian aspects of dissolution. Musing on "this quintessence of dust" (II, 2, 311–12), Hamlet recognizes that the round of nature means that no given state of atoms, even if resident in a body, has precedence over any other state. Utility might matter, however. The "base uses" to which we return are undeniably useful: here is the "noble dust of Alexander . . . stopping a bung-hole" and there "Imperious Caesar, dead and turned to clay," used to "patch a wall t'expell the winter's flaw!" (V, 1, 196–210). Can a living Hamlet best use the atoms he currently employs? Moreover, the new king can be taken down a notch by being reminded that like those megalomaniacs Alexander and Caesar, he too is but worm food on the hoof: a "convocation of politic worms" awaits. "A man may fish with the worm that hath eat of a king, and eat of the fish that hath fed of that worm," remarks Hamlet to the king's puzzlement; Hamlet means only "to show you how a king may progress through the guts of a beggar" (IV, 3, 19–30).

For Sir Thomas Browne, the mid-seventeenth-century physician and philosophical chemist, this kind of thinking is a part of religious consolation, a matching of aspiration to reality. Browne is fascinated by the transformation to come, and even more by the materiality and transitoriness of the self. "*All flesh is grasse*, is not onely metaphorically, but literally true, for all those creatures we behold, are but the hearbs of the field, digested into flesh in them, or more remotely carnified in our selves. Nay further, we are what we all abhorre, *Anthropophagi* and Canibals, devourers not onely of men, but of our selves; and that not in an allegory, but a positive truth for all this masse of flesh which wee behold, came in at our mouths: this frame wee look upon, hath been upon our trenchers; In briefe, we have devoured our selves."[19]

Among the most common themes, particularly of eighteenth-century expressions of postmortem consumption, is egalitarianism. Even more than death, rot is the great leveler. We can all look forward to an existence as filth simply by knowing that everyone else will have the same experience. The presentation recalls the fifteenth-century dances of death, in which each trade or mode of life is summoned in turn to recognize that death and rot are the culmination of all its earthly glory.[20] Thus Robert Blair writes in the much reprinted "The Grave" (1743) of the warrior who once

> fix'd his Iron Talons on the Poor,
> And grip'd them like some Lordly Beast of Prey;
> Deaf to the forceful Cries of gnawing Hunger
> And piteous plaintive Voice of Misery; . . .
> Now! tame and humble, like a Child that's whipp'd,
> Shakes Hands with Dust, and calls the Worm his Kinsman;
> Nor pleads his Rank and Birthright. Under ground
> *Precedency's* a Jest; Vassal and Lord
> Grossly familiar, Side by Side consume. (221–32)

Or the beauty:

> Methinks! I see the with thy Head low laid,
> Whilst surfeited upon thy Damask Cheek
> The high-fed *Worm* in lazy Volumes roll'd
> Riots unscar'd. For this, was all thy Caution?
> For this, thy painful Labours at thy Glass?
> T' improve those Charms, and keep them in Repair,
> For which the Spoiler thanks thee not. Foul-Feeder!
> Coarse Fare and Carrion please thee full as well. (1124–52)

Indeed, the common fate of bodies is typically presented as the only thing that makes inequality and pretension bearable.[21] While this equality is explicitly extended only to humans, the facts that all end up as worm bodies and that worms eat other things too translates into a radical biocentrism in which the human's perspective must somehow be the same level as that of any other creature. Quoting from Job—"*Corruption, thou art my father, and to the worm, Thou art my mother and my sister"*—John Donne speaks of the underground state of "miserable incest, when I must be married to my own mother and my sister, and be both father and mother to my own mother and sister, beget and bear that worm which is all that miserable penury; when my mouth shall be filled with dust, and the *worm shall feed, and feed sweetly.*"[22] Here, in Donne's gloss of the Anglican burial service (taken mainly from Job and 1 Corinthians), all sorts of boundaries are violated in a wholesale enfilthment. We are simultaneously to envision all this from the viewpoint of self and to reject the constituents of self-identity by rejecting the categories it is based on.[23]

As Donne's admission of unavoidable "incest," and Browne's reflections on the relation of food to self suggest, this vermian muse was not just a literary device. It could be a mode of reasoning about human-nature relations in which humans, and particularly individual human selves, are incidental. Thus Blair discovers that the purpose of our bodies is to make the dirt that will bury our successors:

> What is *this World?*
> What? but a spacious *Burial-field* unwall'd,
> Strew'd with Death's Spoils, the Spoils of Animals
> Savage and Tame, and full of Dead Mens Bones?
> The very turf on which we tread, once liv'd:
> And we that live must lend our Carcases
> To cover our own Offspring: In their Turns
> They too must cover theirs.[24]

What can we say about what such images do? A little. First, that however grotesque or macabre we find it, this literature is not mainly intended to horrify or disgust; very little happens in these plots. Second, it is not about damnation or sin: for Quarles, Donne, and Edward Young, for example, the focus on the dissolution of the body simply heightens the contrast with its resurrected glory.[25] (As had been the case with medieval and patristic theologians, the centrality of the doctrine of bodily resurrection focused attention on the fates of particles by raising the question of what exactly was involved in the miraculous reassembly of the dispersed components of human bodies.)[26] The Puritan literature lacks that confident anticipation; there the events of the grave help us reckon with the absoluteness of God's will. Thus Isaac Watts's children's tour of the churchyard: "What a Multitude of Human Beings, noble Creatures, are here reduced to Dust! *God* has broken his own best Workmanship to pieces, and demolished by Thousands, the finest earthly Structures of his own Building. . . . To this Point of Mortality, since 'tis certain and inevitable, let us often direct our Eyes; let our scatter'd Thoughts be recollected from all their Wanderings, and pay a daily Visit to Death."[27]

As a religious discourse about nature, these meditations on self as filth are a far cry from argumentative natural theology. Unrelentingly, these writers deny us the satisfaction not only of material achievement, but also of body, health, and even of self. These meditations are often (though not invariably) sad, but it is a preutilitarian sadness, a fully valid response to the world implying no problem in need of resolution and reflecting an outlook in which happiness is not the benchmark against which all social and natural phenomena are to be measured.[28] The meditations are full of contradiction. The grave is both a place of peace where nothing happens but a form of "sleep" and a place of incessant chemical and biological activity. The desire to merge into something vaster coexists with the terror of losing self. Absolute dignity, with its maintenance of boundaries, is exchanged for absolute indignity. Within the earthly creature highest on the chain of being lie the creatures lowest on the chain, the worms, the fungi, the plants, the dirt; each is made out of the other. What happens to the body is said not to matter, since the soul will be free of it (and perhaps able to look at it from afar), yet it becomes the focus of intense interest, and writers continue to imbue it with senses and reactions: often there is a virtual doubling or even multiplying of self in these accounts. Acknowledgment that the dead will not experience what is going on is followed by a detailed tour of the world of dirt and transformation that awaits. There is clearly destruction, but also construction, of trees, grass, sheep, fish, or even later generations of human bodies.[29]

While the images persist, by the mid-nineteenth century emphasis had shifted from melancholic introspection and ironic statements about the equality of the grave to a utilitarianism that privileges the systems of nature that our bodies happen to sustain. Hamlet's musings about the future productive uses of our atoms take place either as part of an open-ended introspection or as part of a coy assault on his stepfather, but increasingly postmortem productivity is an issue in its own right. A long-standing issue, of whether the raising of "the priest's mutton"— from sheep pastured in churchyards—is or is not desecration, returns, and some even argue that we need to see our atoms as part of the national budget of fertilizing matter.[30] The sources of this shift are surely manifold and complex—a waning of concern with resurrection of the real body, the triumph of Newtonian systems thinking, the ascendency of Liebigian chemistry, the submersion of individuals into a collective nationalist superorganism, and even the view of the self as a firm.[31]

Forerunners of this orientation are evident already in the eighteenth century. Edward Young, trying to refresh the concept of glory, rejects gloomy graveyardism for the beneficent teleology of the natural theologians. Death "Calls for our Carcasses to mend the Soil" (V, 663–64) in the name of some great cycle: "Look Nature through, 'tis *Revolution* all. / All Change, no Death" (VI, 678). "As in a wheel, All sinks, to reascend."

> The world of Matter, with its various Forms,
> All dies into new Life. Life born from Death.
> Rolls the vast Mass, and shall for ever roll.
> No single Atom, once in being, lost,
> With change of counsel, charges the most High. (VI, 688, 696–700)[32]

These themes are also prominent in Pope's "Essay on Man":

> See dying vegetables life sustain,
> See life dissolving vegetate again:
> All forms that perish other forms supply
> (By turns we catch the vital breath, and die)
> Like bubbles on the sea of Matter born,
> They rise, they break, and to that sea return.
> Nothing is foreign: Parts relate to whole.
> One all-extending, all-pervading Soul
> Connects each being, greatest with the least
> Made Beast in aid of Man, and Man of Beast;
> All serv'd, all serving! nothing stands alone. (III, 14–25)

On this basis Pope can conclude in book IV: "God sends not ill; if rightly understood, / Our partial Ill is universal Good" (113–15).[33] If the ontology is still Epicurean, the management is Stoic.

Preoccupation with imagining the courses of atoms as they move in and out of bodies became much more focused in the cremation controversy that began in 1874 and persisted for the rest of the century. By and large, the earlier instances of self-as-filth were expressions of a common idiom; by contrast, what occurred after 1874 was a focused exploration of the implications of that idiom for one's own identity, as well as ecology and technology. Partisans repeatedly insisted that the progress of society required a fixation on the state and fate of the filthy corpse. In retrospect, and with regard to the issues I raised at the outset about the existential and social construction of filth, they succeeded to a remarkable degree, and yet they too engaged filth at the philosophical, rather than the visceral, level.

The cremation controversy was a largely literary conflict between two groups of body-disposal reformers, both of them objecting—on grounds of health, decency, harmony with nature, and wise land use—to an antiseptic embalming mentality of the sort that led to the burial of the Duke of Wellington within three layers of lead. Followers of the eminent urological surgeon and painter Sir Henry Thompson urged the adoption of modern scientific cremation, which had recently emerged in Italy. In Italy, cremation had an anticlerical cast; in Britain, it would attract those of "advanced" views, including some Fabians, progressive Anglicans, and theosophists.[34] A central part of Thompson's argument was that cremation would give the body's atoms, particularly its carbon, maximum mobility to move on to new and beneficent uses as quickly as possible. Thompson's co-reformer and main critic, the eminent gynecological surgeon and lithographer Sir Francis Seymour Haden, urged burial in a biodegradable "earth to earth" wicker casket. Haden's network of supporters is less easily identified than Thompson's Cremation Society, but his ideas appealed to high Anglican organicists, and the scheme was sanctioned by the Church of England Sanitary Association. Whereas Thompson appealed to modern technology in the form of gas (or later electric) furnaces made by such international giants as Siemens, Haden appealed to tradition. Prior to the eighteenth century "unchested" burial had been the norm, he argued.[35] He too was concerned with spiriting our matter on to its next use. Neither, in fact, made much of a dent in Victorian funeral practices, but their controversy was nevertheless highly public—in the letters pages of the *Times*, in the polite monthlies, in the leaders columns of the main medical weeklies, and in the local press around the country.[36]

What makes the controversy so important here is that one of its central issues was whether the buried and rotting corpse was "filth." Owing to the wider range of alternatives for dealing with the bodies of the dead, the concept of filth was contested in a way it had not been in previous burial reform controversies, particularly that of the 1840s, when reformers pressed for replacement of overcrowded urban churchyards by suburban garden cemeteries.[37]

For both sides the question was one of the education of the senses—

or rather of the imagined senses, since the arguments were preponderantly directed toward "imagined" rather than actual encounters with the appearance, odors, or invisible pathological products that might warrant a verdict of "filth." In turn, a good deal of that reeducation concerned transformation. If it could be shown that the stuff of the body was turning, in the most appropriate manner possible, into beautiful new things, then the educated mind would agree that a verdict of "filth" was inappropriate. Thus, an ecological imagination would trump the (presumed) visceral reaction. Both Haden and Thompson agreed that the customary means of disposal of the dead, though based on an attempt to avoid decomposition, was in fact quintessentially filthy and led to the most despicable form of decomposition, slow putrefaction. But each tried also to attach some notion of filth to the other's technology, and for each, the appeal to "nature" was the chief source for filth-escaping rhetoric. This "nature," the entity that administered the cycles that sustained human existence, knew no filth. For both Haden and Thompson, it was indeed a contest of greener than thou.

For both protagonists, and for their many supporters, one of the main modes of argument was a managed alternation between the objective gaze of one who looks upon a body and reacts to it, both viscerally and logically, and the presumed subjective experience of that dead body. That the latter required the attribution of consciousness to an entity that was defined in part by its lack of that very attribute was in fact no great obstacle. One grappled with that anomaly in any discussion of an afterlife, which invariably involved reconciling one's sense of the permanence of self with one's perception (and anticipation) of an insensate and dissolving embodiment. If, logically, the gulf was broad and the concepts irreconcilable, rhetorically it was almost impossible to avoid combining the two acts of cognition: of gazing on the body and reacting to it, and of imagining oneself as that body. Subject and object could not be kept straight.

The language of the debate was itself often unavoidably ambiguous. When a proponent of cremation pointed out that earth burial was "a slow and horribly disagreeable process," surely it is disagreeable not only to behold, but also to contemplate undergoing.[38] William Holder, a surgeon lecturing to the Hull Literary Club, asked, "[Is it] comforting to know that a ton of solid earth is to rest on our body? Does it show much reverence to our dead to place them in the wet clays of our cemeteries, permeated through and through by worms, and laved in the foetid exhalations and exudations percolated from neighbouring graves?"[39] While allusions to the heaviness of the earth have been interpreted, too narrowly in my view, as referring to the widespread fear of premature burial, permeation by worms and washing in "exudations" seem to require a subjective perspective.[40]

Explanation at the chemical level—the self as atoms—was particularly powerful in such discussions because the language of chemical affinity blurred (and in blurring, bridged) the subject-object dichotomy. It left ambiguous and unresolved the question of whether our erstwhile atoms were subjects, acting to free themselves from the confinement of the body, or were objects being acted upon. In vain one locked the body in a coffin, hoping to preserve in "unaltered condition" the body's "elements," noted Thompson, those very elements which were "at that moment so destructive and so mobile!"[41] E. D. Girdlestone, though writing in the context of the disposal of human wastes rather than that of dead bodies, personified the more important elements. The oxygen of the atmosphere was an urgent male wishing to mate ("greatly addicted to polygamy"—"a veritable Brigham Young in the World of Matter"). Nitrogen, an element often seen as the essence of animal life, was female and independent: "she forms the connection with abhorrence, and it is only the awful presence and power of *Life* that restrains her." Once this marriage of life was over, nitrogen, through putrefaction, fought her way back to the air. "The moment that organism, that once living plant or animal, *dies*, that moment the imprisoned Nitrogen . . . begins to reassert, aye, and to enforce, her right to liberty—that moment too decomposition or putrefaction sets in. Putrefaction is the result of the imprisoned Nitrogen seeking to return from her enforced exile to her native sky."[42]

Even if the stuff of self did not liberate itself, we participated as patient in a loving process conducted by God's immediate agents. "Upon it [the buried body] the Almighty Architect is effecting decomposition by the agents of nature; myriads of his microscopic scavengers, microbes, worms, bacilli, fungi, and ferments are breaking up that case of flesh, that we may give back to nature and mankind the elements leased to the body for a period of usefulness."[43]

Both the subjective and the objective point of view could be made either to dictate a verdict of filth or its opposite, a reveling in happiness, beauty, harmony, and utility. In practice, the more subjective accounts were usually the more positive descriptions. Once one worked through the possibilities of molecular transmogrification with an experienced tour guide, one could see much of what was revolting at first glance as a happy atomic afterlife.

Take, for example, a striking passage in Thompson's initial cremation essay, published in the *Contemporary Review* in late 1874, one that recalls the extended meditations of Browne, who had himself reflected on classical cremation in his *Hydrotaphia*. Thompson (famous for his extravagant dinner parties) asked his reader to consider a mahogany dining table, containing, he claimed, particles that had once existed in the bodies of Africans,

> and before the African existed was an integral portion of many a
> generation of extinct species, and when the table, which has borne of
> well nigh some 20 thousand dinners, shall be broken up . . . and
> consigned to the fire, thence it will issue into the atmosphere once more
> as carbonic acid, again to be devoured by the nearest troop of hungry
> vegetables—green peas or cabbages in a London market garden, say—
> to be daintily served on [a new table] where they will speedily go to the
> making of "Lords of the Creation" and so on, again and again, as long
> as the world lasts.[44]

By beginning with humans and by personifying nonhumans—"troop" of "hungry vegetables"—the passage invites us to go along for the ride. And, if one accepts the possibility of a tour of Africa (one without any danger of tropical diseases) as one of the possibilities yet to come, being dead may have a good deal more to offer in terms of interesting experience than being alive. Of course, Thompson had no scientific basis for tracking particular carbon atoms or for presenting so adventurous and liberating a fate—the carbon might as easily have been dissolved in seawater and imprisoned for eons as limestone. He could only say that some carbon atoms would experience any particular fate that could be imagined. And remarkably, no one, as far as I know, took up Thompson's invitation to think that our atoms had once been (or might later be) embodied in persons of another race. It was permissible to think of embodiment in vegetables that Londoners would eat, but most writers presumed some fairly narrow limits for the circulation of their atoms.

All this is, Thompson is also suggesting, a good thing for ourselves as atoms to be doing. We will be busy and not bored, and we are doing some good. And because these cycles may well be eternal, perhaps, if we invest enough of our faith in this material afterlife rather than the vaguer spiritual one, we may well escape having to contemplate the unpleasant judgments that will take place on the last day—surely God cannot really mean to judge carbon atoms?

Haden too would embody our atoms, but in a more overtly Anglican context. The rich were to envy the shroud-wrapped pauper "in his quicker return to Dame Nature's all-teeming, all receiving bosom," noted a *Times* leader on earth-to-earth burial.[45] Even more openly than Thompson, he conflated the afterlife of the soul, the traditional locus of postmortem consciousness, with the body's atoms. We could, Haden suggests, glimpse resurrection in the atoms (again, presumably with the advantages outlined above): "The body, . . . literally as well as figuratively, ascends from the dead and fulfills the cycle of its pilgrimage by becoming again the source of renewal of life." Haden is writing about oxidation here, and yet ascending from the dead is normally the language of resurrection. He goes on to extol the importance of this excursus: "Is it possible to conceive a provision more beautiful, more benign, more suggestive, not of gloomy, but of elevated and consoling trains of thought?"[46]

All this was very nice, to be sure, and the alternative was indeed dreadful. But could one bring it off? As well as highlighting the delights of cremation and earth-to-earth burial, Thompson and Haden needed to depict other modes of disposal (including the other's preferred technology) as truly filthy. Filth, for Thompson, was what happened to you when you were buried, a state so horrid that we could not imagine it: "a glimpse of the reality which we achieve by burial would annihilate in an instant every sentiment for continuing that process," Thompson asserted. "Nay more; it would arouse a powerful repugnance to the more horrible notion that we too must some day become so vile and offensive, and, it may be, so dangerous." That repugnance, he argued, "was surmounted only through the firm belief that after death the condition of the body is a matter of utter indifference to its dead life-tenant." But Thompson's own argument required the absence of such indifference. Imagining such a condition—whether in ourselves or some beloved other—was the source of the repugnance; in telling us that we could not imagine or confront it, he was asking us to do exactly that.[47]

Even though, as Thompson recognizes, partisans of cremation (and equally of earth-to-earth burial) could gain rhetorical advantage by heightening the contrast between the efficient and adventurous afterlife of those lucky enough to be volatilized (or buried "unchested" as the traditional phrase had it), both groups usually avoided both the graphic description of the body as filth and any semisubjective representation of what it might be like to be filth. Usually they only threatened description—recognizing that readers needed only a hint. "Could I paint in its true colours the ghastly picture of that which happens to the mortal remains of the dearest we have lost, the page would be too deeply stained for publication," Thompson wrote, while the *Times* thanked Haden for forbearing to describe too much.[48] Dr. P. H. Holland, the

Home Office's inspector of burials, who felt his own credibility had been undercut by Thompson, argued that, even in life, the biological was best uncontemplated: "Every day processes go on within our bodies, hidden from sight, little thought of, and the less thought of the better . . . ; which if seen would be inexpressibly unpleasant,—for example, the processes of digestion, secretion, etc."[49]

Among the most graphic was Leopold Hartley Grindon, author of *Cremation Considered in Reference to Resurrection* (1874), who thus describes the results of burial: "Let my darling turn into a foetid mass of crawling corruption; let the features once so lovely and loveable become so ghastly and loathsome that my flesh creeps at the very thought; let her become so foul, and hideous, and sickening, that a diseased dog shall be an angel in comparison. . . . Let all go on slowly, slowly, in the way that pleases ghouls; to what end have we placed her in the grave, save that of slow conversion into blue and slimy putrescence?"[50] Grindon, notably, adopts the spectator's role in all this; and yet "blue," "slimy," and "crawling" is the extent of the actual description here—the rest is a series of comparisons and dictated reactions.

By the late nineteenth century, utility was more prominent in such discussions than it had been a century or two earlier, when the emphasis had been on existential truth rather than profitable activity. The nature that had lent us our atoms, which it was now reclaiming, was a corporation, more powerful and efficient than any that humans could create, Thompson explained. Our apotheosis was to play our corporate role; once we learned that, we would cease to resist and instead joyfully participate.

> Nature will have it so, whether we like it or not. She destines the material elements of my body to enter the vegetable world on purpose to supply another animal organism which takes my place. She wants me, and I *must go*. There is no help for it. When shall I follow—with quick obedience, or unwillingly, truant-like, traitor-like [i.e., through burial], to her and her grand design? Her capital is intended to bear good interest and to yield quick return: all her ways show it—"increase and multiply" is her firm and constant law. Shall her riches be hid in earth to corrupt and bear no present fruit; or be utilized, without loss of time, value, and interest, or the benefit of starving survivors?[51]

Speaking on behalf of Haden, a *Times* leader writer stressed the importance of being a good ecological citizen, noting that we were instructed to "return [ourselves] in due time, at the appointed hour, to the earth . . . with cheerfulness, alacrity, and good-will."[52]

While Thompson held as repulsive anything that happened to a body underground and Haden found a fiery dissolution grotesquely technical, industrial, and polluting—he wrote of the "vomitoria" of the stacks of many crematories in language that is disturbingly similar to descriptions of Birkenau—for both, the distinguishing mark between filth and non-filth was speed.[53] Clearly Thompson had the edge here—a cremation got carbon onto its next appointed uses within an hour or two. But Haden countered that a too quick and violent process was wasteful. The narrower concern was that the valuable ammonia, which should be one of the breakdown products, was destroyed in the fire, but Haden's broader concern was that any universal process of nature ought to be invested with an integrity of its own: surely nature knew better than Sir Henry Thompson how to make wise use of the body at all stages of breakdown. Haden partisans, too, contrasted the rapid "transformation"—not, it may be noted, "decomposition"—of true burial with the slow putrefaction of the rich, encoffined in their gross boxes.[54] In a well-aerated soil, what happened underground was as much a purification by fire as what happened in a crematorium—the fire was just flameless.[55]

The makers of utilitarian arguments always risked offending public sensibility, and both sides accused the other of doing just that. But this was the price of understanding one's own death as serving nature's purposes. Nature's units were atoms and molecules, and they were the raw materials of all natural production. Thompson, in repudiating the accusation of callous utilitarianism, made precisely that case. "Seeing [that] the Great Power which has ordained the marvelous and ceaseless action which transmutes every animal body as quickly as possible into vegetable matter and vice versa, and has arranged that this harmonious cycle should be the . . . necessary law for all existence, I have space for no other sentiments than those of submission, wonder, and admiration." Those who complained were to be reminded that their own existence was "solely due to that divine fecundity which pervades all nature." Thompson wondered how Holland, who had made such a criticism, could ignore the fact that an equally utilitarian process was going on in every churchyard. "He knows perfectly well that the presence of abundant plant-growth is essential in the cemetery to assimilate the noxious gases arising from the buried bodies before alluded to, and that those plants owe their life and structure to the very elements of our 'friends and relatives,' about whom he professes to be so utterly shocked." As burial inspector, Holland managed the "largest institution that ever existed for transmuting the human body into vegetable growth of various kinds."[56]

Utility was in fact central to the case that the state of self as filth was a positive one. However good the use we had made of our molecules during our lives, it was hard to deny that God could make something much better of them than could we poor sinners. In advocating earth-to-earth disposal, Haden insisted that we are privileged to be renaturalized in this way. He was pleading "for the dead, . . . for their right to participate in these . . . signal benefits . . . of the friendly operation of the earth."[57]

Perhaps the self might be friendly filth after death, but what about during life? Remarkably, many writers—of popular works on chemistry or hygiene, equally of works on consolation or on the nature of the soul—represented the living body as undergoing much the same processes as the dead one. Even during life the body was continually in flux, replacing its substance, its atoms coming and going. According to most versions, all the matter of our bodies would have been replaced within seven years. Joshua Trimmer, a chemist and natural theologian, reflected on the process in the early 1840s, just at the time the environmental chemistry of Justus Liebig was becoming popular:

> The skin, and flesh, and bone, have been frequently removed and
> replaced. And so it is, more or less, with our whole body. The arms
> and limbs that sustain us in our schoolboy struggles, are long since
> consigned to the dust, have, perhaps, lived over again more than once
> in plant, or flower, or animal. . . . How interesting—how lofty, are the
> reflections which this fact awakens in connexion with our frail being,
> and with our tenure of this mortal life! "We die daily," receives here a
> new sense. Day by day we lay down in the dust a new portion of our
> earthly substance. Day by day we gather up the fragments of former
> bodies, to build up anew our wasting frames. How are we thus daily
> reminded of our true origin, "He formed man out of the dust of the
> earth"; of our true nature,—"Dust thou art"; and of our speedy fate,
> —"To dust shalt thou return." Our connexion with the dead earth is
> never for a moment loosened. We draw upon it for our hourly food. In
> the midst of our most vigorous life, we are connected with it by a chain
> which cannot for a moment be broken.[58]

To religious writers this phenomenon distinguished more clearly the body from the soul, and therefore made a stronger case for the existence of an immaterial soul. If the body was ever changing, its matter could not be the source of our unique self. A common metaphor was body as a river, its form constant, its substance continually changing.[59] In the cremation controversy, the argument was of further service to liberal theologians in making clear that cremation was no threat to resurrection. Nothing would happen to us after death that was not already happening. That we went up the chimney and dispersed ourselves into all other things rather than lying quietly in a box was no problem for God since, in their view, it was the spiritual, not the physical, body that would be resurrected.[60] And yet since no one could quite say what a spiritual body was—the notion was self-contradictory—the imagination rarely escaped the physical body entirely, and the argument could also work in the other direction, in keeping the mind fixed on the atomic self, its ongoing disbursement and replenishment, and the astonishing miracle that would be manifested in its reconstitution (at which stage of life remained a problem) on the day of resurrection. God, Donne noted, echoing the theologians of his own day and the church fathers long before, knew "in what *Cabinet* every *seed-Pearle* lies, in what part of the world every graine of every man's dust lies; and, . . . he whispers, he hisses, he beckons for the bodies of his Saints, and in the twinckling of an eye, that body that was scattered over all the elements, is sate down at the right hand of God, in a glorious resurrection."[61] To represent the matter of the body as transitory was thus to connect us intimately with the world all around. It implied that the molecular experience after death was not altogether different from the molecular experience during life: we had only to learn better to appreciate our material identity with the rest of nature.

Haden and Thompson, their allies and predecessors in British graveyardism, had chosen to navigate in an alluring conceptual territory. It was one that did not demand exploration. They were at the end of a period of several centuries during which the contemplation of the self as the object of putrefaction had been widespread. Ironically, when cremation began to become popular in the 1920s, its supporters kept well away from arguments about the useful services our atoms would perform; this was even the case with the emerging popularity of ash-scattering. In 1874, Thompson had been criticized as an insensitive utilitarian for considering the possibility of ash-scattering, but during the 1920s "gardens of remembrance" became common at British crematoria. That this ash went into the soil and fertilized plants was presumably evident—the brochures of crematoria offer the option of having the ash spaded into flower beds and borders—but there was no waxing eloquent on participation in the great cycles of the universe.[62] Peter Jupp sees the great war as a key cause of the rise of the acceptability of cremation, and perhaps the horrors of the deaths of so many young men had made the issues of atomic destiny simply too frivolous for public consumption.[63] In the mid-1870s, English writers had alluded to the excellent wheat crops grown on the battlefield at Sedan; it seems doubtful that a French or German writer would readily have made such allusions.[64]

Indeed, the promoters of cremation in the 1920s paid hardly any attention to the dead body at all—one of the chief arguments was that cremation was healthier for the living, in part because it was presumed to prevent the spread of epidemic disease, but more because a service in a dry crematorium (and, noted the surgeon Arbuthnot Lane, a *warm* one as well) was much healthier for an aged mourner than was standing by a graveside in a November drizzle.

These earlier writers had chosen to grapple with the very aspect of the dead body, its transgressive quality, that Douglas and Becker regard as the element that warrants the verdict of filth. Indeed, for them, life and death are not binary opposites—the transformations in the soil are simply another kind of life, a perspective that Bloch and other anthropologists of death find more common in non-Western cultures.[65] Although both Hadenites and Thompsonites claimed the high ground of science and eschewed emotion, they were engaging in an interrogation of emotion and sensibility. If one accepts Becker's claim that the denial of death, dissolution, and biologicality is the fundamental neurosis, they were confronting that neurosis in the most direct way. In terms of the history of human relations with the nonhuman, that confrontation is remarkable. These writers invite us to reflect on the ultimate harmony with nature, the recycling of the self, and the abandonment of its boundaries of isolation.

Notes

1. Edward Bickersteth, "First Sermon on Death," in *Works* (New York: Appleton, n.d.), 363.

2. Elizabeth Stone, *God's Acre, or Historical Notices Relating to Church-yards* (London: Parker, 1858), 343.

3. Ernest Becker, *The Denial of Death* (New York: Free Press, 1973), 32; see also 28–31, 51–52, 180–83, 196, 282–84.

4. Mary Douglas, *Purity and Danger: An Analysis of the Concepts of Pollution and Taboo* (London: Routledge and Kegan Paul, 1966).

5. I should note that the presumption of universality seems much stronger in Becker than in Douglas, who makes clear that, while the mechanisms that lead to the "filth" designation operate very widely, the designation of "filth" or "dirt" may fall on a great variety of actions and conditions.

6. See Phillippe Ariès, *The Hour of Our Death* (New York: Knopf, 1981), 110–14, 128, 151–52; Phillippe Ariès, *Western Attitudes towards Death*, trans. Patricia Ranum (Baltimore: Johns Hopkins University Press, 1974), 52; Jack Goody and Cesare Poppi, "Flowers and Bones: Approaches to the Dead in Anglo-American and Italian Cemeteries," *Comparative Studies in Society and History* 36 (1994): 146–75.

7. In seeking an explanation for the preoccupation with resurrection of the real body in the patristic period and the Latin Middle Ages, Caroline Bynum comes close to a Beckerian explanation, but mainly by a process of exclusion: other hypothesized factors do not fit the temporal, spatial, and social character of the evidence: *The Resurrection of the Body in Western Christianity, 200–1336* (New York: Columbia University Press, 1995), especially 113.

8. Lucretius, *On the Nature of Things/De Re Natura*, ed. and trans. Anthony M. Esolen (Baltimore: Johns Hopkins University Press, 1995), bk. III.

9. G. D. Hadzsits, *Lucretius and His Influence* (New York: Longmans, Green, and Co., 1935), 272–317. Cosmo Alexander Gordon, *A Bibliography of Lucretius* (London: Rupert Hart-Davis, 1962), 14–19.

10. For similar themes in the medieval period, see *Erthe upon Erthe, Printed from Twenty-Four Manuscripts,* ed., with intro., notes, and glossary by Hilda Murray (London: Early English Text Society/Kegan Paul, Trench, Trübner and Co., 1911), ix, xxx–xl; Christopher Daniell, *Death and Burial in Medieval England, 1066–1550* (London: Routledge, 1997), 69–70.

11. John Draper, *The Funeral Elegy and the Rise of English Romanticism* (New York: New York University Press, 1929), 5; Hoxie Neale Fairchild, *Religious Trends in English Poetry,* vol. 1, *1700–1740: Protestantism and the Cult of Sentiment* (New York: Columbia University Press, 1939), 231.

12. On the importance of classical models, see *A Century of Broadside Elegies,* ed. John Draper (London: Ingpen and Grant, 1928), 152; Amy Reed, *The Background of Gray's Elegy: A Study in the Taste for Melancholy Poetry, 1700–1751* (repr., New York: Russell and Russell, 1962), 37–38.

13. At least for the earlier period this theme in poetry is well developed by a number of historically minded critics writing in the 1920s and 1930s on the origins of Romanticism. Most important is Draper, *Funeral Elegy*; also Reed, *Background of Gray's Elegy*; Eleanor Sickels, *The Gloomy Egoist: Moods and Themes of Melancholy from Gray to Keats* (New York: Columbia University Press, 1932). See also the delightful and encyclopedic invective of Fairchild, *Religious Trends.*

14. Reed, *Background of Gray's Elegy,* 112; Draper, *Funeral Elegy,* 302. On teenage poets see, for example, Harriet Falcolner, "Extempore on Death" (1787): "O cruel Death, thou fatal canker-worm, / Which on the damask cheek of Beauty prey'st; / With thee the slave and soverign too are one," quoted in Sickels, *Gloomy Egoist,* 137.

15. Sickels, *Gloomy Egoist,* 92; C. S. Northrup, *A Bibliography of Thomas Gray* (New Haven, CT: Yale University Press, 1917).

16. Geoffrey Rowell, *Hell and the Victorians: A Study of the Nineteenth-Century Theological Controversies concerning Eternal Punishment and the Future Life* (Oxford: Clarendon, 1974), 7, 9; Sickels, *Gloomy Egoist*, 38, 92.

17. Ariès, *Hour of Our Death*, 58; Daniell, *Death and Burial*, 83.

18. Edmund Spenser, *The Faerie Queene*, in *The Complete Works in Verse and Prose of Edmund Spenser,* ed. Alexander B. Grosart, 9 vols. (printed for private circulation, 1882), vol. 8, canto VII, lines 421–28, 159–67.

19. Sir Thomas Browne, "Religio Medici," in *Religio Medici and Other Works*, ed. L. C. Martin (Oxford: Clarendon, 1964), 36–37.

20. James M. Clark, *The Dance of Death in the Middle Ages and the Renaissance* (Glasgow: Jackson, Son, and Co., 1950). Nigel Llewellyn, however, notes that order of presentation did represent rank. See his *The Art of Death: The Visual Culture in English Death Ritual, c. 1500–c. 1800* (London: Reaktion Books/Victoria and Albert Museum, 1991), 25. See also the nineteenth-century revival of the dance of death: [William Combe], *The English Dance of Death, from the Designs of Thomas Rowlandson, with Metrical Illustrations by the Author of "Doctor Syntax,"* new ed., 2 vols. (London: Methuen, 1903).

21. At times this muse is defiantly democratic: "Why then, said my working Thoughts, oh! why, should we raise such a mighty Stir about *Superiority* and *Precedence*, when the next remove will reduce us all to a state of equal Meanness? Why should we exalt ourselves, or debase others, since we must all one Day be upon a common Level, and blended together in the same undistinguished Dust?" (James Hervey, "Meditations among the Tombs in a Letter to a Lady," in *Meditations and Contemplations*, 2 vols., 2nd ed. [London: Rivington, 1748], 11). See also Sickels, *Gloomy Egoist*, 137; Adrian Desmond, "Artisan Resistance and Evolution in Britain, 1819–1848," *Osiris*, 2nd ser., 2 (1987): 84–85.

22. John Donne, *Devotions upon Emergent Occasions together with Death's Duel* (Ann Arbor: University of Michigan Press, 1959), 176. Donne draws here on Job 14:17 and 23:20.

23. See, for example, Hervey, who writes that the rich, in their vaults, will "acknowledge Kindred with creeping Things, and *quarter Arms* with the meanest Reptiles" ("Meditations among the Tombs," 49–50). The persistence of belief in spontaneous generation made it possible to think that the body was literally being transformed into worms, rather than being invaded by them (Ariès, *Hour of Our Death*, 120).

24. Robert Blair, *The Grave: A Poem*, intro. J. Means, Augustan Reprint Society 161 (Los Angeles: William Andrews Clark Memorial Library, n.d.). On Blair, see Reed, *Background of Gray's Elegy*, 188.

25. It has been suggested that talk of worms is a reference to "the worm that dieth not" (Mark 9:44) and thus to hell. See Philip Almond, *Heaven and Hell in Enlightenment England* (Cambridge: Cambridge University Press, 1994), 91–92; Michael Wheeler, *Death and Future Life in Victorian Literature and Theology* (Cambridge: Cambridge University Press, 1990), 53. In most cases, I

think, no such referent is intended. One can also find dissolution used for comparative purposes: if you think dissolution is bad, hell is much worse (Hervey, "Meditations among the Tombs," 18–19). Charles Kingsley was insistent that worms be regarded literally, not metaphorically: Frances Kingsley, *Charles Kingsley: His Letters and Memories of His Life, Edited by His Wife*, 2 vols. (London: Macmillan, 1894), 2:59, 309.

26. This is a central theme of Caroline Bynum, *Resurrection of the Body* and *Metamorphosis and Identity* (New York: Zone, 2001). See also D. S. Wallace-Hadrill, *The Greek Patristic View of Nature* (repr., New York: Barnes and Noble, 1968), 69–71.

27. Isaac Watts, "Reliquae Iuvenales," quoted in Draper, *Funeral Elegy*, 68–69; see also 151, 316. Ariès, *Hour of Our Death*, 342–43, takes the Puritan view to indicate a lack of interest in the body. I disagree.

28. It would appear that in France this sadness was associated mainly with secular libertinism; in England, according to Draper, it is a hallmark of Puritan melancholy. Melancholy, while recognized as a pathological condition if in excess, was also respected and cultivated, particularly by Puritans. The melancholic was the realist; there was some expectation, too, that a tendency to melancholic fixation on the grave was a sign of seriousness, and therefore of election. See Draper, *Funeral Elegy*, 16–17, 67, 151–52, 316; Ariès, *Hour of Our Death*, 322, 391–92; J. McManners, *Death and the Enlightenment: Changing Attitudes to Death among Christians and Unbelievers in 18th Century France* (Oxford: Clarendon, 1981), 335–57; Thomas A. Kselman, *Death and the Afterlife in Modern France* (Princeton, NJ: Princeton University Press, 1993).

29. Following Mary Douglas, *Purity and Danger*, one might argue that this literature is a genuine and widely shared struggle to delineate the boundaries of the self by trying to impose a social order on precisely those things that refuse to be categorized. Or, one might note with Maurice Bloch, that this is evidence that his generalization that the living-versus-dead distinction is far from absolute, is applicable in modern western Europe as well. See Bloch, "Death and the Concept of a Person," in *On the Meaning of Death: Essays on Mortuary Rituals and Eschatological Beliefs*, ed. S. Cederroth, C. Corlin, and J. Lindström, Uppsala Studies in Cultural Anthropology 8 (Uppsala: Almqvist and Wiksell, 1988), 16–17.

30. On priest's mutton, see Ariès, *Hour of Our Death*, 56; and Isabella Holmes, *The London Burial Grounds: Notes on Their History from the Earliest Times to the Present Day* (London: Unwin, 1896), 268.

31. Ariès, *Hour of Our Death*, 346, 389, 433–45, 511.

32. Edward Young, *Night Thoughts*, ed. Stephen Cornford (Cambridge: Cambridge University Press, 1989).

33. Alexander Pope, "An Essay on Man," in *The Poetical Works of Alexander Pope*, new ed. (Philadelphia: J. J. Woodward, 1836).

34. Holmes, *London Burial Grounds*, 270. The most recent treatment of the

controversy is J. Leany, "Ashes to Ashes: Cremation and the Celebration of Death in Nineteenth-Century Britain," in *Death, Ritual, and Bereavement*, ed. R. Houlbrooke (London: Routledge, 1989), 188–235.

35. G. V. Poore, *Earth to Earth Burial* (Manchester: Church of England Sanitary Association/John Heywood, 1893); compare Wheeler, *Death and Future Life*, 66.

36. An excellent source is the clippings files (CRE/H) of the Cremation Society Archives held at the University of Durham Library.

37. Deborah Wiggins, "The Burial Acts: Cemetery Reform in Great Britain, 1815–1914" (PhD diss., Texas Tech University, 1991).

38. Rev. R. Ussher, *Lecture on Cremation* (London: The Cremation Society, 1891), 3.

39. William Holder, *Cremation vs Burial: An Appeal to Reason against Prejudice. A Lecture before the Hull Literary Club* (Hull: A Brown, 1891), 3.

40. Wheeler, *Death and Future Life*, 52. One might argue that the preoccupation with premature burial reflects the vividness with which postmortem states were being imagined and the corresponding difficulty of maintaining a clear distinction between alive and dead.

41. Henry Thompson, *Modern Cremation: Its History and Practice to the Present Date*, 4th ed. (London: Smith, Elder, and Co., 1901), 67.

42. E. D. Girdlestone, *Our Debt and Duty to the Soil, or The Poetry and Philosophy of Sewage Utilization* (Weston-super-Mere: Robbins, 1878), 16, 31.

43. Holder, *Cremation vs Burial*, 15–16.

44. Henry Thompson, "The Treatment of the Body after Death," *Contemporary Review* 23 (1874): 319–28, at 320–21.

45. Francis Seymour Haden, *Earth to Earth: An Answer to a Pamphlet on Cremation* (London: Macmillan, 1875), 23–25, 31.

46. Francis Seymour Haden, *The Disposal of the Dead: A Plea for Legislation* (London: Bemrose and Sons, 1888), 4, 7. There were so many naturalistic analogies for resurrection that the boundary between natural and miraculous could be blurred, as in this case. See Wheeler, *Death and Future Life*, 66; Kselman, *Death and the Afterlife*, 128.

47. Thompson, *Modern Cremation*, 91.

48. Thompson, *Modern Cremation*, 90; quoted in Francis Seymour Haden, *Earth to Earth: A Plea for a More Rational Observance of the Conditions Essential to the Proper Burial of the Dead* (London: Earth to Earth Society, 1875), 39–42.

49. P. H. Holland, "Burial or Cremation," *Contemporary Review* 23 (1874): 482.

50. A Truth Seeker [Leopold Hartley Grindon], *Cremation Considered in Reference to Resurrection* (London: James Spiers, 1874), 12–13.

51. Thompson, *Modern Cremation*, 85, 90, 149.

52. In Francis Seymour Haden, *Earth to Earth: An Answer to a Pamphlet on Cremation*, 31.

53. Francis Seymour Haden, *Cremation an Incentive to Crime: A Plea for Legislation* (London: Edward Stanford, 1892).

54. B. W. Richardson, *Hygeia—A City of Health* (London: Macmillan, 1876), 44.

55. Rev. W. H. Lyttelton, *Scripture Revelations of the Life of Man after Death and the Christian Doctrines of Descent into Hell, the Resurrection of the Body, and Life Everlasting, with Remarks upon Cremation and upon Christian Burial* (London: Daldy, Ibister, 1875), 23.

56. Thompson, *Modern Cremation*, 117–19.

57. Francis Seymour Haden, *Earth to Earth: A Plea for a More Rational Observance of the Conditions Essential to the Proper Burial of the Dead*, 6.

58. Joshua Trimmer, "Chemistry in Its Relations to Agriculture," *North British Review* 3 (1845): 276.

59. Frederick C. Bakewell, *Natural Evidence of a Future Life Derived from the Properties and Actions of Animate and Inanimate Matter* (London: Longman, Rees, Orme, Brown, Green, and Longman, 1835); Lyttelton, *Scripture Revelations of the Life of Man after Death*, 33.

60. Ussher, *Lecture on Cremation*, 1–2.

61. Quoted in Almond, *Heaven and Hell in Enlightenment England*, 132.

62. *Cremation in Great Britain* (London: Cremation Society of England, 1909), 40, 43, 49, 68; H. T. Herring, in P. Herbert Jones, and George Noble, eds., *Cremation in Great Britain,* 2nd ed. (London: Cremation Society of England, 1931), 10–11, 17, 22, 27, 35, 43, 47. These authors estimate that ashes were being scattered in about half of the cremations by the end of the 1920s. Most crematoria charged for this service, and charged more for scattering in the Garden of Remembrance, as opposed to other, more generic disposal on the grounds.

63. Peter Jupp and Clare Gittings, eds., *Death in England: An Illustrated History* (New Brunswick, NJ: Rutgers University Press, 2000).

64. Girdlestone, *Our Debt and Duty to the Soil,* 36.

65. Bloch, "Death and the Concept of a Person," 11–29.

Chapter 2

The New Historicism and the Psychopathology of Everyday Modern Life

David Trotter

he histories of sensory experience produced during and partly as a result of the New Historicism's irresistible rise to methodological supremacy might be thought of as the supplement that reveals a lack. Justly celebrated studies like Alain Corbin's *The Foul and the Fragrant* (1982) and Peter Stallybrass and Allon White's *The Politics and Poetics of Transgression* (1986) deploy a model of subjectivity not at all incompatible with that which informs the grand New Historical survey of modern disciplining and punishing.[1] We learn from these studies that the sights and smells of the nineteenth-century metropolis gave rise in the bourgeois subject to a mixture of fascination and disgust, which at times of social and political crisis sharpened into panic. And yet the very richness of the material brought to light by historians of sensory experience makes one wonder about the validity of some of the categories they have used to analyze it. Did fascination always and everywhere infiltrate the disgust provoked in the solid citizen by the prostitute and the overflowing sewer? Should we always and everywhere discern an anxiety about social and political unrest "behind" the sanitary reformer's anxiety about poisonous miasmas?

Esther Lyon's Point of View

I begin with some domestic odors: the smell of old clothes, the smell of tallow, the smell of cooking. The odors are described in George Eliot's

Felix Holt, the Radical (1866), and I begin with them partly because they mattered to Eliot in interesting ways, and partly because they do not feature at all in Catherine Gallagher's fine account of the novel's contexts in the final chapter of *The Industrial Reformation of English Fiction* (1985). That account seems to me one of literary criticism's boldest and most persuasive acts of historical explanation. But the history it clarifies, unlike the novel that prompted the clarification, is oddly odorless: a history of secrets rather than of secretions.

In 1861, a painting in a London gallery provoked a sharp disagreement between two visitors. The visitors were George Eliot and the writer and political economist Harriet Martineau. The painting depicted a stork killing a toad. Martineau attacked it on the grounds both of coarseness and of amorality. Eliot defended it, on the grounds that art shows the world as it is, rather than as it ought to be.[2]

Gallagher uses this encounter in a London gallery to characterize the doctrine of literary realism which shaped Eliot's early fiction. Martineau's faith in Providential design decreed that the uninspiring habits of the stork were remarkable only to the extent that they made Providential design manifest; for her, facts had no meaning at all unless they could be shown to derive from and to exhibit general principles or values. Eliot, by contrast, thought that nothing short of the patient accumulation of evidence of every kind would make manifest whatever inscrutable design there might be in nature. For her, facts were continuous with values: the way to get from one to the other was, in Gallagher's words, "by the process of inclusion, equalization, and acceptance, by the slowmoving narrative method we now call metonymic realism."[3] The writer's job was to accumulate facts. The meaning and value of any principle that, in due course, emerged from the accumulation of facts would depend on its fidelity to the observable social world. Gallagher compares this doctrine of literary realism to the liberal theory of political representation developed in the 1820s by James Mill. Mill's best possible Parliament, like Eliot's best possible novel, would be a detailed proportional rendering of British society. In his view, the meaning and value of Parliamentary representation depended on the closeness of the fit between a representative and the social world (the specific constituency) he represented (222–23). Both the political and the literary doctrine assume an unbroken continuity between facts and general principles.

Gallagher goes on to argue, however, that the novels Eliot published in the 1860s "manifest a deep skepticism about the principles of mere aggregation in literature as well as politics." One source of this skepticism was the critique of liberal theories developed by John Stuart Mill, in "On Representative Government" (1861), and Matthew Arnold, in *Culture and Anarchy* (1869). Mill sought to ensure the disproportionate representation of "instructed minds" by giving plural votes to those who could demonstrate "mental superiority." "His proposed Parliament would not correspond to any empirical social reality," Gallagher explains, "but would, rather, directly express, by distorting what is, that which ought to be." Parliament would thus represent value *to* the people (224–33). Arnold's theory of culture gave a sharper definition to the disinterestedness Mill required from those who represent value to the people. Culture, Arnold maintained, is what enables a man or woman to set aside personal and class interests, and develop that "best self" whose steady and diligent exercise will promote social harmony.[4] The best self, needless to say, was not a principle that could be derived from the accumulation of facts about individual anxieties and desires. Like Mill's theory of government, Arnold's theory of culture rested on a radical discontinuity between facts and principles. Eliot, who followed the work of both men closely, found in their revision of liberal doctrines of government a political role for the writer and a reason to revise her own doctrine of literary realism. Gallagher compares Eliot's later work to the novels of Gustave Flaubert, Thomas Hardy, and Henry James in its readiness to separate fact from value. Like John Stuart Mill's ideal Parliament, these protomodernist works represent value (the value of art) *to* an audience mired in personal and class interests (266).

Gallagher links Eliot to Mill and Arnold most astutely, drawing in particular on passages in Eliot's "The Natural History of German Life" (1856). Like Mill and Arnold, Eliot began in the 1860s to insist on a radical discontinuity between values and facts. Gallagher regards *Felix Holt* as the novel in which Eliot's increasingly Arnoldian politics finally overcame her allegiance to a cumulative or metonymic realism. Her argument turns on the characterization of Felix Holt or, rather, on the near impossibility of characterizing a protagonist whose utter indifference to marks of personal and social distinction altogether disqualifies him from descriptive realism of *any* kind. How does one describe someone who has no self at all apart from his best self?

Felix's indifference becomes an object of analysis in chapter 5, when he visits Mr. Lyon, the dissenting minister. Throughout the visit, he remains indifferent both to social facts (such as household smells) and to social signs (such as the aspiration encoded in the use of candles made of wax rather than tallow). Mr. Lyon does not. He is defined for us by the anxiety with which he points out to Felix that the wax candle is not an "undue luxury," but a result of the loathing his daughter feels for the smell of tallow.[5] It is Felix's indifference to social signs that makes him the embodiment of Arnoldian disinterestedness; he refuses a job that would oblige him to wear a high cravat and straps and thus set him apart from his fellow workers (144). And yet such superficial marks of distinction, which Felix is too cultured to notice, are, as Gallagher points out, all that everyone else, including the narrator and the reader, has to go on (238). We know Mr. Lyon by his momentary alarm about the wax-light. Felix would rather not exist than have his opinions about the smell of tallow or the prestige of wax count for anything. He asks to be known by a different criterion altogether; he belongs to a different world, to a different novel. Thus, when Esther Lyon suggests that there is a good way and a bad way to be refined, Felix condemns refinement out of hand (53). Gallagher's political reading of the novel demonstrates convincingly why its protagonist is as he is. But there is, I think, another point of view embedded in it: Esther Lyon's.

Esther, we might suppose, pays too much attention, or at least more attention than a cultured person should pay, both to social signs (indications of status) and to social facts (the smell of tallow). She is, Gallagher observes, "predefined as a user of conventional codes" (246). Her distaste for the ostentatiously fashionable is itself a fashion statement. For the point of her subtle bonnets is not that they should render modishness obsolete, but that they should extinguish the brazen variety sported by her rivals. "A real fine-lady does not wear clothes that flare in people's eyes, or use importunate scents, or make a noise as she moves," Esther tells Felix: "she is something refined, and graceful, and charming, and never obtrusive." To Felix, however, mere refinement and unobtrusiveness cannot be supposed to constitute authenticity: one sort of "fine-ladyism" is as good, or as bad, as another (153). Indeed, Felix's true authentic culture explicitly defines itself against Esther's false culture, a combination of subtle bonnets and subtle poems: he is appalled to learn that she has been reading Byron (150–51).

However, the indiscriminate vehemence of Felix's "strong denunciatory and pedagogic intention" (150) toward Esther, his rudeness about absolutely everything she says and does, prompts a certain skepticism. One might wonder, for example, whether an aversion to tallow is a "failure" of the same order as caring about bonnets. Felix undoubtedly thinks so; from his point of view, which is the point of view of the Arnoldian best self, mere contingencies of social fact and social sign have neither meaning nor value. The novel, I shall suggest, gives us reason to disagree, for it is remarkably precise about Esther's aversions. Some, such as her objection to the squinting George Whitfield, seem petty enough, and duly fall victim to Felix's scorn (154). Others invite a more complicated response. Thus, Esther feels genuine affection for her father:

> But his old clothes had a smoky odour, and she did not like to walk with him, because, when people spoke to him in the street, it was his wont, instead of remarking on the weather and passing on, to pour forth in an absent manner some reflections that were occupying his mind about the traces of the divine government, or about a peculiar incident narrated in the life of the eminent Mr. Richard Baxter. (161)

Esther's reluctance to walk with Mr. Lyon is attributed, with mild disapproval, to a "horror of appearing ridiculous" (161). Of her dislike for the smoky odor of his old clothes, nothing further is said. Felix, of course, cares as little about smoky odors as he does about appearing ridiculous (it's all contingency). But the contrast between the silence maintained about the first of these aversions and the swift and comprehensive exegesis of the second gives pause for thought. It allows us to acknowledge that a dislike for the smoky odor of old clothes is not self-evidently frivolous, that it bears on the facts of coexistence and cohabitation rather than on a fantasy about status.

That Eliot knew the difference is made plain in chapter 27, when Esther sufficiently overcomes her anxiety about status to walk out for the first time with Felix. The chapter opens on a mundane note, with Esther "left alone in the parlour amidst the lingering odours of the early dinner, not easily got rid of in that small house." On this occasion, the narrator immediately intervenes to point out that such "vulgar details," easily overlooked by rich people who live in large houses, have made or broken many a humble life (358). Esther, who hates the smell of cooking, endures it, now, because she thinks Felix may call. She learns to live with her own disgust, and by living with her own disgust learns to love Felix. She learns not to mind his patched boots and lack of cravat. Endurance of an unpleasant social fact (the smell of cooking) has prepared her, more effectively than any amount of denunciatory and pedagogic intention, to endure an unpleasant social sign (Felix's shabbiness). "Esther was a little amazed at what she had come to" (360).

Esther's amazement occurs during a stroll along the river that rather alarmingly reinstates Felix's best self. "When Felix had asked her to walk, he had seemed so kind, so alive to what might be her feelings, that she had thought herself nearer to him than she had ever been before; but since they had come out, he had appeared to forget all that" (364). Felix's sublime disinterestedness, his forgetting all that, is the source of his superiority, as both Esther and the narrator fervently acknowledge; it expresses true meaning and value to mere women (and mere readers) mired in superficiality. And yet, unlike Felix, we have witnessed Esther's endurance of her own disgust. We do not "forget all that" as easily as he appears to have done. Eliot wrote the scene fluently, making few alterations to the manuscript; she felt both sides of the exchange between Esther and Felix with equal intensity. So, I think, should we.

Fear, Anxiety, and Sanitary Reform

I shall have more to say later about the significance of Esther Lyon's aversion to domestic odors. But I want to turn now to another narrative whose ideological implications have recently become the focus of inquiry: Edwin Chadwick's *Report on the Sanitary Condition of the Labouring Population of Great Britain* (1842).[6] If Henry Mayhew's *London Labour and the London Poor* (1861), with its huge cast of characters, its "many and curious narratives,"[7] and its resemblance to oral history, suited the 1960s, when historians spoke of structures of feeling, of worlds turned (or not turned) upside down, then Chadwick's lugubrious compilation suited the 1990s, when historians spoke of surveillance and discipline. The New Historicism has identified Chadwick as the czar of normalization: the man whose "strategic genius" put in place the elements of a modern disciplinary regime.[8] Peter M. Logan finds in the system of drains Chadwick planned to install in London and other major cities, as Foucault had found in the military encampment, an "architecture that would operate to transform individuals: to act on those it shelters, to provide a hold on their conduct."[9] According to Joseph W. Childers, the 1842 *Report* "belongs squarely within the disciplinary 'tradition' that D. A. Miller eloquently describes in *The Novel and the Police*."[10]

Childers describes the following passage, from observations made by a Dr. J. F. Handley, as "characteristic" of the *Report*'s emphasis on discipline and surveillance.[11]

> When the small-pox was prevalent in this district, I attended a man, woman, and five children, all lying ill with the confluent species of that disorder, in one bed-room, and having only two beds amongst them. The walls of the cottage were black, the sheets were black, and the patients themselves were blacker still; two of the children were absolutely sticking together. I have relished many a biscuit and glass of wine in Mr. Grainger's dissecting-room when ten dead bodies were lying on the tables under dissection, but was entirely deprived of appetite

during my attendance upon these cases. The smell on entering the apartments was exceedingly nauseous, and the room would not admit of free ventilation. (316)

Almost as striking as the passage itself is the commentator's reluctance to comment on it. What we have here, what the New Historicism cannot quite bring itself to notice, is a richly perverse banquet of the senses, or rather, like masque and antimasque, a banquet (in Mr. Grainger's dissecting room) and an anti-banquet (in the slum-cottage). In the dissecting room, appetite flourishes under the protection of a gaze which engenders precise observation from a distance. Anatomy, a science predicated on sight, had of course long been the cynosure of a (modern) desire for knowledge.[12] Immunized twice over, by scientific inquiry and by spectatorship, Handley is able to relish his biscuit and his glass of wine to the full.

In the slum-cottage, however, objects no longer present themselves as discrete entities disposed, like the dissecting room's ten dead bodies, within a coherent visual field. Everywhere, figure lapses into ground. The blackness of the walls cannot be distinguished from the blackness of the sheets, which cannot be distinguished from the blackness of the patients. The children stick together, presenting themselves less to the knowing eye than to the fantasized touch. Confluence is the note not only of the species of smallpox that has struck this family down, but of the scene itself, of the anti-banquet. As the sense of sight loses its way, baffled by confluence, the sense of smell takes over. The nauseating stench kills appetite. For Handley, the scene in the slum-cottage really does take the biscuit.

The emphasis on confluence reminds me of *Bleak House*, the book Miller places at the center of his disciplinary tradition.[13] It reminds me of the "sallow prisoner" who makes a brief appearance in its opening chapter, and whose only function in the novel is to be described as in "a state of conglomeration about accounts of which it is not pretended that he had ever any knowledge."[14] Confluence, conglomeration: in novel and report alike, such flowing or gathering together baffles the panoptic gaze. The fog and the mud, in the opening chapter of *Bleak House*, are not, as Miller maintains, "symbols" of power's ability to pervade and saturate: they pervade and saturate after their own distinct fashions; they belong to the novel's phenomenology of stickiness.[15] Krook combusts, on a "fine steaming night" when there is a "queer kind of flavour" in the air, which may or may not derive from the chops grilling at the Sol's Arms (499–500), in the name of that phenomenology.

Krook combusts so that Dickens may describe the soot on Mr. Guppy's arm, which "smears, like black fat" (505). Krook combusts so that Dickens may describe the "stagnant, sickening oil, with some natural repulsion in it," which oozes down the wall to lie "in a little thick nauseous pool" on the floor (509). Miller's belief that the nature of a disciplinary system shapes the nature of any resistance it may encounter obliges him to regard this combustion as the necessary outcome of the law's pervasiveness. "It is as though apocalyptic suddenness were the only conceivable way to put an end to Chancery's meanderings, violent spontaneity the only means to abridge its elaborate procedures."[16] However, Krook's death, sudden in the event, is remarkably long and drawn out in the discovery. It takes the best part of a chapter before Guppy and Jobling trace the uneasiness that so afflicts them back to its horrific source in Krook's smoldering remains (511). In that time, in the reading of those pages, the black grease they cannot help touching whenever they move exemplifies nothing apart from itself. Continuous with the fog and mud of chapter 1, and with the many other conglomerations described at length in the intervening chapters, it is the world's residue, not Chancery's.

The black confluence in a slum-cottage, the little thick nauseous pool: these representations solicit a new approach. They require, to begin with, I think, an analysis of the meanings and values that have been attributed to sensory perception, and of the moral, social, and political uses to which it has been put. I am indebted at this point to Steven Connor's exploratory work on the relation between the structures of identity and the structure of the sensorium.[17] Connor argues that modernity should be understood not in terms of the subordination of the proximity senses, as typified by the ear to the hegemony of the eye, but in terms of a fraught and continually renewed argument between the powers of ear and eye. His aim is to flesh out, with the help of literary and psychoanalytic descriptions, an "auditory I," a "self imaged not as a point, but as a membrane; not as a picture, but as a channel through which voices, noises and musics travel."[18]

It seems doubtful that there ever was, or ever could be, an olfactory I. Even so, useful points of comparison can be established between the vicissitudes of hearing, as Connor describes them, and the vicissitudes of smell, which are my concern here. Connor points out that sound, unlike sight, has often been understood as a disintegrative principle. We can only see one thing at a time, but it is possible to hear several sounds simultaneously. Sound often carries menace unless and until we trace it back to and locate it in a specific source, or visualize its origin.[19] Similarly, the bad smells that so afflicted sanitary inspectors like Handley were threatening because they were sourceless and composite, a queer kind of flavor in the air. Noise, Connor observes, especially loud noise, is always agonistic: it involves the maximum at once of arousal and of passivity. Thus "noise creates communities of listening sealed by the revulsion and offence of others."[20] Similarly, the stench of the slum engendered in the sanitary inspector both arousal and passivity. What was the slum if not a community of odor sealed by the revulsion and offence of others?

However, there is at least one important difference between hearing and smell. Smell ranks low, as William Ian Miller has pointed out, indeed lowest of all, in the hierarchy of senses. That there are bad sounds need not diminish the glory of hearing. That there are delightful fragrances has done little to elevate smell: traditionally, the best odor is not a good odor, but no odor at all.[21] The sense of smell remained, in the representations that are my concern here, an overwhelmingly disintegrative and agonistic principle. To understand the meanings and values attributed to it, one must be able to think the pure negativity of the nausea it provokes.

The sense of smell has two defining qualities that may help to explain why it featured so consistently as a disintegrative and agonistic principle in the literature of sanitary reform. One has to do with the way smells are conceptualized, the other with the way we remember them. In the first place, smells are hard to define. "Even though the human sense of smell can distinguish hundreds of thousands of smells and in this regard is comparable to sight or hearing," Dan Sperber observes, "in none of the world's languages does there seem to be a classification of smells comparable, for example, to color classification." There is no taxonomy of smells, no "semantic field." When we designate smells, we do so in terms either of their causes (the smell of incense, the smell of excrement) or of their effects (a heady perfume, an appetizing smell). In the domain of color, designations become lexicalized (the term "rose" can be used without bringing the flower to mind); in the domain of smell, "metonymy remains active and infallibly evokes cause or effect."[22] Whereas the tactile possesses its own rich and versatile idiom (oozy, squishy, gummy, mucky, dank, and so on), the odorous does not. "Routine tactile sensation spurs language to inventiveness," Miller points out, "while the olfactory and gustatory reduce us to saying little more than yum or yuck."[23] It is often routine tactile sensation that spurs Dickens to inventiveness in *Bleak House*. When, in passing, he compares a gas lamp seen through fog to the sun seen by husbandman and ploughboy from the "spongey fields" (49), the detail's precision rapidly supplements and clarifies our sense that this is a world in which everyone and everything will stick fast. Indeed, the very richness and versatility of the account somewhat offset its pessimism. Similarly, Dr. Handley's description of the slum-cottage becomes almost Dickensian in tone when it notes the two children "absolutely sticking together." Thus, the phenomenology of tactile sensation both appalls and stimulates at the same time. By contrast, it is the *lack* of an appropriate semantic field that renders the mere allusion to a bad smell in narrative so profoundly unsettling. What would a phenomenology of odor be a phenomenology *of*? Meaning itself falters.

There are two ways, Sperber argues, we can retrieve memorized information: by deliberate recall (without external stimulus) and by recognition (in the presence of some "new" fact, we remember that we already possess it). Some kinds of information are easier to recognize than to recall: we recognize many faces, but recall only a few. Smells are in this respect an extreme case: we recognize them easily, but find them almost impossible to recall. We recall the scent of a rose only by recalling (by revisualizing) the flower; and yet one can, at a distance of years, recognize a scent one has only scented once, and know immediately that one has scented it before.[24] Every time the sanitary inspector enters a slum-cottage, he recognizes its utterly distinctive odor, but he will never be able to recall that odor without external stimulus (he will never be able to re-present it in his written report). A bad smell's other profoundly unsettling quality is that it always comes back from outside, from elsewhere, from beyond the limits of conscious recollection.

The rhetorical function of the shift of emphasis, in Handley's account, from sight and touch to smell is to insist upon negativity. How can we grasp that insistence? The New Historicism's preoccupation with modernity's dominant visual regimes has produced some brilliant analyses of the moment at which those regimes falter: the moment, for example, at which the philanthropist or the colonial administrator finds his gaze turned back against him in menace, in mimicry. However, there is a problem with this form of analysis. The problem lies in the model of affect that the New Historicism more or less uniformly incorporates, whether its object is attitudes to the slum, or orientalism, or homosexual panic. That model is a Freudian model. Freud's insistence that the psyche is incurably split and that ambivalence informs feeling through and through has proved enormously productive in cultural theory. But it obscures the negativity of a feeling like disgust. According to Freud, disgust is a reaction-formation against an interest in and desire for its object; in particular, disgust defends the psyche against a shameful acknowledgment of anal eroticism.[25] It is this faith in the ambivalence of disgust that underpins the New Historicism's account of the nineteenth-century metropolis or the nineteenth-century Orient as a locus of mingled fascination and loathing. Stallybrass and White declare, influentially, that "disgust always bears the imprint of desire."[26] According to Logan, the literature of sanitary reform endlessly reproduces, in its exposure of filth and decay, "a fascination with repugnance."[27]

I do not want to deny that desire exists in a dialectical relation to loathing. However, if we are to understand disgust as a disintegrative and agonistic principle, we must be able to isolate, within the dialectic, its negating or antithetical moment. At this point in my argument, I want to make a knight's move, a move beyond psychoanalysis (beyond ambivalence) into phenomenology. A distinction I have found useful in thinking about Esther Lyon, and about Dr. Handley in the slum-cottage, is the distinction Martin Heidegger develops in *Being and Time* between feeling and mood. One of Heidegger's terms for mood is *Befindlichkeit*: not "state of mind," as it is sometimes translated, but something like "how one finds oneself."[28] "How are you doing?" we say: that is an enquiry after *Befindlichkeit*. My subject is Dr. Handley's *Befindlichkeit*; or, rather, the *Befindlichkeit* he seeks to induce, by such measures as the shift of emphasis from sight and touch to smell, in his readers.

Feelings are directed at specific entities, at people or things; a mood is directed at (or in a sense directed from) the world. Heidegger's favorite moods are of course boredom and *Angst* (anxiety, dread). We might think of the first chapter of *Bleak House* when he observes that profound boredom, "drifting here and there in the abysses of our existence like a muffling fog, removes all things and all human beings and oneself along with them into a remarkable indifference."[29]

Anxiety, too, dissolves or cancels out the identities of subject and object alike. Heidegger distinguishes between fear, which is a feeling, and anxiety, which is a mood. Both are responses to threat, but whereas fear is a response to something specific *in* the world (a gun, an animal, a gesture), anxiety has no object, and is all the more oppressive for that. You can run away from an animal or a gun, and respond to a gesture, but you cannot do anything about the world as such, about being-in-the-world as such. Anxiety confronts *Dasein* with the determining yet contingent fact of its own worldly existence.[30]

For Heidegger, at his most Kierkegaardian, anxiety is oppressive, but also a disclosure, a form of understanding. I want, for my own purposes, to halt his analysis at the moment before it finds in anxiety's oppressiveness a form of understanding, at the moment when it recognizes anxiety as a wholly disintegrative and agonistic principle. *Befindlichkeit*, Heidegger remarks, "makes manifest 'how one is.'" "In anxiety," he adds, "one Feels '*uncanny*' [In der Angst ist einem '*unheimlich*']."[31] Freud's interest in the *unheimlich*, by contrast, centered on the term's semantic density. For him, the uncanny was that kind of terrifying experience that "leads back to what is known of old and long familiar." "Thus *heimlich* is a word the meaning of which develops in the direction of ambivalence, until it finally coincides with its opposite, *unheimlich*. *Unheimlich* is in some way or other a sub-species of *heimlich*."[32] Heidegger's interest in the *unheimlich* was grammatical rather than semantic. It was an interest, not in ambiguity and ambivalence, but in the way language encodes a relation between subject and object, self and world.

> In anxiety, we say, "one feels ill at ease" [es ist einem unheimlich]. What is "it" that makes "one" feel ill at ease? We cannot say what it is before which one feels ill at ease. As a whole it is so for one. All things and we ourselves sink into indifference. . . . At bottom therefore it is not as though "you" or "I" feel ill at ease; rather, it is this way for some "one."

Heidegger wants to know not what uncanniness is, but what it does to the person who experiences it. He wants to know about the "one" it manufactures out of a "you" or an "I." This grammatical inquiry allows him to grasp the uncanny as a disintegrative and agonistic principle rather than as ambivalence. "With the fundamental mood of anxiety," he concludes, "we have arrived at that occurrence in human existence in which the nothing is revealed and from which it must be interrogated."[33]

Heidegger's grammatical inquiry maps onto that taking of position that so absorbs Dr. Handley in the slum-cottage. When a threat emerges, Heidegger says, anxiety, unlike fear, "does not 'see' any definite 'here' or 'yonder'" from which the threat might be thought to come. That which threatens us in anxiety, he goes on, is "already 'there,' and yet nowhere; it is so close that it is oppressive and stifles one's breath, and yet it is nowhere."[34] Dr. Handley, in the slum-cottage, or recalling the slum-cottage, suffers anxiety rather than terror. It is not, exactly, that there is nothing to be afraid of—smallpox is a contagious disease—but he does not represent himself as afraid. He represents himself as anxious and nauseated. In the cottage, he can no longer see any definite here or yonder: people and things no longer appear to him as discrete entities disposed within a coherent visual field. The confluence stifles his breath: he knows it as the stench on which he gags. He knows, we might speculate, not the imminence, but the inevitability, of his own death.

The literature of sanitary reform, taken as a whole, relentlessly con-
verts fear into anxiety. According to the zymotic theory of disease then
prevalent, a bad smell was itself something to be afraid of, a specific
threat; yet in their reports, the sanitary inspectors rarely identify the bad
smells that so afflicted them *in medical terms*, as contagious matter.[35]
Those smells are there, not for diagnostic purposes, but for the anxiety
they have already provoked in the inspector (in "one") and for the
anxiety they may yet provoke in the reader. So pervasive was this conversion of fear into anxiety and nausea that it provoked a counter-
movement, in novels and reports alike: the conversion of anxiety back
into fear, back into a specific threat against which steps could be taken.
Esther Summerson's disfigurement by smallpox, in *Bleak House*, serves
little purpose: it is no test of other peoples' feelings about her, since
those feelings have never been based on appearance. But it does demonstrate that the world's stench can take the concrete and devastating
form of a disease communicated from one identifiable person to another: there is something to be afraid of. It is with such conversions, of
fear into anxiety, and, I shall argue, of anxiety into fear, that historical
explanation can begin.

Fear has hitherto loomed larger than anxiety in New Historicist accounts of the politics and poetics of sanitary reform. Mary Poovey
argues that the emphasis in Chadwick's *Report* on exteriors rather than
interiors constitutes an elaboration of the domestic ideology that the rising middle class had claimed as its own. In eighteenth- and nineteenth-
century Britain, domesticity was one of the most important means by
which middle-class men represented and asserted their social superiority over both the spendthrift earl and the promiscuous and improvident
factory hand. A clean and orderly family life, with its concomitant
separation of spheres, became the norm against which exponents of
middle-class hegemony measured the pathologies only too apparent in
the behavior of aristocrat and proletarian alike.[36] What Chadwick did
in his *Report*, Poovey argues, was to figure domesticity's opposite in
consistently powerful terms: some of its "most graphic and emotionally
charged descriptions" are those of working-class men who do not reside
in anything remotely resembling a middle-class home (121). The Parisian *chiffoniers*, or scavengers, for example, are described as "outcasts
from other classes of workmen" who "sleep amidst their collections of
refuse" and remain idle during the day. These men, Chadwick reports,
"rose in revolt" when the authorities had the streets swept during an
outbreak of cholera. Their British counterparts were the "bone-pickers"

who scavenged for scraps of meat in gutters and dung-heaps. "Often hardly human in appearance," one witness recalls, "they had neither human tastes nor sympathies, nor even human sensations, for they revelled in the filth which is grateful to dogs, and other lower animals, and which to our apprehension is redolent only of nausea and abomination" (163–65).

But why was scavenging such an urgent issue? Poovey finds a political motive. According to her, the *Sanitary Report* mobilized a (largely implicit) domestic ideology in support of an explicit denunciation of social *and* political pathologies. The "precise historical referent" for the figuring of the scavengers was Chartism. It was in 1838, she observes, as Chadwick was laying the foundations of sanitary reform, that William Lovett and Francis Place published the People's Charter. In February 1839, the Convention of the Industrial Classes was held in London. On 6 May, a petition bearing 1,200,000 signatures in support of the Charter was presented to Parliament, and the leaders of the Convention threatened a general strike. Riots broke out in July, and again in September. Despite rigorous suppression, Chartism "had proved by 1842 that working men could and would organize in favor of political enfranchisement." It was these activities, Poovey concludes, that prompted Chadwick's emphasis on the savagery of the bone-pickers (126–27).

There are some problems with this account. Chadwick and Francis Place were in touch throughout the 1830s. On 21 June 1829, Place warmly congratulated Chadwick on an article about poverty in the *London Review*. When Chadwick became Secretary to the Poor Law Commissioners, Place approached him more than once on behalf of friends seeking jobs, or information. On 21 April 1835, he urged Chadwick to enforce the new workhouse regime rigorously. The correspondence continued into and beyond the period of Place's involvement in Chartism.[37] These letters are significant because they articulate, in their forms of address, in the mutual understanding they assume, a professional relationship. Chadwick, no friend to Chartism, was a friend of Chartists. No doubt he disapproved of Place's views, moderate though they were. But it is inconceivable that he would have associated him with bone-pickers.

Furthermore, if anyone was responsible for introducing domestic ideology into the bitter industrial disputes of the 1830s and 1840s, it was the Chartists themselves. Working-class radicals had construed the social world in terms of gender since at least the 1820s.[38] Recent studies have shown that the twin ideals of female domesticity and male breadwinning "developed out of and were in harmony with values which originated in pre-industrial artisanal workshop culture."[39] The separation of spheres was not a middle-class conspiracy. It remained axiomatic in working-class radicalism in the 1830s and 1840s.

My point is not that Chartism posed no threat, in Chadwick's mind, but that the threat it did pose was less than absolute. That threat has to be understood as an element in the complex of fears and anxieties that animated professional relationships among the sanitary reformers in the late 1840s. A remarkable letter written on 1 February 1847 by Dr. Lyon Playfair, one of Chadwick's main collaborators, takes us as close to the center of that complex (as close to sanitary reform's primal trauma) as we are ever likely to get. The letter itself denounces in vigorous terms the "abominable system of cesspools." Its remarkable postscript, however, turns darkly from the cesspools to the men whose job it is to empty them. "Our nightmen are a brutal set of men & fortunate will it be for the public if we can get rid of them." Playfair goes on to describe the evacuation of a cesspool in which matter had been allowed to accumulate for five years.

> During the process of emptying, I saw one of the nightmen actually take up in his hand a quantity of the night soil & swallow it "to see how it tasted." After I left, I understand, in fact I have it in evidence under the signature of the nightman himself, one of the nightmen rubbed the nightsoil into his eyes, "to see if it acted in the same way on the eyes as common night soil." Could the chiffoniers of Paris classed among the "classes dangereuses" equal these nightmen in their bestial habits?[40]

The postscript, which deliberately revives the 1842 *Report*'s allusion to the Parisian chiffoniers, clearly has implications for the debate about the politics and poetics of sanitary reform. It might be taken to confirm Poovey's hypothesis that anxiety about nightmen and nightsoil was determined in the last instance by a fear of social and political unrest, a fear of revolution. Or it might be taken to confirm my hypothesis that the sanitary reformers sometimes sought to control anxiety by converting it back into fear. The point of the comparison, I think, is not to make the nightmen seem even more dangerous than they actually are, by associating them with a politicized lumpenproletariat, but, on the contrary, to humanize them, to find in their otherwise incomprehensible bestiality a semblance of intent, a semblance of identifiable feeling: something to be afraid of. The comparison is Playfair's way of not seeing, or rather of not smelling, his own inevitable death in these shit-eating zombies.

Phenomenology and Historical Explanation

Eliot wants us to acknowledge the force of Esther Lyon's nausea, its justice. The odors do of course have an origin in particular objects or activities. But the condition of simultaneous arousal and passivity they induce in Esther would not be cured merely by the removal of those objects and activities; other objects and activities would soon take their place. The cure lay, as Eliot knew, in public acknowledgment of the condition. One could argue that acknowledgment was taking shape, as Eliot wrote, within a specific institutional context: the Divorce Court. Gradually, in the years after its establishment in 1857, the court began to admit as grounds for legal separation not only the fear in which a violent husband might put his wife, but also the anxiety and nausea he might provoke in her by the "filthiness" of his conduct and attitudes.[41]

The sanitary reformers, too, sought public acknowledgment of something other than the terror aroused by an outbreak of smallpox, or Chartism. They wanted justice for a certain *Befindlichkeit*: one should not have to witness a man swallowing nightsoil or rubbing it into his eyes. Reforms did follow, eventually, though the persistence and the continual diversification thereafter of the literature of sanitary polemic would suggest that they did not and could not address its informing anxiety.

Acknowledgment remains an issue for historical explanation. To acknowledge the novelist's or the sanitary reformer's text is neither to take it at face value nor to reduce it to a symptom. What I have tried to do here is to use the distinction drawn by Heidegger between fear and anxiety as a means of infiltrating those texts. For Eliot's Esther Lyon, as for Chadwick and Playfair, filth is never just filth, that is, something they could stop thinking about if they really wanted to. Nor is it just notfilth; nor just Chartism, as Poovey might argue; nor just an object of repressed desire, as Stallybrass and White might argue. Heidegger's distinction may help us to define the rival fantasies at work in the middleclass Victorian response to filth. With it, historical explanation, hitherto disbelieving of nausea, unable to take it on its own terms, begins. For each enactment of the impulse to convert fear into anxiety, anxiety into fear, is a function of, and in turn illuminates, its particular circumstance.

Notes

1. Alain Corbin, *The Foul and the Fragrant: Odour and the French Social Imagination,* trans. Miriam L. Kochan (London: Picador, 1994); Peter Stallybrass and Allon White, *The Politics and Poetics of Transgression* (London: Methuen, 1986), especially chapter 3. Also of note is Hans J. Rindisbacher's *The*

Smell of Books: A Cultural-Historical Study of Olfactory Perception in Literature (Ann Arbor: University of Michigan Press, 1992). Rindisbacher's main focus is on nineteenth-century French and German realism; he describes the New Historicism as the "line of thinking" in which his study finds its appropriate place (23). All three studies have a common point of reference in the work of Norbert Elias: *The Civilizing Process*, trans. E. Jephcott, 2 vols. (New York: Pantheon, 1978–82).

2. Letter of 7 May 1861 to Henry Reeve; R. K. Webb, *Harriet Martineau: A Radical Victorian* (London: Heinemann, 1960), 39. The staunchness with which Eliot held her ground has led one critic to associate her preference for unheroic subject matter with that of Gustave Courbet, most combative of contemporary realists (Murray Roston, "George Eliot and the Horizons of Expectation," in *Victorian Contexts: Literature and the Visual Arts* [New York: New York University Press, 1996], 114–29).

3. Catherine Gallagher, *The Industrial Reformation of English Fiction: Social Discourse and Narrative Form, 1832–1867* (Chicago: University of Chicago Press, 1985), 221. Subsequent references to this work will be cited parenthetically in the text.

4. Matthew Arnold, *Culture and Anarchy* (Cambridge: Cambridge University Press, 1969), 95.

5. George Eliot, *Felix Holt, the Radical* (Harmondsworth, UK: Penguin, 1972), 139–40. Subsequent references to this work will be cited parenthetically in the text.

6. Edwin Chadwick, *Report on the Sanitary Condition of the Labouring Population of Great Britain*, ed. M. W. Flinn (Edinburgh: Edinburgh University Press, 1965). Subsequent references to this work will be cited parenthetically in the text.

7. Henry Mayhew, *London Labour and the London Poor*, ed. Victor Neuberg (Harmondsworth, UK: Penguin, 1985), 163.

8. The most recent biography, by Anthony Brundage, is entitled *England's "Prussian Minister": Edwin Chadwick and the Politics of Government Growth, 1832–1854* (University Park: Pennsylvania State University Press, 1988). Philip Corrigan and Derek Sayer emphasize Chadwick's "strategic genius" in *The Great Arch: English State Formation as Cultural Revolution* (Oxford: Blackwell, 1985), 127.

9. Peter M. Logan, *Nerves and Narratives: A Cultural History of Hysteria in Nineteenth-Century British Prose* (Berkeley and Los Angeles: University of California Press, 1997), 161. The quotation is from Michel Foucault, *Discipline and Punish: The Birth of the Prison*, trans. Alan Sheridan (New York: Vintage, 1977), 172. One doubts whether Chadwick's drains were meant to *shelter* anyone.

10. Joseph W. Childers, *Novel Possibilities: Fiction and the Formation of Early Victorian Culture* (Philadelphia: University of Pennsylvania Press, 1995), 120.

11. Ibid., 86.

12. See Jonathan Sawday, *The Body Emblazoned: Dissection and the Human Body* (London: Routledge, 1995); Lawrence Rothfield, *Vital Signs: Medical Realism in Nineteenth-Century Fiction* (Princeton, NJ: Princeton University Press, 1992).

13. D. A. Miller, *The Novel and the Police* (Berkeley and Los Angeles: University of California Press, 1988), 58–106.

14. Charles Dickens, *Bleak House* (Harmondsworth, UK: Penguin Books, 1971), 51. Subsequent references to this work will be cited parenthetically in the text.

15. Miller, *Novel and the Police*, 60. There would be worse places to start, if one wished to develop a phenomenology of Dickensian stickiness, than the pages Gaston Bachelard devotes to the "valorization" of mud: *La Terre et les rêveries de la volonté* (Paris: Librarie José Corti, 1948), 105–33.

16. Miller, *Novel and the Police*, 62.

17. Steven Connor, "The Modern Auditory I," in *Rewriting the Self: Histories from the Renaissance to the Present*, ed. Roy Porter (London: Routledge, 1997), 203–23; "Feel the Noise: Excess, Affect, and the Acoustic," in *Emotion in Postmodernism*, ed. Gerhard Hoffmann and Alfred Hornung (Heidelberg: Universitätsverlag Carl Winter, 1997), 147–62.

18. Connor, "Auditory I," 207.

19. Ibid., 213.

20. Connor, "Feel the Noise," 156.

21. William Ian Miller, *The Anatomy of Disgust* (Cambridge, MA: Harvard University Press, 1997), 75.

22. Dan Sperber, *Rethinking Symbolism*, trans. Alice L. Morton (Cambridge: Cambridge University Press, 1975), 115–16.

23. Miller, *Anatomy of Disgust*, 67.

24. Sperber, *Rethinking Symbolism*, 116–17. Psychological research has demonstrated that the association between a smell and its verbal description tends to be weak. See Trygg Engen, "Remembering Odors and Their Names," *American Scientist* 75 (1987): 497–503, and *Odor, Sensation, and Memory* (New York: Praeger, 1991). See also Miller, *Anatomy of Disgust*, 67–68, and Rindisbacher, *The Smell of Books*, 10–20.

25. Letter to Wilhelm Fliess, 14 November 1897, in *The Complete Letters of Sigmund Freud to Wilhelm Fliess, 1887–1904*, ed. Jeffrey M. Masson (Cambridge, MA: Harvard University Press, 1985), 280; *Three Essays on Sexuality*, in *The Standard Edition of the Complete Psychological Works*, ed. James Strachey et al., 24 vols. (London: Hogarth Press, 1966–74), 7:135–243, especially 160–62, 177–78; *Civilization and Its Discontents* (1930), in *Standard Edition*, 21:59–145, especially 99–100.

26. Stallybrass and White, *Politics and Poetics*, 191.

27. Logan, *Nerves and Narratives*, 164.

28. For discussions of the concepts of mood (*Stimmung, Gestimmtsein*) and of *Befindlichkeit*, see Martin Heidegger, *Being and Time*, trans. John Macquarrie and Edward Robinson (Oxford: Blackwell, 1962), 172–79, 388–96.

29. Heidegger, "What Is Metaphysics?" in *Basic Writings*, ed. David Farrell Krell, rev. ed. (London: Routledge, 1993), 93–110, at 99.

30. Heidegger, *Being and Time*, 228–35.

31. Ibid., 233.

32. Freud, "The Uncanny," in *Standard Edition*, 17:219–56, at 220, 226.

33. Heidegger, *Basic Writings*, 101.

34. Heidegger, *Being and Time*, 231.

35. For zymotic theory, see Christopher Hamlin, "Providence and Putrefaction: Victorian Sanitarians and the Natural Theology of Health and Disease," *Victorian Studies* 28 (1985): 381–411. Corbin notes that in France in the middle years of the nineteenth century, a new emphasis on the repulsive smell of the proletariat appears in accounts by doctors and visitors to the poor. "Hitherto, doctors had seemed impervious to disgust; only fear of infection appeared to motivate precautions" (*The Foul and the Fragrant*, 150). He does not develop the distinction between disgust and fear of infection.

36. Mary Poovey, *Making a Social Body: British Cultural Formation 1830–1864* (Chicago: University of Chicago Press, 1995), 117. Subsequent references to this work will be cited parenthetically in the text. Poovey acknowledges a debt to the most influential account of the normalization of domesticity: Leonore Davidoff and Catherine Hall, *Family Fortunes: Men and Women of the English Middle Class, 1780–1850* (Chicago: University of Chicago Press, 1987).

37. Letters of 21 June 1829, 26 August 1834, 21 April 1835, 21 October 1836, in the Chadwick Collection of the Library of University College London: Chadwick MSS, 1587. The collection includes eight letters from Place to Chadwick, 1829–41.

38. Catherine Hall, "The Tale of Samuel and Jemima: Gender and Working-Class Culture in Early-Nineteenth-Century England," in *White, Male, and Middle-Class: Explorations in Feminism and History* (London: Polity Press, 1988), 124–50.

39. Sonya O. Rose, *Limited Livelihoods: Gender and Class in Nineteenth-Century England* (London: Routledge, 1992), 141. See also W. Seccombe, "Patriarchy Stabilized: The Construction of the Male Breadwinner Wage Norm in Nineteenth-Century Britain," *Social History* 11 (1986): 53–76. In 1835, Place himself argued that men should refuse to work alongside women in mills and factories, so that "the young women who will otherwise be degraded by factory labour will become all that can be desired as companionable wives, and . . . the men will obtain competent wages for their maintenance"; quoted in Rose, *Limited Livelihoods*, 147.

40. Chadwick MSS, 1588.

41. I develop an argument to this effect in *Cooking with Mud: The Idea of Mess in Nineteenth-Century Art and Fiction* (Oxford: Oxford University Press, 2000), chapter 8.

Part II

Sanitation and the City

Chapter 3

Sewage Treatments: Vertical Space and Waste in Nineteenth-Century Paris and London

David L. Pike

he exploitation of subterranean space played a formative role in the nineteenth-century city. From the technological novelty of its metropolitan railways, tunnels, arches, and embankments to its mobilization to conceptualize an urban society divided between rich and poor, law abiding and criminal, healthy and diseased, familiar and foreign, the vertical city was a heady mix of physical fact and social fantasy.[1] Different types of underground space combined matter with metaphor in different fashions; this essay focuses on perhaps the most conflicted of them all, the drainage system.[2] While the underground railway, for example, established the urban underground as a novel site for everyday travel by all classes, the sewer remained closely associated with mythic and religious traditions of the epochal, life-altering trip to the underworld. The Paris Métro and the London Underground presented a forward-looking image of urban space as a perfectly controlled network of interlocking tunnels; the sewer operated to channel anything considered backward-looking and recidivist through its conduits and out of the city altogether.

This essay surveys the range of urban conflict that was addressed metaphorically and physically through the image of the sewer as underworld drain in the two metropolises that dominated the imagination of modern Europe: London and Paris. To place anything in a sewer is to define it as the waste product of the world above it; this essay begins with an analysis of this complex term, the effects of its mythic residue, and the paired reactions to it of either disposal or incorporation, generally attributed to the urban spaces of London and Paris, respectively. I test the limits of and relationship between these twin discourses of space through a comparison of Henry Mayhew's *London Labour and the London Poor* (1861–62) and Victor Hugo's *Les Misérables* (1862). Having established a multivalent concept of waste, I consider a rare glimpse of a nonverticalized, and hence positive, portrayal of the London sewer as an underworld space, in contrast both to the predictably negative version and to the more ambivalent Paris counterpart. The essay concludes by suggesting the consequences of this topographical analysis of waste for two topics in modern urban history: the changing nature of contact between the middle and the so-called lower classes, and the debate over prostitution. Rather than a comprehensive history of either of these heavily studied topics, my goal here is to sketch some ways the physically and metaphorically verticalized spaces of London and Paris have contributed, and continue to contribute, to the production of that history.

Waste and the Vertical City

Modeled on the celebrated engineering of the Roman *cloaca maxima*, the city sewer in its modern incarnation pioneered the technology of arched tunnel construction.[3] As a drainage system carrying waste away from the inhabitants, it represented the rational control of an archaic underground past. At the same time, it retained a strong symbolic resonance as a stubbornly irrational space, the most organic, primitive, and uncontrollable part of the modern city. Sewers accumulate waste, not only excrement and offal, but the cast-off and outmoded remains of things, places, people, techniques, and ideas for which physical and conceptual space no longer exists in the world above. As such, they are a primary locus of decomposition and disease, tied to fear of and desire for death, decay, and dissolution. As Ben Jonson suggested as early as 1610 when he parodied the otherworld journey as a perilous descent of the polluted river Fleet, the sewer had incorporated the river Styx into the topography of London. Consequently, the figures associated with the sewer become not only marginal, but mythical as well, analogous to the imaginary beasts that inhabit them: the alligators of Manhattan, the giant pigs of London, the dog-sized sewer cats and cat-sized sewer rats of every major system.

Like the shades ferried across the Styx into the underworld, these creatures have been not only removed from the world above but trans-formed by that removal. Bloated by the sewage on which they feed, their excess size reveals the paradoxical fecundity of waste, just as the souls in hell are both damned for eternity and possessed of frightful power in the eyes of the living. The underworld follows neither the standard rules of time—it endures eternally and mingles every epoch in its depths—nor those of space—it is dark, supernatural, and labyrinthine in its con-struction. Yet because every element of it was once a part of the world above, it maintains the power of that connection, with its former mean-ings recombined in unforeseen ways. Those who ply their trades in the literal or figurative proximity of the sewers become both powerful and alien, and serve as personifications of the powerful and alien qualities of the modern city for which the world above can find no place: the *égoutiers* and *tafouilleurs* of Paris, and the toshers and mudlarks of Lon-don become epitomes, for good or for ill, of urban labor; prostitutes become identified as the sewers of the city, transmitters of disease and immorality, disposal systems for excess libido, thresholds between above and below, between purity and filth. Cholera is held to come from and to be resolvable through the treatment of the drainage system. Rarely, but significantly, the sewer can express utopian dreams as well, if of a conventionally regressive nature: dark, womblike, warm, and safe. In sum, the sewer is the conduit of the archaic and the atavistic in modern urban society.

The modernizing nineteenth-century cities enacted, in the renovation of their subterranean infrastructures, a specific form of a traditional process of purification, creating order by articulating a place for what-ever does not fit that order. The anthropologist Mary Douglas has argued that dirt is simply "matter out of place . . . the by-product of a systematic ordering and classification," and that "pollution behaviour . . . condemns any object or idea likely to confuse or contradict cher-ished classifications."[4] While Douglas tends to underplay the complex identities retained by the detritus of any social system, her structural analysis implies the crucial point that filth and pollution do not exist in static opposition to cleanness and purity, but in their quality as cate-gories are fraught with contradiction. "Seeing 'dirt' as contradiction," writes Michael Taussig, "allows us to deepen our understanding and to move beyond the spellbinding surface of the sensational keywords."[5] The cherished principles and categories that define the world above mask their inherent instability by placing underground as filth anything that does not fit those definitions.

"Where there is dirt there is system," Douglas maintains, but the underground, too, has its own "spellbinding" quality, and it arises as much from the temporary rupture of the system it makes visible as it does from its negative role within that system. Flooding, explosive gases, and clogged drainage passages are riveting spectacle as well as urban disaster. Excrement, disease, and death belie the assurance of a cohesive, unchanging human body, isolated in space, but they also fascinate for that very reason. In a similar way, the categories of prostitution, crime, and foreignness embody contradictions in the economic system that defines the modern world. As Lynda Nead has observed, the prostitute presents a frightening reflection of and threat to the economic system of which she occupies the center: "She is able to represent all the terms within capitalist production; she is the human labour, the object of exchange and the seller at once. She stands as worker, commodity and capitalist and blurs the categories."[6] It is an argument that has been made in various forms since the nineteenth century: because the prostitute employs as exchange value what capitalist ideology tells us is reserved for use value—her body as sexual organ—she makes palpable the inherent contradictions in the conventional divisions between public and private, business and leisure, exterior and interior.[7] Criminal behavior similarly challenges conceptions of equality, demonstrating that not all are content or able to earn through wages, that not all are content or able to dwell within the abstractly perfect space of the capitalist economy. Finally, foreignness must equally be cast as dirty because it brings alien cultures and customs that challenge the myth of a single system of social equality. Just as they are fixed conceptually, so these categories are placed in particular spaces within a verticalized conception of the city, in spaces consequently identified as more or less subterranean, alien in nature although spatially proximate to the world above.

The conception of the city as a vertically divided space began to dominate urban representations as the lives of the inhabitants and the spaces they inhabited began to be divided in increasingly manifest ways. The industrial city posed several problems for the smooth functioning of mainstream society, and their resolution was a primary concern for the governors of nineteenth-century Europe. Large population groups had to be brought together and rationally organized in as efficient a manner as possible. Homogenization and regulation were the primary means for this organization. At the same time, the new concentration of bodies created problems of health, sanitation, and control. The more that the proper operation of capitalism required the denial of the basic facts of life, the more the basic facts of life pressed themselves upon the public eye. The nineteenth-century metropolis was the first in which rich and poor did not live cheek by jowl in a mixed-use urban space. Growing spatial segregation and the increase of single-use spaces went hand in hand with a changed sense that the underground carried specific identities applicable only to certain, now unseen spaces.

Two primary discourses grew up around these strategies of sanitation and underground spaces: one focused on the disposal of waste and was conventionally identified with London, the other focused on its transmutation and was identified with Paris. As we shall see, neither discourse fully accounts for the space of either city, nor can the two models be fully understood separately one from the other. The London model articulated a strategy of flushing out of sight whatever was defined as dirt; what was not suitable to the world above was to be repressed, if not eliminated altogether. The Paris model naturalized the urban space, viewing it holistically and striving to contain, recycle, and profit from what could not be directly incorporated into the world above.

As the many remaining traces of precapitalist social structures were relocated underground as filth, they did not simply disappear. Instead, they gained added power—as allure and as threat—from the act of distancing and rejection, especially as acceptable outlets for the fears and desires they had used to express licitly became increasingly constrained. Peter Stallybrass and Allon White have interpreted this process through a model combining Bakhtin with psychoanalysis, arguing that the "bodily lower stratum," repressed as the bourgeois subject matured, was "transcoded" onto the analogous stratum in the city, its lower depths, "the slums, the labouring poor, the prostitute, the sewer."[8] Hence the nineteenth-century trope of filth as truth, and its end-of-the-century Freudian correlative, the unconscious as the locus of reality.

The psychoanalytic model provides a persuasive explanation for the Victorian obsession with all things subterranean, but the focus on a symbolic topography also risks hypostatizing a change in spatial production as an aspect of individual, middle-class experience. One may well argue, for example, as Charles Bernheimer does, that "the complex fascination [of prostitution] is posited in the denial of what is beneath the female body, which . . . the majority of male writers in nineteenth-century France associated with animality, disease, castration, excrement, and decay."[9] Nevertheless, the bourgeois male, if the carrier of the dominant ideology and the test case for the new subjectivity being worked out through the urban underworld, was only one among many groups involved in the production of the nineteenth-century city. The category of filth cannot be reduced to a single quality without being reabsorbed as an idealized counterpart of the ideology determining what is clean. Put another way, animality, disease, castration, excrement, and decay are alluring not merely because they represent everything denied in the maturation of the bourgeois male, but because they are dialectical categories; they are, in essence, both positive and negative. The underground fascinates not merely because it contains all that is forbidden, but because it contains it as an unimaginably rich, albeit inchoate and intoxicating, brew of other times, places, and modes of being in the world, and because that brew intimates the fragility of the unity claimed by the world above.

It may well be that the underworld continued to function as the locus of truth in the nineteenth century in large part because many writers were working through a desire for their own lost connection to their nether parts. Nevertheless, this argument does not account for the mythic component of the descent to the underworld—as that desire was generally figured—nor for those individuals and social groups that experienced filth in a completely different, if no less conflicted, manner, including, among others, prostitutes, the working classes, the criminal classes, and the many individuals not accounted for by any particular category. The Foucauldian model that dominated readings of the nineteenth-century city over the last two decades of the twentieth century maintains that there was a conventional discourse on filth that served primarily to solidify culturally the changes determined by capitalist exploitation of underground and urban space in the nineteenth century. In its abstract form, the ideology of this discourse is straightforward and, on its own terms, holds an uncomplicated view of filth and the underground. Stallybrass and White's Bakhtinian focus on the materiality of the *monde à l'envers* works to correct the limitations of this approach, but does not depart from the abstractly vertical dichotomy of the model. Nevertheless, if we cease viewing the underground from the standpoint of a unified ideology, if we look past the spellbinding surface words that describe it, we find a dialectic between above- and belowground whereby each term opens up the contradictions within the other, and whereby the apparently cohesive and universal system formed by the pair presents itself as only in fact a partial explanation of the world. The vertical model, whether mobilized affirmatively or inverted critically, will be able to generate a comprehensive image of the modern city in all its contradictions only when also read laterally through traces of those other, nonvertical organizations of space for which it no longer has any use.

Mayhew's London and Hugo's Paris

A good example of the difficulty of reducing the ideology of underground space to a single discourse is Henry Mayhew's *London Labour and the London Poor*, begun as a journalistic survey in the late 1840s, expanded into three volumes published in 1850–52, and into four in 1861–62.[10] Mayhew was fascinated by the social system of the "nomadic tribes" of London as an alternative and a challenge to middle-class society. The authorial voice in *London Labour* alternates between shock at the costermongers' lack of knowledge of religion, disinterest in marriage and refusal to save money, and envy at their freedom from the constraints these very institutions placed on his own social class.[11] In this ambivalent model, occupations such as pure-finding (scavenging "pure," or dogs' dung, for use, paradoxically, to cleanse and purify leather), mudlarking (scavenging the polluted mudflats and drainage entrances of the Thames at low tide), and toshing (scavenging within the sewers themselves for objects and money that had fallen through the drains) were emblematic not simply for their function as an abstract "truth" hidden beneath the veil of filth, but as specific spatial practices within the cityscape of London that, because representable only as filth, expressed the contradictions of the rapidly rationalizing city.

Mayhew divides the various occupations of street-finding and collecting spatially: those who limit their finding to the London streets, those whose labor is confined to the river or "that subterranean city of sewerage" that drains into it, and those who remove waste from the houses as well as the streets.[12] At times, he outlines a social hierarchy between the lumpen grubbers, "vacuous of mind"; the intrepid sewer-hunters, "intelligent and adventurous," working in gangs; the "small master" dredger-men; the working-class dustmen, "of the plodding class of labourers, mere labourers"; and even (although not among those interviewed) the "wealthy contractor for the public scavengery . . . as entirely one of the street-folk as the unskilled and ignorant labourer he employs" (137; see Figure 3.1). At other times, he appears to regard all of them as a challenge to mainstream society, as in the characterization of the grubbers as "with a few exceptions stupid, unconscious of their degradation, and with little anxiety to be relieved of it" (136). Finally, there is a temporal specificity to this spatial practice, for Mayhew implies the eventual disappearance of these "outcast" occupations, since each of them is subject to rationalization into "the occupation of a wealthy man, deriving a small profit from the labour of each particular collector" (136). Mirror of a complex social system, image of underground deviance, metaphor of loss of tradition to progress: these

THE MUD-LARK.

[From a Daguerreotype by BEARD.]

Figure 3.1. "The Mud-lark." The iconography of filth: degraded but free. From *London Labour and the London Poor.*

different discourses and different conceptions of a marginal space of the city coexist in the pages of Mayhew.

It is difficult to reconcile the romantic nostalgia for the vanishing occupations of a previous order of capitalism documented in *London Labour* with the conventional Victorian discourse on the lower depths deployed by Stallybrass and White, or by French historian Alain Corbin, who characterized it as "the incessant vacillation between fascination and repulsion."[13] Nor should we dismiss Mayhew's ambivalence simply because it romanticized the nomadic life of the "dirty" Londoners; rather, we should use that contradiction in the category of London filth to crack open the categories that he was purportedly defending. The life-altering truth with which Mayhew returned from his descent into the underworld of London life was the half-expressed realization that he had not merely viewed something sublimely, terrifyingly true, but seen something that he could both recognize and express as a material desire within himself. In the italicized words of a tosher he interviewed, a former blacksmith's apprentice who had lived off of the sewers for over twenty years: "*The reasons I likes this sort of life is, 'cause I can sit down when I likes, and nobody can't order me about. When I'm hard up, I knows as how I must work, and then I goes at it like sticks a breaking*; and tho' the times isn't as they was, I can go now and pick up my four or five bob a day where another wouldn't know how to get a brass farden" (154).

While Mayhew formulated his relation to filth through identification with a different social organization and a different practice of urban space, Victor Hugo metaphorized the city of Paris as a living organism, a "Leviathan," whose history could best be understood through the study of its "entrails." As befits a city whose inhabitants have always been supremely conscious of its representational spaces, Hugo traced the fifteen years leading up to the 1830 revolution and presented his solution of the rift between *les misérables* and the rest of France, between the ideals of the Revolution and its execution in history, by means of the actual space of its drainage system:

> Paris throws twenty-five million francs a year into the water. This is no metaphor. How, and in what way? . . . By means of what organ? By means of its intestine. What is its intestine? It is its sewer. . . . A great city is the most powerful of stercoraries. To use the town to manure the plain is to ensure prosperity. If our gold is dung [*fumier*], then, conversely, our dung is gold. . . . These heaps of filth around the stone bollards, these tipcarts of muck rattling along the night streets, these

frightful refuse barrels, these fetid streams of underground slime that
the pavement hides from you—do you know what they are? They are
the meadow in flower, the green grass, thyme and sage; they are game,
cattle, the satisfied lowing of great cattle in the evening, perfumed hay,
golden wheat, bread on your table. They are warm blood in your veins,
health, joy, life. Thus is the desire of that mystery of creation which is
the transformation on earth and the transfiguration in heaven.[14]

"This is no metaphor," insisted Hugo, and, indeed, it was not, for the
sewers did in fact contain grains, herbs and cattle, the "warm blood"
and the life of the French countryside within their tunnels, transmuted
into waste through the excretory systems of the city's inhabitants. It
required not an alchemical process but a simple change in perspective
for the filth described in the first half of this passage to transmute into
the pastoral vision purportedly its opposite. Hugo provided practical
directions for this transformation in urging the recycling of Parisian
sewage as fertilizer; the first experiments in "manure-spreading fields"
were conducted only four years after the publication of Les Misérables.[15]

What remains a metaphor, however, is the degree to which Hugo
assimilated France's poor into this natural cycle of consumption, digestion, and excretion; this is the metaphor actualized by the religious language with which the passage concludes, the "mysteries" of creation
and of the transfiguration of wine and bread into flesh and blood. The
true burden of Jean Valjean's character, the ideology with which he
emerged from his odyssey through the sewers, was to persuade the
middle-class reader that the same natural relationship inheres between
the classes as between nourishment and the nourished. As Fred Radford
has suggested, Valjean links the worlds of above and below through the
mythography he performs as well as through his representation as digestive matter: "His underworld flight is also a journey of salvation which
preserves the life of Marius. It is a harrowing of hell: one chapter of the
episode is even called, 'He Also Carries his Cross.' . . . The duality is
also there biologically. . . . Valjean is digested, that is, transformed into
both nutriment (he saves Marius) and excrement (his convict identity is
reconfirmed when he is arrested by Inspector Javert at the sewer exit)."[16]
Radford does not, however, draw the final conclusion of Hugo's social
program, whereby even the convict, even the system's excrement can
potentially be converted into something of value to the body politic.
Whether emerging from the Leviathan as Jonah from the whale in his
individual quality as social prophet within the novel's structure, or
excreted from it as fertilizer for generations to come, Valjean closes the

circle of a perfected and benevolent capitalism in which nothing and no one would go to waste. A counterpart to Baudelaire's equally holistic image of the city as a whore with poisoned sewage coursing through her veins, Hugo's Paris is a Leviathan which feeds on the rich produce of the surrounding country, digesting what is of immediate value and excreting through its sewers as fertilizer for that countryside what it cannot make immediately useful. This is the representational identity of the Paris underground, subsumed within its social space as use value rather than, as in the London model, being carried away as waste product.

The transformation of dirt into gold is a common socialist fantasy and a metaphor for the obscured processes of earlier forms of social organization still buried and redeemable in the present. This is the means whereby Mayhew's scavengers subsisted on the margins of the new economy; in the full-fledged ideology of monopoly capitalism, the metaphor would disappear in favor of the creation of money *ex nihilo*, without the necessity of dirtying one's hands, of processing it through the digestive system first. Exchange value in its purest form uses capital to create further capital, eliminating matter altogether. Hugo, by contrast, aimed to recover the material processes of urban capitalism through the transformative metaphor. So, whereas Radford, for example, writes critically that "even in Hugo the final agent of purification is money,"[17] I would argue that we must read the image dialectically: in comparison with precapitalist systems, this is indeed a frightening process; in comparison with the dematerialized capitalism and the cleansed underground that was developing by the late nineteenth century, it actually provided a critical reminder that such a process of purification was not yet in fact completed.

The Sewer as Domestic Space

While Mayhew may have envied the freedom of the costermonger life and Hugo may have fantasized about modes of recycling the world below, seldom in the writing of London or of Paris does one encounter an extended representation of any positive potentialities of the organic underground as such. Those that exist are quite instructive to examine, for they clearly delineate the contradictory peripheries of the central discourse. One such representation can be found in *The Wild Boys of London* (1866), an infamous penny-dreadful serial so scandalous for its sex and violence that reprints of it were seized by the police.[18] In fact, *Wild Boys* was no more pornographic than many less vilified serials; it did, however, paint an unusually sympathetic portrait of the band of homeless lads that provides its title. The description of the sewer hide-out of the so-called Children of the Night is bereft of the protestations of filth and foul odors that were (and remain) de rigueur for accounts of organic underground urban dwellings.[19] Instead, we find something more akin to an adolescent, makeshift imitation of that innovation of the previous century, the London club:

> It was built in a style of architecture which is rarely seen now; the walls were stone, the roof vaulted, and supported by large pillars. It was furnished with innumerable piles of mats of every description, from the rough rope to the luxurious woolen. On these a number of boys reclined in various attitudes, each according to his inclination. Several lamps hung from chains fixed to the roof, and gave a smokey aspect to the place. A square iron stove stood in the centre, and the smoke was conducted out by means of a pipe, which, with considerable ingenuity, was so placed as to lead downward into an adjacent sewer. A box formed of rough planks, served them for a table, and completed the domestic arrangements, since it also served as a receptacle for provisions.[20]

The introductory architectural note is important, as it grounds the boys' club fantasy in nostalgia for an earlier urban space, "which is rarely seen now." Traces of what might be seen as discomfort remain, as in the "smokey aspect" of the lamps, but they contribute to a picturesque effect in keeping with the nostalgic tone.[21] It is an ingeniously designed, comfortable, and safe space.

It is not so much that the reality of the sewer has been elided, but that the passage has drawn on the positive aspects of the ambivalent qualities of waste in place of the more conventional negative ones. Rather than being assimilated as filth by the sewers in which they live, the Wild Boys move through them at will, in contrast to the streets above, where they continue to be pursued and harassed. "It's nothing when you get used to it," explains Dolphin to the newly arrived refugee, Dick. "We gets wet, and we gets dry again; the mud makes us dirty, and the water makes us clean. And when we gets in, we has a warm bed and a good fire, with something to eat in the bargain."[22] In this description, the boys' identity is in no way fixed by the space in which they shelter. There is a physical ordeal to undergo, a frightening dive and swim through flooded tunnels, but the otherworld within, just under the streets but worlds away, is everything not being offered to these boys in the world above: "a warm bed and a good fire, with something to eat in the bargain," and escape from the authorities a further bonus.

The sensational space the reader expects from the serial's title and from his or her prior knowledge of penny-dreadful muck is there as well, in spades. Chosen for illustration was not the clubhouse scene but the lurid adventure of a new arrival who discovers the body of a man being gnawed upon by rats (see Figure 3.2). The plotting meets all expectations of a verticalized London space as well: the pure boys, those worthy of being salvaged from the sewers, are eventually filtered out and cleaned up, while the dirty ones are shipped off to Australia, which often functioned as a continent-sized garbage dump in the Victorian imaginary. This should not lead us simply to dismiss the original idyll as pure ideology or as simple fantasy, however, for then we must perforce dismiss the same idylls when they appear as pure ideology or pure fantasy in their more familiar place in middle-class discourse. Instead, they can remind us that the utopian aspects of bourgeois desire are no more necessarily joined to capitalist ideology than the negative aspects of filth are inherently lower-class.

The dialectic between the safe haven and the familiar spectacle is not the same as the verticalized play between attraction and repulsion to which the underworld is generally reduced in accounts of nineteenth-century waste, in which the boys would have had to be represented as unthinking albeit pitiable animals in their lair or as above-grounders temporarily and criminally misplaced in the world below. In neither case is the sewer the haunt of the unrepentant villains of the genre, who generally dwell either in the figurative underworld of the slums or as dissolute aristocrats in the mansions high above. The sewer offers shelter and knowledge to those with the misfortune of finding themselves in it. In *The Mysteries of Old Father Thames* (1848), for example, a misplaced youth who will eventually make good is taken in and trained by an old mudlark (popular urban nomenclature was generally more fluid than in Mayhew's taxonomies), who leads him through the tunnels to an abandoned thieves' house on West-street above Fleet Ditch where he inhabits a derelict squat little better than the sewer running just below its floor. Both tunnel and room are equally pervaded by "noxious and pestilential vapours" and "darkness and filth."[23] This view from below is not bereft of critical impetus, but the criticism is expressed solely through the negative formulation of dirt. The old mudlark, it turns out, is actually something of a hermit in retreat from the world above, where, as a shopkeeper with a loving family, he had experienced, as he puts it, "the turpitude with which the competitive system of production and distribution is rife, but the frightful extent of which is known only to those engaged in it" (see Figure 3.3).[24] By contrast to the vitiated existence of the old mudlark, too beaten down even to be granted a name, *The Wild Boys of London* provides us with a glimpse of dispossessed individuals participating on their own terms in a world from which they have otherwise been excluded. At such a moment, admittedly rare in representations of urban poverty, the lower depths exhibit the same contradictory range of experience as any other social space.

THE DISCOVERY IN THE SEWER.

Figure 3.2. "The Discovery in the Sewer." A conventional visual representation of the sensational underworld illustrates a less conventional text. From *The Wild Boys of London* (shelfmark 12620.h.27). Reprinted by permission of the British Library.

Similar spaces in the literature of Paris are more frequent, although they tend, as in the case of *Les Misérables*, to be more ambivalent than this London exception. For example, Erik the Phantom's famous apartments in an underground lake beneath the Paris Opéra, based on a *fait divers* of the late nineteenth century, have much in common with the Wild Boys' crib in terms of safety and comfort. Although never described wholly from Erik's point of view, we see even from the kidnapped Christine's description how it could be seen as a banal space,

THE SEWER-HUNTER.

[*From a Daguerreotype by* BEARD.]

Figure 3.3. "The Sewer-Hunter." The lowest end of the "competitive system." From *London Labour and the London Poor*.

made sinister only by its subterranean location and her position as prisoner: "No doubt I was dealing with some awful eccentric who had mysteriously come to live in these cellars, like others, out of necessity, and, with the silent complicity of the administration, had found a definitive shelter."[25] As with so much in the novel, which plays on dual identities and reflected spaces, the angelic voice and the demonic face, we are given a dual perspective on Erik and his home, and he is allowed to assert an irreducible identity: "I am neither angel, nor genie, nor phantom . . . I am Erik!"[26] Once his mask is lifted to reveal a hideously scarred face, however, Erik, unlike the Wild Boys, *is* reduced, indelibly marked as other, the physical evidence reflected in his underworld life and his ever more twisted behavior. This otherness renders the space romantic, an aristocratic fantasy rather than the homey comfort of the Wild Boys' space, and consequently closer to the conventional vertical discourse of the sewer as underworld.

The Sewer as Technological Space

While the representation of the sewer as home was reserved for locating society's monsters in a distinct space that proactively determined their identity, there was a different code of images applied to those who of necessity shuttled between the world above and the world below: the working classes. In the scientific and journalistic narratives of the sewer worker and the space in which he labors, we find a notable absence of all assertions of filth, disease, and stench. In exchange for such techno-utopianism, however, we find no recognition of physical discomfort whatsoever, nor, conversely, of any aspirations beyond those of doing a job well. These subterranean workers are invariably healthy and happy, the perfect mirror of the behavior desired of their counterparts in the world above. This rationalizing discourse of the organic underground is expressed differently in London than in Paris. In the former, the sewer has always been sealed off as a public utility, requiring, as one account put it, that "in order to investigate that world thoroughly special arrangements will have to be made, and special permissions obtained from various authorities."[27] In the latter, the sewer and its workers have long held their own mythology, with the sewer tour a requisite of any visit to the French capital from the World Exhibition of 1867 on, and the *égoutier* occupying a privileged place in the mythology of the Parisian worker.[28] Beyond these local differences, an ordered relationship with the working classes was the underlying message in both discourses.

As the heroic gave way over the course of the century to the utilitarian in the aboveground representation of the construction and maintenance of the drainage system, the narrative of the London sewer visit stressed more and more the normality of the world below. The residual hint of the otherworld would be contained primarily within the working-class identity of the space of the sewers. Just as the rationalizing city had no space for a dangerous or disruptive underclass, so would its underground spaces be cleansed of any hint of organic matter. Although the period around Edwin Chadwick's influential sanitation report of 1842 was dominated by the rhetoric of danger, filth, and alienness echoed ever since in the literature of sensation, there were already dissenting voices asserting the salubrious effect of sewer gases. In an 1848 letter to the new Commission on Sewers, Edward D'Anson reported that, in addition to being safe from cholera, the sewer workers "are strong, hearty men; they live more than the ordinary duration of life"; their work affected their complexions rather than their health.[29] Mayhew noted similarly of sewer-hunters that, contrary to expectations, they were "strong, robust, and healthy men, generally florid in their complexion," some of them long-term practitioners between sixty and eighty years of age, and all with "a fixed belief that the odour of the sewers contributes in a variety of ways to their general health" (152). Such claims were likely borrowed from the Paris discourse, where, according to Reid, popular wisdom had long asserted the beneficial qualities of raw sewage, and where Parent-Duchâtelet's influential *Essai sur la cloaque ou égouts de la ville de Paris* (1836) had displaced blame for disease from the space of the sewers to the morals of the workers.[30]

By contrast with sensationalistic representations of the still all-too-visible slums, which freely invoked the sewer metonymy whether or not the spatial justification existed, the rationalizing account extended its argument to the entire working class only by implication. One such trope is the sewer worker's costume, which must invariably be donned by the investigator before the descent, and which invariably brings on anxiety over the change of identity. Concern about the costume appears particularly in London articles near the end of the century, as if figuring the transition to a time when the sewer would be totally disconnected from the world above. In "A Gloomy Ramble" (1881), for example, the author is informed by his guide that, in his costume, "Your own twin brother wouldn't know 'ee."[31] An 1888 piece begins with the sighting of a man in "strange clothing . . . emerging through an aperture in the pavement from depths of mysterious darkness below," before continuing with the author's thankfulness for his own outfit's protection against "slimy moisture";[32] what was healthy for the worker was not necessarily so for the reader.

Just as the test of fire in the slumming narrative was whether or not the voyager would shake hands with the denizens and share their food, so the sewer narrative played with two threats: the contact of skin with excrement and the encounter with rats. That the thrill of these narratives could be partially pleasurable is demonstrated by the analogous encounter with the prostitute, in which the physical union is defined positively (since possessing value) as much as negatively (since threatening contamination). Fascination with filth was also a theme of the Parisian sewer tour in both English and French accounts (see Figure 3.4). Rather than highlighting the domination of the organic threat through technology, as the London narratives of the same period did, the Paris tour promised integration with the underworld in a system rational enough to be safe, but still organic enough to thrill. As Maxime du Camp put it, "it has become a sort of pleasure trip to visit the sewers."[33] The photographer Nadar, too, in his description of the sewers, took the tone of a diversion, addressing, as Radford observes, a female audience, rather than the implicitly rationalistic male individual of the London tour.[34] Radford stresses the message of triumph of technology and spectacle over the lower orders;[35] in comparison with the London narrative, we should also note the ongoing desire that each inhabitant experience every aspect of the city he or she inhabited. The Parisian underworld was rendered as spectacle, the *frisson* of otherness was mild, the *égoutiers* served double time as tour guides and mules, but the journey nevertheless remained a material experience of a working urban space otherwise totally segregated from the world above. That the sewer tour could be rather more of a material experience of the urban underground than most accounts suggest is evident in du Camp's offhand remark that a policeman would ride in each sewer wagon to guard the passengers against the risk of another sort of contact: the nimble fingers of a pickpocket.[36]

What could be enjoyed by all in the context of Paris must quickly be flushed out of the space of London: "Sewage," to quote John Hollingshead in 1862, "whether fluid or solid, mixed or unmixed, is very much like our convicts, everybody wants to get rid of it, and no one consents to have it" (11). This was true figuratively as well as literally, for, unlike in Paris, neither sewage nor prostitution was ever given extended, explicit treatment in Victorian fiction of any literary pretension (although crime certainly was). It is tempting to draw an analogy between the poorly integrated Commissions of Sewers, the barely institutionalized systems for the regulation of prostitution, and the lack of overlap between different fictional discourses in London, as opposed to the centralized metropolitan improvements, the highly regulated (and corrupt) institution of prostitution, and the integrated fictional discourse on the underground in Paris. There is no equivalent to Baudelaire's poetic depiction of the whore, to Hugo's history of the sewers, to courtesans such as Manet's Olympia or Zola's Nana in English arts and letters.[37] Consequently, it is the art and literature of Paris that has been richest in drawing out the ambivalent character of filth and the sewers.

It would be a mistake to privilege one space over the other, however, just as it would be a mistake to assume that either space can be comprehended distinctly from the other. To be sure, there are important factual arguments to be made about the differences between London and Paris, between their social structures and physical spaces, between their political histories and roles as imperial centers: these determine the conventional discourses I outlined above, and the representations of city space that dominated both internal and external depictions. But they did not delimit the range of representation any more than the facts delimited the specific experience of the space by each of its inhabitants.

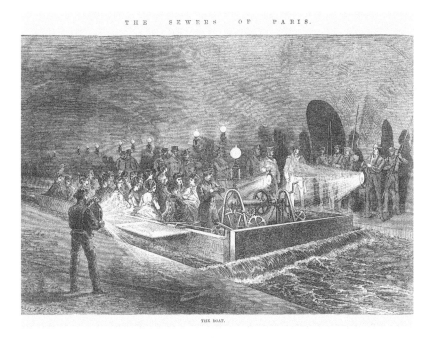

THE SEWERS OF PARIS.

THE BOAT.

Figure 3.4. "The Sewers of Paris." Putting waste to good use: the sewer tour. *Illustrated London News*, 29 January 1870.

Even within middle-class representations, it was common for Parisian writers to adapt London models to their city, and vice versa. For du Camp, compiling in 1870 a panorama of Paris wholly different from the popular examples of the 1840s, Paris had become a better version of London, and London more like the bad old Paris. Although his vast survey did not neglect the much-loved folklore and variety of the city, its ideological focus was on the efficiency of its institutions and the inexplicable and inexcusable choice to act contrary to those institutions. In du Camp's implicit repudiation of the rhetoric of *Les Misérables*, the underground was not ancient, exotic, and exciting, but technologized, perfectly managed, and useful.

Prostitution and the Sewer

The same response is evident with regard to the social phenomenon of prostitution, the occupation most frequently associated with urban filth and with the sewage system. As the most visible as well as the most inimical symptom of the contradictions of middle-class ideology, prostitution was urgently mapped and regulated throughout the century, but nearly always in terms of a verticalized conception of the city that bore little resemblance to the actual interpenetration of the spaces and bodies involved. Identifying the prostitute with the city's drainage system allowed the phenomenon to be graphically visualized, but there were very few whores in the sewers. In the enormous variety as well as in the sheer number of her (and very infrequently his) representations, the nineteenth-century sex worker was by all accounts an omnipresent urban figure as well as an important symbolic one. And while the mid-century calculation by certain authors of some fifty to eighty thousand active prostitutes in London is likely to have been exaggerated, the official count in Paris in 1830, the year public solicitation was outlawed, did give the extraordinary number of sixty thousand, just as the statistical tables in the 1857 edition of Parent-Duchâtelet showed that the number of prostitutes inscribed monthly between 1812 and 1854 never averaged less than a thousand, increasing steadily to more than four thousand monthly by the 1850s.[38]

While the numbers in the two cities are likely to have been roughly comparable, it is unimaginable that one would find an organic image of ordure in Victorian London to match the infamous and influential apology of Parent-Duchâtelet to his study of prostitution, sequel to his exploration of the Paris sewers: "If I have been able, without scandalizing anyone at all, to penetrate into the sewers, handle putrid matter, pass part of my time in dumps, and live after a fashion in the midst of all that is the most abject and disgusting among groups of men, why should I blush to approach a sewer of another sort (a sewer filthier, I admit, than all the others) in the well-founded hope of doing some good while examining it in all its aspects?"[39] The effect of the definition of the prostitute as a sewer was both to naturalize her profession and to consign it conceptually to a specific urban space. As Parent-Duchâtelet expressed this conclusion, "Prostitutes are as inevitable, where men live together in large concentrations, as drains and refuse dumps."[40] This was the conventional nineteenth-century French discourse; most succinct, perhaps, was Louis Fiaux's denomination of the *maison de tolérance* as "the seminal drain."[41]

Just as Belgrand had heroically rationalized the receptacles and conduits of the city's waste and the *égoutiers* now spent their nights sweeping out the drainage tunnels to make sure nothing solid remained to fester, the French "regulatory system" sought to enclose and modernize the drains of its men's bodies, by means of comprehensive inscription and regular inspections to guarantee healthy circulation. Here the resemblance ended, for the material space of the sewers could indeed be mapped and labeled with some degree of accuracy, whereas the regulatory system, notwithstanding the high level of surveillance and documentation, never overcame the difficulty of identifying those who required documentation. *Filles publiques* were defined as those registered and confined to the *maisons de tolérance*, but there was an undefined number of illegal *insoumises* or *non inscrites*, who were, we are told, "everywhere." Because they used codes and signs rather than open solicitation, they were difficult to identify and thus to control. At the same time, and paradoxically, the presence of these women "on the most elegant boulevards," circulating as prostitutes, scandalized members of the public, "who take them for registered prostitutes in breach of the regulations, and . . . are astonished by the inaction of the police."[42] While resembling an open sewer, a slum might at least be a self-contained and hence avoidable space; the illicit *insoumise* brought the chaotic mess of the underworld into the carefully policed space of the boulevards, and in such a manner as to confound the distinctions of the world above with a different experience of space.

To the Parisian system of inscription, as imperfectly as it might function, the French opposed the disastrously "free" system of London, using their attacks on it to express fears about the insufficiencies inherent in their own system. Citing statistics from the English medical journal *The Lancet*, which labeled prostitution in London the worst in

Europe, Richelot wrote in 1857 that the unregulated, unsupervised traffic in London was "a hideous stain . . . an open wound."[43] Not surprisingly, the behavior that shocked Richelot most about London, the overtness of solicitation, can also be found in travel writing about Paris during the same period, which recorded in astonishment the activity of "the semi-mundanes . . . who accost strangers at night on the Boulevards."[44] As Richelot's corporeal metaphor suggests, by legislating the world's oldest profession out of existence, the London model strove to contain a threat of infection for modern society. Rather than the alienness and atavism of the otherworld, the Parisian model attacked the otherworld's threat of transmutation by fixing the identity and place of the prostitute within modern society.

Both the French and the English discourses relied on a vertical segmentation of space in which the prostitute constituted a primary threshold between above and below. To again cite the formative language of Parent-Duchâtelet, "debauchery" would constitute the "passage from an honest life to the state of abjection of a class which cuts itself off from society."[45] The goal of Parent-Duchâtelet's study, as of most such works, was to cross that threshold in order to determine how to eliminate it. In the Parisian model, this meant determining a hard and fast distinction between what he termed "public prostitution" and "public debauchery," between what would be regulated and what would be punished as criminal behavior. In the London model, this meant venturing over the threshold in order to determine which individuals were worthy of salvation, and which ones genuinely did belong below.

What are the consequences of naturalizing prostitution as in the Parisian discourse? For one, it brings out into the open many guiding assumptions of the nineteenth-century city, in particular that the inhabitant of it is defined as a heterosexual male, while the women are defined as part of the infrastructure; discursively, no other permutation can exist. It allows prostitution to be treated as a question of engineering, a matter of the proper organization of abstract space, rather than a social issue. It deflects one moral definition of prostitution—a sinful activity that should be eradicated—by means of another—a defilement of those who are by nature assigned to practice it. On the other hand, one could argue that, like the horrors of the fiction of urban mysteries, naturalizing prostitution acknowledges it as a material social phenomenon and takes some account both of its power in the urban imagination and of the social cost of its dehumanizing aspects. It was certainly a brutal gesture to define women as drains, but it did succeed in expressing a truth of sexual labor absent from the English discourse of the fallen woman.

What are the consequences of individualizing prostitution? It is a discourse well suited to the laissez-faire capitalist system, with which London was identified in the nineteenth century. If each fall was individual, then it was the individual that was blamed or the individual that was a victim, and it was as an individual that the fallen woman must be saved. London regulation of prostitution, such as it was, and London reform of prostitution would operate on a piecemeal basis. On the other hand, we could argue that the refusal to acknowledge the downside of prostitution, the horrors emblematized by the sewage analogy, along with the possibility of casting prostitutes as victims, made available the rare argument that prostitution was actually caused by the desire of men rather than the corruption of women. As Flora Tristan put it in her *London Journal* (1842), "Prejudice, poverty and servitude combine to produce this revolting degradation. Yes, for if you men did not impose chastity on women as a necessary virtue while refusing to practice it yourselves, they would not be rejected by society for yielding to the sentiments of their hearts, nor would seduced, deceived and abandoned girls be forced into prostitution."[46] Tristan remains wholly within the discourse of the fallen woman, individualizing responsibility, and blaming prostitution on seduction, but she mobilized this discourse to combat its primary assumptions.

Because the vertical model is so seductive, it is essential to grasp the positive as well as the negative aspects of its appeal, its contradictions and its limitations. Especially in the partial discourses through which it is generally invoked, the vertical model offers a potent mode for representing crisis and contradiction but, by the same token, no means of assigning agency or of resolving those crises. Read together, the different discourses help to make visible the vertical metaphorics without resolving their contradictions into the opaque ideologies characteristic of nineteenth-century representation. Reading the individualized, free-market treatment of the London streetwalker through the Paris discourse can restore both a sense of the oppressive system obscured by that treatment and a sense of the power of the figure by comparison with its lionized Parisian counterpart, the *flâneur*. Reading the rationalized "seminal drains" of Paris through the London discourse can restore both a sense of individual suffering and a sense of collective power. For instance, in Yves Guyot's *Prostitution under the Regulatory System French and English*, published in France in 1882 and translated into English two years later, we find the personalized narration of the London discourse combined with the holistic perspective of Paris. When Guyot writes of the "common prostitute," he gives the sewage trope a material instead of a moral turn: "Society throws this woman in the river or the sewer, and has no metaphor coarse enough to express all its scorn."[47] The essence of waste lies not in its status as the degraded, debased detritus of society, but in its quality of valuable resources. Guyot expresses a fundamental truth of capitalist exploitation: it uses and discards without regard for what it has used. What the vertical structure provides is the opportunity either to occlude or to make visible the myriad forms of waste, and, once the structure of its spaces is visible, the possibility of reintegrating aspects of both above and below, of constructing a dialectic out of the contradictions in the representation of both spaces that would allow the construction of the space in its actual rather than simply its aesthetic complexity.

Notes

1. On nineteenth-century metaphors of underground space and the vertical city, see Rosalind Williams, *Notes on the Underground* (Cambridge, MA: MIT Press, 1992), and Wendy Lesser, *The Life below Ground* (New York: Faber and Faber, 1987). For a focus on the material aspects, see Benson Bobrick, *Labyrinths of Iron* (New York: Henry Holt, 1994).

2. For two case studies of the different representations of different types of underground space, see David L. Pike, "Underground Theater: Subterranean Spaces on the London Stage," *Nineteenth Century Studies* 13 (1999): 103–38, and "Urban Nightmares and Future Visions: Life beneath New York," *Wide Angle* 20, no. 4 (October 1998): 8–50.

3. For a history of the London sewers, see John Hollingshead, *Underground London* (London: Groombridge and Sons, 1862); Francis Sheppard, *London 1808–1870: The Infernal Wen* (London: Secker and Warburg, 1971), 249–96; and Dale H. Porter, *The Thames Embankment: Environment, Technology, and Society in Victorian London* (Akron, OH: University of Akron Press, 1998). On Paris, see Eugène Belgrand, *Les Travaux souterrains de Paris* (Paris, 1873–77); Emile Gérards, *Paris souterrain* (Paris: Garnier Frères, 1908; repr., Torcy: DMI, 1991), 483–515; David Pinkney, *Napoleon III and the Rebuilding of Paris* (Princeton, NJ: Princeton University Press, 1958), 127–50; and Donald Reid, *Paris Sewers and Sewermen: Realities and Representations* (Cambridge, MA: Harvard University Press, 1991).

4. Mary Douglas, *Purity and Danger: An Analysis of the Concepts of Pollution and Taboo* (London: Routledge and Kegan Paul, 1966), 35–36.

5. Michael Taussig, *The Devil and Commodity Fetishism in South America* (Chapel Hill: University of North Carolina Press, 1980), 112.

6. Lynda Nead, *Myths of Sexuality: Representations of Women in Victorian Britain* (Oxford: Blackwell, 1988), 99.

7. See, for example, Baudelaire's equation of the prostitute with the poet in the alluring sordidness of their relation to the marketplace; Benjamin's analysis

of this equation vis-à-vis the 1930s, particularly in Convolute J of the *Arcades Project* (to which Nead's feminist interpretation is especially indebted); Peter Brooks's argument that the prostitute raises the difficulty of distinguishing between labor and crime, between "the sold body" and "the socially aberrant body" in *Reading for the Plot: Design and Intention in Narrative* (New York: Vintage, 1985), 168; and Amanda Anderson's summary and critique of contemporary versions of this analysis in *Tainted Souls and Painted Faces: The Rhetoric of Fallenness in Victorian Culture* (Ithaca, NY: Cornell University Press, 1993), 5–9.

8. Peter Stallybrass and Allon White, *The Politics and Poetics of Transgression* (London: Methuen, 1986), 125.

9. Charles Bernheimer, *Figures of Ill Repute: Representing Prostitution in Nineteenth-Century France* (Cambridge, MA: Harvard University Press, 1989), 1–2.

10. On the publication history of *London Labour* and the relationship between its various editions, see E. P. Thompson, "The Political Education of Henry Mayhew," *Victorian Studies* 11, no. 1 (September 1967): 41–62.

11. For an excellent analysis of this ambivalence in Mayhew in the context of the different versions of *London Labour*, see Richard Maxwell, "Henry Mayhew and the Life of the Streets," *Journal of British Studies* 17, no. 2 (Spring 1978): 87–105.

12. Henry Mayhew, *London Labour and the London Poor*, 4 vols. (1861–62; repr. New York: Dover, 1968), 2:136. Further citations will be made parenthetically to this edition.

13. Alain Corbin, *Le Miasme et la jonquille: l'odorat et l'imaginaire social 18e–19e siècles* (1982; Paris: Flammarion, 1986), 172. My translation.

14. Victor Hugo, *Les Misérables* (Paris: Laffont, 1985), V.2.i; trans. Norman Denny, *Les Misérables* (Harmondsworth, UK: Penguin, 1980); modified with reference to Fred Radford, "'Cloacal Obsession': Hugo, Joyce, and the Sewer Museum of Paris," *Mattoid* 48 (1994): 66–85.

15. Georges Verpraet, *Paris, capitale souterrain* (Paris: Plon, 1964), 143.

16. Radford, "'Cloacal Obsession,'" 79.

17. Ibid., 75.

18. For a history of the penny-dreadful in England, see E. S. Turner, *Boys Will Be Boys: The Story of Sweeney Todd, Deadwood Dick, Sexton Blake, Dick Barton, et al.*, 1949, new rev. ed. (London: Michael Joseph, 1957). See also John Springhall, "'A Life Story for the People'? Edwin J. Brett and the London 'Low-Life' Penny Dreadfuls of the 1860s," *Victorian Studies* 23, no. 2 (Winter 1990): 223–46.

19. One of the most familiar demonstrations of crisis in a contemporary city is the reportage and photographing of homeless persons dwelling in its sewers, as in a recent *New York Times* report on Angola accompanied by a photo of a well-dressed man emerging through a manhole from the Luandan sewer where, the caption tells us, he sleeps.

20. *The Wild Boys of London, or The Children of the Night. A Story of the Present Day* (London: Newsagents Publishing, 1866), 8.

21. In her study of responses to the Victoria Embankment, Michelle Allen has noted that criticism of the project generally took the form of laments for the loss of the picturesque quality of what was otherwise decried as the dirty and disordered riverside ("The Contest for Salubrity: Embanking the Thames, 1862–1870," conference paper, 17 April 1998, Middle Atlantic Conference on British Studies, New York).

22. *Wild Boys*, 8.

23. *The Mysteries of Old Father Thames. A Romance* (London: W. Caffyn, [1848]), 48–49.

24. Ibid., 179.

25. Gaston Leroux, *Le Fantôme de l'Opéra* (1911; repr., Paris: Livre de Poche, 1959), 240–41. My translation.

26. Ibid., 241.

27. Eric Banton, "Underground London," in *Living London*, ed. George R. Sims, 3 vols. (London: Cassell and Co., 1901), 2:127–32, at 127.

28. For a comprehensive history of the Parisian sewer worker, see Reid, *Paris Sewers and Sewermen*.

29. *A Few Words on the New Commission of Sewers: With Comments on the Reports and Evidence of the Sanitary Commission, by a Farmer, a Lawyer, and an Ex-Commissioner* (London, 1848), 7, 18.

30. Reid, *Paris Sewers and Sewermen*, 98–99.

31. "A Gloomy Ramble," *The Boy's Own Paper*, 17 September 1881, 817–18.

32. Columbus, Jr. "How It Is Done. X.—The Draining of the City," *Cassell's Saturday Journal* (1888): 225.

33. Maxime du Camp, *Paris: Ses organes, ses fonctions et sa vie jusqu'en 1870* (1870; repr., Monaco: Rondeau, 1993), 606. My translation.

34. Radford, "'Cloacal Obsession,'" 72–73; Nadar, "Le Dessus et le dessous de Paris," in *Paris-Guide, par les principaux écrivains et artistes de la France, 1867*, ed. and intro. Corinne Verdet (Paris: Ed. La Découverte/Maspéro, 1983), 154–75. Neither writer makes any reference to London.

35. Radford, "'Cloacal Obsession,'" 74.

36. Du Camp, *Paris*, 607.

37. For a summary of high-cultural French attention to subterranean Paris, see Christopher Prendergast, *Paris and the Nineteenth Century* (Oxford: Blackwell, 1992), 74–101.

38. For 1830, see G. J. Lecour, *La Prostitution à Paris et à Londres 1789–1871*, 2nd ed. (Paris: Librairie de la Faculté de Médecine, 1872), 119; for monthly inscriptions, see Alexandre-Jean-Baptiste Parent-Duchâtelet, *De la Prostitution . . . 3e edition, complétée par des documents nouveaux et des notes par MM. A. Trebuchet . . . Poirat-Duval . . . suivie d'un précis hygiénique, statistique et administratif sur la prostitution dans les principales villes de l'Europe avec cartes et tableaux*, 2 vols. (Paris: J. B. Baillière et fils, 1857).

39. Parent-Duchâtelet, *De la Prostitution dans la ville de Paris, considérée sous le rapport de l'hygiène publique*, 2 vols. (Brussels: Société Belge de Librairie, 1836), 1:6 (my translation). On Parent-Duchâtelet in particular, see Jill Harsin, *Policing Prostitution in Nineteenth-Century Paris* (Princeton, NJ: Princeton University Press, 1985), 96–130, and Bernheimer, 8–33.

40. Parent-Duchâtelet, *De la Prostitution dans la ville de Paris*, *Figures of Ill Repute*, 2:513.

41. Louis Fiaux, *La Police des moeurs en France et dans les principaux pays de l'Europe* (Paris: E. Dentu, 1888), 212, quoted in Alain Corbin, *Women for Hire: Prostitution and Sexuality in France after 1850*, trans. Arthur Goldhammer (1974; Cambridge, MA: Harvard University Press, 1990), 53.

42. Lecour, *La Prostitution à Paris et à Londres*, 145.

43. Supplement to 3rd edition of Parent-Duchâtelet, *De la Prostitution*, 2:395–879, at 629.

44. Thomas Wallace Knox, *Underground, or Life below the Surface* (London: Sampson, Low and Co., 1873), 415.

45. Parent-Duchâtelet, *De la Prostitution dans la ville de Paris*, 1:24.

46. Flora Tristan, *The London Journal of Flora Tristan*, trans. Jean Hawkes (1842; London: Virago, 1984), 81.

47. Yves Guyot, *Prostitution under the Regulatory System French and English*, trans. Edgar Beckit Truman (1882; London: George Redway, 1884), 7.

Chapter 4

Medical Mapping: The Thames, the Body, and *Our Mutual Friend*

Pamela K. Gilbert

> In these times of ours, though concerning the exact year there is no need
> to be precise, a boat of dirty and disreputable appearance, with two
> figures in it, floated on the Thames, between Southwark Bridge which is
> of iron and London Bridge which is of stone, as an autumn evening was
> closing in.

These first lines of *Our Mutual Friend* (1865) portray all of the iconic
elements important to the novel: the degraded man, the pure girl, the
Thames, and, most importantly, filth: a dirty boat on a filthy river, with,
as Dickens's Mr. Mantalini would have described it, a "demd damp, moist,
unpleasant body" in tow.[1] Although Dickens is ostentatiously imprecise
about the year, he is extraordinarily precise about the location on the
Thames, and this is appropriate in a novel in which urban space—a
detailed mapping of the city, its filth, and its main water supply—will
be thematically central. Middle-class Victorians were particularly concerned with filth, and for good reason. Illnesses thought to be caused
by inadequate sanitation were often referred to as filth diseases, and
nineteenth-century London was rife with them. Filth was rotten, decomposing waste, especially animal and human waste, and most especially
feces.[2] Peter Stallybrass and Allon White have argued that the nineteenth-
century city was organized around the binary of filth/cleanliness and
a constant fear of its transgression, or contamination, resulting from

desire.[3] This fear "was articulated above all through the 'body' of the city," which had to be surveyed to be controlled.[4]

By midcentury, this surveillance was institutionalized in the mechanisms of sanitary inspection and had entered both literary and visual culture, the latter principally in the form of sanitary maps. The sanitary movement responded to overcrowding and epidemic disease by emphasizing the dangers of filth. Accumulated waste that earlier had been perceived as an unpleasant but unavoidable reality of life in the city now seemed evidence of a vicious, even murderous, disregard for life. Bodily wastes were seen no longer simply as byproducts of the life process, but as animated and hostile filth that would, given the chance, attack the body itself. The body and its continence, which modeled the boundaries of the middle-class individual self, could only be preserved through a careful policing of the abject and the closure of the boundaries of the body, through which contaminated or contaminating fluids should neither enter nor escape. By midcentury, the "lower bodily strata," which Stallybrass and White show to have been identified with both sewage and underclass populations, were increasingly thematized as both diseased and antimodern. In turn, health and modernity came to be identified with a careful mapping and containment of the city's (and city dwellers') guts.

As a metaphorical description of a population in corporeal terms, the social body had a long history in the early modern period and took on renewed importance in the late eighteenth and early nineteenth centuries as discussions of the social body coincided with a new view of the state's roles as manager of physical health and facilitator of social cohesion. As Foucault's work emphasizes, with the advent of new statistical practices to analyze and measure the population, the figure of the social body divided society into masses of standardized or deviant individual bodies. Vice was configured less as the result of a fallen nature than as the perversion of human nature through unnatural circumstances such as living in urban poverty. Moral health came to be seen as coterminous with physical health. The advent of epidemic disease in urban areas lent both focus and urgency to this understanding of the social body and provided it with a vocabulary grounded in the notion of a physically healthy body as the basis of the modern state. Mary Poovey has argued that the organization of modern space—gridded, uniform, and standardized—was the ideal of a government that conceived of the subjects acting in that space as structurally equivalent and behaviorally similar.[5] Healthy subjects acting rationally would use that space in appropriate ways; in turn, the idea of a rational subject whose behaviors were statistically predictable contributed to the notion of the transparency of modern space. Medical maps both represented the failure of the current social body to attain this transparency and indicated the steps necessary to achieve it. Dickens, in his focus on disciplining the bodies and desires of those who deviated from a bourgeois norm, works toward promoting the similarity of subjectivity that will ideally populate the transparent, disciplined space of the modern metropolis.

The comparison between the novelist and the policeman or doctor as an expert in disciplinary diagnosis and surveillance has been explored by numerous critics following D. A. Miller.[6] Of the many writers who made the sanitary crusade central to their writing, Dickens was foremost. Dickens used both his expert knowledge of London and his sense of human nature to explore the hidden relationships between individuals that both constitute and threaten community. Operating much like medical mappers, Dickens charts human actions onto the urban landscape and traces their hidden connections. As a sanitary activist, Dickens used disease in *Bleak House* (1853) to show those connections; *Bleak House* is a medical map, doing exactly as other medical maps and sanitary narratives did to show how disease spreads from poor to wealthy neighborhoods, in the style of Charles Kingsley's "Cheap Clothes and Nasty" or *Alton Locke*. In *Bleak House*, the contaminated wetness of London miasmatically breeds disease and confusion, but we need not look to metaphor to understand that this moisture is filthy. F. S. Schwarzbach observes that

> the mud [on Holborn Hill] is made up of dirt, rubbish (*dust* in English idiom), and raw sewage, ends up in the Thames and then oozes downstream to the Essex marshes. There it rots and festers, soon producing infectious effluvia that are blown by the raw East Wind back over the city. *This* is the stuff of the novel's dense fog. . . . Dickens is pointing to a literal economy of filth and disease.[7]

The scandal of filth in the heart of the modern city is an actual scandal, covered in the papers almost daily, of the uncivilized, grotesque, leaky body persisting in the midst of managed civilization. This theme would continue to preoccupy Dickens beyond *Bleak House*, when significant changes in medical mapping complicated and extended the novelist's vision of the sick urban body.

Following the paradigm shift set in motion by John Snow's examination of London's contaminated water supply, Dickens carries his portrait of filthy London a step further in *Our Mutual Friend*. Here, the disease becomes explicitly moral, rather than the actual fever that infects

Esther Summerson, while the novel itself animates and narrativizes Snow's second map (of fecal pollution in London's water, which Snow used to argue that cholera was a waterborne disease) and subsequent investigations inspired by it. In London, Snow's work focused public interest on the Thames, long a topic of outcry because of the pollution it made evident to both nose and eye. The confluence of epidemic disease, sanitary theory, and the development of medical mapping, arising from what was perceived as a specifically urban and modern crisis, led to new representations of the city as a body as well. Dickens's work had long been part of this Victorian tradition of narrative topography, and at midcentury the influence of sanitary and medical maps gave a new edge to his precise delineations of characters' itineraries. For Dickens, control of London water's circulation and purity was a goal that both mirrored and was dependent upon the control of individual bodies and selves; *Our Mutual Friend* maps this interrelationship.

The Leaky Body and the Incontinent Self

Dickens uses the midcentury sanitary iconography of London's water supply to elaborate his representation of the urban, social body as well as the individual body in *Our Mutual Friend*. No longer miasmatic, simply emanating from Tom-all-Alone's, disease is also no longer merely a symptom of social ills. Contagion in *Our Mutual Friend* does not require the unlikely proximity of disparate populations that *Bleak House* did, because people no longer catch illness directly from other infected human bodies, but instead from the body of the sick city itself, on which they depend symbiotically. Although Dickens retains the Galenic vision of a body whose fluids and solids must be homeostatically controlled—a vision that supports individual rather than community responsibility for continence—he combines this vision with one of a social body, mapped as London and its surroundings. This body's vital fluid is the Thames, and its contamination serves as index of the incontinence of London society. General physical incontinence, rather than specific disease, becomes the manifestation of a systemic social grotesqueness, and incontinence is persistently linked to the city's polluted water supply.

In *Our Mutual Friend*, then, the straightforward connection between filth and literal disease is replaced by a more subtle portrayal of the body's vulnerabilities. Liquidity, garbage, filth, and waste constantly threaten the unself-contained body, which must shore itself up to build a liberal self with a clear sense of identity.[8] As William A. Cohen writes in the introduction to this volume, "filth is frequently so disturbing that it endangers the subjective integrity of the one who confronts it. By the time one has encountered and repudiated filth, it is too late—the subject is already besmirched by it." In Dickens, desire, especially inappropriate or uncontrolled desire, opens the body to the possibility of filthy encounters; the task of the middle-class male is to control desire and to contain the body so that it cannot either produce or be penetrated by filth.

Uncontrolled desire, thematized as addiction—and greed for money comes under this heading in *Our Mutual Friend*—equates in Dickens with desire for physical dissolution, for the abject. As Julia Kristeva defines it, the abject—those waste products of the body that, by their nature, evoke both excess and the threat of death, especially feces and the corpse—point to the nonclosure and nonsufficiency of the body, its liability, through the mechanisms of desire and need, to take filth into itself and to produce filth.[9] Filth, then, always evokes death, the invasion of the self by nonself; in Dickens, the greater threat is not simply physical death but the absolute dissolution of the individual self, on whose existence—one's ability to *hold oneself together*—the continuation of the social body depends. The unfortunate Mr. Dolls, for example, whose very name is unknown, drinks himself into a shambling and animalistic state of utter dependency; his body fails to hold together as he does finally "shake to bits."[10] As in *Bleak House*, addiction can also manifest as obsession, either monetary or sexual. Eugene, the upper-class gentleman who appears to have a correctly contained bourgeois body but who lacks self-control, succumbs to a sexual obsession with Lizzie—and a sadomasochistic obsession with Bradley Headstone.[11] Eugene is beaten to a bloody and undifferentiated pulp and then dumped, like so much sewage, in the river, from which Lizzie rebirths him (an act that finally rewards her own sexual self-containment, demonstrated by her mastery over the water, with middle-class status).

Bradley Headstone, who cannot control his obsessions with Lizzie and Eugene, is a man drowning in his own bodily fluids. He is unable to contain the blood that periodically spurts from his nose, causing fits: "I can't keep it back. . . . It has happened . . . I don't know how many times—since last night. I taste it, smell it, see it, it chokes me, and then it breaks out like this" (638). Unable to control the "wild energy" that has "heaved up" the "bottom of this raging sea" in his breast (396), Headstone, appropriately, drowns. Incapable of governing his body, he pollutes the river with blood and the fluid excess of his desire; in turn, the polluted river invades his body and transforms it into the wholly abject. Like the city that exudes and reabsorbs its own wastes, the incontinent body dissolves the boundaries of the self into the abject mass of physicality with which London's dangerous classes are associated, and with which Dickens (like other midcentury writers) connects barbarism. A male body that is inappropriately open to its own wastes or that, conversely, allows its vital fluid inappropriately to escape, represents a whole social economy in which individuals only distinguish themselves from the deathly mass of corruption by achieving a high and dry closure.

The leaky body, then, is related in Dickens to incontinence, often to addiction or obsession. It is also the emblem of an imperfectly formed self, a lack of discipline that threatens the very basis of liberal individualism.[12] Herbert L. Sussman has traced in detail Thomas Carlyle's use of images of liquidity and pulpiness to describe the unformed masculine self, which only careful self-cultivation and control could enclose in a relatively firm and clearly defined structure. This structure was constantly threatened by the atavistic and chaotic liquidity of the male psyche; without vigilant self-policing, he suggests, the self was always in danger of dissolution.[13] Sussman traces these anxieties specifically in Carlyle's musings on masculinity, but this imagery was pervasive in mid-Victorian culture. In this light, one might view the basis of the Victorian hierarchy of civilization not as the opposition between the raw and the cooked, but as that between the liquid and the solid. Cholera, a diarrheal disease, literalized this undisciplined evacuation of fluids and linked it to the uncontained human fluids associated with improper drainage, mapping the individual body onto the built environment. As Erin O'Connor notes, "Cholera . . . became the operative term in an entire metaphorics of bodily contamination, a figure for the fluidity of boundaries in metropolitan space."[14]

But this was simply one powerful model of a more widely held understanding of the dangers uncontrolled physicality posed for the social body. Bourgeois individuality—which was not exclusively masculine but certainly masculinized—was based on a model of the body that contained and separated itself from the bodies of others, but the sick, undisciplined body threatened to sink the individual into the unreasoning mass of continuous, embruted embodiment. The pulpiness within was always threatening to burst the bounds of the skin, which defined, contained, and disciplined the individual. If, as Nancy Armstrong argues, combination is troped as sexual scandal in the narratives of the midcentury, then disruption in the social body is translated into a lack of discipline, figured in turn as a lack of bodily self-containment.[15] Wetness and liquidity often ground descriptions of the body disintegrating as a threat to the larger social body.

These images emerge in part out of a Galenic medical vision of the body as dependent for its health on homeostasis and of illness as a deficit or excess that unbalances that equilibrium.[16] Bleeding, for example, might be done by a medic to relieve the pressure caused by excessive richness or volume of the blood. Thus, matter coming out of the body, or going into it by means other than the normal alimentary canal, was itself "matter out of place," as Mary Douglas has famously defined dirt:[17] such matter, though not itself necessarily filthy, indicated a filthy or potentially filthy state within the body. By the mid-Victorian period, this largely humoral model of a body made vulnerable by its own instabilities was being challenged by a model of a healthy body vulnerable to outside filth. Most Victorian medics fell somewhere between these competing perspectives, claiming that illness resulted from a precondition of instability within the body that might be exacerbated by such proximate causes as sanitary nuisances and an epidemic constitution of the environment.[18] Both epidemic and hereditary disease were sites of anxiety, complicating the individualist model; one sees in *Bleak House* that this is where Dickens is able to make his most telling points about social responsibility and interdependence. Still, the model of individual moderation and continence as a means of both self- and social control remained powerful, both in sanitary theory and in political economy.

Dickens's novels of the 1850s and 1860s appeal to this iconography of leakage versus containment in the service of a notion of liberal individualism.[19] He employs traditional narratives of sexual openness (in women), greed, addiction and its psychological double, obsession, to indicate lack of self-containment. The character who succumbs to these dangers risks losing individual identity, becoming part of an undifferentiated and abject corporeal mass.[20] Dickens uses the individual's struggle for bodily continence to stage the development of both the disciplined, self-contained subject and the clean, modern city. In *Bleak House*, the body that is "vicious," not self-contained, engenders in its own humors "the only death that can be died," spontaneous combustion, a death that ruptures and makes meaningless the boundaries of the body that should protect the subject's interiority, leaving a dripping, greasy effluvium.[21] By the early 1850s, then, Dickens already had recourse to the leaky body to relate his treatment of sanitary reform to social responsibility. Between *Bleak House* and *Our Mutual Friend*, however, came an important change in the perception of the city and its own "bodily fluids"—its water supply. Snow's mapping of the fecal contamination of London's water supply redefined the abject as that which cannot simply be expelled but forever threatens to reinvade the incontinent body—social, urban, and individual—through mechanisms of circulation. Following the implications of contaminated water coursing through London's veins, the circulation of the abject becomes central in Dickens's representation of the city and the relationships that constitute it. In order to understand the source of this change, it is important to understand the background and effects of sanitary mapping and the impact of Snow's work.

Mapping the Urban Body

The period from 1830 to 1855 has been termed the golden age of thematic mapping, when maps were used to illustrate specific data sets or arguments; for example, mortality during a particular epidemic could be charted by place.[22] Sanitary reports often included maps to show the location of nuisances. Cartographic historians agree that thematic cartography received an important boost during the cholera pandemic of the early 1830s, which established medical mapping as a standard technique in the West.[23] Thematic mapping resulted from the development of statistics and elaborated upon existing spatial models of social problems. Before the significant use of graphic maps (which mapped not only disease but also poverty, crime, religious practice, and educational access), written narratives described population attributes by parish, neighborhood, street, or house. As Lloyd G. Stevenson observes, such detailed spatial descriptions cried out for visual representation.[24] Social problems, including crime, poverty, and disease, were seen to be especially attendant on urbanization; poverty maps led to the well-known verbal and cartographic mappings of London by Henry Mayhew (whose maps were published in 1862) and Charles Booth (1889). Thematic maps encouraged readers to situate themselves in a geographically defined community; medical maps located readers in a community of vulnerable bodies.

London naturally drew much attention from cartographers, and no community provided more of a market for such representations than Londoners themselves. Since the beginnings of London's accelerated expansion in the late eighteenth century, its inhabitants were fascinated with the mysteries of their own city. Maps and guidebooks strove to give an overview of the city, and narrative mappings traced not only its physical but its social geography as well. Londoners consumed dictionaries of slang designed to initiate them into the mysteries of lower-class communities, enthusiastically read ethnographies like Mayhew's *London Labour and the London Poor* (1861), and entertained themselves with publications ranging from broadsides such as Pierce Egan's *Tom and Jerry* (1821) to urban vignettes such as the young Dickens's *Sketches by Boz* (1836). Victorian commentators tend to cast London as a monster, a huge growth, a confusing profusion. A favorite narrative device was to rely on the initial representation of London as an unmanageable jumble and then to impose order on it through hierarchical binaries used to contain the city's diversity. Often these would rely on well-known geographic symbols such as Tom and Jerry's move from upscale Almack's to All Max in the East End.[25] Early sanitary maps also relied on a simple binary of clean versus filthy.

It is important here to keep in mind the connections Victorians made between disease, morality, and the body. For Victorians, epidemic disease was a sign of filth resulting from poor sanitary practices, which were tied to economic and moral sins; in turn, filth *caused* immorality by so violating the boundaries of the body and psyche as to degrade the self's ability to preserve independence from its surroundings. Especially under the early sanitary movement of Edwin Chadwick, from the late 1840s through the mid-1850s, filth was carefully mapped onto the urban terrain preparatory to intervention, and was an index of moral corruption on the social body and in the individual bodies that composed it. Excise the filth from the urban and individual body, it was reasoned, and the health of the social body must follow. As Lynda Nead points out, London's modernity was "shaped by the forces of two urban principles: mapping and movement," and the mapping had always as its goal the restoration or enhancement of that movement, usually figured as circulation.[26] Sanitary mapping, such as that of sewerage, tended to figure the city as a body that could sicken.[27] As the century wore on and gains were made in the most basic levels of sanitation, medical mapping began to suggest increasingly sophisticated relationships between urban space and disease. Mapping such problems was more than a simple exercise of pinning-the-nuisance-on-the-city, becoming an interpretive practice by which social experts elaborated theories of human behavior and the nature of modern society.

Statistical studies such as Farr's analyses of mortality and morbidity returns sought to standardize a basic human life-trajectory and then grid the city based on variables that affected that standard in a given area—rates of fever, for example, or correlation between elevation and life expectancy. As Poovey argues, such statistical studies sought to transform social space into an abstract space that would be homogenous and transparent.[28] Densely massed populations of the poor and transient who eluded observation—or were perceived to do so—challenged that project of abstraction, a project that was intimately related to Britons' sense of their civilization's modernity. Maps comprised a dual project: the representation of a reality that was, simultaneously, an ordering of that reality. Sanitary maps sought to make transparent or visible the hidden and therefore intractable social or sanitary ills of the day, and representation itself performed a kind of containment, while providing a guide for reformers to achieving that clean, well-lighted translucency that was the ideal of sanitarians. Dickens both was fascinated by and contributed to such representations, while remaining deeply suspicious of what he saw as this project's utilitarian challenges to individuality.

Snow and the Mapping of London's Water Supply

The shift from a simple binary view of the city and sanitation to a more complex mapping coalesces around a dramatic moment in the history of epidemiology. Benjamin Ward Richardson, describing public reaction to the St. James cholera epidemic of 1854–55, remarks, "such a panic possibly never existed in London since the days of the great plague. People fled from their homes as from instant death."[29] Snow's analysis of this epidemic as waterborne and his recommendation to disable the Broad Street pump are canonical in medical histories. Histories of medical maps give prominence to Snow's map of the Broad Street epidemic—in which he showed the distribution of disease near the infected well—as the most important development in medical mapping of its era. Snow positioned himself against the dominant miasmatic model of the sanitarians, mapping not the visible filth whose dangers were easily understood by any layperson, but a hidden relationship between filth and disease: the invisible subterranean pollution of a well by seepage from a nearby cesspool. The Broad Street well water had been visibly clean, and tasted wonderful; Snow's analysis suggested that the reason it tasted so good was precisely the presence of contaminants that oxidized the water. In contrast with sanitary maps that charted some visible, tangible object—say, a dungheap—as the source of disease, Snow's maps redefine urban space by the relationship of disease to hidden features of the cityscape. Whereas earlier sanitary writers had exhorted readers breathlessly to go see for themselves horrors that were hidden only because they were in out-of-the-way places, Snow dryly and professionally observes that the real dangers are those that cannot be seen.

Less attention has been paid to the equally important subsequent portion of Snow's report, which doubles back to 1832, as Snow draws larger connections between water quality and disease. He uses tables to show parish variations in mortality and to connect them to water supply, first in 1832 and then in 1849. Here, too, there is a map, which was to prove important to mid-Victorian public health (see Figure 4.1, reproduced here without color). The original is printed in three flat colors over a black-and-white map of Southwest London, including Putney to the Isle of Dogs to the north, and to the south of the Thames covering Wimbledon on the west to Sydenham on the east. The colors include red (or pink) for areas served by the Lambeth Water Company, blue for Southwark and Vauxhall, and purple where the pipes are mingled. The mortality rates were radically different depending on which company provided the water.

The water company map offers a new definition of a human community, going beyond a neighborhood or even a parish to encompass the entire population of the greater London area. These representations allow new ways of imagining community; they also envision (and thus help to create) a larger spatial entity, which, although hitherto apparently composed of discrete and unrelated monads, could now be understood as vitally connected and participating in the same structure. Whereas earlier sanitary maps, if they offered any detail, tended to concentrate on small areas—parishes, for example—this map offered a new vision of an organically connected city. London, often described in this period as an organism loosely coterminous with the social organism of English society, could be defined, diagnosed, and displayed simultaneously in these documents as a massive entity, organized around the Thames. This map and those that followed it, with their anatomical rhetoric, treat the city as analogous to a body. The city, a fusion of human bodies and geographic setting, sickens with contamination. The human bodies, invisible on the map of homogenous space that is the city, are represented by the personification of the city itself *as* population. Graphically, the monster had an organic unity and a definite structure, organized around a circulatory system.

Sanitary mapping had long focused on water and drainage. Miasma theory posited that wet, low-lying grounds were productive of unhealthy conditions, exacerbated by the filth tending to accumulate in the same places. The filthy state of the Thames had long drawn commentary, and now the additional possibility of underground seepage, as had happened under Broad Street, made almost any urban dampness suspect of being filthy. In short, midcentury medical mapping refocused public attention away from isolated nuisances (though those were still

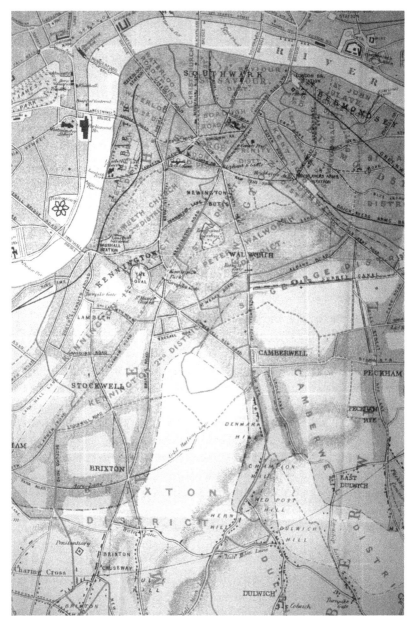

Figure 4.1. John Snow, water company map, from *On the Mode of Communication of Cholera,* 2nd ed. (London: John Churchill, 1855). This detail from the map has been much enlarged and altered to show contrast in black and white format. Differing gray tones represent areas of London whose water and sewerage systems were managed by the Lambeth Company, by the Southwark and Vauxhall Company, or, in the dark-shaded area, by a combination of these companies.

important), transforming the Thames into the primary site of London filth and a symbol of the dangers of uncontained fluids. This shift in the medical and sanitary understanding of water pollution took over a decade to fully penetrate popular understanding of disease, but its impact on those, like Dickens, who were au fait with the sanitary project, was immediate. Although Snow's theories were not accepted at once, they did immediately focus attention on water quality. The Thames in London is a tidal river: the daily tidal changes in the river's banks and the filthy residue of mud it left evidenced the river's tendency to carry the filth of the city's sewers back into the city itself, rather than away to sea. With the hypothesis of fecal-oral contamination, urban residents were forced to consider what had, in fact, long been obvious, if not as feared: that the water of the city traversed and retraversed individual bodies from mouth to anus, just as the city's sewage flowed out toward the sea and back into Londoners' drinking cups with the tides.

The Incontinent City and the Thames

Like the individual characters discussed earlier, the economy of Dickens's London is based not on continence but on greed and fraud—the inflated credit economy of the Veneerings and their ilk. According to the sanitarians, the result of human incontinence is filth, and it results, at the social level, in a filthy city. Organized around the Thames, which gives the city both its structure and its connection to the outside world, medical mappings of London at midcentury, following Snow, began to portray the city as a system vulnerable through its polluted water sources. Dickens was preoccupied with the Thames even as he finished *Bleak House*. Concerned with the recent and returning cholera epidemics of 1849 and 1854, he writes indignantly in a letter of those who would deny that contaminated water causes cholera and anathematizes "those Sewers Commissioners, who . . . really talk more rotten filth . . . than all the sewers of London contain."[30] Dickens's concern with sanitary reform is well documented, and he locates Tom-all-Alone's in one of the hardest-hit areas in the 1849 cholera epidemic (around the St. Giles area). In *Our Mutual Friend*, he is prescient; in the 1866 cholera epidemic, it was the docklands that suffered the worst mortality in the city north of the river.

In this same letter, Dickens mentions the work of George Godwin, editor of *The Builder*. Five years later, Godwin published his popular *Town Swamps and Social Bridges*, which dealt with water pollution and sanitation at some length. Godwin's discussion of the Thames's water quality emphasizes the tidal nature of the river and its effect on pollution. He provides a sketch (see Figure 4.2), showing

> the way in which a dead dog, under our own eyes, traveled. We thought
> he would get away: however, after a time, and after whirling and resting
> amongst the posts and barges, the dead dog came again in sight, moving
> *against the tide*, but much nearer to the shore; he turns off again toward
> the sea this time much sooner than the last; and after describing various
> circles, as shown by the arrows in the sketch, he is deposited in the
> slime, together with other specimens of his and allied families.[31]

Before Snow's work, the Thames's water was popularly thought to sufficiently dilute and then wash the sewage out to sea, but it appears here as an invasive presence—moving, yes, but moving the same wastes into and out of the city repeatedly until its filth simply settles in place. Dickens had pledged in the mid-1850s not to let the cholera issue die or the water companies escape scrutiny. Given that cholera was again advancing toward Britain as Dickens was writing *Our Mutual Friend*, it is not surprising that the Thames and its sewage would become an organizing metaphor for the problems of the city. The tidal nature of the river would become an important sign of the reverses and interdependences of the city's social hierarchies, and the plot would depend on an obsessive and recursive mapping of the river's course.

Figure 4.2. George Godwin, "A Dog in the Thames," from *Town Swamps and Social Bridges* (London: Routledge, Warnes, and Routledge, 1859).

Snow's report examines the role of the water companies in the 1849 and 1854 cholera epidemics, noting that, whereas the Southwark and Vauxhall water company got its water at Battersea, heavily contaminated by sewage and subject to the incursion of seawater from the tide, Lambeth Water moved its supply in the early 1850s to Thames Ditton. The result, as Snow shows, was that the two water companies supplied the same areas, but the customers of Southwark and Vauxhall suffered initially over eight times the mortality rate of those supplied by Lambeth, and nearly five times the mortality in subsequent weeks. Snow asserts, "It is quite certain that the sea water cannot reach to Thames Ditton, any more than the contents of the London sewers" (96); in fact, the normal demarcation between the tidal Thames and the inland river is Teddington Lock, about two miles downriver of Thames Ditton:

> [T]he quantity of water which passes out to sea, with the ebb of every tide, is only equal to that which flows over Teddington Lock. . . . In hot dry weather this quantity is moreover greatly diminished by the evaporation taking place from the immense surface of water exposed between Richmond and Gravesend, so that the river becomes a kind of prolonged lake, the same water passing twice a day to and fro through London, and receiving the excrement of its two millions and more of inhabitants. (95)

In 1866, shortly after the final installment of *Our Mutual Friend* was published, the long-expected cholera struck London. The areas hardest hit were those near where the river was most polluted—Southwark and the East End dock area (see Figure 4.3), the area Dickens maps in *Our Mutual Friend* as the site of identity's loss and construction. Dickens sets the first chapter in one of the Thames's most polluted areas somewhat further west, between Southwark Bridge and London Bridge. In a letter of 7 July 1858, he writes, "The Thames of London is most horrible. I have to cross Waterloo or London Bridge to get to the Railroad . . . and I can certify that the offensive smells . . . have been of a most head-and-stomach distracting nature. . . . In the meantime, cartloads of chloride of lime are to shoot into the filthy stream, and do something—I hope."[32] Eugene masquerades as a lime merchant as a plausible cover for his presence at the docks. Dickens also pays careful attention to the sanitary condition of the river in placing his characters. For example, Riderhood suggests to Headstone that Eugene has lost the tide near "say Richmond" (632), thus stressing that they are at low tide and are therefore above the area in which the city affects the purity of the water. Headstone will wait for the morning and the risen tide to follow.

If Plashwater Weir Mill Lock is above the sewage of London and the tidal influences that can carry it, Greenwich is far enough east in the estuary that the ocean water dilutes and purifies. But this apparent purity is deceptive. In his work on cholera of the mid-1850s, Snow notes:

> The great prevalence of cholera along the course of rivers has been well known. . . . Rivers always receive the refuse of those living on the banks, and they nearly always supply, at the same time, the drinking water of the community so situated. It has sometimes been objected . . . that the epidemic travels as often against the stream as with it. The reply to this is, that people travel as often against the stream as with it, and thus convey the malady. (124)

Eugene and Bradley carry the contagion of the city upriver to the purity of the rural areas there. The filthiest character of all, the Rogue, at one

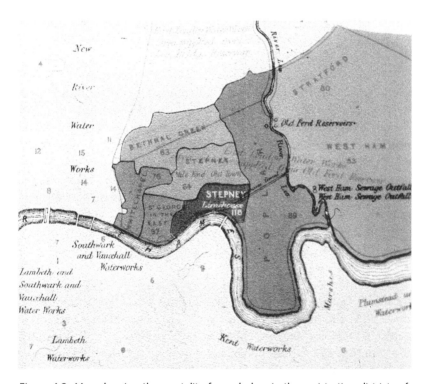

Figure 4.3. Map showing the mortality from cholera in the registration districts of London, 1866 (detail), from *Report on the Cholera Epidemic of 1866 in England: Supplement to the Twenty-ninth Annual Report of the Registrar-General of Births, Deaths, and Marriages in England* (London: George E. Eyre and William Spottiswoode, 1868). From lightest to darkest, the three tones of gray represent mortality rates of 50–75, 75–100, and 100–150 per 10,000 living people.

point tends the lock in a lovely rural area that Dickens says "*looked tranquil and pretty*" (695, emphasis added).

Dickens has Betty Higden live in Brentford (65); around the same time that the Lambeth company moved to Thames Ditton, the Grand Junction water company moved in the 1850s to obtain their water supply at Brentford, a few miles downstream of Teddington where they held it in a settling reservoir, thus cleaning it. "Muddy Brentford" is a liminal point—not itself pure, it at least does not produce poison, as any spot downriver would. Yet Johnny dies of a fever that is likely a filth disease. The Lizzie-Eugene-Bradley plot moves further upriver to the west where the Thames is initially associated with purity. Betty Higden, attempting to evade the Poor Law Guardians, takes "the upward course of the river Thames as her general track" where "you may hear the fall of the water over the weirs . . . and see the young river, dimpled like a child, playfully gliding away among the trees, unpolluted by the defilements that lie in wait for it on its course" (504). Yet she is blackmailed by that urban character Riderhood before she finally dies near the border of Oxfordshire (530).

The apparent cleanliness of the rural river is meaningless; Bradley, fitting emblem for a rotting body, soils it with blood. In insisting on the deceptiveness of the river's apparent purity, Dickens stresses here the *Bleak House* lesson of connection between widely separated places and people, of interdependence between city and suburb, but he uses Snow's connection of the river and pollution to do what a miasmatic model of disease and contagion from Tom-all-Alone's did in the earlier novel. Like Snow, he emphasizes the opacity of those connections to the uninitiated eye; it is the novelist who can map the hidden contamination, while the reader must yield to his expert construction of the city's space.

Seepage and the Self

Catherine Gallagher has argued that identity loss, a key theme in the novel, is tied to immersion in the river.[33] The novel identifies the interpenetration of city and river with this loss as well: individual identity loss is mirrored by the city's boundary diffusion. As Deirdre David notes, Dickens began writing *Our Mutual Friend* as the Thames was being embanked and efforts were being made to establish better drainage near the river in the East End.[34] The novel, however, relies on the river's unembanked state, its pollution of the surrounding land and the uncertainty of its boundaries, to point to the porousness of the selves the principal characters are struggling to contain and define. As in *Bleak*

House's Tom-all-Alone's, social detritus is compared to human waste, and the Thames, as both the organizing metaphor and landmark of the novel, seems at key moments to incorporate the city along its banks: Rotherhithe is "where [the] accumulated scum of humanity seemed to be washed from higher grounds, like so much moral sewage, and to be pausing until its own weight forced it over the bank and sunk it in the river . . . among vessels that seemed to have got ashore and houses that seemed to have got afloat" (21). In this scene, Mortimer and Eugene go to the riverside to *mis*identify John Harmon's decaying body. When Riderhood goes in turn to misidentify Hexam as the murderer, he once again leads Eugene and Mortimer to the water, walking through hail and leaving "marks in the fast-melting slush that were mere shapeless holes; one might have fancied, following, that the very shape of humanity had departed from his feet. . . . It seemed as if the streets were absorbed in the sky, and the night were all in the air" (157).

Riderhood loses the boundaries of his body as the city loses its definition. But it is Hexam's drowned corpse that will emerge from the river, after a long night of transformations in which Eugene impersonates a lime-merchant, Mortimer, in exhaustion, hallucinates, and Eugene himself feels that he is being transformed into a "half-drowned" criminal who has "swallowed half a gallon" of the "wash of the river" (164). On the river itself, "everything so vaunted the spoiling influences of water—discoloured copper, rotten wood, honey-combed stone, green dank deposit—that the after consequences of being crushed, sucked under, and drawn down, looked as ugly to the imagination as the main event" (172). Worse, what goes into the river comes back out and is incorporated into the city's bodies; in the first few pages of the novel, Gaffer responds to Lizzie's river-aversion by insisting that it is "meat and drink" to her. In London, loss of identity also means abjection, the grotesque loss of the body's integrity.

Despite their many trips to the sea or the countryside, the principal characters must still go to this place and face the worst of the river to claim their true identities; that is, they must overcome the filth with which they are contaminated and for which they are in part responsible. Yet damaged as it is, the river represents potential redemption.[35] Harmon loses his identity in his waterside adventure, but is also able to fashion a new and more secure self after his slow rebirth. On a night when the water of the river is blown through the air like rain, blurring boundaries between river and city, he attempts to reconstruct the night he lost himself, having been disguised and drugged: "There was no such thing as I, within my knowledge" (369). Being thrown into the

Thames paradoxically revives him, and he thinks, "'This is John Harmon drowning! John Harmon, struggle for your life. John Harmon, call on Heaven and save yourself!' . . . [Finally] it was I who was struggling there alone in the water" (370). In this struggle to re-form and contain himself, to call himself into being, he confuses himself by actually crossing the river; he cannot reorient himself: "Even at this moment, I cannot conceive that it [the river] rolls between me and that spot, or that the sea is where it is" (370). He is, as the narrator describes him, a "living dead man" (373), as if his soul has been left in hock to the underworld. He attributes some of his unease to the lingering effects of the drug: "even now, I have sometimes to think, constrain myself . . . or I could not say the words I want to say" (371). Retracing his steps and remapping his body's location in relation to the river is part of the process of consolidating his new self.

The metaphors here are all of containment. Like the river, Harmon's subjectivity exceeds its boundaries and he must be "constrained," put back in his container, his body made fast against forces external to it—the drug, for example, or the water. In fact, as with Eugene and Lizzie, Harmon's long, slow birthing out of the Thames cannot be finalized without Bella's love and marriage. It is not until after his marriage, the birth of his child, and the clearing away of the dust mounds that he is able to claim the name he calls out over the river. Not until Bella declares her faith in him and her innocence of any untoward desire for wealth does she, too, in "the state of a dreamer," go to the "low-lying water-side wharves" near London Bridge where all, down to the drunken woman banging on the cell-door, is as it was when Harmon's body was found (762). Again, they go to the Six Jolly Fellowship Porters where, this time, Harmon's living body will be correctly identified. And here, this time, Bella will lose her identity as Mrs. Rokesmith in order that both she and her husband may be reborn as their true selves, the Harmons. The project of embankment, providing definite boundaries between land and water and containing the pollution therein, matches the project of defining and defending clear boundaries of the self.[36]

Dickens's London, the Monster, and the Critics

Much has been made of the chaotic nature of Dickens's urbanism in his later novels, and most of this work insists on the indeterminacy of the monstrous city in the text, its frustrating lack of specificity.[37] In fact, however, the novels are quite specific—even fussily, journalistically so—about locations. I would suggest, following Kay Hetherly Wright, that the grotesque is the structuring mode of these novels, and it is that which makes them seem initially dreamlike and unrealistic in their portrayal of space. But through this mode, Dickens was portraying a very concrete set of conditions in London, which he and his contemporaries perceived as both quotidian and monstrous: human filth is physically present in the very heart of the city. The body is always potentially grotesque in these novels, and the mark of its grotesqueness is waste—excrement, blood, decaying corpses; the city is the material manifestation of the sick social body, and must be grotesque as well.

Franco Moretti points out that Dickens mediates the East End/West End binary by producing a third space, that of the middle class, which occupies the wedge of London including the City, the Inns, and the suburbs north of those points, between the corrupt West End of the aristocracy and the criminal East End.[38] It is a compelling argument, though, as Moretti admits, not completely consistent; for example, Tom-all-Alone's in *Bleak House* sits as uncompromisingly in the middle of Holborn as St. Giles did, and many of Dickens's decent middle class are quite horrifying (for example, Vholes). In locating their homes, Dickens tells us in shorthand a great deal about the characters' social position. But the characters are very often not where they are supposed to be. While *Our Mutual Friend* opens with socially marginal characters from the docklands, they are located between London Bridge and Southwark Bridge—by the City, which Moretti identifies as middle-class space.

One of the most shocking revelations of the 1855 epidemic and Snow's mapping of it was that the single worst local epidemic of this filth disease, so identified with poverty and immorality, happened in rich St. James's—while St. Giles, its abject opposite, was practically untouched. In fact, although many were shocked by the disease striking such an opulent and fashionable West End parish, no one should have been—Berwick Street near Golden Square was one of the worst slums in town.[39] As Henri Lefebvre points out, there is often a disjunction between how social space is perceived and how it is lived.[40] Except for the few people who lived in that slum, the social understanding of Golden Square by most Londoners was assimilated to its general location in a wealthy parish; if people in St. James's could die of cholera, it could happen anywhere, and the binaries of filthy and clean, poor and rich, had collapsed. Snow took advantage of this perception, dwelling on the respectability of the artisans who lived there, rather than on their impoverished living conditions, which would have fueled sanitarian rebuttals to his fecal-oral theory. In this way, perceived space tends to elide some of the complexity of lived space, just as the broad homogenizing tendencies of pitting east and west against each other—or even east, west, and middle—tend to do.

Dickens, then, both employs these binary oppositions and resists them in the interest of particularization. One of his abiding interests is the heterogeneity of local spaces, the surprise that is just around the next corner. To this end, he places characters' homes in locations that take advantage of readers' perceived-space mappings of London and then, like Snow's report, proceeds to demolish those boundaries as he shows just how vulnerable they are to seepage. As in medical maps, the binaries of the first half of the century give way in this novel to a more complex set of spatial relations. Plot interest, as Moretti points out, is often generated by the transgression of boundaries, and certainly some of the disorientation critics complain of is less a result of the novel's atopicality than of the difficulty of reconciling Dickens's meticulous detailing of transgressive itineraries with the binaries of Victorian London as perceived space. Like Snow, Dickens both takes advantage of popular perceptions and challenges them, showing those mythic boundaries to be meaningless in the face of the city's inability to maintain bodily hierarchies. If the West End, with its palaces of government, is the head and mouth of the city, the upper bodily stratum taking in sustenance from the healthy countryside, and the East End is the cloaca, discharging toward the sea (and the Continent) the city's wastes, what does it mean that the corpse of George Radfoot, dumped into the water in Limehouse Hole, washes up in the City? Partially, Dickens wants to emphasize the association of filth with the financial and market districts—the body is hauled up right by London Bridge—to tie the waste-wealth equation together. But this is possible because the tidal river moves from east to west, inverting bodily and imperial hierarchies, just as cholera (both globally and locally associated with the East) appears in St. James's, to the horror of the wealthy and the middle class.

Like the sanitary mapping project, Dickens's novel aimed to challenge the perceived spaces of London—that is, a London of tightly contained and class distinct areas—in favor of an understanding of London as a lived space of heterogeneity and conflict. This demystification is not simply celebratory, however; it is a preparatory step to bringing London into line with what Lefebvre calls "conceived" space—in this case, an idealized vision of London in which disorder is abolished and all areas become homogenously bourgeois. The dominance of middle-class space, which, Moretti demonstrates, emerges in this text, is thus as much utopian inner space as actual geography. Order cannot be imposed simply by cordoning off the dangerous classes—in this novel, mainly because they just jump in a boat and row west—but by transforming them, whenever possible, into continent individuals.

Our Mutual Friend, then, is far more conservative than *Bleak House*. In *Bleak House*, lack of self-containment results in harm through poor sanitation caused by systemic corruption. In *Our Mutual Friend* the systemic corruption practically vanishes from the text except for parenthetic reminders; instead, individual incontinence is mapped directly onto the body of the city without the mediation of a sick government or society at large. Snow has transformed the cholera from a moral issue into an engineering problem, a matter not of prayer or temperance but of simple physical containment. Still, unlike earlier novels, there is no exodus from the sick city, either to Yorkshire or to other garden spots. The city's sick body must be redeemed on its own terms, rather than abandoned. The entropic city faithfully maps subjectivity out of control; the flooding, filthy river bodies forth the desires that erode the boundaries of the embodied middle-class self. The sanitary project of purifying the water supply and the city through careful containment becomes the emblem of a society's attempt to civilize itself through the containment of its constituent bodies, leaving Dickens and his readers gazing, with cautious optimism, at the Embankment.

Notes

1. Charles Dickens, *Nicholas Nickleby* (1839; London: Penguin, 1999), 412.

2. The categorization and value of feces fluctuated with various reclamation programs through midcentury. Still, fecal material within the city was generally viewed with disgust and fear.

3. Peter Stallybrass and Allon White, *The Politics and Poetics of Transgression* (Ithaca, NY: Cornell University Press, 1986), 136.

4. Ibid., 125–26.

5. Mary Poovey, *Making a Social Body: British Cultural Formation, 1830–1864* (Chicago: University of Chicago Press, 1995), chapter 2.

6. D. A. Miller, *The Novel and the Police* (Berkeley and Los Angeles: University of California Press, 1988).

7. F. S. Schwarzbach, "*Bleak House*: The Social Pathology of Urban Life," *Literature and Medicine* 9 (1990): 93–104, at 95.

8. Many scholars have discussed the contents of the dustheaps, and whether we are to take them as containing feces or not. Setting aside the historical question of their contents, we can look at the literary question of their representation. There is little doubt that the dustheaps are waste and represent, at least allegorically, human waste. Critics have noted the anality of *Our Mutual Friend* and the equation of feces with filthy lucre; see Michael Steig, "Dickens's Excremental Vision," *Victorian Studies* 8, no. 3 (1970): 339–54; Catherine Gallagher,

"The Bioeconomics of *Our Mutual Friend*," in *Subject to History* (Ithaca, NY: Cornell University Press, 1991), 47–69.

9. Julia Kristeva, *Powers of Horror: An Essay on Abjection*, trans. Leon S. Roudiez (New York: Columbia University Press, 1982). For a reading of the abject in *Bleak House*, focusing largely on character and sexuality rather than the body per se, see Robert E. Lougy, "Filth, Liminality, and Abjection in Charles Dickens's *Bleak House*," *ELH* 69 (2002): 473–500.

10. Charles Dickens, *Our Mutual Friend* (Oxford: Oxford University Press, 1952), 714. Further citations to this edition will be made parenthetically in the text.

11. Headstone's association with anality and anal rape has been elaborated by Gallagher, "Bioeconomics of *Our Mutual Friend*," and Eve Kosofsky Sedgwick, *Between Men: English Literature and Male Homosocial Desire* (New York: Columbia University Press, 1985).

12. For a related discussion of mess and waste as central to modernity and as signs of the contingency of the self and its reliance on the social in Dickens, see David Trotter, *Cooking with Mud: The Idea of Mess in Nineteenth-Century Art and Fiction* (Oxford: Oxford University Press, 2000), especially 161–75.

13. Herbert L. Sussman, *Victorian Masculinities: Manhood and Masculine Poetics in Early Victorian Literature and Art* (Cambridge: Cambridge University Press, 1995).

14. Erin O'Connor, *Raw Material: Producing Pathology in Victorian Culture* (Durham, NC: Duke University Press, 2000), 41.

15. Nancy Armstrong, *Desire and Domestic Fiction: A Political History of the Novel* (New York: Oxford University Press, 1987).

16. As Gail Kern Paster points out of the early modern period, in "the various disciplinary regimes Foucault has seen as characteristic of emergent modernity, the bodies to be mastered were humoral bodies," particularly the "leaky vessels" of women's bodies. In these bodies, boundaries were always threatened. In the later modernity of the mid-nineteenth century, I would argue that such a vision persisted, but coexisted with the heightened sense that any material entering the body was potentially polluting, and any material leaving the body was filthy and liable to immediately enter surrounding bodies, leading to a new level of anxiety about bodily closure. See Paster, *The Body Embarrassed: Drama and the Disciplines of Shame in Early Modern England* (Ithaca, NY: Cornell University Press, 1993), 7.

17. Mary Douglas, *Purity and Danger: An Analysis of the Concepts of Pollution and Taboo* (1966; London: Routledge and Kegan Paul, 1980).

18. In short, models of illness fluctuated in grossly the same terms as models of economic responsibility: between an individual as a closed system responsible for itself and a communitarian notion of a porous body vulnerable to outside influences often beyond its control.

19. A word is in order here about the use of the term *liberal,* which may surprise readers steeped in Dickens's rejection of classical liberal economics and his

obvious insistence on social connection and responsibility in many of his works. There were many kinds of liberals in mid-Victorian society, and Dickens is more a late Millsian than a Smithian liberal, emphasizing social responsibility while retaining a largely Kantian notion of a core individual self. Most importantly, Dickens is drawing on an iconographic, literary, and medical tradition of the Enlightenment middle-class body (and subject) that emphasizes individualism and separation, a tradition of representation that radically undermines a notion of connected society and, indeed, positions it as a threat.

20. John Kucich, in *Excess and Restraint: The Novels of Charles Dickens* (Athens: University of Georgia Press, 1981), has traced this dichotomy in several of Dickens's novels. He reads the relationship as essentially between the formlessness implicit in death and the conservative impulse toward life. Following Bataille, he sees the novels as staging death—through loss, deaths, overspending, and the like—in order ultimately to recuperate order and restraint. Kucich also remarks the tendency of Dickens's heroes to achieve integration through some scene of disintegration, whether of violence or expenditure (108). Kucich's reading concentrates on a psychoanalytic vision of the self, but his key opposition between excess and restraint, between disintegration and self-control, is one I explore here in terms of the relation of the individual's body to the social body and the city.

21. Dickens, *Bleak House* (Oxford: Oxford University Press, 1986), 479.

22. Arthur H. Robinson, "The 1837 Maps of Henry Drury Harness," *Geographical Journal* 121 (1955): 440–50, at 440.

23. See, for example, E. W. Gilbert, "Pioneer Maps of Health and Disease in England," *Geographical Journal* 124 (1958), 172–83, especially 173; and Saul Jarcho, "The Contributions of Heinrich and Hermann Berghaus to Medical Cartography," *Journal of the History of Medicine and the Allied Sciences* 24 (1969): 412–15.

24. Lloyd G. Stevenson, "Putting Disease on the Map: The Early Use of Spot Maps in the Study of Yellow Fever," *Journal of the History of Medicine and the Allied Sciences* 20 (1965): 226–61, at 240.

25. See Pamela K. Gilbert, "'Scarcely to Be Described': Urban Extremes as Real Spaces and Mythic Places in the London Cholera Epidemic of 1854," *Nineteenth-Century Studies* 14 (2000): 149–72, for an example in sanitary discourse.

26. Lynda Nead, *Victorian Babylon: People, Streets, and Images in Nineteenth Century London* (New Haven, CT: Yale University Press, 2000), 13.

27. Ibid., 15. On the historical portrayal of the city as body and site of proximity to the abject, see Stallybrass and White, *Politics and Poetics of Transgression*.

28. Poovey, *Making a Social Body*.

29. Benjamin Ward Richardson, in John Snow, *Snow on Cholera, Being a Reprint of Two Papers by John Snow, M.D., with a Biographical Memoir by Benjamin Ward Richardson* (New York: Commonwealth Fund, 1936), xxvi. Further citations to this edition will be made parenthetically in the text.

30. Dickens, letter of 10 October 1854, in *The Letters of Charles Dickens*, ed. Graham Storey et al., 11 vols. (Oxford: Oxford University Press, 1965), 7:435–36.

31. George Godwin, *Town Swamps and Social Bridges* (1859; New York: Humanities Press, 1972), 56 (emphasis in original).

32. Dickens, *Letters*, 8:598.

33. See Gallagher, "Bioeconomics of *Our Mutual Friend*."

34. Deirdre David, *Fictions of Resolution in Three Victorian Novels* (New York: Columbia University Press, 1981), 53. See also Dickens's letter of 30 November 1865, in *Letters*, 11:116.

35. See David, *Fictions of Resolution*.

36. The women in the novel, with the exception of Bella and Mrs. Lammle, are largely innocent of the sins for which the men must be purified through a filthy baptism. Although, as Helena Michie has pointed out, women suffer for the sins of others in this novel, women do not have the power to become protagonists in healing the social body, though they can midwife the healing of male bodies; see "'Who Is This in Pain?' Scarring, Disfigurement, and Female Identity in *Bleak House* and *Our Mutual Friend*," *Novel* 22, no. 2 (1989): 199–212.

37. Julian Wolfreys has argued that London is formed in a "discourse always reshaping itself, emerging . . . as a monster" that cannot be fixed but leads us on through desire to "fix it in place, hold it in the gaze forever" (*Writing London: The Trace of the Urban Text from Blake to Dickens* [Basingstoke, Hampshire: Macmillan Press, 1998], 67). Kay Hetherly Wright, in "The Grotesque and Urban Chaos in *Bleak House*" (*Dickens Studies Annual* 21 [1992]: 97–112), finds the key to *Bleak House*'s urban chaos in the grotesque, whereas Allan Pritchard, in "The Urban Gothic of *Bleak House*" (*Nineteenth-Century Literature* 45, no. 4 [1991]: 432–52), seeks an understandable structure to *Bleak House*'s London in the Gothic. All of these readings attempt to account for the pervasive sense of disorientation in *Bleak House* and *Our Mutual Friend* in terms of a lack of realistic specificity or a turn to a mode of representation other than realism.

38. Franco Moretti, *Atlas of the European Novel, 1800–1900* (New York: Verso, 1998).

39. For details, see Gilbert, "'Scarcely to Be Described.'"

40. Henri Lefevbre, *The Production of Space*, trans. Donald Nicholson-Smith (Oxford: Blackwell, 1991).

Chapter 5

Confronting Sensory Crisis in the Great Stinks of London and Paris

David S. Barnes

Londoners began to fret in June 1858, Parisians in July 1880. In each case, a prolonged heat wave braised a rapidly expanding metropolis into a state of extreme vulnerability, and an insidious sensory trigger sparked a blaze that threatened to consume the city. The population demanded relief, the press blared its indignation, and the government was momentarily thrown into crisis. It was neither a foreign invasion nor a natural disaster but rather an *odor*—or, to be faithful to contemporary accounts, not just an odor but an unimaginably foul stench—that caused such an uproar in the British and French capitals. The Great Stink of London lasted for about two weeks in 1858, the Great Stink of Paris for two and a half months in 1880. Was it the same odor in both cases? It is impossible to answer this question with certainty, but chroniclers certainly attributed the two stenches to the same general source: accumulated human excrement.

The imperative of immediate action was quickly perceived in each city. But what kind of action, and how to bring it about? Here the British and French experiences diverged. The aggrieved Englishmen engaged in a brief period of lamentation, accusation, and recrimination before attending to the task at hand. Within weeks a plan had been approved and, shortly thereafter, ground had been broken on an unprecedented public works project to rid London of its shit. The odors never recurred. In Paris, on the other hand, the finger-pointing and disputation dragged on, long past the fading of the stench. Commissions were appointed, conclusions were drawn, resolutions were adopted . . . and nothing was done. What came to be referred to with exasperation as "the odors of Paris" continued to visit the city periodically into the early twentieth century.

Such divergent responses to essentially the same phenomenon raise a number of questions, particularly since the efficient, characteristically modern set of reactions occurred twenty-two years *earlier* than the case of archaic inertia. It is tempting to invoke stereotypes of national "character" or other local particularities (for example, political configurations, fiscal constraints) to explain the contrasting responses, and indeed there were important differences between Londoners' and Parisians' inclinations with regard to major sanitary public works. However, such differences cannot fully account for the French unwillingness to do what the English had readily done: pipe their malodorous waste out of town, out of sight, out of smell, and out of mind. The chief culprit in the French failure to act can be found in an unexpected place: scientific progress, as represented by the nascent germ theory of disease, may actually have blocked rather than accelerated remedial mobilization. Far from complacent or resigned, French authorities were in effect traumatized into virtual paralysis by the odors of 1880. With emotions running high and competing camps of experts promoting different solutions, consensus on the appropriate course of action proved elusive, and nothing was done.

The differences between the Great Stinks of London and Paris cast the early years of bacteriology in an unfamiliar light. Yet the underlying similarities between the two episodes are even more fundamental and of greater long-term historical significance. They highlight the extent to which crises of filth threatened the rapidly growing cities of the nineteenth century and forever changed the way urbanites managed their bodies, their waste, and their environment. Moreover, the magnitude of these two appalling ordeals cannot be explained simply as a straightforward, commonsense reaction to an objective material phenomenon. The fact that they occurred in these places at these times (and not in other places or at other times) calls our attention to the historicity of disgust. The Great Stinks were simultaneously as physically real as the excretions that gave rise to them and as culturally contingent as the political and moral systems that attempted to come to grips with them.

Undertaken from this vantage point, a comparison of these two ordeals and their consequences serves to uncover the fragmentary archaeological traces of a vast and largely unexplored region of historical inquiry.[1] If these sensory crises—seemingly isolated but upon inspection possibly belonging to a larger family of distinct Stinks—could have caused such acute uproar at the time and yet subsequently all but escaped the attention of historians, is it not time to finally listen to what the panicked and revolted inhabitants of Europe's two largest cities were trying to tell us? The following brief narrative overview and comparative analysis of the two Great Stinks suggests that *disgust* represents a promising and underexplored category of historical analysis. The systematic study of disgust traces its lineage back to Darwin and Freud, and, while anthropologists and sociologists have occasionally contributed their insights, the field has been largely left to social and evolutionary psychologists.[2] The result has been a fundamentally *static* understanding of disgust as either a biologicially evolved defense against ingestion of harmful substances or a means of policing human-animal boundaries.[3] The contingency, mutability, and uses of disgust have received very little attention, and our understanding of bodily experience and bodily knowledge—past and present—has been the poorer for it. The Great Stinks of London and Paris hint at the multiple ways this seemingly straightforward emotion, at once biologically and culturally determined, acts as both a *signpost* and an *engine* of historical change.

"The Disgusting State of the River Thames," 1858

In 1858, the bodily waste of Londoners flowed through sewers directly into the Thames. A decade earlier, fearing precisely the spread of odors and disease, local authorities had sought to end the cesspit system, in which pits or containers underneath each residential building collected the excretions of its residents. Under this old sanitary regime, crews periodically emptied the cesspits' contents into carts and transported them to more or less distant depots. In effect, the new system ended up displacing the problem from a multitude of points throughout the metropolis (every residential building) to a single central location: the Thames. Sewers emptied into the river at various points, including central London. Even in the best of times, some observers feared for the safety of drinking water and warned of possible epidemics; if the water level of the Thames were ever to drop significantly, crisis awaited.[4]

There was no shortage of plans for the safe, efficient, and tolerable disposal of the city's waste, but any undertaking of an appropriate magnitude required an unprecedented mobilization of political will, technical expertise, and material resources. An unwieldy and decentralized system of local sanitary authorities was replaced in 1855 by the

Metropolitan Board of Works, intended to facilitate "the better management of the metropolis" through public works. At the top of the
Board's agenda was "the sewage problem."⁵ Insufficient resources and
bureaucratic turf wars between the Government and the Board, however, prevented any real progress until the early summer of 1858.

A prolonged dry spell had left the Thames at an unusually low level,
and a heat wave in June ripened its contents to a peak of pungency. The
effect was catastrophic, if contemporary accounts are to be believed—
not a gradually developing, unpleasant sensation but a devastating and
even incapacitating onslaught. The stench was intolerable; something
needed to be done; the Government and sanitary authorities bore a responsibility to act—without further delay. There was near unanimity on
these points. But agreement was elusive on the key question, repeated
by newspapers and their readers throughout the Great Stink: "What is
to be done?"⁶

Geographic circumstance simultaneously aggravated the impact of
the stench and provided the key to its ultimate remediation. As the
Thames passes through the center of London, many of the most heavily trafficked areas of the city (as well as densely populated residential
neighborhoods) were inescapably suffused with the river's odors. This
was the case, significantly, with the Houses of Parliament in their normally picturesque riverside location in Westminster. Not only did legislators in this instance experience firsthand the problems besetting their
angry constituents, but they were also nearly forced to adjourn the session because of the insufferable odors. The Great Stink rendered the
ordinary work of committees, hearings, and legislation impossible;
meetings were postponed and, in an alarming sign of the magnitude of
the problem (as commentators wryly observed in the press), long-winded
orators cut short their speeches. "Disgust, alarm, and reasonable precautions induced members to stop away," the *Globe* reported laconi-
cally. While sanitation workers dumped tons of lime into the river in a
desperate attempt to counteract the stench, sheets soaked in chloride of
lime were hung over the windows of the Houses of Parliament. MPs
finally understood on a visceral level that something had to be done.⁷

One month after the outbreak of the Great Stink, it was Benjamin
Disraeli, leader of the House of Commons at the time, who (calling the
Thames "a Stygian pool") introduced a bill giving the Metropolitan
Board of Works (MBW) at last the resources and relatively unfettered
authority to undertake a sewerage project of unparalleled magnitude.
Disraeli's bill worked its way through Parliament smoothly and remark-
ably swiftly; according to the *Times*, "the stench of June . . . did for the

sanitary administration of the Metropolis what the Bengal mutinies did for the administration of India." Legislators hostile by nature to major state expenditures or to any significant government intervention in local affairs fell into line, as if dazed by the intensity of the olfactory ordeal. "The Metropolis Local Management Amendment Act: An Act to alter and amend the Metropolis Local Management Act and to extend the powers of the Metropolitan Board of Works for the purification of the Thames and the main Drainage of the Metropolis" became law on August 2, 1858, just eighteen days after its introduction.[8] In time of crisis, smell trumped politics.

The new antistink law empowered the MBW and its chief engineer, Sir Joseph Bazalgette, to undertake a massive plan of sewer construction, eventually completed in 1875 at a cost of £6.5 million. Bazalgette built 83 miles of sewer mains, fed by many hundreds of miles of smaller sewers, so that the waste of London could be evacuated far downstream at high tide and be carried harmlessly to the sea. The centerpiece of Bazalgette's scheme was the construction of the Thames embankments, which, in addition to enclosing the sewer mains, beautified the London riverfront considerably and created new public parks at Charing Cross and Cheyne Walk. Most historians concur in viewing Bazalgette's achievement as a triumph of both sanitation and urban design, a harbinger of a new age of beneficent modern public works.[9]

"The Parisian Infection," 1880

This relatively straightforward response to an olfactory and sanitary crisis presents a sharp contrast to events across the Channel twenty-two years later. Then again, both the causes and geographic focal points of the French stench were more difficult to identify than they had been in London. Paris, too, had undergone a major program of sewer construction in the 1850s and 1860s, as part of the colossal rebuilding plan undertaken by Emperor Napoleon III and the capital's prefect, Baron Haussmann. However, the new Paris sewers (unlike Bazalgette's) drained from the city every kind of refuse and runoff *except* human urine and feces. Haussmann feared that the spacious galleries of the new sewers—whose water pressure was much lower than that of London's smaller sewer pipes—would be incapable of evacuating solids. The chance that "infectious" matter might accumulate, or that sheer disgust would prevent sewermen from doing their jobs, kept him from taking what he saw as the dangerous risk of putting human waste underground.[10] Parisian bodily waste continued to be evacuated by means of cesspits and *vidange* crews, who emptied the cesspits and carted their contents to several waste treatment plants located in the suburbs. (Haussmann expressed no qualms about the disgust of *vidangeurs*.)

One of these plants, in the town of Nanterre west of Paris, became notorious for spreading unpleasant odors throughout the surrounding region. Local residents complained so insistently that on May 14, 1880, the plant's operating permit was temporarily suspended. However, this order seems to have been honored primarily in the breach, as local authorities continued to receive complaints of malodorous activity at the plant. Finally, nine neighboring towns took the plant's operator, the Compagnie parisienne de vidanges et d'engrais, to court for violation of its original license and of the May 14 suspension. The judge found against the company, and ordered the plant shut down permanently. A small victory had been won for the olfactory sensibilities of the population, but it turned out to be short-lived. The suspension and subsequent shutdown of the Nanterre plant caused the Compagnie parisienne, which enjoyed a near-monopoly in Parisian *vidange* services, to transport the waste that would have been treated in Nanterre to other plants in the northern, eastern, and southern suburbs. It was also alleged that some of the resulting surplus waste was simply dumped into the Paris sewers.[11]

In the heat of July, during the suspension of the Nanterre plant's license, complaints about intolerable odors began to arise within Paris itself.[12] Shortly after the final shutdown of the plant in August, the complaints in Paris intensified, particularly in the north-central districts of the ninth, seventeenth, and eighteenth arrondissements. "Fetid emanations," residents claimed in the third week of August, were spreading through the city, particularly in the evening hours, and positively "stinking up" their neighborhoods.[13] By the end of the month, the odors had become an almost daily fixture in the Parisian press, typically under one of two headlines: "The Odors of Paris" or "The Parisian Infection." (The French word *infection* has multiple meanings, including both foul odor and means of disease transmission.) From late August through the month of September and into early October, these two labels came to designate a full-fledged public sensation, an object not just of private annoyance and complaint, but of public policy, official debate, and rancorous accusations.

Parisians sent petitions of complaint to the City Council, which, along with the departmental Conseil général, convened angry hearings at which local administrators were harshly criticized. Echoing the complaints of their constituents and of the press, councillors accused Prefect of Police Louis Andrieux and Director of Municipal Public Works Adolphe Alphand of negligently failing to enforce prohibitions on illegal dumping by *vidangeurs* as well as regulations restricting the operations of the suburban treatment plants. Andrieux commissioned a study by the departmental health council to study the odors; the resulting report (heavily influenced by Alphand) concluded that the odors were unpleasant but harmless.[14] The reassuring report failed to mollify the administration's critics, however.

It did not take long for the local health council's pronouncement to be superseded by that of a higher authority; on September 28, the central government entered the fray. The Minister of Agriculture and Commerce named an eleven-member commission to study the causes of the "infection" of Paris and to recommend remedial measures. Among the commission's members were two leading authorities who had yet to weigh in on the Great Stink: Louis Pasteur and Paul Brouardel. Pasteur was already a nationally and internationally renowned figure in 1880, though his fame would increase considerably in the ensuing years, and Brouardel was one of his staunchest allies in the medical community, professor of public health and forensic medicine at the Paris medical faculty and a preeminent authority on all health matters in late nineteenth-century France.[15]

The commission deliberated from the last day of September 1880 through late June of the following year, identifying an exhaustive array of sites and practices as potential or actual sources of the odors. More importantly, the prestigious commission found that "these odors . . . *can* pose a threat to the public health." In effect, the official voice of French science and medicine, while acknowledging the possibility that foul odors could be harmless, had come down in this instance on the side of their potential danger, and had chosen to take a public stand to that effect.[16]

Sooner or later, every discussion of the Parisian Great Stink came down to an evaluation of *"tout-à-l'égout"* ("everything into the sewers")—the controversial plan to evacuate all of the city's human waste through the sewers, and ultimately into the Seine downstream of Paris and onto sewage farms along the riverbanks. First approved by the City Council in 1876, *tout-à-l'égout* received final legislative approval from the national parliament only in 1894, and even as late as 1914 the connection of each residential building in Paris to the sewer system remained far from complete. Proponents of the plan denounced the cumbersome *vidange* system, and promoted circulation through water rather than accumulation as the safest and least incommodious way to handle human excretions. Landlords, on the other hand, cried foul at the considerable cost of conversion to the new system, while some hygienists feared the health effects of emanations from a permanent excremental stream flowing underneath the streets of the capital.[17]

It was this latter fear that prevailed among the members of the government's Great Stink commission. Brouardel strongly insisted on the likelihood (indeed, he claimed, the demonstrated fact) that fecal emanations spread typhoid fever as well as other diseases. Most curiously, Pasteur cited a recent study he had conducted in which sheep had purportedly contracted anthrax by inhaling germs in the air above a patch of ground where sheep who died of the disease had been buried twelve years earlier. If one accepted that human excrement contained the germs (yet to be identified) of typhoid fever and other diseases, Pasteur reasoned, then the risk of spreading those diseases through emanations from sewers was simply too great to take. This bacteriological neo-miasmatism led Pasteur, Brouardel, and other commission members to reject *tout-à-l'égout* in favor of a hermetically sealed pipeline to the sea, entirely separate from the sewer system, for the evacuation of human waste. The prohibitive expense and dubious feasibility of such a project ensured that it would remain a dead letter outside the deliberations of committees where well-connected opponents of *tout-à-l'égout* held sway.[18]

The stench of August and September had long faded by the time the commission published its final report in June 1881. The urgent pressure for remedial action had faded somewhat as well, and the critical absence of scientific consensus on the one project that seemed to stand a chance of moving forward—*tout-à-l'égout*—spelled doom for any significant response to the Great Stink of 1880. The most that could be achieved were promises from local administrators to keep a stricter watch on the operations of *vidangeurs* and waste treatment plants. For all the outcry, the French essentially did nothing. As for the odors, they returned several times in the subsequent decades with enough intensity to provoke similar complaints, demands for action, commissions, and disputation.[19]

Viewed from afar, the responses to the Great Stinks in Europe's two largest cities could scarcely have been more different. Londoners saw (or rather sensed) a problem, discussed it, and fixed it; Parisians complained, argued, and did nothing. Clearheaded common sense and determination produced results, while quarrelsome deliberation resulted only in future Stinks, great and small. Closer investigation, however, reveals a remarkable degree of parallelism between the English and French reactions. It also suggests a surprising explanation for the one big difference between them.

Disgust and Outrage

The most striking feature of the two Great Stinks is in fact how alike the popular responses were. It is impossible to know precisely what the air smelled like in London in 1858 and in Paris in 1880—and in any case, the capacity of language to represent odors has never matched the emotive power of the experience of smelling them.[20] Nevertheless, whatever the exact chemical composition of the two stenches, they seem to have provoked a nearly identical set of sensations and fears among Londoners and Parisians. In both cases (if we are to believe the contemporary accounts, particularly in the press), the odors were intolerable and disgusting, but also *sickening*, literally as well as figuratively—that is, they were nauseating, and also caused serious illnesses. Both populations demanded urgent government action, and expressed frustration and outrage at governmental authorities' perceived failure to pursue the appropriate measures quickly and resolutely.

On both sides of the Channel, commentators and aggrieved residents took pains to distinguish the olfactory crisis from the everyday, run-of-the-mill urban nuisances to which they were accustomed. In London, one fearful constituent wrote to the Lord Mayor in an attempt to impress upon him the gravity of the situation:

> My Lord,—What is to be done? The stench from the Thames yesterday, even at high water, exceeded anything I have ever smel [*sic*] or noticed before. On leaving the Adelphi Pier I was seized with vomiting, and I really expected some injury would accrue to me.[21]

In a letter to the *Morning News*, another Londoner complained of the "abominable, loathsome, and fever-breeding smells perpetually emitted from that river which was formerly the boast of every Englishman":

> Passing across the bridge yesterday the effluvium was so noxious, and had such an effect on some of the persons who were riding on an omnibus on which I was myself a passenger, that they one and all, to escape the consequences, loudly begged of the driver to quicken his speed to avoid it.[22]

Lest readers (or historians) far from the epicenter of the disaster ascribe such protests to hyperbole, another newspaper warned, "Do not let it be supposed that there is exaggeration in the complaints of the stench of the Thames," and even claimed that "the reality rather surpasses the representations of the nuisance."[23]

On the banks of the Seine, twenty-two years later, a similar tone of disbelief, revulsion, and outrage prevailed, as "the foul stench sweeping down on Paris . . . provoked a general outcry . . . [and] public lamentations." As if anticipating the assumption that their complaints were exaggerated, residents insisted, "The odors are truly unbearable" and "We've never seen anything like this!" By the end of the month, with the arrival of cooler weather, the odors had by all accounts lost none of their intensity, and some Parisians wondered if they would ever end:

> All [last] night we fell prey to these fetid exhalations. In vain we
> hermetically sealed our windows; we couldn't sleep a wink all night.
> This morning, at seven o'clock, the remains of a pestilential mist still
> hung in the air. It was not until nine or ten o'clock that we had any
> relief. This torture is becoming unbearable. What, even in autumn, with
> a clear sky and a cool, dry breeze, which seems to herald winter? [Will
> it last] our entire lives then?! This can't go on![24]

As in London, this was no ordinary urban annoyance, but rather an unprecedented olfactory assault on the population. Also as in London, the sensory stimulus provoked intense feelings of disgust, and its impact far exceeded the boundaries of the tolerable.

Such reactions—like disgust in general—are both natural and man-made, instinctual and learned. What makes this emotional phenomenon so strangely rich in historical significance is precisely the fact that it is experienced as automatic, deeply physical, and unmediated by conscious thought, while it shows distinct variation historically, cross-culturally, and even within an individual's lifetime. Among the relatively few scholars who have devoted sustained attention to disgust, fewer still have offered social or cultural explanations for it. Anthropologist Mary Douglas and others have indeed portrayed the aversive emotion as a deep-seated but flexible strategy for delineating the boundaries separating self from other, life from death, or human from animal.[25] This view of disgust as culturally mutable is in the minority, however. The psychological consensus regards this emotion as an "evolved aversion to potential sources of disease," fundamentally fixed within the species and capable of variation only within a narrow range of specific manifestations.[26]

Evolution, however, cannot account for the dramatically increased urgency attending the public accumulation of feces in the nineteenth-century metropolis. Although this elemental substance seems to have been disgusting to many (if not most) people on some level long before 1858, something changed when hundreds of thousands of human beings began to live in close sensory proximity to one another (and to one another's waste) in a cultural environment that demanded a safe distancing of the senses from bodily substances and odors. It is difficult for historians to make sense of such changes without recourse to simplistic determinisms; it is therefore all the more important to seek guidance from those scholars who have resisted such comfortable certainties if one wishes to understand the sorts of reactions evinced by phenomena such as the Great Stinks in their shifting medical, psychological, social, and cultural contexts.

It has been suggested, taking the very broad view, that the rise of the modern state and the strength of the bourgeois family as building blocks of European civilization in the early modern period rested upon a rejection of excrement, bodily odors, and everything reminiscent of human beings' base, animal origins. Hence the emotionally intense prohibitions against shit—its presence or odor, in public or even in private.[27] Such accounts are intriguing and suggestive, but cannot amount to much more than that in the absence of careful empirical research and detailed, diachronic narrative. In this vein, focusing more closely on late eighteenth- and early nineteenth-century France, Alain Corbin has associated the proscription of fecal and other foul smells with the ascendancy of a distinctly bourgeois class identity and hegemony.[28] His call (echoing Lucien Febvre) for further research on the history of perception has been only intermittently heeded.[29] In the British case, Christopher Hamlin has shown that sanitary authorities were torn in the mid-nineteenth century between the piously progressive desire to put sewage to agricultural use and the fearful conviction that, like all decaying organic matter, human waste, if incompletely disposed of, represented an epidemic waiting to happen.[30] By the late 1870s, however, even their most energetic efforts had failed; the deliberate retention of large amounts of excrement could not be tolerated even outside of cities, even when undertaken for productive ends. The portrayal of this dangerous excretion as disgusting to humans always, everywhere (at least in recent evolutionary time) has come into question at the hands of these and other scholars who have pointed out the local and epoch-specific character of fecal repulsiveness. It is even possible that the sensory and emotional valences of foul odors varied within a single city and within the span of a century or so.

Beyond the emotions it provoked, each of the two Great Stinks also represented a raw affront to the civilization and cultural stature of a great metropolis. As if the physical sensation alone were not horrible enough, the stenches flouted the civilized pretensions of the worldly and urbane in the most egregious fashion imaginable. "Is this atrocious state of a semi-barbarous age to continue?" asked London's *Morning News* indignantly. "A mass of the rankest and most offensive effluvia under the name of a principal river is [being] poured through the metropolis of the greatest city in the world," lamented the *Standard*. The grandeur of the setting simply made the affliction all the more unbearable. Apparently, moreover, the Great Stink not only resulted from, but also precipitated a breakdown in civilization, as the *City Press* pointed out pithily: "Gentility of speech is at an end—it stinks."[31]

In Paris, too, the image of the city as paragon of world culture and civilization made the disgusting odors especially difficult to endure. "[O]ur great and beautiful city . . . [is being] turned into an immense cesspool, which soon . . . will be uninhabitable," warned *Le Siècle*. In the minds of most Frenchmen (and many foreigners as well), no city in the world rivaled Paris as a cultural capital.[32] After the ambitious facelift undertaken during the Second Empire by Napoleon III and his Prefect of the Seine department, Baron Haussmann, the City of Light stood as a model of beauty and order, its wide, handsome boulevards an unparalleled symbol of modern, civilized life. Then suddenly, in the late summer of 1880, this standard of civilization was shattered by "fetid emanations," "unbearable odors," and "horrible miasmas." This transgression was no minor offense; it undermined a basic element of the invisible foundation on which modern civilization rested: the protection of the human senses from contact with the base and vulgar bodily functions.[33]

Perhaps most significantly of all, both Great Stinks were emphatically believed to be deadly. In both cities, individual cases of illness and even death were commonly attributed to the foul odors, and scientific and lay observers alike predicted imminent epidemics. The link between disease and what were commonly referred to as "pestilential" or "fever-breeding" odors was direct and almost reflexive, as if something so unpleasant simply *must* have been a health hazard. In London, the *Examiner* did not hesitate to affirm this equation quite directly:

> Either all that has been said about the effect of bad smells or miasma
> is false, and filth innocuous, or some great mischief to the public health
> will come of this gigantic nuisance. . . . [M]ay we not reasonably
> apprehend that some horrible malady will arise out of the poisoned
> stream flowing through this huge metropolis? In some way or other
> nature is sure to punish such nastiness. It must have consequences either
> in the generation of new disease, or in the aggravation of existing ones.[34]

The satirical newspaper *Punch* depicted "Father Thames" presenting his "Offspring" diphtheria, scrofula, and cholera to the city (see Figure 5.1).

In the same vein, the medical officer of a hospital ship docked in the Thames reported two cases of "fever" and several more of diarrhea caused by the stench, in addition to the general "deleterious effect" it was having on the health of all patients. Even more alarming was the case of fifty-nine-year-old waterman Richard Billingsley, whose death at the height of the Great Stink of 1858 was attributed to the dreaded Asiatic cholera:

> Since the warm weather had set in, he complained of a general debility, and a great nausea, arising, as he stated, from inhaling the poisonous air of the river. He also suffered from diarrhea. On returning from work on Thursday evening, he complained of the increasing stench of the Thames, which had much affected him. He took to his bed, . . . became worse, and on Saturday night, Mr. English, a surgeon, visited him, and found him labouring under all the symptoms of Asiatic cholera. . . . He could not eat anything, as he said he could not get the stench off his lungs.

The surgeon testified at the inquest that "there was no doubt the attack had been brought on by inhaling bad air." The coroner agreed that the prevailing stench was "prejudicial to the public health." They had no trouble convincing the jury at the inquest, several of whose

FATHER THAMES INTRODUCING HIS OFFSPRING TO THE FAIR CITY OF LONDON.
(A Design for a Fresco in the New Houses of Parliament.)

Figure 5.1. "Father Thames Introducing His Offspring (Diphtheria, Scrofula, Cholera) to the Fair City of London." From *Punch*, 3 July 1858.

members shared their own impressions of the condition of the river and docks near where Billingsley worked. Their verdict: "that the deceased died from the effects of an attack of Asiatic cholera, brought on by inhaling the noxious vapour of the Thames."[35]

The Parisian "infection" of 1880 killed too, apparently. During August and September of 1880, residents of the French capital also reported specific cases of "fevers" and "sores" that they blamed on the foul smells. One reader of *Paris-Journal* wrote angrily to the newspaper: "I have three children, who have had the fever for two months now—as have we parents too. If they die, it will be the fault of the city council and the engineers."[36] Most often, however, the claims were more general, warning of an overall deterioration in the health of the population or pointing with alarm to purported recent increases in mortality caused by the odors. The Parisian press accused the local government, in its refusal to commit resources to remedial action, of "speculating on the health of the population . . . exploiting the mortality of poor little children," and "condemn[ing] to death several hundred Parisians, both young and old."[37]

Even if the connection between odors and disease was virtually self-evident, expert opinion was nonetheless marshaled in both London and Paris to bolster this common knowledge. In 1858, Billingsley's surgeon was not the only medical man in London attributing disease to the stench of the Thames. Dr. John Bredall testified at the Court of Queen's Bench that "it would be dangerous to the lives of the jurymen, counsel and witnesses to remain" at the court's chambers; Bredall warned specifically of malaria and typhus fever. The engineer responsible for the ventilation of the House of Commons wrote to the Speaker that he could "no longer be responsible for the health of the house" if it remained in session.[38] In 1880, reports of individual illnesses caused by the Great Stink in Paris found echoes not only in Pasteur's and Brouardel's official and authoritative warnings about the dangers of fecal emanations, but also in innumerable unofficial proclamations of their noxious effects: "all doctors agree" that the odors cause disease; child mortality had tripled; municipal death statistics proved the stench was deadly; mortality was highest in those parts of the city most heavily affected by the odors; infantile diarrhea, dysentery, typhoid fever, cholera, and smallpox were either already on the rise or looming on the horizon.[39]

Of course, the belief that foul-smelling emanations from decaying organic matter spread disease was central to the doctrine of miasmatism, which traced its lineage back to Hippocrates and which served as a broad framework for understanding health and sanitation in both

Britain and France throughout most of the nineteenth century. The perceived connection between bad odors—or, more generally, "bad air" —and disease was both strong and durable.[40] Even the triumph of bacteriology—an ostensibly incompatible causal paradigm—could not entirely displace it, as the French experience of 1880 shows. In fact one of the especially noteworthy features of these two Great Stinks is the continuity of the belief in disease-causing odors across the divide of a scientific revolution.

In addition to disgusted complaints and claims about the odors' pathogenic effects, the Great Stinks of London and Paris had another important element in common: demands for immediate government action. The idea that citizens in a (relatively) democratic polity would collectively seek redress from the state for flagrant and painful assaults on their senses may seem self-evident, but it was not necessarily so in the mid-nineteenth century. Although individual complaints (and resulting legal action) about nuisances caused by neighbors were not uncommon, a mass demand for government protection from foul odors was a novelty. Some combination of the actual intensity and scope of the odors and an emerging sensibility regarding state responsibility and the rights of citizens contributed to a barrage of demands and expectations when stench struck the two capitals.

A *Morning News* reader, for example, wrote to the newspaper in June 1858 to threaten some kind of unspecified citizen revolt "if the Government will not interfere in this matter." The same newspaper editorialized a few days later, "The removal of the cause of this indescribable abomination is not a matter for private speculation, not of strict local interest, but it is for the Government."[41] The same call echoed throughout the press and into the corridors of Parliament. Public demands alone, of course, could not bring decision makers together on a specific solution to the Great Stink, but the accumulated pressure of disgusted public opinion clearly played a role in the expeditious passage of remedial legislation.

Repeated angry demands for government intervention did not have the same result in Paris in 1880. If anything, the French outcry for state action was louder and more insistent than the English equivalent. Parisians began sending petitions to the City Council in mid-August, and a few weeks later newspapers were referring to the odors as a "souvenir of the local administration."[42] "When an entire population complains, quite justifiably," *Le Soleil* lamented, the government is "content merely to order an investigation." "What are our local officials waiting for before they act promptly and effectively?" asked *Le Gaulois*.[43] The theme of government responsibility for prompt action runs throughout the press coverage of the Great Stink:

> Why no action?
> It is incumbent upon our local officials, on the administration of the Seine department, [to recognize their] duty and responsibility to take charge of such a state of affairs.[44]

Especially galling was the fact that, as the odors had struck during the traditional period of summer vacations, prominent officials left the capital in the middle of the Great Stink for various (presumably pleasant-smelling) holiday destinations. While Parisians suffocated, "our local officials are in the countryside, inhaling to the point of intoxication the sweet scent of freshly cut hay," *La Lanterne* remarked acidly.[45] In *La Silhouette*, the city's motto *Fluctuat nec mergitur* ("she is storm-tossed but does not sink") appeared as *"Fluctuat et merditur"* ("tossed in a sea of shit") and suffering citizens looked on while dilatory bureaucrats discussed naming commissions and issuing reports until the crisis ended (see Figure 5.2).

Notwithstanding this steady drumbeat of criticism, complaint, and pressure for action, the Parisian Great Stink of 1880 did not trigger a massive government reaction in the form of public works or improved sanitation. *Tout-à-l'égout* remained in administrative limbo, approved as a matter of principle by local government authorities who lacked the authority to enforce its implementation. The puzzling fact remains that two analogous sensory crises, separated by twenty-two years, a national border, and a sliver of sea, provoked remarkably similar reactions but, in the end, quite different practical results.

Same Shit, Different Day

The drastically divergent outcomes of the Great Stinks of 1858 and 1880—a massive new sewer system and near-total inaction—can be explained in a variety of ways. Although the stereotypes of national character alluded to earlier do little to illuminate this question, particular national trajectories, attitudes, and traditions in politics and local sanitary administration certainly played their parts in shaping events in London and Paris. Most intriguing of all, however, is the role played by medical and scientific developments during the period between the two Great Stinks, which simultaneously clarified and muddied matters when it came to the danger of foul odors.

There were also more proximate, banal causes for the apparent English aggressiveness and French passivity in the face of their olfactory crises. Most obvious of all is the absolute certainty that prevailed in London regarding the source of the odors; all agreed that they came from the Thames, and that they arose from the combination of sewer outflow and the low water level in the river. (This clear localization also had the added effect of stinking out Parliament, thereby increasing the pressure for effective action.) In Paris, the odors invaded disparate parts of the city seemingly at the same time, and appeared and disappeared without warning, only to resurface after a brief respite. One authoritative school of thought blamed a concentration of waste treatment plants in the

Figure 5.2. "Les Odeurs de Paris." From *La Silhouette*, 25 October 1880.

northeast suburbs for the odors, which were putatively carried by an unusual prevailing northeast wind into the north-central districts of Paris. (This hypothesis accounts for the disproportionate number of complaints coming from the ninth and eighteenth arrondissements, but does not explain the near absence of complaints from areas between these districts and the plants, nor for the "infection" of parts of the Left Bank.)[46] Other observers traced the odors to the sewers and sewer vents throughout the city, where *vidange* crews allegedly dumped their cargo.[47] In the absence of a single clear source or culprit, the various parties to the debate on the odors of Paris were able to fall back on established positions and to promote agendas to which they were already committed.

It would seem at first glance that the extremely decentralized English system of government and the highly centralized French system in the nineteenth century ought to have worked in favor of strong administrative initiative in Paris rather than in London. However, political circumstances in these two specific cases conspired to produce the opposite result. In London, the groundwork for remedial action had been laid by years of planning and agitation by engineers, sanitarians, and the Metropolitan Board of Works, all working toward the same general goal: to remove sewage from the Thames. There were sometimes sharp conflicts over jurisdiction, and some disagreement persisted over the most desirable and most feasible kind of sewer system.[48] However, when crisis struck in 1858, it was so obviously due to sewage in the Thames that serious resistance to Bazalgette's plan was no longer possible.

In Paris, the Republican regime was still on quite insecure political footing in 1880. The absence of a mayor, the relatively weak city council and departmental Conseil général, and the division of administrative powers (particularly in matters involving public health) between the Prefecture of the Seine department and the Prefecture of Police all had the effect of diluting the mix of mobilizing factors that had precipitated action in London. Moreover, the precedent of Haussmann's audacious reach in urban public works may actually have worked against an aggressive response in 1880. Haussmann's (and the imperial regime's) political opponents were now in power, and many of them had established their reputations by contesting the Prefect's autocratic style and the possibly corrupt financing of his rebuilding schemes. In 1880, to look for inspiration to the hated fallen regime was all but unthinkable. Finally, in contrast to the prevailing situation in London in 1858, years of debate over *tout-à-l'égout* in Paris had laid the groundwork not for consensus in time of crisis, but rather for an entrenchment of positions on both sides of the question. The Great Stink of 1858 brought bickering constituencies together; its counterpart in 1880 drove opponents even farther apart.

Another development that would eventually cause cataclysmic change had also intervened between the Great Stinks of London and Paris. By 1880, in the wake of pathbreaking research by Pasteur in France and Robert Koch in Germany, physicians and scientists were beginning to believe that the secrets of human disease—in addition to those of silkworms and the spoilage of beer and wine, among other phenomena— might lie in the activities of microscopic living organisms. Although it would be another decade or more before many skeptics in the medical profession were convinced, the possibility that invisible germs in the air, soil, and water (as well as in the bodies of sick people) could spread deadly illnesses gave serious pause to some in Paris in the aftermath of the Great Stink. One might expect that the identification of specific microbes as the causes of specific diseases would definitively put to rest the highly *unspecific* (and, to later observers, highly unscientific) notion that foul odors spread disease. In 1880, however, this was far from the case.[49]

While Alphand and other advocates of *tout-à-l'égout* seized upon the odors of Paris as proof of the *vidange* system's defects, then, other prominent voices brought forth their own scientific arguments to denounce the proposed reform as, in effect, heralding a permanent—and deadly—Great Stink. The pressure of popular disgust and health warnings actually pushed in opposite directions simultaneously; the intensity of the stench, the disgust, and the fear raised the stakes of the debate and had the effect of hardening positions on both sides.

In a consummate irony, it is possible that the advent of the germ theory of disease actually *hindered* the realization of significant sanitary reform in 1880. It is commonplace to credit the new (and presumptively truer, better) understanding of disease causation with the validation, revival, and reorientation of older sanitary agendas, such as clean water supplies, sewerage, garbage removal, and slum clearance.[50] In the case of the Great Stink of 1880, however, Pasteur's science supported *tout-à-l'égout*'s opponents. The road to sanitary salvation was exceedingly difficult to discern; each path seemed strewn with frightful dangers. In contrast, authorities in 1858—a time that Pasteur would have seen as the etiological Dark Ages—saw no basis for opposing the disposal of human waste through sewers. (British proposals for the agricultural use of human-produced fertilizer still depended on evacuation and treatment through sewers.)[51] Even in the midst of jurisdictional and fiscal debate, few Londoners doubted in which direction progress lay. Across the Channel two decades later, as the bacteriological revolution gathered steam, it was not a paucity but rather a surfeit of science that blocked sanitary reform.

Filth as Crisis

Urbanites of the mid- and late-nineteenth century refused to tolerate the smell of shit. And why not? Isn't it just disgusting, period, no matter the place and time? This obvious conclusion must be taken seriously, and indeed there is a record of popular complaints and government regulations concerning the public presence of excrement in European cities stretching back centuries before the Great Stinks. From the Middle Ages on, there are periodic complaints from residents and travelers along with royal edicts and local ordinances decrying the careless handling of urban urine and feces, and prohibiting the emptying of chamberpots into the streets.[52] It may be that the public presence of human waste in cities was always denounced—by someone, somewhere. Nevertheless, the fact that the protests tended to fall on deaf ears and the ordinances invariably went unenforced speaks louder than the complaints themselves. The descriptions of unexceptional everyday conditions are lurid —in Paris in 1667, "all streets from the Porte Saint-Martin to La Villette are infected with stenches coming from the fecal matter which has been left on the ground, without having been taken to cesspits or waste treatment plants"[53]—but when such protests recur regularly (decade after decade) without any appreciable response or change in conditions, one can only infer a substantial background level of resignation (if not acceptance) in the population as a whole. Nobody went on record to approve of the situation, but nobody took great pains to change it either. Official pronouncements remained moot.

The Great Stinks triggered collective protests different in both quantity and quality from anything that had come before. Refusal of the excremental presence in the city had reached a critical mass; the unloved but tolerated status quo was no longer tenable. Complaints were so widespread, so loud, and so sustained that they could not be ignored. Even in Paris after 1880, inaction in the short term seems to have masked an intensified enforcement of regulations governing waste treatment plants, and Pasteur's rejection of *tout-à-l'égout* only delayed what was made inevitable by the outcry against the dreadful odors.[54] It may well be that the smell of shit has always been disgusting on some level. But it took a particular configuration of material, social, and cultural conditions for that disgust to become active, relevant, and urgent.

The history of excremental aversion may not be able by itself to disprove the evolutionary defense-against-disease theory of disgust, but it certainly suggests that this emotion has been historically variable in its manifestations. Corbin in particular has shown that all odors—pleasant and unpleasant, alluring and revolting—acquired a heightened social significance between the mid-eighteenth and mid-nineteenth centuries. As deodorization of public space came to be associated with health, and perfumes signified refinement, foul smells (and that of excrement in particular) became an acute menace, emblematic of decay, disease, and the dangerous classes. Odors that had previously been tolerable—or, if not tolerable, bothersome on an individual or strictly local scale—now represented a genuine social crisis and provoked widespread, angry protest.[55]

Moreover, the meanings of unpleasant odors continued to change even after the two Great Stinks discussed here. For example, a stench reminiscent of that of 1880 hit Paris again in the early summer of 1895. Disgust, outrage, and fervent demands for governmental intervention all surfaced in response to the odors, just as they did in 1880. However, one key element of the earlier reaction was missing: the belief that the stench could spread disease. Doctors, government officials, and press commentators agreed in 1895 that the smell of excrement was revolting, intolerable, and incompatible with a civilized way of life—but it simply was no longer a health hazard.[56] The transmission of disease by fecal means received more medical attention than ever; cholera and typhoid fever, among other deadly scourges, were well known to be spread through contaminated food and water. The bacteria responsible for these diseases, first identified in the 1880s, could be found, isolated, and cultured in the controlled environment of the laboratory. Their presence in the excretions of sick people (and, later, of healthy carriers) could be incontrovertibly demonstrated.

In effect, this demonstrable and measurable infection—in the new sense of transmission of pathogenic microorganisms—took the place of the more diffuse, impressionistic "infection"—in the old sense of contamination—of the Great Stinks.[57] Excrement and other disgusting substances still caused disease, but they did so henceforth in a more narrowly circumscribed fashion—not through odors. Alleged vehicles of disease that could not be specifically identified, isolated, and manipulated no longer attracted the attention and fear that now accrued to bacteria, the culprit seemingly behind every disease in the closing years of the nineteenth century.

To some degree, certainly, taboo behaviors and violations of socially accepted prohibitions have always been perceived as pathogenic.[58] This apparently universal fact begs the question, however, of how particular health threats wax and wane in the public consciousness (as well as in medical orthodoxy) under certain historical circumstances. Although foul-smelling emanations had been thought to cause disease for centuries in the Hippocratic medical tradition, it took a particular nineteenth-century confluence of material, political, and cultural developments for the smell of excrement to become an urgent health crisis in London and Paris. The unprecedented urban population implosion that accompanied the first phases of industrialization in England and France, for example, dramatically increased the sheer amount of human excreta per square mile in the two metropolises.[59] Roughly contemporaneously, democratic ideals and electoral realities had created in both countries at least a minimal expectation of government responsiveness to the core concerns of its constituents.[60] Events such as economic crises, food shortages, and epidemics demanded immediate action; unprecedented sensory assaults also fell into this category. Finally attitudes toward the excretion and disposal of bodily substances had changed to the extent that what had been an annoyance had become an abomination. Absent any one of these historical elements—material, political, cultural— the odors of 1858 and 1880 would not have caused the disruption that they did.

It is important to note that where cultural change is concerned, such crises do not tell us what was happening *at the time* (London in 1858, Paris in 1880) as much as they reveal changes that had *already* taken place or had been ongoing for several decades or more. In the middle of the nineteenth century, a perceptual shift had taken place (or was in the process of taking place) whereby the smell of excrement in public, previously unpleasant but apparently bearable, became absolutely anathema. By century's end, the odor of excrement remained utterly intolerable, but it no longer caused disease. Thereafter, fecal transmission of illness took place through ingestion of contaminated food or water rather than through emanations.

Moments of filth-induced crisis can also do more than simply reflect past cultural shifts. In their formidable power to shock and to disgust, they can also intensify or accelerate those shifts, and thereby act as triggers of change in the technological and/or political realms. Bazalgette and his Thames Embankment offer the clearest evidence in this regard, but even in gridlocked Paris, the traumatic experience of 1880 cannot have failed to linger in memory, subtly altering expectations concerning human waste and its disposal. Changes in behavior and public policy in turn *reinforced* cultural prohibitions on the public perceptibility of disgusting bodily products. Disgust—the powerful, collective disgust of the Great Stinks—could galvanize or paralyze, but it could not be ignored.

It is possible to perceive through the stinking summer air of London and Paris the conflicts and negotiations through which recognizably modern forms of accommodation with the bodily exigencies of huge urban agglomerations took shape. Perhaps even more fundamentally, one can see in these episodes the collective articulations of demands and boundaries that established modern (civilized, sanitized) bourgeois identities, and identified threats and prohibitions that would henceforth define the social body's boundaries of acceptability. These nineteenth-century crises of filth, in other words, simultaneously revealed and reshaped the shifting collective values of the populations that lived through them—values that would in turn condition the modalities of urban life for decades to come.

Notes

1. The term "archaeological" may call to mind a specifically Foucauldian methodology, but it is meant here in its most general, metaphorical sense.

2. Among the most significant contributions are Charles Darwin, *The Expression of the Emotions in Man and Animals* (1872; Chicago: University of Chicago Press, 1965); Sigmund Freud, *Civilization and Its Discontents* (1930; New York: W. W. Norton, 1962); Andryas Angyal, "Disgust and Related Aversions," *Journal of Abnormal and Social Psychology* 36 (1941): 393–412; Mary Douglas, *Purity and Danger: An Analysis of the Concepts of Pollution and Taboo* (1966; London: Routledge, 2002); William Ian Miller, *The Anatomy of Disgust* (Cambridge, MA: Harvard University Press, 1997); and the work of Paul Rozin, including "Disgust," in Rozin, Jonathan Haidt, and Clark R. McCauley, *Handbook of Emotions,* 2nd ed., ed. Michael Lewis and Jeannette M. Haviland (New York: Guilford, 2000), 637–53.

3. A useful overview of this work, and an argument for the defense-against-disease hypothesis, can be found in Edward B. Royzman and John Sabini, "Something It Takes to Be an Emotion: The Interesting Case of Disgust," *Journal for the Theory of Social Behaviour* 31 (2001): 29–59; see also Valerie Curtis and Adam Biran, "Dirt, Disgust, and Disease: Is Hygiene in Our Genes?" *Perspectives in Biology and Medicine* 44 (2001): 17–31.

4. Stephen Halliday, *The Great Stink of London: Sir Joseph Bazalgette and the Cleansing of the Victorian Capital* (Stroud, UK: Sutton, 1999); John D. Thompson, "The Great Stench or the Fool's Argument," *Yale Journal of Biology and Medicine* 64 (1991): 529–41; Roy Porter, *London: A Social History* (London: Hamish Hamilton, 1994), 262–65.

5. Porter, *London,* 262–63.

6. For example, *The Standard,* 15 June 1858, and *The Morning News,* 30 June 1858.

7. Halliday, *Great Stink*, 71; Porter, *London*, 263; *The Morning News*, 24 and 26 June 1858; *The Globe*, 24 June 1858.

8. Halliday, *Great Stink*, 73–75 (including quotation from *The Times*, 21 July 1858); Porter, *London*, 263; Francis Sheppard, *London: A History* (Oxford: Oxford University Press, 1998), 284.

9. Porter, *London*, 263–64; Halliday, *Great Stink*; Sheppard, *London: A History*, 280–84; Steven Inwood, *A History of London* (London: Macmillan, 1998), 433–35. In contrast, the contemporaneous public works projects of Baron Haussmann in Paris—considered the *ne plus ultra* of nineteenth-century urban public works—also built extensive new sewer lines, but in prohibiting the evacuation of human waste through them, merely postponed this vital sanitary question for future decades of administrators to deal with.

10. Georges Eugène, Baron Haussmann, *Mémoires* (1890–93; Paris: Seuil, 2000), 969.

11. Commission de l'assainissement de Paris instituée . . . en vue d'étudier les causes de l'infection signalée dans le département de la Seine ainsi que les moyens d'y remédier, *Rapports et avis de la Commission* (Paris: Imprimerie nationale, 1881), 158–59; *Conseil municipal de Paris: Procès-verbaux*, 1880, 2:339 (session of 9 October 1880).

12. *Conseil municipal de Paris: Procès-verbaux*, 1880, 2:148 (session of 27 July 1880).

13. *Le Siècle*, 21 August 1880. Unless otherwise specified, all translations from the French are by the author.

14. Conseil d'hygiene publique et de salubrité du Département de la Seine, "Commission spéciale pour l'étude des causes de l'infection de Paris," report to Prefect of Police, 29 September 1880, in *Journal officiel de la République française*, 7 October 1880, 10333.

15. Commission de l'assainissement de Paris, *Rapports et avis*, 5–6. On Brouardel, see Lion Murard and Patrick Zylberman, *L'Hygiène dans la république: La santé publique en France, ou l'utopie contrariée, 1870–1918* (Paris: Fayard, 1996), 198–203; Olivier Faure, *Histoire sociale de la médecine, XVIIe–XXe siècles* (Paris: Anthropos, 1994), 180; Jacques Léonard, *La Médecine entre les pouvoirs et les savoirs* (Paris: Aubier, 1981), 252–54, 292–95.

16. Commission de l'assainissement de Paris, *Rapports et avis de la Commission* (Paris: Imprimerie nationale, 1881) [in Archives de la Préfecture de Police, Paris, DB1: 434], 13–23 (emphasis added).

17. Gérard Jacquemet, "Urbanisme parisien: La bataille du tout-à-l'égout à la fin du XIXe siècle," *Revue d'histoire moderne et contemporaine* 26 (1979): 505–48; Donald Reid, *Paris Sewers and Sewermen: Realities and Representations* (Cambridge, MA: Harvard University Press, 1991), 58–65, 79–83, 118–20; Roger-Henri Guerrand, "La Bataille du tout-à-l'égout," *L'Histoire*, February 1983, 66–74.

18. Commission de l'assainissement de Paris, *Rapports et avis*, 93–108; "Sur la longue durée de la vie des germes charbonneux et sur leur conservation dans

les terres cultivées," *Comptes rendus de l'Académie des sciences* 92 (1881): 209–11 (session of 31 January 1881).

19. Most notably in 1895, 1911, and 1926. See Alexandre Le Roy des Barres (Commission d'Etudes dite des Odeurs de Paris), *Rapport préliminaire sur les causes des émanations odorantes de Paris et de la banlieue* (Paris: Chaix, 1896); O. Boudouard, "Recherches sur les odeurs de Paris," *Revue scientifique* 50 (1912): 614–21; *Compte rendu des séances du conseil d'hygiène publique et de salubrité du Département de la Seine*, 1911, 2:102–3, and 1926, 164; and A. Trillat, *Commission des odeurs de Paris: Rapport général* (Paris: Chaix, 1928).

20. Miller discusses the impoverished lexicon of smells in *The Anatomy of Disgust*, 67–68.

21. *The Standard*, 15 June 1858.

22. *The Morning News*, 19 June 1858.

23. *The Globe*, 21 June 1858 (quoting the *Examiner*).

24. *Le Siècle*, 4 September 1880; *Paris-Journal*, 4, 11, and 28 September 1880.

25. For example: Angyal, "Disgust and Related Aversions"; Douglas, *Purity and Danger*; Miller, *Anatomy of Disgust*; Rozin, "Disgust."

26. For example: Royzman and Sabini, "Something It Takes," 50; Curtis and Biran, "Dirt, Disgust, and Disease," 22–29.

27. Dominique Laporte, *History of Shit*, trans. Nadia Benabid and Rodolphe El-Khoury (Cambridge, MA: MIT Press, 2000), 76–89.

28. Alain Corbin, *The Foul and the Fragrant: Odor and the French Social Imagination*, trans. Miriam Kochan (Cambridge, MA: Harvard University Press, 1986).

29. Noteworthy among recent work are William M. Reddy, *The Navigation of Feeling: A Framework for the History of Emotions* (Cambridge: Cambridge University Press, 2001), an extremely rigorous attempt to historicize emotions (which nevertheless focuses relatively little on sensory perception per se), and John E. Crowley, *The Invention of Comfort: Sensibilities and Design in Early Modern Britain and Early America* (Baltimore: Johns Hopkins University Press, 2001), an exemplary integration of the histories of technology, material culture, and bodily practices.

30. Christopher Hamlin, "Providence and Putrefaction: Victorian Sanitarians and the Natural Theology of Health and Disease," *Victorian Studies* 28, no. 3 (1985): 381–411.

31. *The Morning News*, 21 June 1858; *The Standard*, 17 June 1858; *City Press*, 19 June 1858, quoted in Halliday, *Great Stink*, 71–72.

32. The multiple (and sometimes conflicting) representations of Paris as cultural mecca are discussed in Christopher Prendergast, *Paris and the Nineteenth Century* (Oxford: Blackwell, 1992).

33. *Le Siècle*, 21 and 22 August and 3 September 1880; *Paris-Journal*, 11 September 1880.

34. *The Globe*, 21 June 1858 (quoting the *Examiner*).

35. *The Globe*, 23 June 1858; *The Morning News*, 23 June 1858.

36. *Paris-Journal*, 9 and 12 September 1880.

37. *Le Siècle*, 22 August and 4 September 1880.

38. Halliday, *Great Stink*, 72–73.

39. *Paris-Journal*, 4 September 1880; *Le Siècle*, 4 and 15 September 1880. There are no clear traces of the putative correlations between mortality and odors in the published (monthly and annual) statistical compilations for 1880.

40. Corbin, *Foul and the Fragrant*, especially 22–56; Caroline Hannaway, "Environment and Miasmata," in W. F. Bynum and Roy Porter, eds., *Companion Encyclopedia of the History of Medicine* (London: Routledge, 1993), 1:292–308; George Rosen, *History of Public Health*, expanded ed. (Baltimore: Johns Hopkins University Press, 1993), 263–66.

41. *The Morning News*, 19 and 21 June 1858; similar sentiments are expressed in, among others, *The Globe*, 18 June 1858, and *The Morning News*, 26 June 1858.

42. *Le Siècle*, 21 August and 26 and 28 September 1880; *Paris-Journal*, 11 September 1880 (quoting *Le Soleil*).

43. *Paris-Journal*, 11 September 1880 (quoting *Le Soleil* and *Le Gaulois*).

44. *Paris-Journal*, 12 September 1880.

45. *Paris-Journal*, 28 September 1880 (quoting *La Lanterne*).

46. Information concerning the geography of complaints during the Great Stink of 1880 is drawn from a review of five Parisian daily newspapers (*Le Siècle*, *Paris-Journal*, *Le Figaro*, *Le Petit Journal*, and *Le Temps*) from July through October 1880, including material that these newspapers reprinted from other publications.

47. For example, see *Le Siècle*, 6, 9, 19, and 22 September 1880; *Paris-Journal*, 20 September 1880.

48. Porter, *London*, 259–66.

49. Only Adolphe Alphand, Director of Municipal Works, expressed this view in discussions of the Great Stink of 1880; he referred to Pasteur by name, suggesting that the new science of germs should reassure Parisians with respect to the putatively pathogenic effects of odors: Conseil d'hygiène publique et de salubrité du Département de la Seine ("Commission spéciale pour l'étude des causes de l'infection de Paris"), report to Prefect of Police, 29 September 1880, in *Journal officiel de la République française*, 7 October 1880, 10333–37. This argument seems to have been less than fully convincing at the time, given that Pasteur himself was on the other side of it.

50. For example, see Nancy Tomes, *The Gospel of Germs: Men, Women, and the Microbe in American Life, 1880–1930* (Cambridge, MA: Harvard University Press, 1998).

51. Hamlin, "Providence and Putrefaction," 393–94.

52. On Paris, for example, see the catalogue of miseries recounted in Martin Monestier, *Histoire et bizarreries sociales des excréments des origines à nos jours* (Paris: Le Cherche Midi, 1997), 85–118. On London: Inwood, *History of London*, 422; Porter, *London*, 125; Sheppard, *London: A History*, 251–58, 281–84;

Michael Leapman, ed., *The Book of London: The Evolution of a Great City* (New York: Weidenfeld and Nicolson, 1989), 178.

53. Monestier, *Histoire et bizarreries*, 95.

54. When the odors returned in 1895, members of the departmental Conseil général insinuated that regulatory authorities clamped down on the plants whenever elected representatives or other prominent Parisians complained, thereby diminishing the odors quite effectively—until the crackdown eased: *Conseil général du département de la Seine: Mémoires et procès-verbaux*, session of 8 July 1895, 539–44. On the long and tortured history of *tout-à-l'égout*, see Jacquemet, "Urbanisme parisien"; Andrew R. Aisenberg, *Contagion: Disease, Government, and the "Social Question" in Nineteenth-Century France* (Stanford, CA: Stanford University Press, 1999), 105–12; Lenard Berlanstein, *The Working People of Paris, 1871–1914* (Baltimore: Johns Hopkins University Press, 1984), 56; Reid, *Paris Sewers and Sewermen*, 78–83; and Guerrand, "La Bataille du tout-à-l'égout."

55. Corbin, *The Foul and the Fragrant*.

56. See, for example, *Le Temps*, 4 June 1895; *Le Figaro*, 7 and 26 June 1895; *Le Siècle*, 16 June 1895; *Paris-Journal*, 4 August 1895; *Conseil général du département de la Seine: Mémoires et procès-verbaux*, session of 8 July 1895, 539–44; Alexandre Le Roy des Barres (Commission d'Etudes dite des Odeurs de Paris), *Rapport préliminaire sur les causes des émanations odorantes de Paris et de la banlieue* (Paris: Chaix, 1896), 6.

57. Owsei Temkin, "An Historical Analysis of the Concept of Infection," in *The Double Face of Janus and Other Essays in the History of Medicine* (Baltimore: Johns Hopkins University Press, 1977), 456–73.

58. See, for example, Douglas, *Purity and Danger*, and the essays in *Morality and Health,* ed. Allan M. Brandt and Paul Rozin (London: Routledge, 1997).

59. Francis Sheppard, *London 1808–1870: The Infernal Wen* (Berkeley and Los Angeles: University of California Press, 1971), 1–2; David H. Pinkney, *Napoleon III and the Rebuilding of Paris* (Princeton, NJ: Princeton University Press, 1958), 151–52.

60. Porter, *London*, 239–56; Inwood, *History of London*, 389–407; John Davis, *Reforming London: The London Government Problem, 1855–1900* (Oxford: Clarendon Press, 1988), 1–67; Philip Nord, *The Republican Moment: Struggles for Democracy in Nineteenth-Century France* (Cambridge, MA: Harvard University Press, 1995), 133; see also Judith F. Stone, *Sons of the Revolution: Radical Democrats in France, 1862–1914* (Baton Rouge: Louisiana State University Press, 1996), beginning at 88.

Part III

POLLUTING THE BOURGEOIS

Chapter 6

Victorian Dust Traps

Eileen Cleere

In addressing you on the subject of the Fine Arts in relation to
Sanitary Reform, I am met by two difficulties, a Scylla and Charibdis
that might well appall one who had not set out with a determined
purpose, or was not sure of his way. The first difficulty is that the
work of the artist and of the sanitary engineer seem to stand so very
far apart in our minds, that I may be challenged with the question,
"What have they to do with each other? Speak about either of the
two things, and we will listen. But let us have one thing at a time." The
second difficulty is that the two—Art and Sanitation—are so nearly
identical, are so interwoven in their action and re-action, that it may
be too hastily assumed that anything I may have to say regarding
their relation to each other must necessarily be obvious and trite.
—*Wyke Bayliss, "Sanitary Reform in Relation to the Fine Arts"*

*I*n 1889, Wyke Bayliss, F.S.A., confronted his audience at the
Hastings and St. Leonard's-on-the-Sea Health Congress with
the same unlikely topic I take up in this essay: sanitation
and decoration.[1] Somehow, by the last decades of the nineteenth century, the apparently dichotomous topic of art and sanitation had
become "obvious and trite" to artists like Bayliss, as well as to some of
the most influential advocates of British aesthetic reform. I have argued
elsewhere that aesthetic philosophy was significantly transformed in the
years immediately following the 1842 publication of Edwin Chadwick's
Sanitary Report, when the Romantic celebration of sublime decay and
picturesque dilapidation suddenly seemed out of keeping with the new
Victorian reverence for health.[2] Embrowned pictures, architectural ruins,
and "moving" scenes of poverty and distress could not remain aesthetic
vehicles for reform-minded Victorians who saw dirt as a social embar-
rassment and a material danger, a sign of oppression, disease, and moral
degradation. Yet while John Ruskin's celebration of modern painters
worked in tandem with the pre-Raphaelite movement to institutionalize
a "cleaner" style for fine art, an ideological struggle between aesthetic

and sanitary practitioners lingered for most of the nineteenth century. Optimistic artists like Bayliss may have insisted upon the obvious simultaneity of art and cleanliness, but in the pages of popular novels, art journals, architectural essays and home-decoration guides, art continued to be haunted by its dirty, disreputable past.

For Edwin Chadwick, the connection between art and dirt was topographically obvious: art was dirty because its cherished environments were dirty. Venice, that revered paradise of aesthetic culture, was "pestilential and foul" in Chadwick's assessment, and the art it contained and inspired must necessarily be degraded and contagious.[3] Chadwick's sanitary understanding of Europe is standard in a variety of nineteenth-century literature; from Nathaniel Hawthorne's *The Marble Faun* to Samuel Smiles's *Character*, celebrated cities of art (Rome, Paris, Florence) are repeatedly identified as centers of human disease and aesthetic contamination.[4] But mapping the unsanitary status of distant European capitals was not the primary geographical effect of Chadwick's sanitary idea; as Peter Stallybrass and Allon White have influentially argued, Victorian reformers like Chadwick and Henry Mayhew were central in the ideological mapping of London for the Victorian middle class.[5] By locating, exploring, and evocatively describing slums, sewers, cesspools and other so-called fever nests for the cleanly bourgeois reader, Chadwick, Mayhew, and other reformers engineered a city plan that drew imaginary safe, sanitary borders around middle-class shopping districts, neighborhoods, and finally, around the apex of cleanliness, the middle-class home. For the bourgeois citizen, the domestic sphere was not only a haven in a heartless, unhygienic city; as Stallybrass and White argue, it was a snug, hermetically sealed zone of middle-class comfort and smug, scopophilic pleasure in the filthiness that resided just around the corner.

Already a self-contained moral universe, as Nancy Armstrong, Catherine Gallagher, and Mary Poovey have argued, the Victorian home was under increased pressure in the second half of the nineteenth century to appear hygienically inviolable, impermeable, and unassailable.[6] Yet after the development and general acceptance of germ theories in the 1870s, the impenetrable Victorian home became an anxious fantasy rather than a predictable ideological construct. Mid-Victorian sanitary geographies of the city turned inward, eventually producing analogous geographies of the overdecorated, architecturally busy middle-class interior. Although aesthetic history and sanitary reform are rarely explored as coterminous cultural narratives, artists like Wyke Bayliss and decorators like Lewis Day insisted that they could only be understood in tandem.

As Day explained in his 1882 article "How to Hang Pictures," "If we hang pictures to slope downward, there would be a shelf above for porcelain, terra cotta, and the like, or condemned for being a 'dust trap' according as one were bitten with the aesthetic or the sanitary mania."[7] Sanitary "maniacs" not only condemned the nooks, crannies, tunnels, dark rooms, narrow hallways, and turrets cherished by Gothic revivalists, they also dismissed the favored features of aesthetic decoration—dados, decorative carving, shelving, cornices, tapestries, curtains, and carpets—as "dust traps" or, in other words, "the forcing beds for disease germs."[8] More genteel addresses ran afoul of sanitary regulators, and the decorative artist and architect joined the painter and fine artist as the suspected enemies of health, hygiene, and cleanliness. Ultimately the domestic "dust trap" replaced the urban fever nest as the primary locus of pollution anxiety within sanitary geographies of the Victorian home. Inside the dust trap an aesthetic philosophy became a material household canker, a site where the opposing claims of art and hygiene collided, with potentially dangerous effects. However, by the end of the nineteenth century, the claims of cleanliness appeared to have triumphed. The transition to a sleek, seamless modernism in British art and architecture looked less like an aesthetic revolution than the inevitable effect of Victorian sanitary reform.

Sanitation and Decoration

By the middle of the Victorian period, Chadwick's sanitary idea was already redrawing aesthetic borders and remapping the philosophy of art and design. Despite widespread cultural suspicion that artists were thoroughgoing fans of filth, many Victorian artists like Bayliss were calling for the creation of an aesthetic "City of Hygiea" as the necessary remedy for increasing industrial pollution and moral degradation. As early as 1871, Ruskin himself was arguing that "the beginning of true art was to get your country clean and your people lovely,"[9] an environmental perspective that would be adopted a decade later by William Morris: "Of all the things likely to give us back popular art in England, the cleaning of England is the first and most necessary."[10] For Ruskin, the sanitation of fine art first required a recognition and refusal of the aesthetic values represented by the Renaissance Old Masters. The Old Masters were dangerous and degraded because the pictorial worlds they revered—sunless, filthy, environmentally compromised—threatened to contaminate the aesthetic values of British painting. Certainly the yellow-brown tones of the dirty Old Masters could only have been inspired by the most unsavory, unhealthy shades of local color, and, according to Ruskin, these colors were reminiscent of a setting especially reviled by the Victorian middle class:

> The sky, with the sun in it, does not usually give the impression of being dimly lighted through a circular hole; but you may observe a very similar effect any day in your coal cellar. The light is not Rembrandtesque, usually, in a clean house; but it is presently obtainable of that quality in a dirty one. . . . It is the aim of the best painters to paint the noblest things they can see by sunlight. It was the aim of Rembrandt to paint the foulest things he could see—by rushlight.[11]

Ruskin's "Rembrandtesque" house existed not only as a descriptive metaphor. Mellowed by time, warmed by a fine golden tone, paintings by the "brown" and even "black" Renaissance masters imposed a formidable aesthetic standard on both pictorial art and the still life of home decoration favored by late-Victorian aestheticism.[12] Although Ruskin is often identified as the founder of the aesthetic movement, aestheticists generally believed art had the power to make life not more moral but more beautiful, with Walter Pater's notion of "art for art's sake" standing as the unofficial motto of Aesthetic practitioners. While Pater never mentions Ruskin in his idiosyncratic, solipsistic aesthetic manifesto, *The Renaissance*, Ruskin's distaste for the pagan darkness and moral indifference of the fifteenth century is critiqued and rejected on every page.[13] Much like the Romantic idea of sublimity, aesthetic and decadent philosophy valued art for its ability to allow the viewer to achieve a personal transcendence untrammeled by moral, social, or even sanitary feelings. As Talia Schaffer and Kathy Alexis Psomiades explain, "aestheticism's interest in artifice, intense experience, the mixing of beauty and strangeness, and the desire to experience life as an art" easily yielded an artistic concept of decadence, "with its fascination with the unnatural, death, decay, the body, and the exotic other."[14] Not only did Pater's theories revive aesthetic interest in the Renaissance, they reanimated some of the dirty interests Ruskin had found so appalling in art criticism written at the end of the eighteenth century, especially the notion that beauty could be found in the contemplation of dirt, disease, or even death.

For Ruskin, and also for William Morris, art ceased to be beautiful when it ceased to be useful; Pater, on the other hand, had no use for use. At its most decadent, the aesthetic design for living was highly ornamental, artificial, and above all Rembrantesque. Dirty browns, muddy yellows, and livid greens were favorite shades for household decoration, and these unsanitary colors had corresponding human hues; because the most exquisite feelings were usually sensations of sorrow, fatigue, or pain, sickly, sallow complexions were considered more expressive of aesthetic "intensity" than the robust faces of health. As Mr. Chaloner, the villain of Rhoda Broughton's satiric novel *Second Thoughts* explains, in aesthetic philosophy, "There is nothing so beautiful as the passionate pulsations of pain!"[15] Accordingly, Victorian sanitarians had little patience for the decorative choices of the aesthetically inclined. "Most houses in London are dark naturally and helplessly," Mrs. Florence Caddy explains in her 1881 novel and home-design guide *Lares and Penates, or The Background of Life.* "People generally regret this, but some affect darkness and even increase it to gain 'tone' and 'repose'; which are often euphemisms for dirt and idleness."[16] As the narrator of *Lares and Penates* visits a series of aesthetically noteworthy houses, she creates a sanitary map of London and its suburbs: at Alford House near the South Kensington Museum, she satisfactorily notes bright lights and colors, but in South Hampstead, the "younger rival" of South Kensington, Mrs. Caddy finds red brick houses clustered like "carbuncles," and in the home of Belinda Brassy, she discovers colors like "a symphony in boiled vegetables," and "spinach in an advanced state of decomposition" (172). Conversely, at the suburban house of sanitary architect and engineer Mr. Newbroom, the narrator is able to inspect an alternative background for life. "We don't allow any dust here," said Mrs. Newbroom. "None of your matted paint and embossed papers—all of them dust-traps" (244). But while Mr. Newbroom's house is light, bright, and polished to a high gloss, our reporter admits that something more intangible and less sanitary may be missing:

> The beds were curtainless, of course, and the floors, equally of
> course, were uncarpeted. The partequeterie floors were waxed to icy
> slipperyness; the very rugs only stood still by being buttoned to the legs
> of the bed. . . . Life in this house may not be beautiful—it is not, indeed
> —but it is cleanly. It is scarcely even comfortable; the air is too freely
> changed, and too much according to rule, not allowing human nature to
> indulge a weakness, one petted sin. It is no grovelling, dust-coloured
> life, but one of perpetual stimulant, a mental pepper. (254)

In Mr. Newbroom's house, cleanliness has defeated beauty, and constant circulation has banished stillness and repose. "But what would the disciples of the tone school say to you?" our narrator inquires of the architect. "Poets and Artists enjoy the peacefulness of dust." "Were I an independent man," Newbroom replies, "I should call them a pack of savages. . . . It is modern sanitary science versus dust, or choked knowledge . . . and your art work is most of it a dust-trap" (243–46).

The dusty corners of Victorian middle-class houses were thus important nodes of sanitary and aesthetic controversy, simultaneously places of artistic imagination and filthy accumulation. This ideological battle is distinctly visible in Charlotte Mary Yonge's 1873 *The Pillars of the House*, where an apparently simple argument about wallpaper is transformed by sanitary rhetoric into a controversy about dust traps. Of the orphaned Underwood siblings, two—Cherry and Edgar—are painters, trained by Romantic-era art criticism to appreciate the dark sublimities of Renaissance art. Wilmet, their practical elder sister and housekeeper, has just repapered the parlor in a pattern her brother calls "Philistine"; Edgar deplores the domestic incarceration of sister Cherry "among the eternal abortive efforts of that gilded trellis to close upon those blue dahlias, crimson lilacs, and laburnums growing upwards, tied with huge ragged magenta ribbons."[17] Edgar, a fledgling Bohemian, and Cherry instead wax rhapsodic about the old wallpaper, "which could only be traced by curious researches in dark corners," and the color, which was "soft, deepening off in clouds, and bars, sunsets and stormclouds, to make stories about." "Where it was most faded and grimy!" Wilmet replies in Ruskinian recognition of aesthetic pretensions. "It is all affectation not to be glad to have clean walls." "Clean!" cries Edgar. "Defend me from the clean!"[18]

By the 1880s, it was apparent that sanitation consisted of more than adequate plumbing and good ventilation; cleanliness was an aesthetic and architectural decision that had converted the ephemera of taste into the science of health. Hefty instructional manuals appeared throughout the decade, containing design tips that could have been penned by Mr. Newbroom himself. Architect Robert Edis's contribution to the 1883 volume *Our Homes and How to Make Them Healthy* was called "Internal Decoration," and it contains the clearest call for a modern simultaneity of decoration and sanitation:

> For many years, we have been content to cover the whole floor surface of the rooms with carpets, under which dirt and filth naturally accumulated, to exclude light and air by heavy fluffy curtains, to form resting places for blacks and dust by the use of internal Venetian blinds, and to fill our rooms with lumbering old-fashioned furniture, with flat or sunken tops, which formed dirt and dust traps, rarely cleaned out. We have covered our walls with papers absolutely deleterious to bodily

health, and have had but little regard to the mental effect of jarring colours and patterns, or the nervous irritability which is almost unknowingly excited by the use of badly designed furniture, incongruous and staring decoration, and vulgar anachronisms in household taste, all of which, I believe exercise to an important degree an influence equally damaging to our mental as bad drainage and improper ventilation do to our bodily health.[19]

According to Edis, old-fashioned colors and contours could produce both physical and mental disease; indeed, anachronism itself was a trap where much filth could fester. Joint art and health exhibitions began to be held all over England, with artists, scientists, and doctors hosting discussions on "Healthy Furniture and Decoration," "Dress in Its Relation to Health and Climate," and "The Hygienic Value of Colour in the Dwelling." Moreover, architects, engineers, and furniture designers like Phillip Webb, Norman Shaw, and E. W. Godwin joined Edis in an attempt to theorize the "Healthy House," a modern living environment that eliminated architectural nooks, decorative crannies, and the dust-trap anachronism.

Edis's 1881 lecture "On Sanitation in Decoration" followed a William Morris doctrine of utility in furnishing, advising that

> Everything in the House should be made useful; all ledges and unnecessary dust spaces should be carefully avoided, and everything so arranged that may be cleaned with as little labour or trouble as possible. All furniture which has superfluous carving or moulding should be avoided, and simplicity and utility should take the place of excessive ornamentation. . . . There is no reason why we should convert our homes into pest houses by a style of furnishing which renders accumulations of filth not only likely but positively inevitable.[20]

At the same conference, Dr. Alfred S. Carpenter agreed, and added that "carpets, curtains, and comforts of all kinds retained the debris from our skin and our pulmonary membranes," and that "the excreta from our sweat glands are allowed to settle on our uncleaned windows, on out of the way cornices, useless ledges, and so-called architectural and upholstering ornaments."[21] Such decorative dust-traps were perceived as the hiding places of diseases from typhus to measles to scarlet fever; as the editor of *Our Homes and How to Make Them Healthy*, Shirley Forster Murphy, explained in his introduction, poisonous disease particles could live indefinitely in the beautiful borders of the Victorian home. "It may be enclosed in woolen materials, it may be concealed in adhesive material, on the walls, in the ceilings, on the floors . . . it may be a solid particle, and dried up as mere dust, it retains its poisonous properties."[22] Murphy goes on to tell story after story about people who bought new houses in suburbs and soon died from pulmonary disease. This was not surprising to architects Percival Gordon Smith and Keith Downes Young, who devoted their own chapter in Murphy's anthology to the modern practice of wallpapering rooms with papers and pastes "almost entirely composed of vegetable substances . . . and, frequently, not of the purest description," adding that "the readiness with which a mass of half a dozen layers decays and ultimately becomes putrid is easily understood."[23]

Some of the anxiety about hidden pockets of putrescence in the Victorian home seemed to stem from a desire to prevent the middle classes from encroaching upon decorative styles previously reserved for the upper classes. Improvements in mechanical reproduction made rich tapestries and flocked wallpapers much more accessible to homeowners on a budget; however, as Rhoda and Agnes Garret advised in their *Suggestions for Home Decoration* (1877), even if a middle-class family could afford to purchase such furnishings and fittings, they would not be able to afford their sanitary upkeep. "Now nothing compensates in a house for dirtiness," the sanitary sisters warned, "and for moderate incomes it is therefore better to have the walls and ceilings treated in such a manner that they may take their turn to be cleaned and done up without any very serious outlay."[24] Indeed, it is clear that many Victorian home-decoration guides were meant to harness the potentially wayward tastes of untrained middle-class domestic designers, especially in the choice of wallpapers, and that the disciplinary mechanism used to produce aesthetic taste was often sanitary reform. "When we choose wallpapers," advised William White, F.S.A., "those that are the most beautiful in form and colour are to be preferred. We should, however, satisfy ourselves that the patterns on the papers with which our rooms are hung have not a look of motion. Nothing is more distressing than to be in a room where the pattern of the paper seems always to be moving like a drop of dirty water under the microscope."[25] The Garret sisters agreed that the choice of wallpaper, especially in the bedroom, was crucial to the inhabitant's health, but for them the danger was not limited to invisible germs under a metaphoric microscope: "select a paper that has an all-overish pattern that cannot be tortured into geometrical figures by the occupant of the chamber, who, especially in hours of sickness, is well-nigh driven to distraction by counting over and over again the dots and lines with endless repetition before his aching eyes."[26] Edis also discouraged the choice of strongly repetitive or monotonous patterns in wallpaper on the grounds that "such patterns would be a source of infinite torture and annoyance in times of sickness and sleeplessness, would materially add to our discomfort and nervous irritability, and after a time would have a nightmare effect upon the brain."[27]

Architectural Anachronism: The Haunted House

In the context of such testimony, it is impossible to resist revisiting Charlotte Perkins Gilman's 1892 "The Yellow Wallpaper" as not just ghost story or feminist protest, but as a psychological revolt against bad design. The already depressed American protagonist is initially struck by the "repellent, almost revolting" color of the wallpaper in the up-stairs room where she is placed for postpartum "rest" by her doctor husband: she describes "a smouldering, unclean yellow, strangely faded by the slow-turning sunlight. It is a dull yet lurid orange in some places, a sickly sulphur tint in others."[28] She also says she knows something "of the principle of design," and that not only is the furniture in her room "inharmonious," but the wallpaper is "committing every artistic sin" by not adhering to "the laws of radiation, or alternation, or repetition, or symmetry, or anything else that I ever heard of" (9). Gradually the wall-paper begins to torment her already strained nerves. She sees morbid images (broken necks, bulbous, unblinking eyes) in the paper, and even-tually fancies the ugly trellis design to be a prison or cage, from which a creeping woman is trying to escape. While this "debased Roman-esque" wallpaper has been read as a metaphor for patriarchy and as an icon of psychological entrapment, within the nineteenth-century con-cept of the healthy home, this wallpaper is a sanitary menace. Although the protagonist is ostensibly assigned this room at the top of the house because it is the most healthy, the sulphurous paper not only stains the clothing of all who go near it, but it gives off the "subtlest, most endur-ing odor" in damp weather, an odor the heroine can only identify as "like the color of the paper! A yellow smell" (15). Even though she can-not identify the exact scent given off by the rotting wallpaper, a sanitary investigator would be more interested in the fact of the smell itself: "When you perceive a bad smell," explains Florence Stacpoole in her 1905 tract *A Healthy Home and How to Keep It*, "something unclean, and perhaps poisonous actually touches you."[29]

Importantly, the house featured in "The Yellow Wallpaper" is a colonial mansion, an old, hereditary estate, "empty for years," which the middle-class doctor has been able to lease for his wife's recovery because it is mysteriously cheap. The protagonist wonders briefly if it is haunted at the beginning of her stay, and perhaps the answer to her question, from a sanitary point of view, is yes. Sharon Marcus has noted that the Victorian ideology of the home as an "impenetrable, self-contained structure" had much to do with public health warnings about overcrowding, and has argued that ghost stories proliferated in the late nineteenth century because anxieties about "mixed" lodging houses and semidetached villas suggested that even new middle-class residences were already too populated with "souls."[30] Marcus adds, "in many stories, illness and death follow as consequences of seeing a ghost,"[31] and while this is certainly true, I would argue that overcrowding is just one explanation for such unsanitary hauntings. For example, in William Bardwell's sensationally titled *What a House Should Be, versus Death in the House*, we are warned that "the pabulum of disease lies festering in unremoved heaps" inside even the wealthiest, single-family homes, and that the untimely deaths of whole families in a single residence are less mysterious than most people suppose.[32]

> Look again how the members of families in certain streets gradually disappear, until a forlorn survivor is left to transport his pining frame to another quarter, and give room to a fresh family supply, which in turn feeds the domestic demon—an unhealthy home. If you care to examine the component parts of this monster, you will find prominent the fatal soil pipe, the water closet, the sink and rotting boards, and tainted wall papers, the dust-bin, filled with decomposing vegetable and animal matters, or defective and trapped drains; all or any of which send up deadly emanations to poison the air in the house.[33]

A home may indeed be cursed, Bardwell warns, and as an architect and sanitary engineer, he is quick to locate the domestic demon in the "fatal" bowels of the Victorian house. Nooks and crannies, bins and toilets, wet apertures and decaying decorations are deadly from a sanitary rather than supernatural perspective. Certainly the "unclean" spirits of many unlucky, abandoned, rotting, nineteenth-century haunted houses in fiction seem to be no more than the foul emanations of aristocratic filth, dirty decorating styles, and a variety of organic decompositions. In J. E. Murdock's 1887 *The Shadow Hunter: The Tragic Story of a Haunted Home*, Miss Tryphena Sabine inherits the ancient family mansion of her former (rejected) suitor, an old eccentric named Mr. Jerrald. From the moment she crosses the threshold, she is seized with "unaccountable" shuddering; the house is in a state of general dilapidation, smells moldy, and most of the rooms are sealed up. Soon after their arrival, Tryphena and her sister Flo begin hearing dripping noises, and seeing gauzy vapors and spots of blood. Both women get nervous, irritable, and eventually ill, and a doctor is called in for consultation. Dr. Trapmore is not superstitious, and is less interested in the bloody, floating head Tryphena claims she sees than in an apparently bricked-up part of the wall, which he advises her to tear down. His advice goes unheeded, Flo and Tryphena become sicker and finally die, and Dr. Trapmore inherits the haunted estate. The first thing he does is tear down that suspicious false wall, and he discovers a sealed-off room at the center of the house from which emanates an odor "peculiarly sickening and foetid."[34] The aptly named Dr. Trapmore discovers that the "place was a charnel house" with two dead bodies festering in the very spot Mr. Jerrald had bludgeoned and decapitated them. At the end of the tale, Trapmore decides that the only way to purify the house is to raze it, and the doctor accomplishes sanitation and exorcism simultaneously.

Wilkie Collins's 1878 story "The Haunted Hotel" also features foul smells that emanate from an ancient family mansion, but this haunted house is a damp, moldy Venetian palace with a bloody history of Inquisition-era crimes.[35] The palace is destined to be turned into a lavish hotel by a group of English speculators when Lord Mountbarry, his new wife, the former Countess Narona, and her brother, the Baron Rivar, rent it for several months. Lord Mountbarry dies suddenly while in residence, the Baron and the Countess emigrate to America, and, through a series of plot twists, the remaining members of the Mountbarry extended family are the first guests in the new hotel. The only two rooms in the hotel that have escaped renovation are the bedchamber where Lord Mountbarry died and the Baron's bedroom directly above. These rooms are the most luxurious in the hotel, with original fittings and sumptuous antique furnishings, but each Mountbarry family member who attempts to sleep in the dead man's room fails to rest comfortably. First Henry Westwick loses both sleep and appetite to the room, and decides that something in the room must be "unhealthy." Mrs. Norbury, Henry's sister, falls asleep but has frightful dreams that feature her dead brother: "she saw him starving in a loathsome prison; she saw him pursued by assassins, and dying under their knives; she saw him drowning in immeasurable depths of dark water; she saw him in a bed on fire, burning to death in the flames; she saw him tempted by a shadowy creature to drink, and dying of a poisonous draught" (172). Mrs. Norbury moves upstairs to the former bedroom of Baron Rivar, but is pursued by the same nightmares. The hotel manager changes the number on the dead man's room, but Francis Westwick, another Mountbarry brother, is driven from it by an offensive odor. Finally, Agnes, the dead lord's jilted lover, wakes in the night to a vision of a bloody head, floating in the air above her bed, and a sickening smell that penetrates the entire room. Henry Westwick opens an investigation, and discovers that Baron Rivar's room contains an ornate mantelpiece with a hidden cavity; the doors of the cavity spring open when the heads of two sculptured caryatids are pressed. Inside the cavity is the source of the foul odors: a partially decomposed human head, eventually identified by false teeth as Lord Mountbarry's. Like the mansion in *The Shadow Hunter*, the Palace Hotel is a charnel house; Henry discovers that the rest of Lord Mountbarry's body was mutilated and hastened to decomposition by chemicals in the Baron's vaults, and that the unclean spirits that haunt the palace are the putrid gases of organic decay.

Importantly, moreover, the Palace Hotel is haunted by both evil deeds and bad taste: while the hiding place in the Room of the Caryatids dates from the bloody days of the Inquisition in Venice, the mantelpiece itself is a degenerate design of the eighteenth century "and reveals the corrupt taste of the period in every part of it" (208). In late-nineteenth-century literature, bad designs of previous centuries habitually appear as hiding places for a variety of contaminants. Jane Ellen Panton, the well-known purveyor of healthy domestic decoration, uses the language of supernatural uncleanliness to describe her visit to the former home of Thomas Carlyle and his wife Jane.

> I penetrated with awe into the dirty, dark chamber of horrors which had been sacred to the master, and I climbed up into the so-called drawing-room, where even the glass in the windows was obscured to hide the view, such as it was: where the drab paper and paint gave me the horrors as I thought of dark November and December afternoons and evenings and thought how much better they might have been had pink or blue replaced the drab; or a cheerful yellow brought sunshine into the nest of murky cobwebs; and when I saw the bedrooms, where the ghastly ghosts of all their sleepless nights seemed still to linger; and as I contemplated them, and finally descended into their damp, stone-floored awful kitchen; I quite understood why there were so many domestic catastrophes, and so much ill-health, low-spirits, ill-temper, and dyspepsia, for no one could have possibly been well or happy in a house which was arranged and decorated . . . as that one was.[36]

Here, Panton clearly links bad health with the familiar accoutrements of Gothic anxiety; dirt and darkness, murky cobwebs, and ghastly ghosts all reveal the Carlyles' mid-Victorian townhouse to be a medieval "chamber of horrors," replete with the dusty decorative anachronisms that are the obvious cause of so much bad temper and disease.

Even novels that steer clear of the supernatural contain old houses that are haunted by unclean spirits. In Thomas Hardy's 1881 novel *A Laodicean*, Paula Power inherits the ancient De Stancy castle from her father, an enormously influential and wealthy railway engineer, who purchased it from an aristocratic family in economic and moral decline. For the romantic hero, architect George Somerset, Paula represents an exciting new spirit of eclectic modernism coupled with a return to the physical development of the Greeks: she outfits her ancient castle with both a telegraph for rapid communication and a gymnasium for healthful exercise. But Mr. Woodwell, the Baptist minister who keeps trying to baptize Paula according to the deathbed wishes of her father, suspects prolonged residence in the medieval walls of the De Stancys will corrupt the "indomitable energy" of the Power family.[37] Woodwell warns Somerset that "The spirit of old papistical times still lingers in the nooks of those silent walls, like a bad odour in a still atmosphere, dulling the iconoclastic emotions of the true Puritan" (64). For Woodwell, the entire castle is a dust trap: the ancient Catholic heritage haunts the De Stancy mansion like an unsanitary smell, collecting in the Gothic chinks and gaps and producing spiritual dullness in the reformed Christian inhabitant. Indeed, thoroughly modern Paula soon begins to believe that "feudalism is the only true romance of life" (92). Moreover, when the dispossessed De Stancy heir begins to court her in an attempt to regain lost family land and monies, Paula is struck by his romantic resemblance to a portrait in her picture gallery, and begins to desire a legitimate place for herself upon the venerable yellow walls. The possession of Paula by the unclean feudal spirit of the De Stancy legacy draws her away from her suitor-architect, Somerset, who originally had been hired to restore the castle to its original state; eventually, however, Paula realizes that she has been deceived by false romanticism into a regard for William De Stancy, and returns to her slighted lover. But the nooks and crannies of De Stancy castle still present a significant threat to the possibilities of modernism, and must be burnt to the ground in the final pages of the novel. Somerset comforts Paula with promises of a new, "eclectic" home on the same ground, and the possibility that she will yet represent the "modern spirit" in English life: "You, Paula, will be yourself again, and recover, if you have not already, from the warp given to your mind (according to Woodwell) by the medievalism of that place" (431).

Architectural Exorcism: The Healthy House

The dust of ages was a deadly feature of ancient mansions, haunting, possessing, and infecting the healthy spirit of modern life. Yet the picturesque dust traps so inevitable in old castles had unfortunately been reproduced in the design of relatively new, suburban middle-class houses; indeed, one sanitary complaint that might be legitimately lodged against John Ruskin was that the critic's impassioned reverence for Gothic architecture had inspired a revival of dirty medieval eccentricities in new construction. For Ruskin, Gothic architecture was a powerful ecclesiastical testament to medieval faith and joy in individual labor. For mid-Victorian enthusiasts, on the other hand, the Gothic style was perfectly appropriate for shops, warehouses, individual residences, and even pubs. William Bardwell noted that many "model" cottages built for tenants on large estates reflected the designers' "admirations of medieval architecture," and "are irregular in plan and hence irregular in outline, from an idea of being picturesque; and hence all the chimneys are outside, involving loss of heat, and the roof all hips and valleys, and dormer windows requiring constant repair, and exhibiting an utter ignorance of the very first principles of a Healthy House."[38] But of particular concern were the pseudo-Gothic suburban villas that were springing up like our contemporary McMansions on the whims of speculative builders for middle-class families; then, as now, substandard construction materials and shoddy workmanship yielded Romantic decay and picturesque dilapidation much faster than anyone desired. Describing the construction of these suburbs, Robert Edis insisted that the plaster was often mixed with trash, road rubble, and a wide variety of accidental impurities, and that the other fittings were similarly contaminated:

> The woodwork is of the trashiest and most flimsy character, unseasoned and utterly unfit for its purpose, so that in a year or two all the joints are shrunk, leaving places for the lodgement of dirt and dust; the paint, and the oil with which it is mixed, of the cheapest and nastiest kind; the size used in the distempering of the walls and ceilings decomposed and stinking; the plumbing work of the cheapest possible character. . . . It is not to be wondered that in such houses there is constant sickness, and a general sense of depression fatal to any sound state of bodily or mental health.[39]

For Edis, such houses were bound to be filthy, regardless of housekeeping efforts. At the 1881 Brighton Health Congress, he asked, "How is it possible to be cleanly or tidy in a house in which the walls are breaking out into patches of damp, the woodwork of the floors or doors opening into yawning cracks, resting places for dirt and dust, which no amount of cleaning should get rid of? How can floors be kept clean where the joints and crevices are filled with decomposing filth?"[40]

In the context of such heightened anxiety about dust traps in both ancient and modern Gothic homes, architects Norman Shaw and E. W. Godwin took on the design and creation of Bedford Park, an entire sanitary suburb constructed in modified Queen Anne style, without basements, carpets, or curtains for the hygienically conscious but aesthetically minded middle class. The community was financed by Jonathan T. Carr, who was closely associated with the new Grosvenor Gallery, and motivated by the idea that the domestic environment could provide ordinary, middle-class lives with backgrounds that were both beautiful and clean. As sanitary expert Dr. Richardson explained, "Hitherto, it has been generally supposed that perfect sanitary arrangements and substantial construction are inseparable from ugliness. But it is especially claimed for Bedford Park that it is the most conspicuous effort yet made to break the dull dreariness of the ordinary suburban villa."[41] A variety of tasteful William Morris wallpaper designs were available to be installed with clean pastes; matting was used instead of carpet, and decorative tile was the preferred substance for most flooring. When stained glass was used, it was used sparingly, and never when it could impede the emission of light. One of the first advertisements for the suburb pronounced it "The Healthiest Place in the World" and proudly described the "gravelly soil" and "the most approved Sanitary arrangements" alongside the encouraging statistic that its "Annual death rate is under 6 per Thousand." Despite its prosaic pedigree, painter Edward Abbey reported that walking into this Chiswick area suburb was just "like walking into a water-colour,"[42] and writer Moncure Conway, in his 1882 *Travels in South Kensington*, insisted that "the spirit of artistic inspiration" had been preserved in this mecca of sanitation, "which had come into existence so swiftly, yet so quietly that the building of it has not scared the nightingale I heard yesterday, nor the sky-larks singing while I write."[43]

Like Abbey and Conway, other proponents of sanitary architecture insisted that a smoother, shinier, seamless design for living was absolutely compatible with artistic inspiration and production; the narrator of *Lares and Penates*, for example, finds the ideal design for a fireplace in the Holland Park home of pre-Raphaelite painter Lord Leighton: "a single slab of massive milk-white marble, one perfectly plain polished smoothness, with nothing to catch the dust, and no detail to worry eyes needing rest from study of form and colour" (57). By continuing to link excessive decorative detail to ocular and psychological distress, supporters of the seamless, fully integrated aesthetic of home design not only banished the dust trap, they banished the fear of "permeability," which Tamar Katz has identified as the defining dilemma of both the Victorian home and the Victorian subject.⁴⁴ Moreover, the filthy Romantic concept of "tone" was divorced from the more desirable domestic and psychological effect of "repose." This uncoupling is clearly seen in George Halse's *Graham Aspen, Painter* (1889), a novel that fully repudiates decadent aesthetic preferences for darkness and decay by linking them with mental weakness and bodily disease.⁴⁵ Aspen is described as a modern Pygmalion, who devotes enormous "abnormal" energy to the realization of an ideal study of a beautiful woman he supposedly never met; eventually, however, we learn it is a picture of his dead mother. The artist's obsession with this picture as well as with other sublime images of death and decay render his mind morbid, his body sickly, and his colors "false." The heroine, Hester, is so moved by watching Graham faint in a doctor's office that she becomes a nurse; however, the two do not actually meet until some time later, when she intrudes upon a picture he is painting of dead trees in the woods and his assistant suggests that Aspen add her to it. Hester's healthy, living image gradually displaces the dead mother's idealized presence, and their marriage plot ultimately coalesces around a project that formally recognizes the healthfulness of Aspen's new art: they jointly purchase a former health farm. Long celebrated for its excellent drainage, fine air, and pure water, Flinders Farm is transformed by painter and nurse into a famous art school, where enfeebled British painting will be cleansed and revived.

Such resolutions are paradigmatic in popular Victorian literature after 1870, where the sanitation of morbid artistic sublimity brings both marriage and the repose of a clean environment. But in *Graham Aspen, The Pillars of the House, The Shadow Hunter, Lares and Penates, A Laodicean,* and other works, environmental cleanliness also requires a veritable exorcism of the psychological depth and architectural space inspired by the concept of sublimity. While praising the cleanliness of Alford House in South Kensington, Caddy's narrator notes its thoughtful architectural design: "There is no loss of space, no bewilderment, as in our pseudo-Jacobean houses, no tracasserie, no labyrinth of shady passages" (49). Indeed, E. W. Godwin had associated the revival of past historical periods in architecture with both filth and pre-Enlightenment confusion, and had insisted that such architecture made "our modern houses already look weird, as if with forebodings of ghosts and haunted chambers."[46] As Juliet Kinchen argues, "Godwin's modern house was the enemy of secrets and possessions" because its transparency and easy circulation of air and people made Gothic anxiety an architectural impossibility.[47] Even Harriet Martineau lobbied for the elimination of decorative dust traps from the modern Victorian home on the grounds that hiding spaces concealed both ancient dust and Gothic terror: "We in our tight houses, whose walls have no chinks and no cracks, may better hang our apartments with clean and light and wholesome paper, which harbors no vermin, screens no thieves, and scares no fever patient with night visions of perplexity and horror."[48] In the minds of such Victorian sanitarians, the connection between Gothic architecture and psychological disease was clear, and so was its remedy: in order to evict the madwoman from the attic, you had to eliminate the attic. Banishing domestic nooks and crannies gave the pestilence of psychological distress nowhere to fester.

On one hand, the evacuation of mental vicissitudes appeared to displace the Victorian concept of interiority onto the modern body. In G. K. Chesterton's 1908 cult classic *The Man Who Was Thursday*, for example, Bedford Park appears in the guise of Saffron Park, an artistic colony that "Never in any definable way produced any art."[49] Saffron Park is the home of poet Gabriel Syme, who, as the son of a sanitarian mother and an artist father, now believes "our digestion . . . going sacredly and silently right, is the foundation for all poetry. . . . Yes," he exclaims feelingly, "the most poetical thing in the world is not being sick."[50] In the sanitized aesthetic philosophy of late-Victorian culture, artistic inspiration is ironically founded upon the healthy body rather than the diseased mind, and the best art is measured by its good effect on human physiology. Mr. Newbroom of *Lares and Penates* asks the narrator why she does not "write whitewashing up as a fine art," explaining that in addition to being the most hygienic varnish for walls and ceilings, "lime has a natural affinity with the acids which cause diseases of body and mind. Let a gouty man try a day's whitewashing and see if it will not draw the acids out of his joints" (242). The sickly human body is as fraught with pockets of contamination and disease as the unsanitary house, but the performance of cleansing the latter will also heal the diseases and weaknesses of the former. Indeed, Mrs. Caddy reports that a new trend in middle-class homes involves training the daughters of the family in the healthy exercise of house cleaning: "If children can do nothing else, let them fetch and carry—and dust the furniture. A year passed in spying out dust and learning the poisonousness of it, would train the eye to purity for life. Here is the true kindergarten. . . .

It is exercise versus exercise book" (77). Within modern conceptions of cleanliness, intellectual pursuits interfere with health and produce deformity; daughters might be healthier for the physical activity of housework, and, after all, who better than a diminutive child for infiltrating the obscure nooks and crannies of the Victorian middle-class home? "I have but two daughters," mourns one Mrs. Gay in *Lares and Penates*, "and very valuable they are to me; but a house with nine daughters, what might it not be made!" (17).

On the other hand, however, although the dark corners of aesthetic sublimity had been thoroughly exorcised by the end of the century, John Ruskin would not have been entirely satisfied with the style of healthy subject that stood in its place. In fact, the late-Victorian sanitation of subjectivity ushered in a theory of "impressionist" consciousness that was much closer to Pater's solipsistic aestheticism than to Ruskin's social realism. The late-nineteenth-century impressionist movement in both art and literature—which Katz and other recent critics have characterized as being mistrustful of traditional structures of realist representation—suggested that individual perceptions of the world were invariably at odds with cherished mid-Victorian models of linear history, narratology, and mimesis.[51] While such intellectual paradigms were crucial to Ruskin's understanding of Old Masters and modern painters, Pater's ahistorical celebration of the Renaissance avoided Ruskinian periodization, classification, and binarization. Renaissance artists "do not live in isolation" in the fifteenth century, Pater insisted, "but breathe a common air, and catch light and heat from each other's thoughts."[52] Like Godwin's healthy house, Pater's aesthetic subjectivity was built for the easy circulation of air and people; "permeability" no longer represented the threat of contamination—it implied the promise of transcendence. In fact, within Pater's philosophy, Ruskin's rigid periodization of art emerges as a process of intellectual and imaginative ghettoization, a confinement of artistic genius to the dust traps of period, fashion, and trend. The artists of Pater's ongoing Renaissance transcend the petty details of history and "work quite cleanly, casting off all *débris*, and leaving us only what the heat of their imagination has wholly fused and transformed."[53]

Pater's newly modern self responded to a steady stream of ephemera, "impressions" of everyday life that were sometimes decadent, sometimes banal, and sometimes even unsanitary. In Pater's famous aesthetic narrative, *The Child in the House*, Florian looks out his window at the fog and soot from the nearby city without condemnation or disgust; in fact, the child is touched by the beauty produced by the rolling, shifting clouds and smoke. Unlike Ruskin, Pater insists that true aesthetic appreciation of beauty should resemble Florian's, and should not be "dependent on any choiceness or special fitness in the objects which present themselves to it."[54] Like the "physiological aesthetics" of Grant Allen, or the "psychological aesthetics" of Vernon Lee, Pater's aesthetic philosophy converted banal and commonplace things into beautiful "aspects" without reference to social or sanitary utility.[55] This admiration of impressions over objects was often satirized at the end of the century, especially in novels like J. Fitzgerald Molloy's *It Is No Wonder: A Story of Bohemian Life* (1882): "Do you think the sky too yellow?" aspiring painter Marcus Phillips asks his friend and fellow painter. "You see, the public likes a good sunset, something between Turner and eggs and bacon."[56] Clearly, such aestheticism bordered on decadence, and threatened to replace the intellectual rapture provided by art with physiological responses to feelings that were much more corporeal in origin and inspiration: "These kidneys are delicious," exclaims an Oscar Wilde–like Mr. Amarynth while eating breakfast in R. S. Hichens's 1894 satire, *The Green Carnation*. "They are as poetic as one of Turner's later sunsets, or the curved mouth of the La Giaconda. How Walter Pater would love them."[57]

Notes

1. Wyke Bayliss, "Sanitary Reform in Relation to the Fine Arts," in *Transactions of the Hastings and St. Leonard's-on-the-Sea Health Congress, 1889* (Hastings: F. J. Parsons, 1890), 238.

2. Eileen Cleere, "Dirty Pictures: John Ruskin, *Modern Painters*, and the Victorian Sanitation of Fine Art," *Representations* 78 (Spring 2002): 116–39.

3. Edwin Chadwick, "The Manual Laborer as an Investment of Capital," in *The Journal of the Statistical Society* (London: Harrison and Sons, 1862), 504.

4. Nathaniel Hawthorne describes Rome, that other exalted Italian city, as malarial and oxygen-poor, and suggests that whenever the term "picturesque" is applied to a landscape, its inhabitants are suffering slow and steady genocide: "There is reason to suspect that a people are waning to decay and ruin," he mourns, "the moment that their life becomes fascinating either in the poet's imagination or the painter's eye" (*The Marble Faun* [1860; New York: Oxford World's Classics, 2002], 232). Samuel Smiles argued that if art education were truly necessary for the advancement of a civilization, European cities of art would not be so unsanitary and debased. If there was any real connection between beauty and social improvement, Smiles insisted, "Paris ought to contain a population of the wisest and best human beings," and Rome would not be so "inexpressibly foul" (*Character* [London: John Murray, 1890], 263).

5. Peter Stallybrass and Allon White, *The Politics and Poetics of Transgression* (Ithaca, NY: Cornell University Press, 1986), 129–30.

6. See Nancy Armstrong, *Desire and Domestic Fiction: A Political History of the Novel* (New York: Oxford University Press, 1987); Catherine Gallagher, *The Industrial Reformation of English Fiction, 1832–1867* (Chicago: University of Chicago Press, 1985); Mary Poovey, *Uneven Developments: The Ideological Work of Gender in Mid-Victorian England* (Chicago: University of Chicago Press, 1988).

7. Lewis F. Day, "How to Hang Pictures," *The Magazine of Art* (London) 5 (1882): 58–60.

8. Alfred S. Carpenter, "Domestic Health," in *Transactions of the Brighton Health Congress, 1881* (London: E. Marlborough and Co., 1881), 228.

9. John Ruskin, "The Relation of Art to Use," in *Lectures on Art* (New York: John W. Lovell, 1900), 73.

10. William Morris, "Address Delivered to the Wedgewood Institute," in *The Wedgewood Institute Reports of the School of Science and Art* (Burslem: Warwick Savage, 1881), 19.

11. John Ruskin, "The Cestus of Aglaia," in *On the Old Road: A Collection of Miscellaneous Essays, Pamphlets, etc., etc., published 1834–1885* (London: George Allen, 1885), 499.

12. For more on the development of the aesthetic movement in the context of British domesticity, see Talia Schaffer and Kathy Alexis Psomiades, *Women and British Aestheticism* (Charlottesville: University of Virginia Press, 1999).

13. Walter Pater, *The Renaissance* (1873; New York: Oxford University Press, 1998).

14. Schaffer and Psomiades, *Women and British Aestheticism*, 3.

15. Rhoda Broughton, *Second Thoughts* (London: Macmillan and Co., 1899), 60.

16. Mrs. Florence Caddy, *Lares and Penates, or The Background of Life* (London: Chatto and Windus, 1881), 43. Subsequent references will be cited parenthetically in the text.

17. Charlotte Mary Yonge, *The Pillars of the House* (London: Macmillan, 1873), 1:301–2.

18. Ibid., 302. Edgar's dirty propensities in art are matched by an equally decadent moral philosophy, and negative reviews of his painting "Brynhild" at the Royal Academy exhibition send him into a downward spiral of degradation; he eventually runs away to the American West where he dies an appropriately horrible death at the hands of Indians.

19. Robert Edis, "Internal Decoration," in *Our Homes and How to Make Them Healthy*, ed. Shirley Forster Murphey (London: Cassell and Company, 1883), 313.

20. Robert Edis, "On Sanitation in Decoration," in *Transactions of the Brighton Health Congress, 1881* (London: E. Marlborough and Co., 1881), 324.

21. Carpenter, "Domestic Health," 228.

22. Shirley Forster Murphy, *Our Homes and How to Make Them Healthy*, 8.

23. Percival Gordon Smith and Keith Downes Young, "Architecture," in *Our Homes and How to Make Them Healthy*, 127.

24. Rhoda and Agnes Garrett, *Suggestions for Home Decoration* (Philadelphia, PA: Porter and Coates, 1877), 89.

25. William White, "Hygienic Value of Colour in the Dwelling," *International Health Exhibition Literature*, vol. 7, *The Sanitary Construction of Houses* (London: William Clowes and Sons, 1884), 142.

26. Garrett, *Suggestions for Home Decoration*, 69.

27. Robert Edis, "Healthy Furniture and Decoration," *International Health Exhibition Literature*, vol. 1, *Health in the Dwelling* (London: William Clowes and Sons, 1884), 321.

28. Charlotte Perkins Gilman, "The Yellow Wallpaper," in *The Charlotte Perkins Gilman Reader*, ed. Ann J. Lane (New York: Pantheon Books, 1980), 5. Subsequent references will be cited parenthetically in the text.

29. Florence Stacpoole, *A Healthy Home and How to Keep It* (London: Wells Gardner, 1905), 39.

30. Sharon Marcus, *Apartment Stories: City and Home in Nineteenth-Century Paris and London* (Berkeley and Los Angeles: University of California Press, 1999), 94.

31. Ibid., 125.

32. William Bardwell, *What a House Should Be, versus Death in the House* (London: Dean and Son, 1873), ii.

33. Ibid., 5.

34. J. E. Murdock, *The Shadow Hunter: The Tragic Story of a Haunted Home* (London: T. Fisher Unwin, 1887), 131.

35. Wilkie Collins, *The Haunted Hotel* (New York: Oxford World's Classics, 1999). Subsequent references will be cited parenthetically in the text.

36. Jane Ellen Panton, *From Kitchen to Garret: Hints for Young Householders* (London: Ward and Downey, 1893), 12.

37. Thomas Hardy, *A Laodicean* (New York: Oxford World's Classics, 1991), 64. Subsequent references will be cited parenthetically in the text.

38. Bardwell, *What a House Should Be*, 8.

39. Edis, "Internal Decoration," 310.

40. Edis, "On Sanitation in Decoration," 319.

41. Benjamin Richardson, quoted in Ian Fletcher, "Bedford Park: Aesthete's Elysium?" in *Romantic Mythologies*, ed. Ian Fletcher (London: Routledge and Kegan Paul, 1967), 177.

42. Ibid., 171.

43. Moncure D. Conway, *Travels in South Kensington* (New York: Harper and Brothers, 1882), 230.

44. Tamar Katz, *Impressionist Subjects: Gender, Interiority, and Modernist Fiction in England* (Urbana: University of Illinois Press, 2000), 31.

45. George Halse, *Graham Aspen, Painter* (London: Hurst and Blackett, 1889).

46. E. W. Godwin, quoted in Juliet Kinchen, "E. W. Godwin and Modernism," in *E. W. Godwin: Aesthetic Movement Architect and Designer*, ed. Susan Weber Soros (New Haven, CT: Yale University Press, 1999), 106.

47. Ibid.

48. Harriet Martineau, *Health, Husbandry, and Handicraft* (London: Bradbury and Evans, 1861), 463.

49. G. K. Chesterton, *The Man Who Was Thursday* (New York: Dodd, Mead, and Co., 1975), 7.

50. Ibid., 12.

51. See Katz, *Impressionist Subjects*, 5; Murray Roston, *Modernist Patterns in Literature and the Visual Arts* (London: Macmillan, 2000), 10–13; David Weir, *Decadence and the Making of Modernism* (Amherst: University of Massachusetts Press, 1995), 55–56. Katz's book treats Pater's relation to literary and artistic impressionism thoroughly, especially with regard to *The Child in the House*.

52. Pater, *The Renaissance*, xxxiii.

53. Ibid., xxxi.

54. Pater, *The Child in the House* (Oxford: H. Daniel, 1894), 12.

55. See Grant Allen, *Physiological Aesthetics* (New York: Appleton, 1877); Vernon Lee, *The Beautiful: An Introduction to Psychological Aesthetics* (Cambridge: Cambridge University Press, 1913).

56. J. Fitzgerald Molloy, *It Is No Wonder: A Story of Bohemian Life* (London: Hurst and Blackett, 1882), 30.

57. R. S. Hitchens, *The Green Carnation* (New York: Mitchell, Kennedy, 1894), 27.

Chapter 7

"Dirty Pleasure": *Trilby*'s Filth

Joseph Bristow

rilby, George Du Maurier's bestseller of 1894, assuredly counts among the dirtiest and most disorderly of those well-known fin-de-siècle novels whose grease and grime besmear their decadent and naturalist worlds. But unlike the bulk of such fictions from the late nineteenth century, *Trilby* hardly deplores the working-class deprivation associated with urban squalor. Du Maurier's initially humorous narrative wishes to preserve a variety of filth belonging to a particular place and time: Paris's less than salubrious *quartier latin* of 1856–57. These were the years immediately before Imperial Baron Georges-Eugène Haussmann, whom in 1853 Louis Napoleon appointed prefect of the Seine, would demolish many of its tortuous alleys as part of his wholesale modernization of Paris.

Not surprisingly, Haussmann's perspective differs considerably from Du Maurier's on the unreformed Latin Quarter, since this district, probably more than any other part of the city, appeared to him in particular need of reconstruction. In his *Mémoires* (1890–93), Haussmann recalls his student days of the 1830s, when he made his way from his parents' home on the Right Bank across the Seine to the Place du Panthéon at the corner of the School of Law. En route he passed the "filthy mass of pot-houses" and the "meanders of the Rue de la Harpe."[1] Quoting this passage, David H. Pinkney suggests that the *quartier latin* exemplifies how Paris had by 1850 become a decidedly "inconvenient city" (18).

Even though at the time of the July Monarchy (1830–48) sidewalks were built, their sandstone edges crumbled into black mud. What is more, pedestrians trying to cut a path along "the narrow ways" would often depend "on the hospitality of shop doors to avoid being run down or splattered with mud and the filthy water that flowed in the gutters" (18). But, as Pinkney points out, Paris was not just "inconvenient" in its dirty lack of design; it was also extremely "smelly" (18). The sweeping movement of Haussmann's boulevards would literally clean up areas such as the Latin Quarter through a systematic arrangement of sewers (engineered by Eugène Belgrand), raising the city, as it were, out of the gutter.

Du Maurier's initially exuberant novel begins by refusing to imagine that the muck that characterized the *quartier latin* is the repulsive matter that Belgrand would eventually sanitize. Instead, Du Maurier at first champions the dirt and disorder of this legendary locale for its ebullient style of artistic living, which involves, in rather frivolous ways, Du Maurier's bunch of budding painters ingenuously mingling with lively riffraff whose scummy origins pose no threat. In the early chapters of *Trilby*, Du Maurier devises some striking techniques to conjure up an agreeable impression of the *boue* of *la bohème*. His talkative narrator provides an unforgettable description of the high-ranking atelier where Du Maurier's three young Britons—jovially nicknamed the Laird, Taffy, and Little Billee—learned the tools of their trade. In spite of its eminence, Carrel's atelier looks almost unsanitary: "there were many large dirty windows, facing north, and each window let the light of heaven into a large dirty studio."[2] In this, the "largest" and "dirtiest" studio, "some thirty or forty art students drew and painted for the nude model every day but Sunday from eight to twelve" (53).

As one might predict, there are limits to how far these cheerful British chaps are willing to get down and dirty among the studio's detritus, not to say its nudes. In the bustling bohemia that at first captivates these rather naïve young blades, filth of all kinds begins to accumulate in such thickening quantities that Du Maurier soon takes his novel through some fantastic twists, in a grudging admission that it is not entirely proper to revel nostalgically in the bohemian *boue*. No matter how much its chatty narrator attempts to preserve the glory of the "dirtiest" atelier, the outlandish story of *Trilby* is driven by historical forces that demand that it turn at last away from Carrel's grubby windows. As its attention shifts to its best-known scenes of spectacular mesmerism, the narrative ultimately pursues a somewhat lifeless path that concludes in an austere, though in all respects purified, scene: the completely transformed cityscape of Haussmann, which ruthlessly pushed its clean, unexciting lines through the spirited mess of *vieux Paris*. Du Maurier displays a remarkable ambivalence toward the Parisian filth of yore. At the start of the novel, his narrator is more than ready to admit that the most admirable kinds of artistic energy once had their basis in a coarse, rough, indeed tainted way of life. Yet, at the same time, the stumbling plot discloses that the attempt to absorb the vivacious gaiety of *la bohème* into the highest realms of bourgeois culture depends on exploitative manipulation. If *Trilby* sets out to impress a moral, then it upholds one that rests upon a compelling contradiction: any desire to make the artistic brio of mucky streets appear neat, clean, and tidy remains an unprincipled—if not, by extension, polluted—affair.

Trilby is hardly alone in depicting the Latin Quarter with such jolly vivacity, and it is useful to begin by showing why the novel should be transfixed by a down-at-heel domain that had for years generated many a memorable artistic legend. By the 1840s the inhabitants of this renowned part of Paris were synonymous with diverse *bohemians*—a term, as Marilyn R. Brown observes, that "could occupy multiple positions and contain numerous associations" in nineteenth-century France.[3] Brown contends that this highly inclusive word, which derived from fanciful ideas about the gypsies of fifteenth-century Bohemia, typified a colorful cast of itinerants that provided ready-made subjects for French art and literature. It encompassed "*saltimbanques* (vagabond circus performers), the *commedia dell'arte*, beggars, vagrants, street people, tramps, brigands, *chiffoniers* (ragpickers), ambulant musicians, charlatans, the Wandering Jew, and urban *flâneurs*." As Karl Marx knew from his Parisian years, this was the "whole amorphous, jumbled mass of flotsam and jetsam that the French term bohemian."[4] Water Benjamin, however, would qualify this claim: "A ragpicker cannot, of course, be part of the *bohème*"[5]—insofar as the *chiffonier* remained a pauper rather than a producer of the midcentury art that willingly depicted him. Rather, as Benjamin would observe, "everyone who belonged to the *bohème* could recognize a bit of himself in the ragpicker," since the "*littérateur*" was "in a more or less obscure state of revolt against society" (18).

Certainly, French poetry and fiction of the period shows bohemian artists as figures of shabby rebellion who seek to resist the forces of capitalist modernization exemplified in what *Trilby* calls Haussmann's "mania for demolition and remolition" (207). Amid the "mass" that Marx identified lay the melancholy stereotypes familiar to Théophile Gautier's lyrics of the mid-1850s. In "Le Mansarde" ("The Garret"), for example, the poetic voice declares: "Alike for artist and grisette . . . / A garret—save to music set— / Is never otherwise than sad."[6] Here we find the impoverished "poet-youth whom fame awaits," together with the working-class "Rigolette," whose "broken glazing mirrors yet / A portion of her pretty brow" (163). These lines allude to Eugène Sue's popular *roman-feuillton Les Mystères de Paris* (1842–43), where the original Rigolette can only make ends meet as a seamstress by taking up life with an art student. Besides Sue, authors as diverse as Honoré de Balzac and Alfred de Musset had already woven a number of touching legends about the loose morals of the Latin Quarter. Perhaps the most memorable images of *la bohème* came from Henri Murger's *Scènes de la Vie de Bohème* (1845), together with the various *physiologies* that Gavarni illustrated in the 1840s.[7]

The opening chapters of *Trilby* draw on these vivid myths, though Du Maurier scarcely sends the boyish Britons crashing immediately into the arms of an artist's model. Instead, the *"trois* Angliches" (69), as the bohemian natives style them, enjoy the seemingly innocent camaraderie in a nicely decorated apartment that contains an appealing farrago of canvases, drawings, and other souvenirs. In the evening, they stroll arm in arm through the city, crossing the Seine where they are eventually "surfeited with classical beauty" at the Louvre (9). Later, over dinner, they engage in chatter about the likes of Titian, Rembrandt, and Veláz-quez. Little Billee listens with "rapt attention and reverentially agree[s]" with each and every "beautiful thing" that they say (11). Later, Little Billee preserves these "beautiful things" in "beautifully drawn" pen-and-ink sketches that "he sent to his mother and sister at home" in England (11). The narrator's exuberant depiction of a "beautiful" life that prospers both indoors and outdoors among the bohemian dirt sustains its enthusiasm in an unsophisticated style whose amateurism becomes plain through the daft repetition of such epithets. But these unprofessional locutions should not be construed as Du Maurier's inability to rise to a slightly more polished level of authorship. To the contrary, the gabby narrator continually casts doubt on the need to produce elegant, well-finished art. Although Little Billee presumes that he is about to acquire the skills that will "make himself the great artist he long[s] to be" (8), the narrative voice suggests that these ideas amount to little more than naïve, though admirable, idealism: "Good honest, innocent, artless prat-tle—not of the wisest, perhaps, nor redolent of the very highest culture" (30). Even if it lacks philosophical insight, such jabbering remains wholly acceptable, since "higher culture"—he advises—"can mar as well as make" (30).

Accordingly, the avowed "literary shortcomings" of *Trilby* (36) have ensured that critics have seldom taken much notice of its low-grade tittle-tattle. In fact, the gossipy style gave grave offense to one of Du Maurier's oldest and most irascible acquaintances from Gleyre's. On reading the serial version in *Harper's New Monthly Magazine*, the American painter James Abbott McNeill Whistler exploded with rage when he recognized himself in one of the characters. Joe Sibley, we learn, was a "vain, witty, and most exquisite and original artist" who proved the "most irresistible friend in the world as long as his friendship lasted—but that was not for-ever."[8] Even though Whistler prided himself on the numerous enemies he made, he probably had, as his best biographer suggests, good reason to accuse Du Maurier publicly of "pent-up envy, malice and furtive intent."[9]

Du Maurier's send-up of Whistler's infamous anger was not just a taunt. As Whistler knew, the caustic joke also originated in Du Maurier's experiences as an art student that painfully excluded him from the world of high culture. In the summer of 1857, after the author of *Trilby* departed from Gleyre's for the Antwerp Academy of Fine Arts, he was "drawing from a model, when suddenly the girl's head . . . seemed to dwindle to the size of a walnut."[10] The retina had become detached from one of his eyes. His Belgian doctors feared that he might turn blind. Understandably, this traumatic event had serious consequences for his career. "He was not," wrote his fellow student Felix Moscheles, "to become a painter."[11] Thus there was all the more reason for Du Maurier to look back longingly to the bohemian moment because its heyday fostered his youthful ambition to proceed to a career that may well have rivaled Whistler's eventual success.

Recording these details, Leonée Ormond observes that Du Maurier "was to remain obsessed as a result with a sense of failure and inadequacy."[12] He was, however, able to "adapt . . . himself quickly to the attitudes and prejudices of the English art world" while establishing a reputation as a capable illustrator: employment that gradually led to a senior position on the satirical journal *Punch*. From the 1860s onward, Du Maurier's cartoons would indulge in mocking the pretentiousness of artistic types associated with venues such as the Grosvenor Gallery (1877–91), where aspiring painters sought to make their mark. It was only much later in life, at the urging of Henry James, that Du Maurier came to public attention with three novels: *Peter Ibbetson* (1891), *Trilby* three years later, and *The Martian* (which started serial publication in 1896, the year of his death).[13] By far the most popular of his fictions, *Trilby* helps to explain the source of his antipathy to artistic prestige. Du Maurier, after all, built his career as a satirist whose cartoons poked fun at the profession from which distressing personal circumstances had bitterly distanced him.

Obligingly, Du Maurier removed Sibley from the tale. But Whistler pressed as hard as he could for damages. (He received ten guineas, plus an apology in *Harper's*.) Little did Du Maurier's publisher anticipate this unholy row, which revealed that the author had violated professional decorum by submitting to the magazine what threatened to become a libelous roman à clef. Yet Du Maurier's "literary shortcomings" would tarnish his reputation in other respects. As one early reviewer put it in the Boston *Literary World*, the noticeably undisciplined "wordy enthusiasm" of the novel was a key component of its commercial prosperity. [14] (The single-volume edition probably earned Harper's, owing to a contract that weighed much in its favor, around $600,000 in the first year.)[15]

Trilby certainly rollicks in chaotic loquacity. One of the novel's most unruly features is the long-winded pleasure that the narrator takes in recording the characters' adulteration of the English and French languages, thus contributing to the polyglot—culturally hybrid—verve that characterizes bohemia's joie de vivre. Time and again, the Britons fall short of even adequate French pronunciation. (One of them, for instance, contorts "embonpoint" horribly—and thus hilariously—into "ongbongpwang" [193].) And when *les trois Angliches* are not fumbling in French, they join their cronies at gatherings like the uproarious Christmas party where nearly everyone breaks into a rackety tune. The Laird, true to his Scottish origins, croons "Hie diddle dee for the Lowlands low" (115), while Taffy carols a "Somersetshire hunting ditty" (116). The bohemian atmosphere is undoubtedly full of jollity, where everybody lends his voice to what appears to be an agreeably cosmopolitan world, where diverse cultures do not so much commingle as amusingly clang and jar. So far the filth of *la bohème* can only thrill— not defile.

But it was not for this cheerful clangor among the raggedy scraps of *la bohème* that modern scholars would remember *Trilby* when they began to reflect on why anyone might take what starts out as a lively Parisian romp with any measure of seriousness. By any account, *Trilby*'s filth has scarcely proved an enduring source of scholarly pleasure. For the most part, critics have viewed the novel's muck as a contemptible substance that remains ingrained on the skin of its most stigmatized character. It is true that the young Britons who wander through the *quartier latin*, no matter how much paint from their palettes has spattered their clothes, do at least take pains to get clean. In this respect, they remain dissimilar from the *bohémien* whose overwhelming grubbiness the narrator will not tolerate. The filthy figure in question is the gifted musician Svengali who makes his memorable entrance as "a tall bony individual of any age between thirty and forty-five, of Jewish aspect, well-featured but sinister. He was," the narrator observes, "very shabby and dirty" (11).

Svengali's dirtiness appears extreme, even amid the charming squalor of *la bohème*. Inhabiting a "dilapidated garret," Svengali appears as a "grossly impertinent" man whose "egotism and conceit were not to be borne," not least because "he was both tawdry and dirty in his person" (41). Somewhat later, a typically blustering exchange makes it look as if this Jewish personage is morally and physically corrupt. When Svengali spies Little Billee enjoying a good scrub in a hip-bath, he immediately asks: "Why the devil are you doing that?" (47). Little Billee tries his best to explain: "Why, to try and get myself *clean*, I suppose." "Ach!" exclaims Svengali (in his exasperated "German-Hebrew-French" [47]): "how the devil did you get yourself *dirty*, then?" The speedy dialogue shows that Svengali possesses absolutely no understanding of how, where, or when one's body might be considered uncontaminated.

This episode proves particularly debased because it seeks to provoke laughter by exploiting the dirtiest stereotype of the Jew. In obvious ways, Svengali conforms to the loathsome habits of his equally maligned literary forebear, the sexually exploitative Fagin of Charles Dickens's *Oliver Twist* (1836–37). As Juliet Steyn remarks, Fagin's "dirtiness" together with his "bad smell" (the historical "*foetor Judaicus*") "is both a reminder of the primitive sexuality of the Jew and a threat to sociality."[16] But apart from extending a tiresome literary tradition that makes such a stink out of the Jew's indelible dirt, Du Maurier's potboiler would appear to concentrate on Svengali's abhorrent mind and body for one clear reason: Svengali's dirtiness focuses the narrator's desire to maintain identifiable borders between purity and pollution. Edgar Rosenberg, for example, suggests that the narrator's stress on Svengali's dirtiness might be viewed as part of a racially and nationally inflected "allegory on art" where *les trois Angliches* enjoy strength in numbers against the isolated "horrible Jew."[17] As Rosenberg sees it, Svengali — who remains forever "walking up and down the earth seeking whom he might cheat, betray, exploit, borrow money from" and "bully if he dared" (*Trilby*, 42) — typifies the wanderlust of the timeworn Eternal Jew who never deserves a moment's rest in Christian nation-states. Rosenberg, however, fails to mention that the Wandering Jew belongs to the larger itinerant company depicted in the art and literature of *la bohème*.[18]

The marked distinction between the purified Britons and the polluted Jew, despite the lifestyle they share in Bohemia, looks plain enough to Daniel Pick as well. "Filthy Svengali," he puts it bluntly, "is contrasted with the clean Englishmen."[19] But Pick, it must be said, quickly apprehends that the contrast remains to some degree unsteady. "As so often in Du Maurier," he writes, Svengali's filthiness "becomes, in its very excess, rather intriguing." Pick alleges that the narrator does more than make Svengali "dirty, ill-mannered and gross" for the sake of elevating the taintlessness of *les trois Angliches* above the Jew's corruption; Svengali's "desire and fury," he says, "keep spilling over, implicating others, like the critical painters at the studio who seem to watch, disapprove, but also to participate in certain lascivious rituals." Readers soon learn that Svengali's filth proves inextricable from his lust. In the past, Svengali was the paramour of "the mysterious Honorine, of whose conquest he was much given to boast, hinting" — deceitfully, of course — "that she was *une jeune femme du monde*" [a decent young woman of the world] (43).

It is not, however, just Svengali's sexual repulsiveness that intrigues his fellow *bohémiens*. Pick's analysis encourages us to see how Svengali's filthy spectacle becomes altogether more entangling in an early episode when he picks up an "elastic penny whistle" in order to execute "Ben Bolt" — an otherwise "poor old twopenny tune" of the 1840s — with "thrilling, vibrating, piercing tenderness" (23). The "shrill scream of anguish" that Svengali produces from the "little flexible flageolet" sounds "more human almost than the human voice itself" (23). Despite the fact that his coarse "Hebrew-German accent . . . sounded much more ghastly in French" (92), Svengali's professional skills generate poignant emotions that entrance his audience. In this instance, exquisite artistic pleasure arises from an unacceptable fountainhead of filth. For the first time, the great cultural worth that *Trilby* would rebelliously like to accord to bohemian muckiness betrays that it might have unpalatable — if not wholly disgusting — origins.

This entrancing interlude anticipates how Svengali, some five years later, will manipulate his far more valuable instrument, Trilby: the unwary drudge who falls prey to his mystifying mesmerism. Under his demonized spell, she unsuspectingly transforms from a gregarious *grisette* who fails to hit "a true note" when struggling to sing "Ben Bolt" into a dispassionate diva whose "great contralto" (216) is like a "chromatically ascending rocket" that reaches "E in alt" (220). Trilby, however, in some ways knows that she should—if only she could—resist him: before she succumbs to his hypnotic seduction, Trilby calls Svengali a "big hungry spider" (52; see Figure 7.1). So provocative is this image that Pick has devoted an impressive full-length study titled *Svengali's Web* in order to elaborate "a particular British bemusement and ambivalence" toward "Jewish-gentile relations."[20] There is, it seems, no escape for anybody—Du Maurier's characters and critics alike—from fixing their gaze on how the dissolute Jew enchants only to entrap his otherwise untainted onlookers.

Trilby without question contains plenty of material that supports Rosenberg's and Pick's respective accounts of how and why it represents the "horrible Jew" as the "alien enchanter" around whom many a fin-de-siècle cultural fantasy might be amplified. But as my opening comments have indicated, the squalor visible right at the start of the story remains hardly exclusive to Svengali's ensnaring web. His "greasily, mattedly unkempt" body (41) forms only one—if vital—part of a novel that frolics around bohemia in the name of reveling in *la boue*. Consequently, it is not always possible for Du Maurier's narrative to distance itself from Svengali by jumping into the bath and washing off the mud from an exclusively British or even Gentile perspective. The talkative narrator sometimes catches himself off guard when he fails to resist the temptation to perform what amounts to nasty muckraking. On occasion, he indicates that Svengali is hardly alone in taking filthy delight in what Pick has called the Jew's "lascivious rituals."

The *boue* of Du Maurier's *bohème* can at times coagulate into an erotic sludge that morally imperils the narrator—since it can and does arouse him. *Trilby*'s filth takes on its most unsettling sexual guise in a passage that considers a habitual antagonism between reputable painters and the disreputable press. Here the narrator deplores how unprincipled critics talk "in hissing dispraise of our more successful fellow-craftsman" (144). It is not, he pronounces, "a clean or pretty trade." "It is," he asserts, "something like the purveying of pornographic pictures"—which belong of course to proverbially dirty books (144). While some people may "look" at this carnal smut and "laugh, and even buy," it remains the case that to "be a purveyor thereof" appears much worse—"ugh!" (144).

If this divagation on obscenity were not enough, the narrative voice sustains its polemic by characterizing the contemptible critic as a "cracked soprano" who has been thrown out of the "Pope's choir" (144). The only places left for such infidels are "the harems still left in Stamboul" where these implicitly impotent wretches can "sweep and clean," making "women's beds" and emptying "slops" (144). Garrulous as ever, he proceeds to embellish this orientalist fantasy. In his view, the emasculating labor of cleaning up the seraglio compares favorably with "the basest instinct of all": "the dirty pleasure we feel (some of us) in seeing mud and dead cats and rotten eggs flung at those we cannot but admire" (145).

In the matter of a few sentences, the narrator has shifted quickly from symbolically castrating the purveyor of filth to cautiously admitting

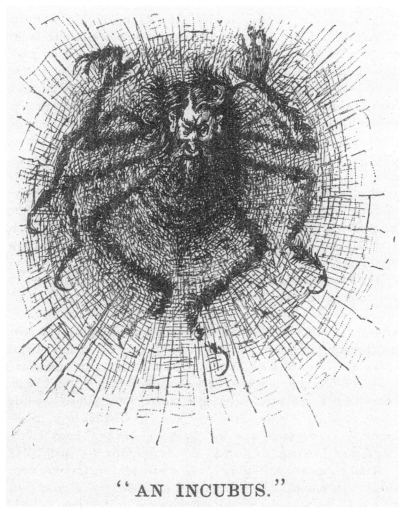

"AN INCUBUS."

Figure 7.1. George Du Maurier, "An Incubus," *Trilby, Harper's New Monthly Magazine* 88 (March 1894): 576.

the "dirty pleasure" that he takes in his own mudslinging. And when we consider the critical delight that Du Maurier himself often relished in satirizing artistic pretentiousness, this polemic looks like an admission of guilt. *Trilby* therefore operates a double standard with regard to the *boue*. What repulses the novel can also inspire it—if in carefully qualified ways. In this regard, the most "dirty pleasure" that both the narrator and *les trois Angliches* experience in the Latin Quarter is Trilby: a distinctly bohemian figure whose hodgepodge of attributes turns out to be not quite as quaint as it might seem.

It may sound eccentric to suggest that *Trilby* basks in "dirty pleasure" when describing its eponymous heroine. Svengali, after all, would seem to be the one who enjoys the filthy penetration of her body when he starts making her "spellbound" while ostensibly helping to cure the "neuralgia in her eyes" (49). Once she comes out of her trance, she recalls "the touch of his soft, dirty fingertips on her face" (53). But, as I will explain here, the narrator progressively makes it clear that Trilby also maintains an intimate acquaintance with a less visible, but nonetheless troubling, strain of squalor.

At the outset, her peculiar appearance enshrines the shopworn heterogeneity of *la bohème* (see Figure 7.2). Accoutered in "the grey overcoat of a French infantry soldier" (12) and a "huge pair of male slippers" (13), Trilby wears a "medley of clothes" that suits "the atmosphere of French studios" (13). Unusually tall, she is in every respect oversized: "the eyes were too wide apart, the mouth too large, the chin too massive, the complexion a mass of freckles" (13). Even though her other features supposedly compensate for this distended oddness, the "very fine brow" together with her "full, broad cheeks" suggest that she "would have made a singularly handsome boy" (13). Tall, boyish, and sensual, Trilby in some respects possesses the symbolic constituents of a Freudian phallic mother. Such an interpretation makes complete sense, especially when we recall that Trilby's first utterance is the cry "Milk below!" (12). (One of her many odd jobs involves delivering the students' groceries.) In some ways coded with masculine qualities, she tramps into the studio—figuratively at least—like a large, life-giving breast. Yet, as Nina Auerbach suggests, Trilby may be a "virtual giantess," but her size cannot overwhelm the company of men; instead, her working-class *grisette*'s body "can be parceled into fragments with a self-contained totemistic value of their own."[21]

In this regard, there is one aspect of Trilby's unusual physique that the narrator reserves as his *pièce de resistance*: her "astonishingly beautiful feet," which many famous artists are said to have "facsimilied in pale plaster of Paris" (15). Everyone admires these appendages—so much so that copies can be subsequently found on sale at galleries in London. At a later point, Svengali celebrates them in a rhyme: they are her *"süssen füssen"* (92). But it is Little Billee, the most talented of the art students, who grows most obsessed with this part of her anatomy. It is worth asking why. Mary Russo suggests, given Trilby's "boyish and irregular features," that it proves hard for the *grisette* to fit into Little Billee's "artistic frame."[22] Thus the "heterogeneity of her body suggests a level of conflict that can only be resolved by severing her foot from the rest of" Trilby's unusual physique (137). Such severing, according to Russo, represents a distinctly psychoanalytic mode of fetishism where Little Billee's repeated idealizing of Trilby's feet amounts to "hiding the nothing, castration"—that is, his "earlier perception of the [female] genitals as mutilated or lacking a penis" (140).

Little Billee's fetishism, however, turns out to be doubtful for a historical reason that helps to reconfigure Russo's theory of how the idealized female foot serves to mask what Freud sees as a typically male form of psychic disavowal. Trilby spends time rubbing her feet clean, and thus they do not disclose to the gullible Little Billee the dirt that has often stuck to their soles. Her careful cleansing removes the stains that were often associated with the *grisettes* who earned their keep as studio models. In this connection, Eric Homberger has examined a number of midcentury calotypes and photographs of Parisian nudes that formed part of a movement that aimed at greater accuracy (and thus realism) in visual culture. Taken by Gustave Le Gray, J.-F. Boitouzet, Bruno Braquehuis, and others, these pictures feature female models whose dirty soles and heels, together with their loosened stockings and scuffed slippers, remain conspicuous in each frame. Such details, Homberger remarks, "tell us much about the *bohème* world of young Parisian artists, their models and *grisettes*."[23] "They also hint," he adds, "at the large and highly visible world of commercial sex in Paris." In other words, it was not uncommon for prostitution (linked with sexual filth) and modeling (itself a physically dirty form of work) to draw on the same pool of labor.

Displaying her *"süssen füssen"* to an enraptured Little Billee, Trilby breezily remarks that she works as a model for Durien. "I pose for him in the altogether," she says (15). By the "altogether" she means the "*l'ensemble*"—in other words, the nude (15). The thought of her naked body deeply troubles him. Two days later, when he meets her again, Little

"WISTFUL AND SWEET."

Figure 7.2. George Du Maurier, "Wistful and Sweet," *Trilby, Harper's New Monthly Magazine,* 88 (December 1893): 175.

Billee surveys "the full-bosomed young *grisette*" with trepidation, since he realizes that the "thrill" she arouses in him is "only half aesthetic" (30). Looking into "the tender mirthfulness of her gaze," he perceives first of all her "well of sweetness" (30), then proceeds to her "heart of compassion" before recognizing "at the bottom of all—a thin slimy layer of sorrow and shame" (31) that at once attracts and repels him.

It is worth pausing for a moment with the "slimy layer" that Little Billee detects in the depths of Trilby's soul, since it resonates with the literal meaning of *la boue*: the mud that clogs the bottom of a canal. Almost everything about Trilby turns out to be in some respect degraded—and, by implication, sexually arousing. Assuredly, there is no evidence that Trilby earns money from commercial sex. But she nonetheless belongs to a disreputable class of women whose feet have touched the lowest rungs of society. Jerrold Seigel contends that "by the early 1840s, the mythology of the *grisette* had become a staple of romantic fantasy: available, grateful and understanding, unencumbered by bourgeois morality."[24] Such women had left the countryside in search of work. "From a middle-class perspective," Seigel observes, "the lives of *grisettes* often seemed attractive, independent and free from restraint" (41).

Trilby conforms to this type. Even though "her heart was not large enough to harbour more than one light love at the time" (37), she followed "love for love's sake . . . in a frolicsome spirit of camaraderie" (36). Little Billee does his utmost not to cloud his mind with this knowledge. His attention remains on the "momentary gleam and the dazzle of a pair of over-perfect feet" (35). But, as the narrator's adjectives suggest, Little Billee proves mistaken in his awe. Erroneously, he "idealized from the base upward" (35). By implication, he should have peered down on her murky depths, since such a headlong gaze would have prevented him from falling in love with her. Little Billee's "liberal education," however, led him to maintain a "democratic scorn" of social hierarchy (35). As a result, he fails to appreciate what it means for a ragpicker and a dealer in a bric-a-brac—traders in bohemian trash—to shelter a *grisette* whose rent comes in part from the "altogether." Their trade intimates Trilby's questionable origins. Laughably, she tells tall tales about her father, one "Patrick Michael O'Ferrall," claiming that he was a "Fellow of Trinity, Cambridge" (18). Soon after, the narrator states on good authority that Trilby was a "posthumous child," born ten months after the "drunkard" O'Ferrall's death (37). Illegitimate, Trilby, particularly to the late-Victorian eye, looks like the progeny of a squalid Irish Catholic. We learn next to nothing about her mother—"a beautiful Highland lassie of low degree" (37)—from whom Trilby has learned to speak her distinctive form of English.

Like everything else about her, Trilby's spoken voice sounds eccentric, not least because of its distinctive timbre. Completely inescapable is her "incipient *tenore robusto*" (13) that booms her hardly dulcet mode of speech. More than any other character, Trilby mangles practically every sentence that she chooses to articulate. Her embroiled heritage (dubiously Irish, Scottish, and French all at once) contributes to her carnivalesque expressions. Early in the story, she produces an outlandishly disordered utterance when trying to conciliate one of *les trois Angliches*. "I've brought you these objects of art and virtu to make peace with you," she says. "They're the real thing, you know. I borrowed 'em from le père Martin, chiffonier en gros et en détail, grand officier de la Légion d'Honneur, membre de l'Institut et cetera" (32). Appropriately enough, the various *objets d'art* in her possession are nothing more than junk that her ragpicking landlord swept off the streets. Noticeably, however, the narrator stresses the difference between her respective use of English and French. While speaking English, she displays "none of the ungainliness of so many Englishwomen" sharing her mother's "humble rank" (64). Her French, by comparison, is quintessentially of the *quartier latin*—"droll, slangy, piquant, quaint," insisting that she was "no lady" (64).

It is these linguistic blemishes that *les trois Angliches* determine to efface. While she dutifully darns their socks, they commence on a program of restoration, which attempts to convert her from a "slangy" *grisette* into a literate Englishwoman. First of all, they lend her books that will further cultivate her mother's tongue. Once she starts to consume the canonical works of Dickens, Thackeray, and Walter Scott, radical changes occur. The more she reads in English, the more she thinks in it as well. And the "nice clean English" (82) that runs through her head supposedly speaks to her better conscience. Thus the trio strives to extend the United Kingdom to this bastard child of Ireland who has strayed onto the streets of a disreputable foreign land. Yet, regardless of how many novels by Dickens, Thackeray, and Scott they place in her hands, their program of conversion to refined British culture remains incomplete. She tries to clean up her reputation as a dirt-removing *blanchisseuse de fin* (85) and, as a consequence, undergoes a "strange metamorphosis" (91), which ensures that she no longer resembles one of Gavarni's types (90). Yet Little Billee's mother recognizes that a mere "washerwoman" (123) would only "drag" her son "down" (126). Thus

Trilby frees Little Billee from the stigma of marrying a *grisette* by departing for the country with her young brother, Jeannot. In a sense, she has cleaned up perfectly by leaving no trace whatsoever of her whereabouts.

Trilby's exit hardly brings relief to a narrative in which her increasing moral cleanliness appears to undermine her authentic—because so crossbred—bohemian vitality. As her purity intensifies, she becomes practically lifeless, and the remaining chapters deplete what little vigor remained in the young men's listless desertion of Paris. The later part of *Trilby* culminates in the amazing scenes of mesmerism whose hypnotic power took hold of an equally transfixed readership in the mid-1890s. Yet much of the story from this point on discloses Du Maurier's conflicting, somewhat exhausted responses to the cultural associations that link *la bohème* with the *boue*, on the one hand, and bourgeois life with professionalism, on the other.

On leaving the station of the Chemin de Fer du Nord, Little Billee embarks on a respectable career that he soon despises because it isolates him from the mixed company and creative enthusiasm of the *quartier latin*. His consequent enfeeblement in England dramatizes a commonplace in the critical literature on *la bohème*: the cultural appeal of bohemian aesthetics lies in its perceived opposition to bourgeois economics. César Graña pinpoints the key question arising from this phenomenon. "[H]ow did it happen," he asks, "that while one section of the bourgeoisie was efficiently gathering profits with unbending matter-of-factness, another was giving itself over to philosophical despair, the cult of sensitivity, and the enthronement of non-utilitarian values?"[25] To Elizabeth Wilson, the answer is plain. By the time of Orléanist France, lackadaisical bohemia resisted the bourgeois imperative that art should become "just another commodity, to be produced speculatively in the hope that it would sell."[26] "Thus the artist," Wilson asserts, "was set against the bourgeois 'philistine': that crass and undiscriminating individual, for whom art was a status symbol" (17). Further, this standoff between bohemian and bourgeois resulted in a paradox "in which to succeed was, for the artist, to fail" (18) because commercial success betrayed the high ideal to create art for art's sake.

Only Little Billee's affiliation with a Jewish heritage, which the narrator associates with artistic genius, temporarily fortifies his creative energies. "[I]n his winning and handsome face," we learn, "there was just a faint suggestion of some possible very remote Jewish ancestor—

just a tinge of that strong, sturdy, irrepressible, indomitable, indelible blood which is of such priceless value in diluted homeopathic doses" (6–7). Elaine Showalter remarks that Little Billee thus embodies "elements of sexual and racial hybridization," which are "signs of his artistic potential," as well as "clues to his latent kinship with Svengali."[27] But Showalter does not show how these mongrel attributes connect him with the heterogeneity of *la bohème* while putting him at odds with his English homeland.

Were it not for the fact that the "Oriental blood kept him straight" (157), Little Billee would have been seduced by the hordes of pandering ladies of leisure, among them the "[h]ideous old frumps (osseous and obese, yet with unduly bared necks that made him sick)" (156). Making many such unpleasant asides, the narrator explains why Little Billee would abscond in order to savor "London life at its lower end—the eastest end of all" (157). In Whitechapel, the Minories, Ratcliffe Highway, the Docks, and Rotherhithe (areas rendered especially fearful in the late-Victorian imagination), he rediscovers a working-class culture that provides an English equivalent of the cheerful rowdiness that *Trilby* associates with the *quartier latin*. "He was," we learn, "especially fond of frequenting sing-songs, or 'free-and-easies,' where good hard-working fellows"—filled with "manly pluck"—"met of an evening to relax and smoke and drink and sing" (158).

Little Billee's encounters with "manly pluck," however, cannot brace his health, since the hysterical "brain fever" that has previously made him swoon continues to afflict him. True to his "girlish" side, he undergoes an "everlasting chronic plague of heart-insensibility" (160), in which he curses himself as a "puny, misbegotten shrimp" (162). Disillusioned with life, he displays what the narrator calls Little Billee's "unhappy portion of *la maladie du siècle*" (181). The only means of escaping a supposedly clean life based on English respectability and bourgeois professionalism is for Little Billee to rendezvous with his old pals in *la bohème*.

Thus we reach what promises to be the longed-for return to Paris. But it becomes immediately evident that the Britons' tour of old bohemian haunts results not in the recuperation of nostalgic bliss but in what can only be described as even more mortifying bourgeois monotony than Little Billee endured in London. After a lapse of five years, *les trois Angliches* attempt to reenact their student days as they pass "along the quay and up the Rue de Seine," following "well-remembered little mystic ways to the old studio in the Place St. Anatole des Arts" (197). Yet while they wander through the Left Bank they find "many changes": "A row of new houses on the north side, by Baron Haussmann—the well-named—a boulevard was being constructed right through the place" (197). When they locate the atelier where they shared such fun, they learn from the landlord that Carrel is dead. On this occasion, the shabby condition of the studio appalls them: "the window so dirty you could hardly see the houses opposite; the floor a disgrace" (200). The trio experience greatest heartache when they ponder Little Billee's lovelorn poem, "Pauvre Trilby," whose elegiac stanzas, together with a drawing of her shapely foot, have been preserved under glass. Saddened, they make their way down the appropriately named Rue Vielle des Trois Mauvais Ladres only to discover that, in this old leprous space, "about twenty yards of a high wall had been pulled down" just at the point "where the Laird had seen the last of Trilby" (204).

It is not long before they reencounter the *grisette* who vanished inexplicably from their lives. She, too, emerges in what is now Haussmann's Paris, and she, like its renovated cityscape, appears utterly transformed. During their evening at the fashionable Salles des Bashibazoucks, the Britons have no idea that she will tower before them as Madame Svengali: the diva who is about to sing a number of airs, including Schumann's "Nussbaum," a traditional French song, and "un impromptu de Chopin, sans paroles." This is, as the narrator states, "a somewhat incongruous bill of fare" (208). Overwhelmed, the Britons hear her "absolutely, mathematically pure" voice (211). Likewise, her phrasing is pure—"just as a child sings" (211). Throughout her beautifully executed performance, she shows no "expression whatever" while her eyes remain transfixed on Svengali, who keeps "beating time," "conducting her, in fact, as if she had been an orchestra" (210). Afterward, when they watch her pass in a carriage, Trilby responds to an anguished Little Billee "with a cold stare of disdain" (235). How could such transmogrification occur in Trilby? Why does she perform such an "incongruous" repertoire with mathematical precision?

The answers of course take us back to Svengali and those aspects of the novel that have absorbed most critical attention since its earliest publication. Much of the initial excitement that surrounded *Trilby* lay in the fervid discussion of whether Svengali's use of hypnotism was plausible. Throughout the fin de siècle, there was an immense amount of European debate about mesmerism that frequently concentrated on what Chas. Lloyd Tuckey in 1891 identified as the conflict between two leading French schools of thought: "That of the Salpêtriére, enunciated by the eminent physician, Charcot, is, that hypnotism is pathological, and, in fact, a form of hysteria, and occurs in hysterical subjects only; while the Nancy school contends that hypnosis is a physiological condition analogous to natural sleep, and that nearly all persons of sane mind can be hypnotised."[28] Mindful of these sources, not only the literary press but also medical journals like *The Alienist and Neurologist* eagerly asserted that "such vocalists as Trilby . . . are possibilities."[29] Some publications, however, were skeptical: *The Medical News* in Philadelphia would contend that Trilby's transformation into a diva was infeasible because "no matter what her vocal powers might be, she would be utterly incapable of harmonious song unless she could hear and correctly appreciate the tones of her own voice."[30]

Meanwhile, avid followers of what one journalist called "The Trail of 'Trilby'" would learn that Svengali's mesmeric manipulation of the credulous *grisette* originated in the experiments that the Jewish Moscheles practiced at the back of his mother's Antwerp shop.[31] "You'll see that I've used up all your Mesmerism," Du Maurier told his old friend about *Trilby*. (Moscheles's *In Bohemia with Du Maurier* [1897] recorded the fact [9].) But such biographical information hardly helps to explain Svengali's exploitation of Trilby. The novel's unquestionable anti-Semitism scarcely wreaks vengeance on Du Maurier's old Jewish friend. Nor do the late-nineteenth-century scientific disputes elucidate why hypnotism should be the powerful instrument of a Jewish maestro.

What hypnotism does relate to is artistic professionalism, which the narrative constantly associates with doses of Jewish blood. In *Trilby*, such doses are frequently in the wrong quantities. They are exaggerated in Svengali and diminished in Little Billee. Bearing this point in mind, Dennis Denisoff maintains that both Little Billee and Svengali—whatever other distinctions come between them—occupy different points along "a spectrum of genius," one that is "imbued throughout by ethnicity, sexual unconventionality, and musicality," which becomes "tainted by concerns with fame, money, and self-advertising."[32] Svengali's moneymaking proves especially tainted because it arises from a midcentury suspicion of a particular profession. As Alison Winter shows, the rise of the "baton conductor" in the 1820s and 1830s whose "powerful ability to unite and direct a group" characterized him as a controversial figure.[33] Demanding complete silence, the "baton conductor" was often perceived as an almost oppressive source of authority over orchestra, performer, and audience alike.

Under Svengali's baton, the hypnotized Trilby represents not only oppression under Jewish professional prowess; her flawless presentation is also like a façade that attempts to block our view of her bohemian dirtiness. In making several references to the architectural transformation that Paris rapidly underwent in the 1860s, the narrator indicates that Trilby's "mathematical" presentation—both historically and physically—relates to a larger shift in Parisian life: Svengali's attempts to depurate Trilby correspond to the numbing effects of Haussmann's urban scheming. At midcentury many critics saw that the Second Empire's accelerated methods of refurbishing—and, indeed, deodorizing—Paris produced what Christopher Prendergast calls "a city without surprise": a place whose "rectiligne" streets and "géométrique" boulevards produced a persistent feeling of "monotone."[34] Likewise, Svengali's hypnotic sway over Trilby makes her far too sanitized—to the point that her colorlessness can seem almost inhuman.

Far from literally dirtying Trilby, Svengali—now donning "irreproachable evening dress" (208)—would appear to have done quite the opposite by making everything about his presence and her performance appear as clean and professional as possible. But as her fame spreads, we soon detect that this polished act is at base "incongruous" not just in its "bill of fare." Certainly, La Svengali inspires awe. Du Maurier takes the liberty of imputing that Gautier wrote a poem that wondered if she were "*Ange, ou Femme*" ["Angel or Woman"] (220). So phenomenal is her success that no one can fully understand the seeming perfection that she embodies. But no matter how much her performance crescendos "like the lovely bouquet of fireworks at show" (220), it becomes noticeable that she wears so much "rouged and pearl-powered" maquillage that the kohl around her eyes makes them look like "disfigurements" (234). The artificial, distorting sheen of makeup soon appears on the celebrity photographs that implicitly degrade her image even further in the shop-windows of London where "presentments of Madame Svengali in all sizes and costumes" await the clamoring crowds (243–44).

How, then, might the narrative retrieve Trilby from her clean-looking, entrancing, but ultimately debasing relationship with Svengali? Would it be best to return her from the hypnotizing world of professional performance to the buoyant *boue* where she screeched "Ben Bolt"? In the closing pages, the narrator must confront the plain truth that there are limits to the "dirty pleasure" that he might derive from either slinging mud at bourgeois pretentiousness or purging the less palatable filth of *la bohème*. Thus in the final chapters the once-enthusiastic storyteller fails in his efforts to get Trilby back to where she belongs without contaminating her any further. Having shown how celebrity has made

Trilby into a mass-reproducible commodity, the narrative voice recalls how she was released from Svengali's entrapment when her artificial edifice as an aloof diva crumbled into the dust. By breaking Svengali's spell, the narrator wants to reveal that the illusory spectacle of professional prowess—like hypnosis itself—amounts to a temporary entertainment whose despicable trickery can only end in ruin. When Svengali drops dead during Trilby's London debut, her voice degenerates into the "most lamentably grotesque performance ever heard out of a human throat" (250), and thus her native filthiness spills back into the streets from whence it came. Once the audience starts laughing, Trilby scorns everyone as "*tas de vielle pommes*" ["rotten old potatoes"] (250).

This excruciating episode embarrassingly reveals that the only means of terminating Svengali's bourgeois hold over Trilby involves dragging her back into the bohemian *boue*. And yet the filth of *la bohème*, no matter how preferable it might appear to bourgeois cleanliness, contains adulterated elements from which the narrator knows she must be reclaimed. Since Du Maurier proves unwilling to rehabilitate the heroine among the scum of the earth, he pushes his narrative toward an indecisive compromise whose meandering melancholia offsets the exuberance of the novel's rather maudlin first half. Toward the end, the onetime *grisette* remains transplanted in England, the nation of constipated values, which would seem hardly propitious for her revitalization. She thus rests, awaiting death, in the care of Mrs. Bagot, whose maternal love cherishes her as a "fast-fading lily" raised on "very questionable soil" (271).

The far-from-shapely ending of the novel may seem in keeping with the unfinished, amateurish, and antiprofessional aesthetic that Du Maurier strives to establish at the start. But his muddied nostalgia remains predicated on the knowledge that what it would like to retrieve proves irrecoverable because it is simply too filthy to handle. Thus death also is the only option for Little Billee, who, like Trilby, has suffered greatly throughout the narrative's erratic exchanges between purity and pollution, given its intermittent movement back and forth between bourgeois London and bohemian Paris.

The aftermath of Little Billee's demise sets Taffy and the Laird at an even further distance from their beloved bohemia. By this point Du Maurier remains uncertain whether his novel can ever recuperate any of its previous gusto by returning to what little Haussmann has left of *la bohème*. While the Laird retreats to a marriage in Dundee, Taffy weds Little Billee's sister. Twenty years on, long after Haussmann retired from his prefecture, Mr. and Mrs. Wynne "laze and flane about the boulevards, and buy things, and lunch anywhere" (290). But, for all their bourgeois habits, they remain haunted by bohemian legend—especially the elusive events that occurred between Svengali and Trilby after the three young Britons departed for their homeland. Thus the honorable couple retrace the steps of *les trois Angliches*, discovering that the studio where they thrived in 1856–57 is "now very spick and span, and most respectable," inhabited by two "coldly civil" American artists who resent the Wynnes' disruption of their work (290). The very fact that the studio looks clean, clinical, and professional leaves them feeling "quite chilly" (301)—to the point that they decide to depart from streamlined Paris forever.

Before they take their leave, however, the respectable Wynnes continue to "flane" along the "rectilinge" boulevards (consuming, whenever they can, such cultural glories as the Sèvres factory and the Hôtel de Cluny). All the while, they remain mindful of the enduring mystery of Trilby. And through an act of distinctly bohemian serendipity, an answer of sorts comes from Svengali's Hungarian accompanist Gecko ("a gypsy, possibly—much pitted with smallpox" [11]), whom the British trio knew in their youth. "*There were two Trilbys*," Gecko informs the Wynnes (298). One was a "singing-machine . . . the unconscious voice that Svengali sang with," the other knew "nothing at all" of the likes of Schumann and Chopin (299). One dead, another asleep: this explanation of Trilby's divided condition provides the novel's final effort to wipe off the mud and put what happened in clear perspective. Aptly, once they make this discovery, the Wynnes watch the dawn rise over Paris, peering out at "the deserted boulevards, where an army of scavengers, noiseless and taciturn, was cleansing the asphalt roadway" (300).

This spectacle, however, does not throw perfect light upon the divided Trilby: a figure torn asunder, like the novel itself, between purity and pollution, England and France, and the bourgeoisie and *la bohème*. The dawn illuminates a troubled image of the changes wrought by Haussmann's Paris. Here the Britons no longer perceive this trader in trash as a member of the ambulant camaraderie that characterized the *quartier latin*. For the first time, Taffy witnesses the *chiffonier* as a downtrodden scavenger whose ragpicking keeps the clean-cut boulevards free of litter. This bleak prospect leaves it unclear as to which is worse: the clean "asphalt" that has regimented Paris of the Second Empire or the abject misery of the *chiffonier*—whose wretchedness formed the basis of Marx's powerful concept of the "passive dungheap" that comprised the lumpenproletariat.[35]

Where Marx's "Eighteenth Brumaire of Louis Napoleon" (1852) proposed a theory of *la bohème*, Du Maurier's *Trilby*, published over forty years later, possessed none. The same was true of Du Maurier's response to mesmerism. "Of the mechanism of *Trilby*," he informed one of many pestering journalists, "I can tell you nothing."[36] The fact that neither he nor his novel remained able or willing to explain how the maestro transformed the *grisette* into his instrument meant that thousands of readers rushed out to consume the narrative as a magical commodity worthy of speculation. But *Trilby*'s runaway success—together with the bric-a-brac it spawned (puzzles, games, sweets, even toothpaste), in addition to a stage play and numerous burlesques[37]—could not compensate Du Maurier for the vanished bohemia that he wished but could only fail to revivify. In his tribute to Du Maurier, Henry James remarked in 1897 that the "violence of publicity" that surrounded *Trilby* did not leave Du Maurier's failing health "untroubled and unadulterated": it "darkened all [Du Maurier's] sky with a hugeness of vulgarity."[38] The "landslide of obsessions, of inane, incongruous letters, of interviewers, intruders, invaders, some of them innocent enough"—in all their "irresponsible chatter"—proved "maddening."

The blatant irony is that Du Maurier was at last subjected to a type of gossipy vulgarity that *Trilby* would like to preserve in his 1850s bohemian Paris but not in his 1890s bourgeois London. In a sense, the obnoxious commercialism that was aroused by *Trilby* generated for him an unbearable type of "dirty pleasure" that could not have come at a worse time. As his physical vitality waned, Du Maurier had to contend with the paradox that his contamination as a celebrity arose from his impossible desire to sink back, as much he could, into the *boue*.

Notes

Several colleagues have offered me guidance on a number of sources. My thanks go to Malcolm Baker, Paula Gillett, Ruth E. Iskin, Margaret D. Stetz, and Thomas Wortham. For materials on late-nineteenth-century debates about mesmerism, I am particularly grateful to Jill Galvan. I have also benefited from listening to Chris Waters discuss how the periodical press of the 1880s and 1890s engaged the controversies surrounding hypnotism. At UCLA James Walter Caufield provided invaluable research assistance.

1. G. E. Haussmann, *Mémoires du baron Haussmann*, 3 vols. (Paris, 1890–93), 3:535–36, quoted in David H. Pinkney, *Napoleon III and the Rebuilding of Paris* (Princeton, NJ: Princeton University Press, 1958), 16 (Pinkney's translation); further page references appear in parentheses.

2. George Du Maurier, *Trilby*, ed. Elaine Showalter and Dennis Denisoff (Oxford: Oxford University Press, 1998), 53; further page references appear in parentheses. This edition is based on the first single-volume, illustrated edition that was published in London by Osgoode, MacIlvaine in 1894. As I explore

later, the 1894 text differs in some important respects from the text that appeared in serial form in *Harper's New Monthly Magazine* 88 (1893) and 89 (1894).

3. Marilyn R. Brown, *Gypsies and Other Bohemians: The Myth of the Artist in Nineteenth-Century France* (Ann Arbor, MI: UMI Press, 1985), 3; further reference appears on this page.

4. Karl Marx, "The Eighteenth Brumaire of Louis Napoleon" (1852) in Marx, *Later Political Writings*, ed. and trans. Terrell Carver (Cambridge: Cambridge University Press, 1996), 78. Marx's discussion focuses on "the dregs, refuse and scum of all classes" (78) that Louis Napoleon rallied in his Society of 10 December 1850, which displayed the "unconditional support" of the dispossessed classes for the Bonapartist bid for power.

5. Walter Benjamin, *Charles Baudelaire: A Lyric Poet in the Era of High Capitalism*, trans. Harry Zohn (London: New Left Books, 1973), 17; further page reference appears in parentheses.

6. Théophile Gautier, "The Garret," in *Enamels and Cameos*, trans. Agnes Lee, *The Works of Théophile Gautier*, 24 vols. (New York: George D. Sproul, 1900–1903), 24:164; further page reference appears in parentheses.

7. See, for example, Honoré de Balzac, "Un Prince de la Bohème" (1840); Alfred de Musset, "Mimi Pinson" (1844); and Louis Huárt, *Physiologie de la grisette—vignettes de Gavarni* (1842). Murger's *Scènes* inspired Giacomo Puccini's famous opera *La Bohème* (1896).

8. Du Maurier, *Trilby, Harper's Monthly Magazine* 88 (1894): 577.

9. James McNeill Whistler, *Pall Mall Gazette*, 15 May 1894, quoted in Leonée Ormond, *George Du Maurier* (London: Routledge and Kegan Paul, 1969), 466. For a comprehensive reading of Whistler's indignation, see Stanley Weintraub, *Whistler: A Biography* (New York: Weybright and Talley, 1974), 385–94. Weintraub points out that "the *Trilby* affair damaged Whistler" (394), who eventually realized that his loud protests to Du Maurier's publisher could not prevent its immense commercial success. Whistler's infamous hostility toward his contemporaries—such as John Ruskin and Oscar Wilde—appears in his *Gentle Art of Making Enemies* (1890).

10. Robert H. Sherard, "The Author of 'Trilby': An Autobiographic Interview with Mr. George Du Maurier," *McClure's Magazine* 4 (1895): 397.

11. Felix Moscheles, *In Bohemia with Du Maurier: The First of a Series of Reminscences* (New York: Harper Brothers, 1897), 29; further page reference appears in parentheses.

12. Ormond, *George Du Maurier*, 86; further reference appears on this page.

13. In March 1889, Henry James made a notebook entry that recorded Du Maurier's outline of the plot of what would become *Trilby*: in *Complete Notebooks of Henry James*, ed. Leon Edel and Lyall H. Powers (New York: Oxford University Press, 1987), 51–52.

14. [Anonymous,] Review of George Du Maurier, *Trilby, The Literary World* (Boston), 22 September 1894, 299.

15. See L. Edward Pearsall, "Trilby and Trilby-Mania: The Beginning of the Bestseller System," *Journal of Popular Culture* 11 (1977), 69.

16. Juliet Steyn, "Charles Dickens's *Oliver Twist*: Fagin as a Sign," in *The Jew in the Text: Modernity and the Construction of Identity*, ed. Linda Nochlin and Tamar Garb (London: Thames and Hudson, 1995), 48. Svengali appears at one extreme of a range of Jewish characters in Du Maurier's novel. Svengali's "ghastly French, pronounced with a Hebrew-Jewish accent" (92) associates him with the Yiddish-speaking Ashkenazim, whose desertion of Russia after the pogroms of the early 1880s ultimately led in Britain to the Aliens Act of 1905, which aimed to restrict Jewish immigration. By contrast, the great singer Gloriori, depicted as a "human nightingale" or "male rossignol" (168) is praised as "the biggest, handsomest, and most distinguished-looking Jew that ever was"; his dignity arises from the fact that he is "one of the Sephardim," which the narrator playfully celebrates as "one of the Seraphim" (168). In some respects, Glorioni occupies a median point between Svengali and Little Billee; he combines, as they do not, artistic preeminence with commercial prosperity (he has a share in his family's wine business).

17. Edgar Rosenberg, *From Shylock to Svengali: Jewish Stereotypes in English Fiction* (Stanford, CA: Stanford University Press, 1960), 241; further reference appears on this page.

18. On the figure of the Wandering Jew in midcentury French art and literature, see Brown, *Gypsies and Other Bohemians*, 61–62. In this context, Brown mentions Eugène Sue's serial novel *Le Juif errant* (1844–45) and Edgar Quinet's prose poem *Ahasvérus* (1833), among other works, in relation to Gustave Courbet's self-presentation as a "wandering artist" in his painting *The Meeting* (1854).

19. Daniel Pick, "Introduction," in George Du Maurier, *Trilby*, ed. Daniel Pick (Harmondsworth, UK: Penguin, 1994), xxii; further references appear on this page.

20. Daniel Pick, *Svengali's Web: The Alien Enchanter in Modern Culture* (New Haven, CT: Yale University Press, 2000), 15.

21. Nina Auerbach, *Woman and the Demon: The Life of a Victorian Myth* (Cambridge, MA: Harvard University Press, 1982), 17.

22. Mary Russo, *The Female Grotesque: Risk, Excess, and Modernity* (New York: Routledge, 1992), 137; further page references appear in parentheses.

23. Eric Homberger, "The Model's Unwashed Feet: French Photography in the 1850s," in *Artistic Relations: Literature and the Visual Arts in Nineteenth-Century France*, ed. Peter Collier and Robert Lethbridge (New Haven, CT: Yale University Press, 1994), 140.

24. Jerrold Seigel, *Bohemian Paris: Culture, Politics, and the Boundaries of Bourgeois Life, 1830–1930* (New York: Viking Penguin, 1986), 41; further page references appear in parentheses.

25. César Graña, *Bohemian versus Bourgeois: French Society and the French Man of Letters in the Nineteenth Century* (New York: Basic Books, 1964), 17.

26. Elizabeth Wilson, *Bohemians: The Glamorous Outcasts* (London: I. B. Tauris, 2000), 17; further page references appear in parentheses.

27. Elaine Showalter, "Introduction," in Du Maurier, *Trilby*, xvi.

28. Chas. Lloyd Tuckey, "The Applications of Hypnotism," *Contemporary Review* 40 (1891), 672. Tuckey's essay counts as one of dozens on hypnotism and mesmerism that appeared in the late-Victorian periodical press. For a survey of these materials, see Alan Gauld, *A History of Hypnotism* (Cambridge: Cambridge University Press, 1992).

29. *The Alienist and Neurologist*, July 1895, quoted in "Is the Hypnotic Episode in 'Trilby' Possible?" *Literary Digest* 11 (1895), 645.

30. "The Pathologoic Novel," *Medical News*, 5 October 1895, quoted in "Is the Hypnotic Episode in 'Trilby' Possible?" 733.

31. Albert D. Vandam, "The Trail of 'Trilby,'" *Forum and Century* 20 (1895), 429–44. Vandam claims that Trilby's experience is based on Jean-Martin Charcot's experiments on "a girl of great plastic beauty"—Élise Duval—who was a "favorite model of MM. Gérôme and Benjamin Constant" (435).

32. Dennis Denisoff, "'Men of My Own Sex': Genius, Sexuality, and George Du Maurier's Artists," in *Victorian Sexual Dissidence*, ed. Richard Dellamora (Chicago: University of Chicago Press, 1999), 154.

33. Alison Winter, *Mesmerized: Powers of Mind in Victorian Britain* (Chicago: University of Chicago Press, 1998), 310. It is valuable to compare Winter's powerful discussion with Jonathan Freedman's discussion of Svengali's central position as both mesmerist and musical genius. "Mesmerism," Freedman observes, "has been habitually associated with the figure of the Jew in contemporary [i.e., nineteenth-century] discourses. . . . His hypnotic power combines with his sexual appetencies"; moreover, "the connection of the Jew to musical genius (or lack thereof) was a particularly hot topic in the nineteenth century, both in England and on the Continent, and one that places Svengali in the middle of a full-scale cultural debate about Jewishness and artistry negotiated in terms of music" (*The Temple of Culture: Assimilation and Anti-Semitism in Literary Anglo-America* [New York: Oxford University Press, 2002], 108).

34. Christopher Prendergast, *Paris and the Nineteenth Century* (Oxford: Blackwell, 1992), 10–11. Prendergast offers as a representative example of the use of "monotone" to describe Haussmannization the words of Pierre-Joseph Proudhon: "la ville neuve, monotone et fatigante de M. Haussmann, avec ses boulevards rectiligne," quoted in George Duveau, *La Vie ouvrière en France sous, le Second Empire* (Paris: Gallimard, 1946), 206. Prendergast's line of inquiry appears to owe much to T. J. Clark, *The Painting of Modern Life: Paris in the Art of Manet and His Followers* (New York: Alfred A. Knopf, 1984). Clark comments that "the city that resulted from this fever [of Haussmannization] was supposed to be regular, empty, and boring." "There was," he adds, "no more multiformity in Paris, no more surprise, no more *Paris inconnu*" (43).

35. Marx, "Manifesto of the Communist Party" (1848), in Marx, *Later Political Writings*, 11. The etymology of *lumpenproletariat* derives from the

German *Lumpen* (rags) of the Latin *proletarius* (progeny). It was from this "ragged" mass that Marx's revolutionary proletariat would arise.

36. Addison Bright, "Mr. Du Maurier at Home," *The Idler* 8 (1895), 429.

37. Paul Potter's stage version of *Trilby* opened at the Boston Museum on 4 March 1895 and at the Haymarket Theatre, London, on 30 October 1895. There were countless burlesques of the play, including William Muskerry's *Thrillby* (with a lead named Spaghetti) at the Garrick Theatre, London. For an account of these dramatic spin-offs, together with a survey of the commercial detritus that circulated in light of the novel's success, see J. B. Gilder and J. L. Gilder, *Trilbyana: The Rise and Progress of a Popular Novel* (New York: The Critic, 1895) and Pick, *Svengali's Web*, 41–43.

38. Henry James, "George Du Maurier," *Harper's Monthly Magazine* 45 (1897): 607; further references appear on this page.

Chapter 8

Merdre! Performing Filth in the Bourgeois Public Sphere

Neil Blackadder

> We dare not speak about shit. But, since the beginning of time,
> no other subject—not even sex—has caused us to speak so much.
> — *Dominique Laporte*, History of Shit

It was "the word" which, greeted by the spectators with laughs or
whistles, with applause and boos, played the starring role. It fluttered
about from the stalls to the circle, and was exchanged from seat to seat.[1]

The word to which Henri de Régnier refers, in his 1933 memoir about
Alfred Jarry, is *merdre*, the young writer's playful and provocative defor-
mation of *merde*, which figured prominently both in Jarry's play *Ubu
Roi* and in the audience response when the play premiered in Paris in
December 1896. The two performances were among the most uproarious in the history of the French theater, and led to an outpouring of
indignation from the critics, most of whom dismissed *Ubu Roi* as, for
instance, a "filthy fraud [*fumisterie ordurière*] that deserves nothing but
the silence of contempt."[2] Yet the public reaction generated by Jarry's
taboo-breaking play was anything but silent, and the confrontation
between *Ubu Roi* and its first spectators constitutes a singular site for
the performance of turn-of-the-century bourgeois attitudes toward filth.
Reflecting afterward on the audience response, Jarry wrote: "It is because the public are an inert and obtuse and passive mass that they need
to be shaken up from time to time so that we can tell from their bear-
like grunts where they are—and where they stand."[3] By bringing filth
into the public sphere with *Ubu Roi* at a time when the bourgeoisie

increasingly treated excretion as a private matter, Jarry induced the spectators to a revealing display of their own ambivalence toward bodily functions.

The five acts of *Ubu Roi* depict the rise and fall of Père Ubu, an obese, foul-mouthed buffoon who leads a plot to kill the Polish king, usurps the throne, and briefly rules with an uncompromising and frequently cruel devotion to enriching and gratifying himself. The king's son and heir returns (with the help of Bordure, one of Ubu's co-conspirators whom he had promptly betrayed), defeats Ubu in battle, and takes back the throne; but Ubu's cowardice enables him to survive and escape into exile. This cartoon-like parody of *Macbeth* unfolds through a series of short scenes of seldom plausible, often funny, and more often crude dialogue. And the word *merdre* recurs throughout. In the first act alone, Père Ubu says the word ten times; his wife, Mère Ubu, six; by the end of the complete text, *merdre* has been pronounced thirty-three times. This eccentric play was unlike the work of any other dramatist in 1890s France, bearing little resemblance either to the earnest treatment of social issues in realistic theater, or to the static, elusive would-be poetry of symbolist drama. Most of Jarry's contemporaries regarded his play as a hoax that would be remembered as such, if not forgotten entirely; beginning in the 1920s, however, *Ubu Roi* came to be recognized as a startlingly prescient representation of human beings' capacity for selfishness and brutality.

By the time it premiered, the text of *Ubu Roi* had been published three times in different versions, and Jarry had mounted a publicity campaign that in literary and artistic circles excited great eagerness to see the much-talked-about and already-controversial new play. If a Parisian in December 1896 knew only one detail about *Ubu Roi*, that detail was its opening and most characteristic word: *merdre*. Not surprisingly, that single element of the play's vocabulary became the primary focus of its supporters' expectations before the performances, and of their opponents' outrage during and after them. As Géroy put it in his recollections of salon conversation in 1896: "everyone was waiting with curiosity to see what effect would be produced first by the work and second by the 'word,' the famous word enriched with a sixth roaring and sonorous letter."[4] The very distinction between the play as a whole and this single word is a dubious one: there was no way for *Ubu Roi* to have an effect without *merdre* doing so. Then as now, the word *merde* was used, with varying degrees of frequency and openness, by French people of high as well as low social rank—as reflected by the euphemism "le mot de Cambronne," which alludes to one of Napoleon's generals who reportedly exclaimed "Merde!" during the defeat at Waterloo. Émile Zola, in an 1891 article, captured both the widespread usage and the force of the word in advising young writers to "dire merde au siècle" ["say shit to the century"].[5] Yet it was one thing to write this widely used though transgressive word, another to utter it in public: it was still virtually inconceivable that what Laurent Tailhade dubbed "the essential word of French parlance" might be spoken in a play performed by one of Paris's respectable theaters.[6] It is a striking illustration of the radical nature of Jarry's decision to highlight this word that, even half a century later, Géroy, like Régnier in the 1930s, repeatedly refers to it as "le 'mot,'" and avoids spelling it out. A more recent critic explains that in the 1890s the stage was still regarded as a "privileged site for the conservation of fine language, which has always been above common practice," so that Jarry's act of writing *Ubu Roi* amounted to "the laying waste of theatrical language."[7]

While the significance and status of the word *merde* may have remained largely unaltered in the course of the nineteenth century, the treatment of human and other waste in French society had changed considerably. As cities rapidly grew, the inadequacy of existing sanitation systems had become increasingly apparent. During the Second Empire in particular, much ingenuity and technology was employed to improve waste management. As part of the Haussmannization of Paris, the city's sewer system was expanded during the 1850s and 1860s to more than five times its previous size and grew further during the Third Republic. Yet there was substantial resistance to the *tout-à-l'égout*, and it was not until 1894 that the city was authorized to require property owners to connect their buildings to the system.[8] By the turn of the century still fewer than ten percent of Paris houses were hooked up, and "two out of every three lodgings in France had no lavatory at all." Eugen Weber demonstrates that conditions in many parts of the country in the 1880s and 1890s showed virtually no sign of progress in sanitation: "Many things were performed in the street, as they had been for centuries, including the natural functions of men and beasts"; large as well as small cities "saw their household garbage, sewage, and kitchen waste discarded in the gutters, chamberpots emptied in alleyway or street, the contents of cesspits removed in open tipcarts."[9]

Improvements in municipal waste management were accompanied by a shift in attitudes toward various kinds of dirt and to the odors associated with them; but on that level, too, change was gradual and uneven. As Weber puts it, "cleanliness forged ahead—slowly, like everything else, hesitating before established prejudice reinforced by antediluvian facilities." In the 1890s, it was still the case that few French people, even among the wealthiest, washed with any frequency, and all of them smelled; "Around 1900 a Parisian noted that a maid newly arrived in town could not even distinguish between what is dirty and what is not: 'For the distinction is not evident for everybody, and it has only started to be made during the last few years.'"[10] That new preoccupation with cleanliness among the dominant classes did not simply derive from the realization that better sanitation would help minimize the spread of disease. Alain Corbin writes: "In the nineteenth century modesty and shame were important determinants of behavior," and the fears lying behind those feelings "led to self-discipline, as people sought to prevent any organic manifestation of the body's existence."[11] An ever greater premium came to be placed on privacy: as Georges Vigarello observes, "The exclusion of others became an obligatory element in the cleanliness of the elite at the end of the nineteenth century."[12] In one clear manifestation of that mindset, around 1900 lavatories and bathrooms began to be equipped with locks.[13]

As many historians and other critics have pointed out, the aspirations of the French middle and upper classes to an unaccustomed degree of fresh-smelling cleanliness also composed part of a crucial social and political development: in Corbin's words, "the elite was impelled by a desire to distinguish itself from the foul-smelling populace."[14] One of Weber's general remarks in a brief introduction to his study of fin-de-siècle France is that "those details that helped maintain the difference between social orders were being whittled down." By way of an example, he later includes two pictures of street-car interiors from the 1890s which "illustrate the new democracy of public transport, where elegant ladies and men of the world rubbed shoulders with the lower classes."[15] As Peter Stallybrass and Allon White remark in analyzing changes in the nineteenth-century city, that unprecedented intermingling among social classes was anything but welcome to many of the better off: "The tram, the railway station, the ice rink, above all the streets themselves, were shockingly promiscuous." The aversion to such promiscuity manifested itself as a fear of being touched and thus contaminated, but also through self-serving disgust; in Stallybrass and White's formulation, "Disgust was inseparable from refinement: whilst it designated the 'depraved' domain of the poor, it simultaneously established the purified domain of the bourgeoisie."[16] Jarry's forceful foregrounding of bodily functions in *Ubu Roi* thus contravened both the bourgeoisie's efforts to embrace new standards of cleanliness and their wish to regard such standards as setting them apart: he brought into the public arena of the theater an aspect of life that the Parisians who formed the audience were trying to make more private than ever before.

In breaking the taboo surrounding the use of *merde* in the bourgeois public sphere, Jarry chose not to preserve the word in its established form, but to add an extra *r*. The neologism *merdre* was one of the many features of *Ubu Roi* that Jarry drew directly from the schoolboy pranks in which his play originated: at the *lycée* Jarry attended in Rennes, pupils had for some years devised mock epics ridiculing a fat, incompetent physics teacher called Hébert. The hero became *le père Heb* or *Ébé*, and a range of invented and altered words developed, including *merdre*. The additional *r*, far from diminishing the force of *merde*, makes the obscenity both more effective and more complex. Most simply, the extra letter augments the acoustic effect of the word. The two syllables of *merde* sound like only one because the second is a mute *e*; the addition of the extra *r* makes the second syllable more distinct. This elongates the word and the obscenity, and provides the speaker with greater scope for enunciating "merd-re" in an expressive and aggressive manner. Furthermore, by modifying *merde*, Jarry accentuated the offensiveness of the word. If the extra letter ostensibly changes and thereby disguises *merde*, it does this so ineffectually that the addition actually serves to underline rather than camouflage the obscenity. A word that has been disguised but remains absolutely recognizable draws attention to itself. As one reviewer wrote—in a punning remark whose degree of irony it is difficult to gauge—"It was in vain that Mr. Jarry put in *r* [air]—it did not smell good."[17] Finally, in retaining the schoolboys' idea of adding the extra *r*, Jarry made the word *merdre* the keystone of Père Ubu's inventive and idiosyncratic vocabulary. Ubu's language features many resonant—and virtually untranslatable—neologisms such as "rastron" and "cornegidouille," whose distinctiveness contributed to the notoriety author and play acquired before and after the first production. (In her biography of Jarry, for instance, Rachilde—an important friend and supporter of the young writer—recalls that Père Ubu's lexicon was borrowed not only by journalists but even by "carters who, from time to time, added the *r* to accentuate the swear-word!"[18]) When *merdre* was first introduced to the public, part of the effect of the supplementary letter was to make Jarry's assault on the audience via Père Ubu more direct and personal: just as *merdre* simultaneously is not and yet is *merde*, so *merdre* is simultaneously a word that only Père Ubu uses and one that everyone uses.

Ubu Roi was performed twice in December 1896 by the avant-garde Théâtre de l'Œuvre: the actual premiere took place on Thursday, December 9, one day after the *répétition générale*—the public dress rehearsal attended largely by Jarry's fellow writers and artists as well as the most prominent and influential drama critics. Tailhade compared the fracas over Jarry's determinedly unconventional work with the famous premiere of Victor Hugo's Romantic drama *Hernani* in 1830: "a battle of *Hernani* between the young schools of Decadence and Symbolism, and the bourgeois critics."[19] Certainly the conflict between mostly young artists and their associates on the one hand and the older representatives of established cultural standards on the other underlay the pandemonium, especially at the *générale*. Yet both houses of close to a thousand spectators also included, between those two poles, many who were not predisposed either to support or oppose Jarry's play. And however much the audiences may have varied in age and aesthetic orientation, almost all the spectators belonged to a quite limited cross section of the Paris population. By 1896, fringe theaters [*théâtres à côté*] like the Théâtre de l'Œuvre had formed part of the capital's theatrical landscape for almost a decade—since André Antoine founded the Théâtre Libre in 1887—yet remained the province of a minority. Commercial theater flourished in fin-de-siècle Paris by providing a range of formulaic entertainment. The boulevard theater, which had come into being half a century earlier, continued to thrive on the well-made plays of authors like Sardou—writers described by one contemporary critic as "makers of digestive plays, for whom theater is a complement to dessert."[20] Increasingly spectacular productions of melodrama drew large audiences, and suburban theaters catered to the limited resources and particular tastes of the lower classes. Organizations like the Théâtre de l'Œuvre, by contrast, offered occasional productions of new work that interested only those who followed the latest artistic developments. Few if any working-class Parisians were likely to attend productions by the Œuvre, and the same appears to be true for members of the aristocracy; so although Tailhade characterizes only the critics as bourgeois, most members of the two audiences brought to *Ubu Roi* the expectations and values of the bourgeoisie.

Jarry himself—only twenty-three at the time—directed the first production of *Ubu Roi*, and ensured that the script's pronounced antirealism was further enhanced by the staging: a single decor was maintained throughout in spite of the play's multiple settings, armies were represented by just a few actors, and the principal characters were played with masks and heavy accents. Both performances prompted considerable uproar: one reviewer described the house as "turbulent, very combative, curious, bursting into applause and protests, laughter and whistling mixed in with the bravos."[21] Reviews and memoirs provide a less detailed picture of the premiere than of the *générale*, though it seems that on the second evening, when the audience comprised fewer people inclined to support Jarry, and more who were genuinely surprised and shocked by his play, the reactions were more consistently negative. Many critics and other observers of the two evenings commented that the performance in the auditorium supplanted the one on stage: "the performance [*le spectacle*] was the auditorium itself."[22] One contemporary review depicted the conflict during the *générale* between those for and those against the performance through a succinct sampling of utterances: "'Bravo!' 'It's disgraceful!' 'It's superb!' 'It's idiotic!' 'You wouldn't understand Shakespeare!' etc."[23] The mode of description adopted by Catulle Mendès highlighted the range of reaction prompted by *Ubu Roi*: "Whistling and hissing? yes; yells of rage and groans of malicious laughter? yes; seats ready to fly onto the stage? yes; occupants of boxes screaming and shaking their fists? yes; and in a word a whole throng, furious at being the victims of a hoax, jumping with a start toward the stage."[24] While Mendès's and some other reviews indicate a considerable degree of tension in the auditorium during the *générale*—"From the middle of the first act one senses that things are going to turn nasty"[25]—most of the critics represented the skirmish as quite good natured. That impression emerges even from some of the negative reviews, which expressed satisfaction at the way the spectators had resisted Jarry's attack on established notions of propriety. Thus prominent conservative critic Francisque Sarcey wrote: "I noted with pleasure that the audience (this nonetheless very special audience one finds at performances by the Œuvre) eventually rebelled against this excess of ineptitude and obscenity."[26] Sarcey's explanation for the spectators' failure to immediately protest against Jarry's play appears to be that these were not typical spectators, but the exceptional patrons of the Œuvre, who were prepared to tolerate more than the average audience. But part of the reason is that, for much of the *générale* at least, *Ubu Roi* entertained many in the audience for some time before it offended them.

Many of the contemporary critics who regarded *Ubu Roi* as an elaborate and tasteless practical joke further argued that the audience's counterperformance was superior to the spectacle on stage; for example, "beginning in the second act, the evening was nothing but a series of jibes in the auditorium, the least witty of which was without question less inept, and above all less disgusting than what was being said on stage."[27] In fact, many of the shouted retorts adopted the vulgarity of Jarry's script, and in particular of its most prominent word *merdre*; in some instances the spectators took up Jarry's neologism with humor, in others with real hostility. Although Régnier's account of the starring role played by *merdre* should perhaps be taken with a grain of salt, given that it was written almost forty years later, one of the contemporary reviews confirms his basic contention: "the first word of the play recurs all the time; the audience gets angry and sends it back."[28] Jarry had promoted such a response first by giving the modified obscenity pride of place in the script, second by having the characters employ it in an aggressive manner. The play begins in medias res: Père Ubu says "Merdre," and since there is no indication of what he could be responding to, the curse might well appear to be directed at the spectators. Mère Ubu's reply is "Oh! well that's very nice, Père Ubu, you great big lout," which, rather than clarifying the situation and Père Ubu's motivation for saying *merdre*, reinforces the impression that her husband had aimed the word outward and therefore into the auditorium.[29] No doubt many spectators were astonished by the mere fact of hearing the word *merdre*, and even those who knew to expect it would probably not have foreseen such a forceful first utterance. The audience members who chose to throw the forbidden word back at the stage were of course assisted by the fact that *merdre* at once is and is not *merde*, so that they could experience the thrill of transgression and yet feel that they were not actually violating a prohibition.

Two of the most noteworthy verbal protests during the *générale* entailed emulation of the play's crude language and themes, the first through a pun combining the name of Aurélien Lugné-Poe, the director of the Œuvre, with *pot de chambre*, the French term for a chamber pot: "when in the midst of the uproar one interrupter was heard to exclaim, 'A bas [Down with] Lugné-Poe . . . de Chambre,' the approbation was virtually unanimous."[30] And at another point, an audience member shouted a wordplay devised even more in the spirit of the play: "At the cry of 'Merdre,' someone replies 'Mangre!'"[31] Thus Jarry's provocative hurl of "Shit!" elicited the still more aggressive "Eat shit!" Presumably the wordplay "A bas Lugné-Poe de Chambre!" was intended as a protest against the director of the Œuvre for having sanctioned the performance of *Ubu Roi*; but in imitating the play's vocabulary of excretion, the pun actually served to underline how much that audience member and his supporters had in common with the foul-mouthed and ill-mannered Père Ubu. Both interventions seem to have been received by the other spectators with approving amusement, suggesting that most audience members regarded them as playful acts of resistance to the performance. But clearly the effectiveness of both as protests was severely compromised by their own scatology: "A bas Lugné-Poe de Chambre!" and "Mangre!" extended more than they opposed the filth in Jarry's play.

Moreover, if the shout of "Mangre!" was designed to protest against *Ubu Roi* by outdoing its obscenity, then strictly speaking it could not succeed, since Jarry had already brought together *merdre* and eating in the third scene of the play, where the final item on the dinner menu Mère Ubu announces, and which the Ubus and their guests proceed to eat, is "choux-fleurs [cauliflower] à la merdre." And Père Ubu augments that element of the meal by throwing on to the table a "balai innommable [unnamable brush]"—that is, a lavatory brush—from which he tells his guests to take a taste.[32] One critic focused on this scene as an example of how repugnant the play's dialogue is: "You will have an idea of what was dared when you know that King Ubu, at table with his guests, has them served an ordinary dinner of excrement. And the meal takes place on the stage!"[33] But Jarry's reasons for including this detail were not as primitively offensive as such reactions presume. "Choux-fleurs à la merdre," rather than simply representing the extreme of Jarry's desire to gratuitously force his audience into contact with bodily functions, is the most explicit illustration of Père Ubu's elemental nature. At the start of scene 4, Ubu and Bordure compare notes on the meal:

PÈRE UBU: Well, Captain, did you enjoy your dinner?
CAPITAINE BORDURE: Very much, monsieur, apart from the merdre.
PÈRE UBU: Eh! the merdre wasn't bad.

In a different context, it might seem as if Ubu's intention was to provoke his guest, to put him in the position of having either to lie about the dinner or to be honest and risk insulting his hosts. But in fact Père Ubu is perfectly sincere when he claims to have enjoyed the "choux-fleurs à la merdre." For him, unlike for Bordure or for the others who "fall down poisoned" after tasting from the brush, consumption and excretion are two sides of the same, basic, life-sustaining process, so that eating feces symbolically brings the two together.[34]

A couple of writers who wrote firsthand accounts of the *générale* reflected on the shout of "Mangre!" and the reaction it prompted, and both regard the incident as representative of a predominantly good-natured mood in the auditorium. Henry Bauer, one of the established critics who wrote most favorably about *Ubu Roi* before as well as after the performances, suggested that more than one audience member shouted "Mangre," and remarked that "it does not displease me that some jokers collaborated with the protagonists on stage, and, when the latter added an R to the Cambronne illustration, felt obliged to reply 'Mangre' to the Poles. What was taking place on the boards was only a suggestive appearance and theme for those who approached it with goodwill."[35] And Francis Jourdain, recalling the "epic" first performance of *Ubu Roi* many years later, writes that "The first few *Merdre!*s from Monsieuye Ubu and his spouse made the spectators less indignant than the more unexpected riposte from one of them, *Mangre!*, made them laugh."[36] That intriguing combination of outrage and amusement in the initial reception of Jarry's play has largely been overlooked as theater history has come to cherish the notion that "*Ubu Roi* was greeted by a riot."[37] The audience response to Jarry's taboo-breaking play is all the more revealing because it was not uniformly hostile, especially in relation to filth.

The mixed reaction to *Ubu Roi* and to *merdre* appears to provide evidence in support of various theoretical writings on human beings' relationship to excrement. Freud observed that small children are interested in, even proud of their excretions, but that "under the influence of its upbringing, the child's coprophilic instincts and inclinations gradually succumb to repression; it learns to keep them secret, to be ashamed of them and to feel disgust at their objects."[38] However, as Freud wrote in a different context, "Certain forms of mental activity such as joking are still able to make the obstructed source of pleasure accessible for a brief moment, and thus show how much of the esteem in which human beings once held their faeces still remains preserved in the unconscious."[39] According to this view, the performances of *Ubu Roi* triggered not only the learned response of disgust in many audience members, but also in others a return of the repressed coprophilia. Those spectators who repeated Jarry's scatology or invented their own evidently took childlike enjoyment from uttering and even playing with the taboo term.

Jacques Lacan wrote briefly about the connection between *merdre* and Freud's ideas. Commenting in passing on the extra *r*, Lacan represents it as a playful addition that serves to get at the truth: "one letter sufficed to give to the most vulgar of French jaculations the joculatory value, verging on the sublime, of the place it occupies in the epic of Ubu: that of the Word from before the beginning." Lacan brings out particularly well the way in which the conversion of *merde* into *merdre*—like Jarry's play as a whole—is at once simple and resonant. He goes on to remark that "the fool is the one, oh Shakespeare, in life as in literature, for whom the destiny was reserved of keeping available through the centuries the place of truth that Freud was to bring into the light."[40] In keeping with the ages-old technique of pointing to the truth via irreverent humor, the modification creatively brings to the fore a deeper meaning behind the obscenity, shedding light on human beings' fraught relationship with their physical selves.

While Freud focused on the gradual repression of coprophilia in the development of the individual, other more recent critics have demonstrated that an analogous process has taken place on the level of culture. Broadly speaking, the more "civilized" a culture becomes, the more it repudiates any positive relationship to excrement. Stephen Greenblatt has shown how not only in primitive tribes but also throughout Europe up until the Renaissance, feces could signify "abundance as well as humiliation, magical medicine as well as corruption, renewal as well as death." But between about the sixteenth and nineteenth centuries, the body in general and excrement in particular were subjected to various forms of regulation that gradually deprived feces of any positive connotations. "Eventually," Greenblatt writes, "all of the body's products, except tears, become simply unmentionable in decent society."[41] Yet just as the individual cannot but retain some of his or her coprophilic inclinations, so too does the collective continue to associate positive feelings with those bodily products that have been banished from social discourse. That duality inevitably leads to mixed feelings; as Dominique Laporte states in his *History of Shit*, "Civilization does not distance itself unequivocally from waste but betrays its fundamental ambivalence in act after act."[42]

Stallybrass and White draw on Greenblatt's work for their argument about the relationship between cultural categories of high and low in various contexts from the seventeenth to the twentieth centuries. As they write in the conclusion, "The bourgeois subject continuously defined and re-defined itself through the exclusion of what it marked out as 'low.' . . . But disgust always bears the imprint of desire. These low domains, apparently expelled as 'Other,' return as the object of nostalgia, longing and fascination."[43] *Ubu Roi* and its reception seem to conform to Stallybrass and White's model and in a most concentrated and direct form: a play in which the "low" was unusually explicit was performed only twice at a time when the bourgeoisie was pursuing cleanliness with unprecedented determination. The spectators at the Œuvre were confronted by insistent verbal and other references to an element of human existence from which they were endeavoring to dissociate themselves. The audience's fervent opposition to Jarry's highlighting of *merdre* might appear simply consistent with that exclusion of the "low" were it not undermined by such clear indications of ambivalence on the part of those spectators who shouted the taboo term.

Some accounts of the anticipation preceding the two performances even suggest a degree of self-consciousness in the bourgeois public's capacity to enjoy what they were conditioned to reject. According to Jehan Adès, an actor who witnessed the *générale* from the wings, "the audience was informed, and well disposed. People expected obscenities and desired them. And even the ladies were not about to take offence."[44] Thus it seems that advance warning about the taboo-breaking language and themes of Jarry's play not only enabled some Parisian theatergoers to brace themselves against a spectacle that might otherwise merely have given offense, but actually brought to light a distinct appetite for engagement with the prohibited. A fascinating commentary on the excited anticipation surrounding *Ubu Roi* was written by Rachilde, herself the author of successful and often scandalous novels. Half a year after the performances, Rachilde reflected on the apparently contradictory situation that Jarry had contrived through his highlighting of the word *merdre*: "A full house, the elite of humanity, of journalism, come to hear *that* like flies go you know where." Those were the unprecedented circumstances Jarry had succeeded in bringing about: a large number of the more privileged members of society flocked to witness a work of art whose language placed the most unsavory bodily functions in the foreground. For Rachilde, the public's expectations went as far as imagining that the stage debut of *merdre* would bring out and even transform "all the red hatreds of the old toward the young, of the young toward the old, of the young toward the young, all the kinds of sexes, newly discovered, hoping to set themselves up thanks to a dawn of more direct obscenities." She also recalls the spectators' "concupiscent terror of finally hearing *the word*" and describes the finely dressed female audience members as "divine clay shivering with voluptuousness in expectation of *the magic word*."[45] There is little evidence that this potential to catalyze some kind of social change for women in particular was fulfilled, unless one counts the action of the lady audience member who according to one account assailed Sarcey during the *générale* by shouting at him: "Vieux c. [i.e., *con*]" ["Bloody old fool"].[46] Rachilde's focus on women, and her piece as a whole, no doubt reveal more about her own preoccupations than about the reception of *Ubu Roi*; but her overwrought reflections do confirm that some of Jarry's contemporaries recognized that *merdre* belonged to a psychologically and sociologically complex field of meaning.

Yet if we consider the actual audience reaction to *Ubu Roi*, the form in which ambivalence manifested itself better accords with Freud's terms than with Stallybrass and White's: it seems more fitting to conceive of the spectators who uttered, and in some cases played with, the taboo term *merdre* as taking advantage of the chance to reconnect with an "obstructed source of pleasure" than as acting on the basis of more earnest drives such as "desire" or "longing." What characterized the response of a significant number of audience members at the Œuvre, especially at the *générale*, was enthusiastic embrace of play. By the 1890s, normative behavior in theater catering to the middle and upper classes in France had grown quite subdued—so much so that one lecturer complained about the "sovereign indifference, that banal, soft-spoken politeness which has superseded the fine tumults of yesteryear."[47] The uproar generated by *Ubu Roi* violated the newly established restraint, to the indignation of some of the reviewers, for example, "Yesterday, at the Œuvre, the audience did not set an example of reserve and of good conduct. It is true that the play had started. But is not the most natural protest, and above all the most dignified, to get up and leave?"[48] According to another review, instead of leaving, "People booed and hissed, meowed, barked, played whistles, all of this with enough sincerity and persistence that . . . I find that I've come away having understood no more than fragments of *Roi Ubu*."[49] Such descriptions suggest that Jarry's introduction of filth into the public sphere did have a liberating effect for some spectators, reflective not so much of the weighty issues Rachilde later wrote about, but rather of a more straightforward impulse to behave with a kind of abandon no longer customary in the theater.

The enthusiasm with which some audience members shouted "*merdre*" at each other, and their attempts to outdo the primitive humor of the play, remind one more of the uninhibited uproar of the nursery than of the ordinarily decorum-bound environment of the theater auditorium. This is ironic given that one of the most common criticisms leveled at Jarry's play was that it was childish. If *Ubu Roi* was an "enfantillage," was not the spectacle in the auditorium also? Jarry would no doubt have agreed that his play, and certainly its main character, were in some respects childish; the spectators, by contrast, would probably have denied any significant resemblance between their behavior and the events on stage. Alain Corbin points to the interplay between conceptions of maturity and social class in relation to filth in nineteenth-century France: "Most contemporary discourse associated scatological behavior with instinct, that is, with childhood and with the masses; it contrasted it with the behavior of the educated, mature bourgeoisie, who had been able to assimilate the somatic discipline necessary to remove excrement from the realm of sight and smell."[50] Jarry's carefully planned assault on the standards and expectations of the public coaxed at least some of the bourgeois spectators into invalidating such generalizations.

The reviewer who described *Ubu Roi* as a "scatophile insanity"[51] was not the only one who apparently construed the play as some kind of positive statement about excrement. Another observed that "the attitude of a good number of my fellow guests showed me that I am not the only one who does not at all appreciate the charm of filth."[52] That statement itself implies that other members of the same audience responded differently; and indeed, some of the spectators at the first performances demonstrated that they did appreciate, if not the charm of filth, at least the appeal of the scatological. There are more grounds for calling some of the audience members "scatophile" than for applying the term to the play or its author. Certainly the label fits Père Ubu, and the reviews suggest that many in the audience identified the author with the play's central character, rather than considering that Jarry might have created Père Ubu in order to expose and indict certain attitudes and behavior. Conflating Père Ubu and Jarry also allowed reviewers to declare with satisfaction that the audience proved themselves to be wittier than Jarry; for example, "wit has not lost its rights among the spectators. Lord knows, it was certainly necessary to make up for what was absent from the stage."[53] Jarry himself derided that simplistic response after the performances: "Really, there's no reason to expect an amusing play. . . . And above all no-one understood . . . that Ubu was not meant to utter witticisms, as various little ubuists demanded of him, but stupid remarks, with all the authority of the Ape."[54]

Those critics who took offence at *Ubu Roi*—and, presumably, those spectators whose point of view they represented—often regarded Père Ubu as a misconceived satire on the bourgeoisie. Jarry's own reflections on his play and the public's response make clear that for him the figure had much farther-reaching significance; and there emerges from those various writings a quite nuanced conception of filth. Writing on the eve of the premiere about the character of Père Ubu, Jarry clarified that

> *He is not* exactly Monsieur Thiers, nor the bourgeois, nor the boor: he is rather the perfect anarchist, with that which prevents *us* from ever becoming the perfect anarchist, that he is a man, whence cowardice, filthiness, ugliness, etc.[55]

Jarry was trying to forestall the efforts of critics and others to regard Ubu as a satirical portrayal of a particular kind of person, emphasizing instead how much Ubu has in common with all people—and through the pronoun "us" he includes himself. The "not exactly" acknowledges that Ubu possesses something of the bourgeois, just as he does something of its opposite, the anarchist; for Jarry it is fundamental to being human that one cannot actually make the transition from conformist bourgeois to lawless anarchist. The three properties Jarry names as characteristic of human beings each represent the opposite of how most people no doubt like to think of themselves, i.e., as brave, clean and beautiful. Yet the second term, "filthiness," is the least expected and most provocative, and best reflects Jarry's desire to confront the public with a representation of, as he later put it, "their ignoble double, which had never before been completely presented to them."[56] Elsewhere too, Jarry made clear the connection between Ubu's baseness and the fundamental nature of our species: in the program, for instance, he wrote: "M. Ubu is an ignoble being, which is why (from underneath) he resembles all of us."[57] So it would appear that in this context Jarry is referring to a kind of natural filthiness, an unavoidable engagement with the body and its products that it is customary, yet absurd, to deny. For Jarry, that kind of "filth" characterizes not only Père Ubu, but humans in general.

In the essay Jarry wrote after the performances, he again employed the term "sale" (filthy), but to make another, complementary point. Reflecting on the audience's response, Jarry wrote:

> It would have been easy to fit *Ubu* to the taste of the Paris public by making the following minor modifications: the opening word would have been Zut (or Zutre), the unspeakable brush a pretty girl going to bed, the army uniforms would have been First Empire style, Ubu would have formally embraced the Czar, and various people would have been cuckolded—but that would have been filthier [*mais ç'aurait été plus sale*].[58]

Jarry may well have been responding to the frequent use of the term *sale* in spoken and written objections to his play, such as this complaint, which encapsulates the common dual charge of offensiveness and pointlessness: "It is not only that it is filthy [*sale*], but it takes up space."[59] Whereas for most of the public, filth connoted vulgar language and the bodily functions to which it referred, for Jarry, filth in this context would consist of presenting the audience with precisely what they expected and wanted: inoffensive language, erotic titillation, mild satire, a happy ending, and plenty of adultery. Jarry's reference to the "coucher de petite femme" may well have been an allusion to a genre of entertainment that evolved following the 1894 success of *Le Coucher d'Yvette*, shows which, as Weber writes, "turned around the actions of a young woman undressing to go to bed or else rising from bed to dress."[60]

In both instances where he used the word *sale,* Jarry argued for a definition of filth that contradicted conventional thinking: first, that a certain kind of natural filthiness defines all and not just some human beings; second, that in artistic creation the most filthy is the most predictable and least challenging. In other words, Père Ubu is filthy, like the rest of us, but *Ubu Roi* is not. The majority of the audience failed to make such distinctions, yet all the while their very behavior, their exuberant display of supposed resistance to filth, corroborated Jarry's point that there is a filthiness from which human beings can never entirely sever themselves.

Rachilde also wrote about *saleté* in considering the audience response to *Ubu Roi*. According to her analysis, "People whistled above all at the lack of real filth. They had thought that this Punch of an Ubu would function sexually." The kind of filth Rachilde refers to is that of transgression, filth as an appealing violation, and she implies a distinction between degrees of such filth, some more "real" than others because more radically transgressive. Yet far from sharing this opinion, regretting that *Ubu Roi* had not proven more "filthy," that is, more extreme in its breach of theatrical and social norms, Rachilde suggests that those spectators whose excited anticipation she depicted were foolish to associate Jarry's taboo-breaking treatment of excrement with sexuality. From her own writing career, Rachilde had ample experience of the public dwelling on "scandalous" treatment of sexuality to the exclusion of everything else. (Had she been writing some years later with psychoanalytic theory in mind, she might have pointed out that the infantile Ubu does by implication function sexually since, for Freud, the child's coprophilic and sadistic-anal inclinations are integral to pregenital sexuality.) In general, Rachilde found the response to *Ubu Roi* disheartening: "Traits that are almost marks of genius did not carry at all, and the deliberately idiotic received the customary success"; and she writes that once all the whistling was over, "there was a general malaise."[61] Throughout her account of the public's excitement before and reactions during the performances of *Ubu Roi*, Rachilde highlights the simplifying effect of filth-as-scandal, the way in which the focus on *merdre* led to a polarized and unsubtle audience response. Ultimately Rachilde seems disappointed that the whole episode, in spite of, but also perhaps because of, the filthiness of Jarry's play, only brought out truths about the public that were already well known.

Yet while the performances of *Ubu Roi* left Rachilde and other supporters of the avant-garde disappointed, Jarry was pleased with the scandalized response of most of the audience (for the scrapbook of reviews that he put together, he omitted the few favorable notices). His objective had been to present the spectators with an unvarnished, authentic image of themselves:

> I wanted the scene that the audience would find themselves in front
> of when the curtain went up to be like that mirror in the stories of
> Madame Leprince de Beaumont, in which the depraved see themselves
> with bulls' horns, or a dragon's body, each according to the exaggera-
> tion of their vice; and it's not surprising that the public should have
> been aghast at the sight of their ignoble double.

He finds it entirely understandable that the audience should have been taken aback by this unprecedentedly direct representation of human baseness, but at the same time he is frustrated that their habitual way of perceiving and understanding drama impeded their readiness to recognize in Père Ubu their "ignoble double." He argued that the public "got angry because they understood only too well, whatever they may say"—and that combination of recognition and denial that Jarry discerned in the spectators is mirrored by their ambivalent response to *merdre*.[62] Père Ubu makes no bones about preoccupying himself with shit; the spectators joined in with him, yet disavowed any bond between his behavior and theirs. Père Ubu exists in an infantile state virtually unaffected by the repression that leads us to reject excrement as filth; the spectators responded at once in that same childlike spirit and from the point of view of an adult, civilized culture that is founded on the repudiation of bodily products.

Notes

1. Henri de Régnier, "Alfred Jarry," in *De mon temps* (Paris: Mercure de France, 1933), 152. Unless otherwise indicated, all translations—often intentionally literal—are mine.

2. Francisque Sarcey, review of *Ubu Roi* (Jarry) at Théâtre de l'Œuvre, Paris, *Le Temps,* 14 December 1896, reprinted in Henri Robillot, "La Presse d'*Ubu Roi,*" *Cahiers du Collège de 'Pataphysique* 3–4 (1950): 75.

3. Alfred Jarry, "Questions de théâtre," in *Ubu*, ed. Noël Arnaud and Henri Bordillon (Paris: Gallimard Folio, 1978), 346.

4. Géroy, "Mon ami Alfred Jarry (Souvenirs)," *Mercure de France,* 1 July 1947, 508.

5. Quoted in Norman L. Kleeblatt, "MERDE! The Caricatural Attack against Emile Zola," *Art Journal* 52, no. 3 (1993): 54.

6. Laurent Tailhade, *Quelques fantômes de jadis* (Paris: Éditions française illustrée, 1920), 216.

7. Henri Béhar, *Jarry Dramaturge* (Paris: Nizet, 1980), 75.

8. Donald Reid, *Paris Sewers and Sewermen: Realities and Representations* (Cambridge, MA: Harvard University Press, 1991), 30, 35, 82.

9. Eugen Weber, *France, Fin de Siècle* (Cambridge, MA: Harvard University Press, 1986), 57–59.

10. Ibid., 101, 62.

11. Alain Corbin, "Backstage," in *From the Fires of Revolution to the Great War*, ed. Michelle Perrot, trans. Arthur Goldhammer, vol. 4 of *A History of Private Life* (Cambridge, MA: Harvard University Press, 1990), 491.

12. Georges Vigarello, *Concepts of Cleanliness: Changing Attitudes in France since the Middle Ages*, trans. Jean Birrell (Cambridge: Cambridge University Press, 1988), 216.

13. Corbin, "Backstage," 482.

14. Ibid.

15. Weber, *France*, 5, 73.

16. Peter Stallybrass and Allon White, *The Politics and Poetics of Transgression* (Ithaca, NY: Cornell University Press, 1986), 135, 140.

17. "Un Sarcisque," review of *Ubu Roi* (Jarry) at Théâtre de l'Œuvre, Paris, *L'Événement,* 11 December 1896, reprinted in Robillot, "La Presse," 78.

18. Rachilde, *Alfred Jarry, ou le Surmâle de lettres* (Paris: B. Grasset, 1928), 89.

19. Tailhade, *Quelques fantômes*, 214.

20. Jean Carrère, "Les Théâtres," *La Plume,* 1 April 1894, 137.

21. Review of *Ubu Roi* (Jarry) at Théâtre de l'Œuvre, Paris, *La Lanterne,* 12 December 1896, reprinted in Robillot, "La Presse," 81.

22. Georges Rémond, "Souvenirs sur Jarry et autres (fin)," *Mercure de France,* 1 April 1955, 666.

23. "Coquerico," review of *Ubu Roi* (Jarry) at Théâtre de l'Œuvre, Paris, *La Patrie,* 12 December 1896, reprinted in Robillot, "La Presse," 82.

24. Catulle Mendès, review of *Ubu Roi* (Jarry) at Théâtre de l'Œuvre, Paris, *Le Journal,* 11 December 1896.

25. Jules Renard, *Journal (1887–1919)* (Paris: Gallimard Pléiade, 1960), 363.

26. Sarcey, review, 75.

27. Edouard Noël and Edmond Stoullig, *Les Annales du théâtre et de la musique,* vol. 22 (1896) (Paris: Ollendorff, 1897), 423–24.

28. "Coquerico," review, 82.

29. Alfred Jarry, *Ubu Roi*, in *Ubu*, ed. Arnaud and Bordillon, 31.

30. "C' de N.," review of *Ubu Roi* (Jarry) at Théâtre de l'Œuvre, Paris, *Paris,* 11 December 1896, reprinted in Robillot, "La Presse," 78.

31. Renard, *Journal*, 363.

32. Jarry, *Ubu Roi*, 37, 39.

33. Review of *Ubu Roi* (Jarry) at Théâtre de l'Œuvre, Paris, *Petit Parisien,* 11 December 1896, reprinted in Robillot, "La Presse," 79.

34. Jarry, *Ubu Roi*, 40–41, 39.

35. Quoted in Noël Arnaud, *Alfred Jarry, d'Ubu roi au Docteur Faustroll* (Paris: La Table Ronde, 1974), 317.

36. Francis Jourdain, *Né en 76* (Paris: Pavillon, 1951), 204.

37. Richard Schechner, *Performance Studies: An Introduction* (London: Routledge, 2002), 208.

38. Sigmund Freud, "Preface to Bourke's *Scatalogic Rites of All Nations*," in *The Standard Edition of the Complete Psychological Works*, ed. and trans. James Strachey, 24 vols. (London: Hogarth Press, 1958), 12:336.

39. Sigmund Freud, "Dreams in Folklore," in *Standard Edition*, 12:187.

40. Jacques Lacan, *Écrits* (Paris: Seuil, 1966), 660, 661.

41. Stephen Greenblatt, "Filthy Rites," *Daedalus* 111 (1982): 9, 10.

42. Dominique Laporte, *History of Shit*, trans. Nadia Benabid and Rodolphe el-Khoury (Cambridge, MA: MIT Press, 2000), 32.

43. Stallybrass and White, *Politics*, 191.

44. Quoted in René Druart, "Un témoignage sur la générale d'*Ubu Roi*," *Cahiers du Collège de 'Pataphysique* 20 (1955): 53.

45. Rachilde, review of *Les Jours et les nuits* (Jarry), *Mercure de France*, August 1897, 143–44.

46. Quoted in P. Lié, "Notes sur la seconde représentation d'*Ubu Roi*," *Cahiers du Collège de 'Pataphysique* 20 (1955): 52.

47. E. Rodocanachi, quoted in F. W. J. Hemmings, *The Theatre Industry in Nineteenth-Century France* (Cambridge: Cambridge University Press, 1993), 99–100.

48. "Un Spectateur," review of *Ubu Roi* (Jarry) at Théâtre de l'Œuvre, Paris, *La Presse*, 12 December 1896, reprinted in Robillot, "La Presse," 78.

49. "L.-B.-D.," review of *Ubu Roi* (Jarry) at Théâtre de l'Œuvre, Paris, *Gil Bas,* 11 December 1896, reprinted in Robillot, "La Presse," 77.

50. Alain Corbin, *The Foul and the Fragrant: Odor and the French Social Imagination,* trans. Miriam Kochan (Cambridge, MA: Harvard University Press, 1986), 214.

51. Review, *Le Petit Parisien*, 79.

52. "L.-B.-D.," review, 77.

53. "Pompier de Service," review of *Ubu Roi* (Jarry) at Théâtre de l'Œuvre, Paris, *La Paix,* 11 December 1896, reprinted in Robillot, "La Presse," 76.

54. Jarry, "Questions," 345.

55. Alfred Jarry, "Les Paralipomènes d'Ubu," *Revue Blanche,* 1 December 1896, reprinted in *Ubu*, ed. Arnaud and Bordillon, 323.

56. Jarry, "Questions," 344–45.

57. Alfred Jarry, "Programme d'*Ubu roi*," reprinted in *Ubu*, ed. Arnaud and Bordillon, 337.

58. Jarry, "Questions," 344.

59. Noël and Stoullig, *Annales*, 424.

60. Weber, *France*, 162.

61. Rachilde, review, 144.

62. Jarry, "Questions," 344, 346.

Chapter 9

Foreign Matter:
Imperial Filth

Joseph W. Childers

By the middle of the 1870s, many Victorians were convinced that the influx of immigrants into England was a direct cause of the vice, degradation, and filth that plagued its cities. Focus had shifted from the northern 1840s shock cities, such as Manchester, with its large Irish population, to the East End of London, that bottleneck of empire, where streets, alleys, homes and businesses were clogged by thousands of refugees and immigrants, as well as travelers simply passing through on their way to points west. The presence of these foreigners was palpable, and as the century advanced, the press, in encouraging passage of "aliens acts" to regulate the flow of immigrants into England, regularly circulated inflated figures. One East End newspaper claimed that a "total of 836,280 foreign aliens" had settled in the United Kingdom between 1891 and 1901—an impossible and entirely fabricated figure.[1] Regardless of the exact numbers, these foreigners became easy targets for writers who routinely proclaimed their amazement that "these people can exist—and even thrive—in an atmosphere and amid surroundings which to the more highly-developed Englishman and Englishwoman mean disease and death."[2]

Such attitudes helped reinforce not only the *presence* of these foreigners, but their fundamental difference as well, resulting in a combination of antifilth and antiforeigner rhetoric that resonates throughout a host of works of the late Victorian period, especially in the Sherlock Holmes stories.[3] Arthur Conan Doyle introduced Holmes in *A Study in Scarlet* in 1887. Over the next four decades, he produced four novellas and fifty-six short stories featuring the redoubtable detective; well over half the narratives were written and published before 1905 and the passage of the first Aliens Act.[4] These enormously popular tales, fictively narrated by a wounded veteran of the Afghan wars, characteristically insist on the association of the exotic, the alien, the foreign, with the "filth" of crime and the London underworld. As a result, Englishness is always on display as the standard for right-minded human behavior, an essence that must be kept free from the impurities of the other. Simultaneously, these stories also write Englishness—and its metonym England—as dangerously susceptible to just this sort of contamination. They remind their readers that even the apparently most stalwart Englishmen (and women) run the risk of losing their way and falling under the influence of outside forces, which—because alien and unclean—threaten to change England and Englishness into a quagmire of degradation.

The task these tales often set for themselves—the protection and display of English national identity—is complicated by their overdetermined understanding of Englishness. The Holmes stories are about saving the national culture and character from being transformed into something menacing and unrecognizable as English. Yet these stories also imply that Holmes and Watson's job is so important *because* degradation, impurity, and hybridity are endemic, familiar, even desirable to the English character. From the first pages of *A Study in Scarlet*, well before Watson or the reading public has met Holmes, the doctor establishes that internal danger, describing the culmination of his imperial wanderings in terms suggesting that London has already been contaminated. With neither "kith nor kin in England [he] naturally gravitated to London, that great cesspool into which all the idlers and loungers of the Empire are irresistibly drained."[5] Having circulated through the empire, Watson returns wounded and spent to attempt to improve his ruined health. The London to which he returns is indeed the heart of the empire, but that organ no longer functions efficiently. Rather than the pump that keeps men and materials moving along the arteries feeding the farthest-flung extremities of empire, it has become a backwash of imperial detritus, susceptible to infection from without and sepsis from the pool of filth that has accumulated within.

The implications of Watson's statement seem clear enough at first, but on closer inspection they raise serious difficulties, especially when considering the connections among the English, immigrants or foreigners, and English conceptions of filth. The affiliations of filth and foreignness that emerge in several of the Holmes stories, particularly *The Sign of Four* and "The Man with the Twisted Lip," are the direct concern of this essay. In thinking about the mutual exchanges between these two important cultural signifiers of the late Victorian period, I want to argue that in reading back through foreignness and issues of national identity we can begin to understand the depth of the fascination and revulsion the Victorians had with filth. Julia Kristeva has argued that filth reveals the "frailty of the symbolic order," exposing the very boundaries and prohibitions out of which the subject is constituted.[6] That order is specifically threatened by the ambiguity of Watson's description of London as the cesspool of empire, which potentially jeopardizes the subjectivity that can function within it. While I would not embrace the transhistorical assumptions that follow from Kristeva's theory and that William A. Cohen has discussed in the introduction to this volume, I do propose that the boundaries complicated within Watson's statement provide an important starting point for examining the "trouble" with Englishness —a trouble Doyle identifies as existing on both sides of the line separating English from other, which is inextricably bound up with English representations and perceptions of filth.

Watson's connection of London to its periphery, the somewhat hazy "Empire," as well as to its extreme interior accentuates the problem I have identified, raising a number of interpretive questions in the process. Was London the rotten center of empire because of the English—that is, simply because it was London and therefore attracted imperial vagabonds? Or was it those transients who were the polluting influence and who, in finding their way back to the metropolis, carried with them the residue of the crimes committed for and against empire, infecting London by their presence? Who were these throwaways—colonizers or colonized? Is a distinction made, and does it matter? When Watson counts himself among the "idlers and loungers," he insinuates not only that the answers are much more complicated than merely distinguishing English from other; he also implies that the very boundaries defining what it means to be English (and therefore ostensibly pure and untainted) were increasingly indistinct and permeable. Consequently, Englishness must not only face infiltration from without, but also confront an even more serious risk to its coherence: the presence of the taint from within, that which can be neither repudiated nor absorbed. This internal filth threatens to expose the limits of Englishness, the national character, as permeable and unstable. The resulting dilemma is how to protect Englishness from external defilement while also saving it from itself.

Ronald Thomas has pointed out that in the midst of fin-de-siècle concerns about national identity and responsibility, detective fiction and the Holmes stories in particular brought England "face to face with the specter of its own criminal guilt and impending colonial revenge, and the means with which to defend itself against both."[7] For Thomas the answer Doyle offers is to focus on the foreignness of the traces of the criminal body left at the scene of the crime. What, then, are the limits of foreignness? As so many of the Holmes stories imply, these limits are not easy to determine. Even Watson's reluctance to distinguish himself from the human waste of empire suggests that the marks left from having taken "the Queen's shilling" in the colonies are not easily erased. Throughout the Holmes canon, Watson reminds the reader of his time in service, of the lessons he learned among the "savages," and of the bullet he took (sometimes in the shoulder, other times in the leg) during the Afghan wars. Yet Watson's link to empire building, and the potential despoliation of his national identity because of it, only further complicates attempts to draw a clear line between what does and does not count as foreign. For, despite Watson's voluntary identification as victim — because defender — of empire, his time spent in the colonies makes him rather more than less stereotypically English. Morally upright, and somewhat pristine in that regard, Watson is the reintegrated colonial. His references to his various imperial experiences and his knowledge of native ways should make him a resource to Holmes, but in fact the detective is often much better informed about the specifics of life — and death — beyond the borders of England than is the good doctor. *The Sign of Four* is a case in point. It is Holmes who has the information about the Andaman island prison colony ready to hand, not the well-traveled Watson. And when queried by Holmes about blowpipes and poison darts, Watson incorrectly guesses their origin to be South America.

Watson, then, is no encyclopedia of knowledge about the various colonies or the habits and customs of their indigenous peoples. The imperial patina left upon him is only a few shades removed from the complexion of those Anglo-Indians T. N. Mukharji describes having met in London: "queer characters" who "pompously displayed their acquaintance with the Hindi language, however slight it might be, and their power and superiority over us."[8] Like that of the condescending Anglo-Indians, Watson's Englishness is highlighted by the imperfect impressions his colonial experiences made on him. He performs national identity so vigorously precisely because of his exposure to foreignness, to the potential of penetration and contamination by that which is most un-English. It is always Watson, rather than Holmes, who observes the fine points of common courtesy, or who protests when Holmes's behavior becomes so eccentric that it threatens to upset their cozy domesticity at 221B Baker Street. Also, it is usually Watson who is in charge of protecting the pair in dangerous situations, often being reminded by Holmes to bring his pistol, that remnant of his days as a military officer. Further, if any blemish remains as a result of his time in service, Watson typically either ignores or struggles to repress it by overcompensation. He is the moralist, the exemplary Victorian, who reminds the readers and Holmes alike of their ethical responsibilities as well as their failings. For instance, in the famous opening of the *The Sign of Four,* Watson asks Holmes, "Which is it today . . . morphine or cocaine?" (107). Although cocaine did not have the cultural stigma that was increasingly associated with opium, to Watson there is little moral difference, as he makes clear when he upbraids Holmes, telling him to "Count the cost [of injecting cocaine]. . . . Surely, the game is hardly worth the candle. Why should you, for a mere passing pleasure, risk the loss of those great powers with which you have been endowed?" (108). Whatever concern Watson may have for the impairment of Holmes's powers, the doctor also immediately implies the connection of drugs to the dangers associated with foreignness, for when asked by Holmes if he would like to try it, Watson brusquely replies, "No indeed. . . . My constitution has not got over the Afghan campaign yet. I cannot afford to throw any extra strain upon it" (107). Because he is so acutely aware of the fine boundary between foreignness and Englishness, Watson operates narratively to reassert the physical and moral superiority of the English as well as to warn against infiltration by the other, even in the recreational use of cocaine, which most contemporary readers would have judged innocuous.[9]

Watson's function in this regard is complex. It suggests that Englishness is most formidable after being "touched" and potentially contaminated by the other; only against the face of foreignness can it show its true mettle. In pushing this analysis farther, it is easy to see that, again, the underlying apprehension in the narratives is over the relative permeability of Englishness as an identificatory discourse. Like so many things, Englishness cannot define itself in terms of presence alone; it needs its other to articulate what it is *not*. By the same token, the ability to distinguish the other as such also means that there must be some kind of identification with it—something shared that allows for recognition: the unrecognizable that is also the familiar. The necessity of this connection means that Englishness itself, whether as a purely discursive or empirically defined category, constantly runs the risk of legitimizing that connection, extending its limits to be so inclusive that the category itself becomes meaningless—or worse, impure. In actuality, of course, this alloying had already and always taken place. The constant presence of ethnic others helped to create a kind of hierarchy of national identity based partly on visible marks of difference—what we might today call race—and partly on cultural difference. The Irish are more like the English than the Jews, who are more like the English than Indians, who are more like the English than Africans, and so on.

This ethno-cultural chain of being is common in the Holmes stories and even instrumental in a work like *The Sign of Four,* in which Holmes and Watson uncover the story of the treasure of Agra. The treasure was stolen by the English soldier Jonathan Small and his three Sikh companions from a murdered rajah's servant during the Mutiny in India more than thirty years earlier. Captured and convicted for the murder, the four of the story's title offer to disclose the whereabouts of the treasure to Major Sholto and Captain Morstan, their jailers, in return for the officers' help in escaping from their Andaman Island gulag. Sholto, however, betrays them all, absconding to England with the treasure. Holmes and Watson become involved when the late Morstan's daughter enlists their services regarding an anonymous note in which the author tells Mary she is a "wronged woman" and expresses a wish to meet her in order to explain. Ultimately, Holmes and Watson not only discover the treasure, which Small and his pygmy accomplice steal back from Sholto's heirs (murdering one in the process), but they also capture Small in a wild boat chase down the Thames. The story begins with only the smallest reminders of outside infiltration and difference: Holmes's indulgence in his seven percent solution of cocaine, which he is injecting to ease his boredom, and Watson's remarking Mary Morstan's beige turban. The narrative quickly moves to the more eccentric exoticism of Sholto's son, the aesthete Thaddeus, then to the Major's London home (Pondicherry Lodge), next to prison colony escapee Jonathan Small, then to his Sikh accomplices, and finally to Tonga, Small's Andaman islander companion, who is so far removed from the familiar that he is mistaken by Watson for a "Newfoundland dog" lying on the deck of the river launch he and Holmes are pursuing. With each succeeding exposure to the influence of the other, the danger to Mary, as well as to Holmes and Watson, increases, just as their proximity to the treasure grows nearer.

The arrival of foreign horror is explicitly tracked in another story, "The Five Orange Pips," in which Holmes solves the mystery of the deadly letters to Elias Openshaw, his brother, and eventually his nephew.

Rich from his exploits in America, the somewhat irascible Elias returns to England. After some years, he receives an anonymous letter containing five orange seeds, or pips, and the demand that he relinquish some papers. Rather than follow the instructions, he burns several documents and becomes ever more reclusive. In a few weeks, however, he is found dead, apparently due to an accident. Openshaw's brother inherits his wealth, and after a year receives a similar letter with five orange pips. Having no idea what papers the letter refers to, he ignores the message. A few days later, he too dies, supposedly by accident. Elias's nephew, now in possession of his uncle's property, has received yet a third letter and comes to Holmes and Watson for help.

Although the death of each of the Openshaws takes place on English soil, it is clear from the outset that whoever is sending the letters, and is apparently responsible for these deaths, is at least initially acting from outside England. The map of empire emphasizes the way in which the murders themselves are becoming increasingly English in origin. The first demand for the papers is posted from Pondicherry in India, the next from the Scottish port of Dundee. By the time the ill-gotten Openshaw fortune has fallen into the hands of the genteel and thoroughly middle-class nephew, John, the warnings are being posted from *east* London. The hint of the empire that lingers from the East End postmark stresses that the crime is stalking England as much as the Openshaws, illustrating how easily the line between the fastidious civilization of the domestic and the murderous savagery of empire is crossed.

Homicide does not respect either racial or national lines in the Holmes stories, and charting the threats' points of origin in "The Five Orange Pips" speaks directly to the fear of moral contamination that the filth of empire presents. Bad enough that murders are perpetrated on English soil in reaction to crimes committed elsewhere; but when alien turpitude is perceived to originate in England, then an entire way of life is threatened. Similarly, in *A Study in Scarlet*, Doyle's awkwardly constructed narrative of the revenge murder of an American in London, the insinuations of ethno-cultural contamination — though more subtle — use the American West and Mormonism as the points farthest from the English norm, then return to Europe through erroneous speculations about secret German and Italian political societies in London. As each of these tales demonstrates, the cesspool of London that can contain, even nurture, those who would commit such crimes has seeped into the norm of Englishness, potentially sullying it beyond recognition. In response to just such concerns, newspapers shout their xenophobic opinions in *A Study in Scarlet*. The *Daily Telegraph* admonishes the government for not maintaining "a closer watch over foreigners in England"; the *Daily News* surmises that the crime was no doubt political, carried out by one of the "number of men" driven to English shores by the intolerance of their governments (39–40). Only after the crime has been solved does the *Echo* warn "all foreigners" to "settle their feuds at home" and not carry them "on to British soil" (103). The problem is that when the etiology of a crime is finally exposed, the trail often leads not outward to some aboriginal savage, but home, to a crime committed by one or more Englishmen while in service to the building and maintenance of the empire. By the time Watson and Holmes come onto the scene, it is usually years after the original misdeed has been absorbed and the malefactor has returned to England. The crimes the detective is asked to solve are subsequent, and in many ways subordinate, to the original transgression. The Englishness performed so thoroughly by Watson, which is the true jewel to be protected by Holmes, has already been desecrated on the voyage out. The contamination that the newspapers and Watson fear with the arrival of foreigners is really accomplished by the return of the Englishman. Holmes as detective, and Watson as doctor of the social body, are always treating the symptoms rather than the disease itself.

When John Harmon returns from the colonies in Dickens's *Our Mutual Friend*, he is literally flushed into the Thames, barely escaping with his life. For much of the rest of the novel, he teaches management, both professional and domestic, disguised as John Rokesmith. The novel implies not only that his years as a colonial have helped him to save himself from the filthy Thames, but that they also trained him in the art of managing the garbage that is both his personal legacy and England's. By Doyle's time it is not as clear that these lessons are so well taught or perfectly absorbed. Watson does indeed seem to learn, or at least to fortify, his Englishness in the colonies, but his return is by no means a signal that everything will be set right, or that it would even be possible to learn how best to run anything other than a scam in the remote reaches of empire. Rather, the mismanagement of empire by the English is increasingly apparent, and these stories appear at the moment when "the English were being confronted by the accusation of acting less like the moral policemen of the world and more like its lawless economic exploiters."[10] Although Watson is figuratively plucked from the sewer that is London by his happenstance introduction to Holmes, it is one of the few times the English are saved from themselves. As a matter of discretion, transgressions, even murder, are often allowed to go without public resolution. The open secret of the financial health of those middle-classes returning to England from the colonies is that their wealth is likely to be the product of some crime. Joseph Kestner makes this point when he writes of *The Sign of Four* that "Doyle is asserting that bourgeois security and identity rest on secret criminality."[11] Stephen Arata calls this "the pathology of bourgeois life," which Holmes proves "surprisingly powerless to address."[12]

Holmes's failures on this front are symptomatic of the ambivalence about empire expressed as helplessness over the transgressions committed by the English. It is easy enough to assign culpability; rectifying matters is another thing altogether. In *The Sign of Four*, for instance, Jonathan Small's story plainly incriminates him and all English. The Sikhs who persuade him to join them in murder and larceny make that clear when they declare, "We only ask you to do that which your countrymen come to this land for. We ask you to be rich" (191). Small explicitly links his fortunes with his "countrymen" when he and the Sikhs make their pledge to share the treasure with Captain Morstan and Major Sholto. Yet rather than being a redemptive move, their pact with the English officers is their undoing when Sholto, from whom the "four" had hoped to get an early release from prison, betrays them all, decamps with the treasure, and returns to England. Important in this narrative is the moral pollution that is tied to the English from the start. When the Sikhs give Small the opportunity to join them, clearly they are emulating Englishmen and Englishness in India. Sholto's actions underscore how morally defiled the English already are. As threatening as this may be to the boundaries of Englishness, as familiar as it may be as an endemic, and perhaps even inherent, pollution of national character, it is essentially ignored. Though the officers are guilty of all manner of treachery on the subcontinent, the onus for their offenses seems to melt into air once they have managed to get to English soil. The Major's wealth is tacitly legitimated; Watson frets that Mary, Captain Morstan's daughter, will inherit half the jewels, thus putting her out of his romantic and economic reach. Never is her claim to the jewels questioned. No one suggests that the Agra treasure should be returned to its Indian owner. Regardless of how it was obtained, it now has become English. Dramatizing that fact, Small tosses the gems into the Thames while being chased by Watson and Holmes. They will never be recovered, and the English taint upon the treasure has made it a permanent denizen of the river bottom. Through it all we should remember that Small is not being pursued for his crimes in India or even for his escape from the prison colony. His crime is his part in the slaying of Bartholomew Sholto—though he declares he had no quarrel with the old major's son and curses the "savage" Tonga for his bloodthirstiness—and in the theft of a treasure that had already been stolen twice before: once by Small and his accomplices from its rightful owner, and once *from* Small while he languished in his tropical prison.

Finally, too, in a rather heavy-handed metaphor, Small is actually captured by English muck. An "active" and "agile" man, he leaps onto the banks of the Thames when the police boat carrying Holmes and Watson overtakes his launch. But Small has a peg leg which sinks, hip deep, into the mire. "In vain," reports Watson, "he struggled and writhed."

> Not one step could he possibly take either forward or backward. He
> yelled in impotent rage and kicked frantically into the mud with his
> other foot, but his struggles only bored his wooden pin the deeper into
> the sticky mud. When we brought our launch alongside, he was so
> firmly anchored that it was only by throwing the end of the rope over
> his shoulders that we were able to haul him out and drag him, like some
> evil fish, over our side. (178)

The quagmire of Small's plotting, and for that matter England's, is inescapable. A fen of filth, it not only corrupts but effectively castrates the villain, making him powerless and immobile. The description of his capture also foreshadows the scene of his death, when he will once again kick frantically and impotently as he swings from the hangman's noose. Small is one with the swampy filth that holds him fast. Like that mud, he washed up on the shores of England, a victim of his own devices.

As the drifter, the loafer, the lounger drained back into the cesspool of Watson's London, Small contributes to its putrefaction; yet the scene of Small being caught by and in English filth suggests that, as much as he may have added to the pollution, it was already there and is inescapable. At the moment of his greatest abjection, when he is most likely to define clearly the line between purity and filth, when he is most susceptible to being expelled from the metaphorical body of Englishness, he is engulfed by the literal excrescence of London, and by extension England. It is only when he is hauled back into the boat, like some "evil fish," and the symbolic order reestablished, that Englishness once again is defined by Holmes and Watson rather than by the criminal they are chasing. The foul and filthy "cesspool" portion of England has become central to constituting Englishness. The resulting admixture of the polluted and pristine in Englishness makes it difficult to adduce what (or who) counts as English or who possesses true English traits. For those attempting to identify with Englishness, the stakes are raised and the desire to cling to undeniable English characteristics becomes ever more important. It is as though by demonstrating (and thus claiming) such attributes as honesty or courage the pollution of one's English-ness is somehow mitigated. Complicating matters is Small's unshakeable loyalty to the Sikhs and to the Andaman islander. His compacts with these men put him in league with the other and thus place him forever outside of what for Doyle is an increasingly permeable line of English-ness. Small crosses over into the abject, ironically distinct from men like Morstan and Sholto, for whom protestations of loyalty are nothing more than means to an end. Sworn to black men, Small is irredeemable, forfeiting his Englishness, irrevocably fouling it with the very feature he hopes will preserve his claim to it.

This is difficult terrain for Doyle to navigate. Small and his accom-plices are savage and murderous. Additionally, Small and Tonga trade on that savagery, maintaining themselves by displaying Tonga "at fairs and other such places" as a "black cannibal" who eats raw meat and dances a war dance (203). Yet these men display a sense of honor and obligation to each other that is usually depicted as quintessentially Eng-lish—although it is lacking in Sholto and Marston. While the narrative insists that Small's connection to the Sikhs and the Andaman islander does a great deal more to bring out the criminal in him than otherwise, it also puts forward the possibility that it is the depth of those connec-tions that makes Small more sympathetic than the two English officers who betray him. Read in this way, *The Sign of Four* is more than a "scathing indictment" of the "grasping nature of imperialism and the economic impetus of the ideology of 'great expectations'";[13] it defines the space in which Englishness is imperiled, establishing the dual assault on national identity. First is the threat from without, especially when the empire comes "home" to the metropolis. Second, and perhaps more troubling for the late Victorians, is the relative weakness of Englishness as a sustainable set of principles, its tendency to become virtually unrec-ognizable at the merest hint of a smudge or stain.

It is arguably this tendency of Englishness that helps to secure nation-alism: its ability to absorb various subject positions that would other-wise stand solidly outside the boundaries of English national identity extends its reach and therefore creates stronger rather than weaker bonds. Simon Gikandi and Ian Baucom have made similar arguments about the consolidation of Englishness throughout the empire, tracking its func-tioning into the postcolonial era, and noting apprehensions over the for-mation of Englishness that arose in the nineteenth century and earlier.[14] Baucom argues that as the definition of Englishness expanded and shaped itself to accommodate a changing imperial constituency, discourse about it remained intent on expressing its essence. From Daniel Defoe to Tony Blair, all who speak or write of Englishness assert its uniqueness. There is always the sense of trying to save it, even if only to use it as the antithesis of postcolonial identities. The narratives of trying to secure and preserve Englishness from external contamination, as well as from its own essential corruption, drive the Holmes stories. Regardless of the ultimate *ideological* effect of Englishness, the *narrative* effect of the Holmes tales provides an opportunity to examine some of the tactics available for making sense of a national identity perceived to be endangered from internal as well as external pollution.

One especially prominent tactic is the attempt to come to terms with English place as well as English subjects as possible sources of filth and corruption. With spatiality in the Holmes stories so often taking narrative precedence, London, from virtually the beginning of *A Study in Scarlet*, functions as more than just the soul of Englishness, defining its essence for all of the empire, allowing the colonial other to "know" the "Feringhee"; it is also the site that most threatens whatever remains salvageable of Englishness (such as Watson).[15] Struggling with this paradox, Doyle goes directly to the heart of the matter in "The Man with the Twisted Lip." In this story, the limits of Englishness are ineluctably tied to London: Neville St. Clair's "business" in town provides him with his thoroughly middle-class home in the suburb of Lee, where he lives in his "large villa" with his wife and two young children. Each day he commutes into the city to earn his living, unbeknownst to his wife and family, as an entertaining but remarkably filthy beggar in the East End. London offers the opportunity for realizing middle-class aspirations while simultaneously contaminating those who work or dwell there. The city harbors secrets not easily deduced, even for Holmes, who until quite late in the story insists that St. Clair must have been murdered and his body dumped into the Thames. St. Clair's crime of begging in disguise in London's East End is as double as the life he secretly leads. As Audrey Jaffe points out, he is guilty of blurring the social distinctions between gentleman and beggar, falsely taking advantage of the middle class's feelings of responsibility for the "worthy poor."[16] More fundamentally, however, he is guilty of keeping the secret in the first place and of involving, indeed depending upon, the cooperation of an ethnic other in order to do so. Here again is one of the loafers and loungers of empire who has been drained into the London cesspool, but this is a case of the imperial lounger never really leaving home. As with his counterparts in other stories, however, the damage done to St. Clair is an effect of his knowledge of the other, knowledge he gained when investigating begging as a reporter. As such he belongs in the same category as Jonathan Small, Watson, and Jefferson Hope, the murderer in *A Study in Scarlet*. By expressing exoticism and foreignness in class as well as in ethnic terms, "The Man with the Twisted Lip" adds another delimiter to complicate notions of national identity.

Foreign matters, then, are also domestic matters. Of special concern are the dangers of the connections between the English and the empire within London. Watson begins the story with the declaration, "Isa Whitney . . . was much addicted to opium" (306). At the time of the 1891 publication of this story, a new sense of the dangers of opium had already emerged somewhat sensationally in English popular culture. Essentially uncontrolled until the Pharmacy Act of 1868, the drug, which had always been associated with India and China, in the 1870s also became linked in the public imagination to demoralization and degradation. One result of the representation of East End opium dens in "a manner soon accepted as reality" was a rise in anti-opium societies that themselves helped to perpetuate visions of the evil Asian keeper of the den luring the English inside, leading them to a life of addiction, lassitude, and irresponsibility.[17] In this way the empire perilously infiltrates England and London, and English bodies as well. Even this danger, however, is not the problem so much as the allure of the other situated in the East End. Whitney's wife arrives distraught at Watson's home late one evening, but her husband's addiction to opium concerns her less than the fact that he has been in an opium den for three days. Watson's own domestic life is disturbed. He is obliged to raise himself from his easy chair and his after-dinner reading, kiss his wife on the cheek, and begin a search through the filthy, infamous East End haunts. Whitney's and Watson's experiences at the opening of the story are of course paralleled by St. Clair's when he too leaves his wife and home to earn his living on the streets of the metropolis. He, like Whitney, disappears into the opium den, and like Whitney, it is his wife who undertakes to save him. This association between the dangers of Whitechapel and the disruption of home life emphasizes the story's concern with spatial threats to national identity. Not only do they exist *in* London rather than at the opposite end of the earth; they also intrude upon the home, which gets pride of place in Victorian conceptions of Englishness.[18] At issue here is the way the East End asserts itself over London. Rather than being contained and surrounded by the rest of the metropolis, its irresistible force has the ability to draw all London into it, and in doing so destroys and devalues the constructions upon which national identity is based.

Doyle was apparently uncomfortable with this possibility, and after this story kept Holmes fairly clear of the East End. As Franco Moretti has pointed out, unlike Doyle's first two novels, "which take place mostly south of the Thames . . . the short stories published in the *Strand Magazine* from 1891 onward focus almost entirely on the West End and the City." In fifty-six stories, Holmes goes to the East End "exactly once."[19] Moretti speculates that the incredible popularity of the stories, especially in relation to the reception given the novels, may well be due to Doyle's accurate "guess" of the "right space for detective fiction" (134). Beyond the narrative needs that Moretti identifies for detective fiction, which necessitate the London of privilege as the locus of crimes, there is also the very real threat to English bodies and English identity that was associated with the East End of London, a reality that was pressed home by sensational accounts of crime and poverty in that area. As Moretti says, *"fictional crime in the London of wealth; real crime in the London of poverty"* (136, emphasis in the original). Middle-class London faced daily reminders of the propinquity of this threat, the "riverside city of a hundred thousand souls, where the tenement houses swelter and reek with the outcasts of Europe" ("Adventure of the Six Napoleons," 815). It is hardly surprising that Doyle would find his readers much more willing to accept Holmes's work in drawing rooms and great banks than to be forced to follow the detective into the heart of the urban jungle.[20]

St. Clair's case reveals the extent of that threat, thus suggesting why Holmes so rarely ventures into the East End. When St. Clair enters the opium den, managed by a lascar of "the vilest antecedents" and situated in "the farthest east of the City," he transforms himself into Boone, the lame beggar with the twisted lip (314, 307). Although contaminated by the place, St. Clair is also able to exploit it. Making more than seven hundred pounds a year as a panhandler, he can afford to pay the lascar well to keep his secret. His income resembles guilt money, for by placing himself directly in the way of the city's denizens, he holds their attention and gaze, reminding them of the proximity of the risk to their own respectability, class status, and cleanliness. The pennies and halfpence he brings in every day signify their attempts to stave off the peril stalking England: the loss of distinction relative to the other existing in its midst, the forced association with those who are perceived as less English, the increasing permeability of the boundaries of Englishness. Those coins are the weight of guilt that kills St. Clair in a double sense. First, they are his motive for replacing his true identity with that of one who earns a handsome if tainted living. They are also the means by which his coat is weighted to sink into the Thames. Because of that burden, it does not wash away and is found on a mud bank, convincing Holmes that St. Clair drowned, having been "sucked away into the river" (316).

Once again a treasure is heaved into the Thames and sinks into the mud. This time, however, rather than being scores of feet beneath the water, like the Agra jewels, it is stuck on the bank, like Small. And, like Small, the coat is recovered and made to tell its tale, one Holmes cannot read correctly. Instead of understanding the metonymic link between St. Clair and the coat as one of disavowal and the money as evidence of St. Clair's challenging the limits of middle-class respectability, and thus Englishness, Holmes construes the coat as proof of foul play, the money helping to hasten St. Clair to a watery grave. As if underscoring the temptations of filthy lucre, Holmes literally cleans up the mystery by scrubbing Boone's grimy face to reveal St. Clair. Just as Watson is apparently saved by his association with Holmes, St. Clair is made whole by having the detective wash his face to reveal his true Englishness—in this case founded upon his place among the bourgeoisie. Characteristically, Holmes has come to the rescue of the middle classes, providing them the means by which to maintain both their wealth and the secret of its source. After being exposed, St. Clair confesses to Holmes that he has never told his family the origins of his wealth. He could not bear to think of the shame it would bring his children. Holmes suggests to St. Clair and to the police that the man really committed no crime and that the entire matter can easily be handled internally by the police without involving the courts and journalists. St. Clair is consequently allowed to keep his dirty little secret, as well as his money, though the police insist that this must be the end of Hugh Boone.[21] Holmes's solution to St. Clair's dilemma is once more emblematic of the helplessness of the detective to deal with the causes of the crime. He may be able to infiltrate the opium den, but he cannot contain its seductive powers. Nor, for that matter, can he enforce a distance between the contaminating effects of the exoticness of the city and the members of the middle classes who work and live there. All he can do is hope to protect Englishness by helping it to keep its secrets. Even those efforts, however, are confounded by the myriad associations across social boundaries to dirt, otherness, and the lowest classes that all combine to fight against anything resembling an English essence. For Holmes and for the late Victorians alike, the difficulty arises from the paradox of those connections serving to create a more protean version of Englishness while concurrently operating as the means the middle class uses to consolidate its wealth and respectability, even more vigorously fortifying and asserting its claim to national identity.

In masquerading as the beggar, Boone, St. Clair moves with impunity across social boundaries, thus confusing the significance of dirt, which for the late Victorians was deployed in a system of surveillance that established a norm and its counterpart, and policed the borders between the two.[22] Add to this St. Claire's transgression of the boundary between clean and dirty money, and it is apparent that the line separating the clean (male, middle-class, English) from the dirty (female, working-class, colonized) has been blurred; the normative limits of national identity are at stake. The dirt, acting as St. Clair's mask, shielding him from the surveillance of his wife, Holmes, and the police, is also the material condition upon which Boone constructs his identity, and that marks him as the object of surveillance. Holmes's act of wiping the beggar's face clean does not simplify matters; it merely makes them evident. The wet, soapy rag across Boone/St. Clair's face both dissolves and accentuates the boundaries that the fetishization of dirt establishes, permitting Holmes to warn of as well as to reaffirm the tenuousness of operative, normative constructions of national identity.

The tenuousness of national identity continually confronts Holmes, and it is at least partially connected to his relative helplessness to address the causes rather than the symptoms of crimes threatening it. Holmes and Watson together are the ostensible prophylaxis for maintaining the health of Englishness, but in fact their function is primarily cosmetic. They can do very little to prevent the contamination of an already sullied national identity. Their responsibility is to clean up after the fact and to ensure, as much as possible, that no trace remains of the link between the filth helping to prop up Englishness and the face it displays to the world. Holmes, therefore, is a *private* detective, for these secrets must remain in limited circulation. He, like Watson, is always a participant in the duplicity of Englishness. His own abilities as a mimic point to the motility within the discourse of Englishness available to one cognizant of its limits. His impersonations illustrate how very slippery categories of identification within the discourse are and consequently how feeble a grasp Englishness itself has on its claims to cultural and moral superiority. They also reveal the necessary cooperation between Holmes and Watson in their attempts to contain national identity within easily recognizable boundaries.

Holmes and Watson depend on each other, as the narratives themselves depend upon them, to reassure one another of the proper performance of Englishness. Holmes's disguises endanger his own identity precisely because he is so good at mimicry. Indeed, his ability not only to become another but *the* other has no real narrative value unless he can reveal himself, usually to Watson. Without that crack in the performance, that moment of recognition, narratively he becomes another character. When not even the reader can see through Holmes's performance, the detective discursively disappears. Watson is his narrative lifeline and as such becomes the touchstone of Englishness, always able to pull Holmes back to his true self. The men's relationship is a symbiotic one, although the two are not really so dissimilar as they may appear, for Holmes too is a bit of a lounger and a loafer. Watson regularly refers to Holmes's long bouts of inactivity, at times pathologizing them as melancholia, but more often they resemble ennui. Holmes's active mind must be stimulated; when nothing in the "professional way" presents itself, he either lies about or indulges his taste for cocaine. Despite Martin Booth's claim that "addiction was not censured in Victorian times, as it was subsequently," Watson clearly disapproves.[23] In the opening of *The Sign of Four*, when he finally musters the nerve to remonstrate with Holmes about his habit, he tells him, "It is a pathological and morbid process which involves increased tissue change and may at least leave a permanent weakness." He goes on, "Remember that I speak not only as one comrade to another, but as a medical man to one for whose constitution he is to some extent answerable" (108). Man to man, friend to friend, doctor to patient, Watson sees the potential for his friend to be absorbed into a life at the edge of Englishness, which he himself barely escaped. This loss of identity would be easy for someone like Holmes, whom not even Watson recognizes in the opium den in "The Man with the Twisted Lip." Holmes understands this too, gently chiding Watson after revealing himself to the doctor: "I suppose, Watson, . . . that you imagine that I have added opium-smoking to cocaine injections, and all the other little weaknesses on which you have favoured me with your medical views" (312). It would not be a surprising assumption on Watson's part since, as the opening of the *Sign of Four* indicates, Holmes does indeed dabble in opiates.[24]

A number of arguments have been made about the function and import of Holmes's addiction, including its association with the upper classes, its operating to identify Holmes as an aesthete, and the need to provide the detective with a crack in his rational armor.[25] At least as significant as all of these are the broader implications of the ingestion of the other, the link to the alien that potentially destroys English identity even as it inoculates it against further contamination. It is as though Holmes's dalliances with exotic drugs work as vaccines, allowing him to push the limits of Englishness, to move about the London cesspool with relative immunity, to explore the ambiguities of his own identity and still be able to return, and to help to define what Englishness is and how it should function. If the problem for all these stories is where Englishness leaves off and foreignness begins, one could profitably answer that it is in the body of Holmes himself. The salutary result, however, is that foreignness is never able completely to overcome that particular English identity—one based in class as well as national characteristics. If Holmes (and London) does not ingest the empire with impunity, then he does so with the understanding that what he takes into himself may undeniably change his character but also will make him more functional in a world that increasingly demands that identities be fungible.

The problem of Englishness in the Holmes stories finds only functional solutions, and the space in which national identity can potentially exist is expressed as between the eccentric, experimentally venturous Holmes at the one pole, and the more stolid, conventional, skeptical Watson at the other. It is not an identity that can do without either, however, because one without the other always runs the risk of infection and loss. Englishness can only be maintained in a kind of flux that always tests its limits, and alone, Holmes or Watson is incapable of making it back across those boundaries. The protection they actually provide is not to an already in-place and functioning national identity. It is too late for that. As Small, Sholto, Morstan, St. Clair, and scores of others in the stories repeatedly demonstrate, contamination by the other—whether in class or ethnic terms—is too much for any one person to defend against. The result is an imperial filth that has become, like the Agra treasure, peremptorily English, inhering in Englishness itself. All the water in the Thames and all the Pears soap in London cannot scrub clean the English soul. The best Holmes and Watson can do is to offer a glimpse of what lies beneath the dirt and to be, as Watson says, "to some extent answerable" for each other. In withdrawing from the most pernicious spaces of London danger to the middle- and upper-class bastions of the West End, Holmes can safely indulge his fascination with drugs and Watson can enjoy domestic bliss with only intermittent interruptions spearheaded by his deductive friend. There they can complement each other's performance of Englishness and service the moneyed classes with their discretion.

In the years between *A Study in Scarlet* and *The Case Book of Sherlock Holmes* (1927), five significant Alien Bills were passed restricting immigration to England and defining British nationality. A World War was fought and the stage set for a second one. The foreign matters that bedevil Holmes and Watson, testing the flexibility of Englishness in the late Victorian period, became matters of course for an empire on the wane. But no satisfactory answer to the question of the limits of foreignness or the problem of Englishness has been forthcoming. Consolidated by world wars and issues of national security during the twentieth century, they became even more premier concerns with the breakup of the Commonwealth and the migration to England of former colonials after the Second World War. In the wake of attempts to refigure English national identity in the 1980s, the Holmes stories enjoyed a resurgence of popularity as a result of the Granada Television productions. Seeing particular conceptions of Englishness performed and embodied by Jeremy Brett's Holmes and Edward Hardwicke's Watson revisited the issue of imperial filth and its origins. And while we may have much to say about the ideological limits of Doyle's approaches to these problems, we can almost certainly agree that there was a particular prescience in his understanding of the need to address them at precisely the moment when the stains on England's imperial legacy were about to become too large to ignore.

Notes

1. Bernard Gainer, *The Alien Invasion: The Origins of the Aliens Act of 1905* (New York: Crane, Russak, and Co., 1972), 11.

2. W. H. Wilkins, *The Alien Invasion* (London: Methuen, 1892), 95.

3. Wilkins writes: "Cleanliness and sanitation are peculiarities of Western rather than of Eastern nationalities. When Peter the Great went back to Russia after his famous visit to London two centuries ago, he left behind him such a filthy habitation, that the cleansing of it had to be defrayed by an especial grant from the Exchequer. . . . A similar experience in connection with the visit of an Oriental potentate has occurred in very recent years. If this sort of thing is incidental to the visit of Eastern Princes, how much rather then is it liable to accompany the wholesale inundation of poor and degraded foreigners, who flock into London . . . from every country in Europe?" (95).

4. *A Study in Scarlet* (1887) was followed by *The Sign of Four* (novella, 1890), *The Adventures of Sherlock Holmes* (1891), *The Memoirs of Sherlock Holmes* (1892), *The Hound of the Baskervilles* (novella, 1902), and *The Return of Sherlock Holmes* (1903). Doyle published *The Valley of Fear* (novella) in 1914, *His Last Bow* in 1917, and *The Case Book of Sherlock Holmes* in 1927.

5. Arthur Conan Doyle, *A Study in Scarlet*, in *Sherlock Holmes: The Complete Novels and Stories,* 2 vols. (New York: Bantam, 1986), 1:6. All further parenthetical references to Doyle are to this edition.

6. Julia Kristeva, *Powers of Horror: An Essay on Abjection*, trans. Leon S. Roudiez (New York: Columbia University Press, 1982), 69.

7. Ronald Thomas, *Detective Fiction and the Rise of Forensic Science* (Cambridge: Cambridge University Press, 1999), 220.

8. T. N. Mukharji, *A Visit to Europe* (Calcutta: W. Newman, 1889), 106.

9. See Paul Gootenberg, ed., *Cocaine: Global Histories* (London: Routledge, 1999); Tim Madge, *White Mischief: A Cultural History of Cocaine* (London: Mainstream Publishing, 2001).

10. Thomas, *Detective Fiction*, 220.

11. Joseph Kestner, *Sherlock's Men: Masculinity, Conan Doyle, and Cultural History* (Aldershot, UK: Ashgate, 1997), 67.

12. Stephen Arata, *Fictions of Loss in the Victorian Fin de Siècle: Identity and Empire* (Cambridge: Cambridge University Press, 1996), 143.

13. Kestner, *Sherlock's Men*, 67.

14. Ian Baucom, *Out of Place: Englishness, Empire, and the Locations of Identity* (Princeton, NJ: Princeton University Press, 1999); Simon Gikandi, *Maps of Englishness: Writing Identity in the Culture of Colonialism* (New York: Columbia University Press, 1996).

15. For a less pessimistic view, see Arata, *Fictions of Loss*, 143.

16. Audrey Jaffe, "Detecting the Beggar: Arthur Conan Doyle, Henry Mayhew, and 'The Man with the Twisted Lip,'" *Representations* 31 (1990): 97. See also Rosemary Jann, *The Adventures of Sherlock Holmes: Detecting Social Order* (New York: Twayne Publishers, 1995), 91–92.

17. Virginia Berridge and Griffith Edwards, *Opium and the People: Opiate Use in Nineteenth-Century England* (New Haven, CT: Yale University Press, 1987), especially 196–97.

18. This is such an important aspect of Englishness that it is commented upon at length by visitors to Britain during the nineteenth century. Mukharji devotes a long section of his book to the "Banker at Home," further accentuating the links between particular notions of domesticity, the middle classes, and national identity.

19. Franco Moretti, *Atlas of the European Novel: 1800–1900* (New York: Verso, 1998), 133. Further parenthetical references are to this edition.

20. Remarking on the use of the south of England as the launching point for marches on the capital in the popular "invasion literature" of the period, Moretti points out that "the crimes occurring south of London (all murders) begin to look like Doyle's trope for a foreign invasion" (137).

21. Compare this resolution with the relative ignorance of so many of the heirs of ill-gotten gains in the Holmes stories.

22. See Anne McClintock, *Imperial Leather: Race, Gender, and Sexuality in the Colonial Contest* (New York: Routledge, 1995), 153–54.

23. Martin Booth, *The Doctor and the Detective: A Biography of Sir Arthur Conan Doyle* (New York: St. Martin's Minotaur, 2000), 149.

24. Cocaine, Holmes's drug of choice, was often prescribed for addiction to opium in the late nineteenth and early twentieth centuries. See Jack Tracy and Jim Berkey, *Subcutaneously, My Dear Watson: Sherlock Holmes and the Cocaine Habit* (Bloomington, IN: James A. Rock, 1978), 43.

25. For these and other readings of Holmes's drug use, see Booth, *Doctor and the Detective*; Ian Small, *Sherlock Holmes Detected: The Problem of the Long Stories* (London: David and Charles, 1974); Daniel Stashower, *Teller of Tales: The Life of Arthur Conan Doyle* (New York: Henry Holt, 1999); Joseph McLaughlin, *Writing the Urban Jungle: Reading Empire in London from Doyle to Eliot* (Charlottesville: University of Virginia Press, 2000).

Part IV

DIRTY MODERNISM

Chapter 10

The Dustbins of History: Waste Management in Late-Victorian Utopias

Natalka Freeland

To collect facts about the past, and to leave the social application
of this information for any one or no one to give it a philosophical
meaning, is merely to encumber the future with useless rubbish.
—*Frederic Harrison,* Autobiographic Memoirs *(1911)*

This is how one pictures the angel of history. His face is turned
toward the past. Where we perceive a chain of events, he sees one
single catastrophe which keeps piling wreckage upon wreckage and
hurls it in front of his feet. The angel would like to stay, awaken
the dead, and make whole what has been smashed. But a storm is
blowing from Paradise. . . . This storm irresistibly propels him into
the future to which his back is turned, while the pile of debris
before him grows skyward. This storm is what we call progress.
—*Walter Benjamin, "Theses on the Philosophy of History" (1940)*

*V*ictorian futurists have their minds in the gutter. One
after another, utopian novels describe improved systems for waste management as cornerstones of their
fantasies of alternate worlds. This impulse is so strong that, faced with
a future lacking any evidence of rubbish removal, the narrator of H. G.
Wells's *The Time Machine* (1895) imagines it must be just out of sight:

A peculiar feature, which presently attracted my attention, was the
presence of certain circular wells. . . . I was at first inclined to associate
it with the sanitary apparatus of these people. It was an obvious
conclusion, but it was absolutely wrong. . . .

In the matter of sepulture, for instance, I could see no signs of crematoria nor anything suggestive of tombs. But it occurred to me that, possibly, there might be cemeteries (or crematoria) somewhere beyond the range of my explorings. This, again, was a question I deliberately put to myself.[1]

In fact, the "waterless wells" (35), which continue to intrigue the traveller for most of his stay in the future, serve as the only conduit between the bucolic idyll on the earth's surface and a mechanical, violent world of subterranean tunnels; the reason he cannot find any human remains in this "social paradise" (27) is that the bestial Morlocks regularly ascend through the "wells" to cannibalize the childlike Eloi. When he discovers his mistake, the traveller concedes that literary convention prompted his automatic equation of the central mysteries of the future with sanitation: "I must admit that I learned very little of *drains* and bells and modes of conveyance, and the like *conveniences*, during my time in this real future. In some of these visions of Utopias and coming times I have read, there is a vast amount of detail about building, and social arrangements, and so forth" (34, emphasis added; "convenience" was a Victorian euphemism for a water closet). The traveller's familiarity with this generic cliché begs the question: why does waste removal figure so prominently in late-Victorian utopias? A generation earlier, social problem novelists had justified their graphic descriptions of filth and rubbish by appealing to the dictates of realism: true accounts of industrial poverty and urban slums needed to describe refuse.[2] But utopian fiction assumes an opposite imperative: exotically "other" places and projected futures make no claims to verisimilitude, and the worlds they depict are characteristically defined by the absence of nineteenth-century Britain's most intractable problems. Why would these heavily sanitized elsewheres and nowheres insist on calling attention to the drains?

It is precisely utopian fiction's escapism that fuels its emphasis on refuse. The invocation of imaginary (or impossible) futures responds to a cultural anxiety about the crushing accumulation of history and its material artifacts—in utopian novels, the weight of the past is represented (both metaphorically and metonymically) by the weight of the objects it has left behind. For utopian fictions, then, scenes of disposal literalize the genre's efforts to abandon the constraints of historical precedent. Even in their fantastic departures from contemporary reality, however, utopias continue to insist on the need for systemic disposal, betraying a suspicion of the iterative force of this accumulative paradigm. In this chapter, I first trace the literary commonplace identified by Wells's traveller, exploring the connections between refuse and history in H. Rider Haggard's *She* (1887), William Morris's *News from Nowhere* (1890), and Richard Jefferies's *After London* (1884); I argue that the utopian rejection of history does not just shift settings from past to future but, more radically, constructs an open temporality in contradistinction to the teleological determinisms of nineteenth-century theology and science—and of the realist novel. I then turn to a more detailed analysis of *News from Nowhere* in which I suggest that Morris develops a particularly creative response to the challenge of accumulative excess: instead of sending superabundant goods (or people) to the dustheap—or its figurative geopolitical equivalent, the colonies—Morris advocates eliminating material waste through art. Where planned obsolescence and emigration simply delay the crises of accruing refuse, in *News from Nowhere*'s utopian future, surplus productive capacity is absorbed by labor-intensive craftsmanship, and this waste *of time* produces no detritus. In Morris's vision of workaday transcendence, art provides a genuine escape from history.

One of the least expected accounts of waste management in Victorian fiction appears in Haggard's African adventure *She*. While Haggard's narrator, Holly, dismisses the fact in a footnote, it comes as a shock when we learn that the ancient Kôr civilization, in the midst of an unspecified swamp in sub-Saharan Africa, had "reservoirs and sewers."[3] A well-developed sewer system was one of nineteenth-century Britain's claims to global preeminence, and discovering one in the heart of Africa forces a reevaluation of the relations among geography, history, and civilization.[4] On closer examination, Haggard's Africa is not primitive, but degenerate, a point the novel highlights by insistently Orientalizing these "yellow" Africans: the tribal elder wears a pigtail "like a Chinaman's" (123); the carvings on the cave walls "looked more like Chinese writing than any other" (132); She's rooms are hung with "Oriental" curtains (139). This spatial displacement from Mozambique to the Far East implies an even greater temporal dislocation: if, in the Victorian imagination, Africa was ahistorical—or at best prehistorical—the Orient, as Edward Said has argued, was decidedly posthistorical.[5] In other words, the Amahagger tribe are suffering not from a dearth of history, but from its surfeit—and, consequently, from the accumulated refuse that history has left behind.

While much of *She* relies on a Hegelian narrative of universal history, the novel's explanation of the Amahagger's latter-day degeneracy remains thoroughly materialist. The Amahagger do not progress technologically because they are glutted with the artifacts of the civilization that preceded theirs. Echoing Ernest Renan—"forgetting . . . is a crucial factor in the creation of a nation"[6]—Holly presupposes a strict dichotomy between the persistence of relics and the development of any new industry: "[Their] vases are of a very ancient manufacture, and of all sizes. None such can have been made in the country for hundreds, or rather thousands, of years. They are found in the rock tombs . . . and my own belief is that, after the fashion of the Egyptians . . . they were used to receive the viscera of the dead" (97). The Amahagger's recycling—a strange mix of applied archeology and ecological economics—can only lead to decline and decay: a people whose everyday appliances are erstwhile burial equipment, and who live literally in the tombs of their extinct forerunners (who themselves rehearsed the customs of the necrophilial Egyptians) cannot join the nineteenth century's march of progress. Moreover, considering the central role of textile manufacture in Britain's headlong industrial expansion, the Amahagger can hardly be expected to follow suit so long as their own clothes all come ready-made: "the yellowish linen whereof those of the Amahagger who condescended to wear anything in particular made their dresses . . . was taken from the tombs, and was not, as I had at first imagined, of *native* manufacture" (130, emphasis added). In Holly's tellingly inaccurate phrase, morbid—but local—relics become imports, making the Amahagger the colonized outpost of their own history.

By contrast, Morris's *News from Nowhere* foretells the decolonization of the future: the death throes of industrial Britain inaugurate a communist paradise. While the Nowherians know better than to dress in or eat out of Victorian hand-me-downs, they nonetheless retain some of the nineteenth century's more symbolically charged cultural residue. Notably, Morris's narrator, William Guest, discovers the Houses of Parliament intact. As his tour guide Dick explains: "You may well wonder at our keeping them standing. . . . [M]y old kinsman has given me books to read about the strange game that they played there. . . . [Now] they are used for a sort of subsidiary market, and a storage place for manure."[7] The special exception made for the Houses of Parliament, in a culture that regards monuments as "worthless, and public nuisances" (69), effectively conflates history and garbage. Morris's well-known antipathy for Charles Barry's and Augustus Pugin's Gothic Revival design adds an aesthetic critique to this political statement: anachronistic styles, like antiquated forms of government, are best left in the dustheap. The classic definitions of refuse emphasize location: "dirt is matter out of place."[8] In *News from Nowhere*, dirt, or at least dung, is also matter out of time.

Jefferies' *After London* highlights the dangers of this kind of atavistic materiality. The residents of Jefferies's imaginary future do not need to condemn the past by using its monuments to store their refuse: nature does it for them. The entire first section of Jefferies's utopia celebrates a "Relapse into Barbarism," which is above all a reassertion of nature against man-made things. Beginning with the announcement that "it became green everywhere in the first spring, after London ended," this characterless and plotless exposition runs through five chapters detailing the reverse arc of English civilization.[9] London is the locus of ruin and decomposition: "For this marvellous city, of which such legends are related, was after all only of brick, and when the ivy grew over and trees and shrubs sprang up, and lastly, the waters underneath burst in, the huge metropolis was soon overthrown. . . . Trees and bushes covered [the ruins of houses]; ivy and nettles concealed the crumbling masses of brick" (32). The loving catalogs of natural life that make up most of *After London* notwithstanding, Jefferies's account of the end of the city does not give all of the credit to trees and ivy. Before nature takes over, civilization collapses under its own accumulated weight: "vast quantities of timber, the wreckage of towns and bridges . . . was carried down by the various rivers, and by none more so than by the Thames. These added to the accumulation, which increased the faster because the foundations of the ancient bridges held it like piles driven in for the purpose" (32).

Surprisingly, the very drains and tunnels that might be expected to relieve this build-up of matter exacerbate its implosive effect: "when this had gone on for a time, the waters of the river, unable to find a channel, began to overflow up into the deserted streets, and especially to fill the underground passages and drains, of which the number and extent was beyond all the power of words to describe. These, by the force of the water, were burst up, and the houses fell in" (32). In this not-quite-logical account of the city flooding and collapsing because of its extensive drainage system, *After London* slips into a familiar scatological tropology. The intangibly dangerous weight of history is concretely embodied in its residue of human filth: "all the rottenness of a thousand years and of many hundred millions of human beings is there festering under the stagnant water, which has sunk down into and penetrated the earth, and floated up to the surface the contents of the buried cloacae" (34). The causal link between history and stagnation—accumulated artifacts block waterways, in turn leading to destruction and decay—is matched by a syntax that fails to distinguish between years and corpses as poisonous and festering things. For the residents of the future, avoiding history and avoiding corruption become synonymous:

[T]he sites are uninhabitable because of the emanations from the ruins. Therefore they are avoided. Even the spot where a single house has been known to have existed is avoided by the hunters in the woods.

. . . And thus the cities of the old world, and their houses and habitations, are deserted and lost in the forest. If the hunters, about to pitch camp for the night, should stumble on so much as a crumbling brick or a fragment of hewn stone, they at once remove. (35)[10]

Jefferies's protagonist later comes to London, and, after picking up some blackened coins that he finds amidst the skeletons and ruins, almost dies from "the decay of the ancient city . . . the decomposition of accumulated matter" (175) — "the very essence of corruption" (169). Money, the record and repository of past values and a claim on the future for their repayment,[11] is as dangerously corrupting in Jefferies's pastoral fantasy as in John Ruskin's dystopian allegory of capital:

[L]ately in a wreck of a Californian ship, one of the passengers fastened a belt about him with two hundred pounds of gold in it, with which he was found afterwards at the bottom. Now, as he was sinking — had he the gold? or had the gold him? . . . [M]any of the persons considered wealthy, are . . . operating for the nation, in an economical point of view, either as pools of dead water . . . or else, as mere accidental stays and impediments, acting not as wealth, but (for we ought to have a correspondent term) as "illth."[12]

Conflating economic and hygienic rhetorics, Ruskin's portmanteau word defines money as a fatal composite of dirt and disease.

Like a good amateur historian, Jefferies's hero takes the filthy lucre and runs. The archeophobic hunters are more suitable emblems for the genre as a whole: by definition, utopian fictions abandon the cultural remains of contemporary Britain for other places or, more often, for a future that ignores, fears, or hates the past it left behind. John Sutherland has argued that Victorian historical fiction presents a critical anomaly: "a surprising number of Victorians would have claimed that . . . historical romances were the very greatest literary works of the age. On no matter relating to the Victorian novel has posterity more diverged from contemporary nineteenth-century thought."[13] But the trend that Sutherland identifies goes back to the Victorians themselves, who registered their ambivalence about the Macaulayan narrative of progress in the waning popularity of historical novels at the end of the century. The Victorian preoccupation with history reemerges, inverted, in the fin-de-siècle fad for novels of the future. This major generic reorientation from history to utopia goes much deeper than a change of setting. Theorists of the novel have routinely defined it as an open form, a "genre of becoming" (Bakhtin) that emphasizes open-ended possibilities instead of deterministic causality (Lotman).[14] But in the standard nineteenth-century realist novel (from which these theoretical models are derived) the usual arsenal of narrative strategies (plot, themes, character development) ensures that the beginning, middle, and above all ending cohere. Critics such as Frank Kermode have read this literary historical peculiarity as a universal truth, not only of genre, but of human nature: "fictions, whose ends are consonant with their precedents, satisfy our needs." In Kermode's analysis, even our desire to imagine the future is a wish "to see the structure whole," thereby giving meaning to the otherwise unpatterned and incoherent middle.[15]

This model of closural poetics recalls theorists like Walter Benjamin, who argued that the best stories culminate in death, because fixed endings retrospectively organize and contain what preceded them. Kermode's deterministic "sense of an ending" also, more surprisingly, echoes late-Victorian millennialists like Patrick Fairbarn, who insisted on the importance of prophecy to motivate the present in light of the future: according to Fairbarn, God "informs the minds of his people in respect to the end, that they may come also to know better than they could otherwise have done, the beginning and the middle."[16] This closed futurism is structurally identical to the most conservative models of deterministic historicism. Thomas Carlyle's "On History" (1830), for example, makes claims for the epistemological importance of the past that are nearly indistinguishable from those Fairbarn makes about the future: "Let us search more and more into the Past; let all men explore it, as the true fountain of knowledge; by whose light alone, consciously or unconsciously employed, can the Present and the Future be interpreted or guessed at."[17] In both cases, the emphasis on continuity (with the past or with a predicted future) disables the potential of the present to deviate from a prescribed narrative.

By contrast, utopian fiction invites newness into the world by rejecting the genealogical continuity that characterizes realist narrative in favor of temporal rupture. Late-Victorian utopias like Morris's *News from Nowhere* imagine radically alternative futures that do not depend upon (and so do not explain) the pasts that they reject. The point applies equally to *After London*, Anthony Trollope's *The Fixed Period* (1881–82), Edward Bulwer-Lytton's *The Coming Race* (1871), W. H. Hudson's *A Crystal Age* (1887), Edward Bellamy's *Looking Backward* (1887), and scores of lesser-known fantasies—though Wells's *Time Machine* is an exception that proves the rule. The closing lines of *News from Nowhere* underscore this idea when Ellen assures Guest that his preview of the future should not change how he conducts his present: she tells him to "Go back" to his own life, adding, "go on living while you may, striving, with whatsoever pain and labour needs must be, to build up little by little the new day" (228). Wells's *The Time Machine*—where the future hypostatizes (in order to diagnose) the present instead of rejecting it—ends on a markedly similar note: after his journey, the traveller "thought but cheerlessly of the Advancement of Mankind, and saw in the growing pile of civilization only a foolish heaping that must inevitably fall back upon and destroy its makers in the end. If that is so, it remains for us to live as though it were not so . . . to me the future is still black and blank" (76). These matching imperatives to go on living in the present despite having seen the future are all the more surprising when we consider the diametrically opposite contexts in which they occur: where Morris's Guest has to avoid complacency while remembering the future, Wells's narrator has to avert despair by forgetting it.

In *News from Nowhere,* rejecting the past is not only a formal device but also one of the central tenets of an imagined ideal society. As the title—punning on the term "utopian novel"—suggests, Nowhere places a high premium on innovation. This principle is enshrined precisely where most Victorian novels stake the strongest claims for continuity: in the structure of families and the biology of inheritance. Nowhere's chief antiquarian, Hammond, explains the difference between Victorian and twenty-second-century models of heredity: "In times past, it is clear that the 'Society' of the day helped its Judaic god, and the 'Man of Science' of the time, in visiting the sins of the father upon the children. How to reverse this process, how to take the sting out of heredity, has for long been one of the most constant cares of the thoughtful men amongst us" (95). By rejecting these key nineteenth-century metanarratives—religion and (evolutionary) science—Hammond effectively eschews both of their versions of temporal determinism. While religion refers backward to an original revealed truth, science points forward to future discoveries. This apparent antinomy conceals a deeper congruence, since both religion and science argue from time-bound events (recorded in scripture or in the fossil record—or observed in the laboratory) to timeless laws. For religion, nothing after the revealed truth matters; for science, nothing before the latest discovery counts. History as the medium of lived experience—and as the site for potential change—becomes irrelevant.[18] This is historicism in the service of eternity, where, in Gerard Manley Hopkins's memorable phrase, "All things counter, original, spare, strange" point back to a principle "whose beauty is past change" ("Pied Beauty," 7, 10). In Hopkins's poem, this changeless principle is identified with God; uniformitarianism plays the same role for the scientists challenging the timeline (though not the structure) of revealed history.

Nowhere's antihereditarian social policies also call attention to the rigid structure of continuity underlying Darwin's model of dynamic change. Hammond's rejection of historical determinism is twofold: children are freed from their parents' pasts, and, analogously, Nowhere is released from its Victorian epistemological legacy. Paradoxically, Hammond escapes the grip of nineteenth-century historicism by historicizing it: in his account, science and religion are not revealed or discovered (in either case, timeless) truths but contingent political positions.[19] Victorian defenses of presentism often oddly equate a person's historical moment with his biological ancestors, as in George Eliot's censure of "Looking Backward" (1879): "Most of us, who have had decent parents, would shrink from wishing that our father and mother had been somebody else whom we never knew; yet it is held no impiety . . . for a man to wail that he was not the son of another age and another nation, of which he also knows nothing except through the easy process of an imperfect imagination and a flattering fancy."[20] Morris stands this reasoning on its head, suggesting that precisely as we might wish to escape the consequences of being our parents' children, we can try to reject the wider implications of our cultural and historical situatedness.[21] In this light, the utopian novel is ironically cast as the logical heir to the nineteenth-century bildungsroman and its tradition of Smilesian arrivistes.

The avowed aim to escape the implications of history is, moreover, strangely at odds with the atavistic medievalism of Morris's anti-urban and anti-industrial future. The first denizen of Nowhere whom we meet, for example, "would have served very well . . . for a picture of fourteenth-century life . . . he seemed to be like some specially manly and refined young gentleman" (47). This becomes the novel's refrain, as each new mode of life, costume, decoration, or architecture is found to resemble a past (almost invariably fourteenth-century) model, and approved accordingly. For many readers, Morris's nostalgic idealism recalls Marx's critique of "feudal socialism" as "half lamentation, half lampoon; half echo of the past, half menace of the future." Marx's denunciation of the medium as well as the message of the feudal socialists' half-hearted and disingenuous campaigns—"a serious political contest was altogether out of the question. A literary battle alone remained possible"—makes the applicability of his comments to Morris's nostal-gic futurism seem difficult to deny.[22]

News from Nowhere, however, carefully qualifies its analysis of the relation between past and present. We might almost be tempted to ascribe Morris's defensive disavowals to an anxiety of influence: "their dress was somewhat between that of the ancient classical costume and the simpler forms of the fourteenth-century garments, though *it was clearly not an imitation* of either" (53, emphasis added); their architec-ture "seemed . . . to embrace the best qualities of the Gothic of north-ern Europe with those of the Sarcenic and Byzantine, though *there was no copying* of . . . these styles" (62, emphasis added). This stridently post-Romantic rejection of imitation may seem incongruous coming from the man who spent most of his career painstakingly reviving lost handicrafts: teaching himself to loom tapestries from eighteenth-century manuals, experimenting to reproduce forgotten dyeing arts, building and operating the hand-press that turned out Chaucer's fourteenth-century masterpiece in an appropriately Gothic typeface that Morris himself designed. This apparent contradiction—like the equally vehe-ment opposition of the Society for the Preservation of Ancient Buildings to restoration and support for preservation—recapitulates the distinc-tion between a historicism that venerates the lifeless detritus of the past and an organic utopianism that consumes its own history. Thus, Mor-ris contrasts Renaissance classicism, irremediably "bound to the dead corpse of a past art," with its "genuine new birth," which was "the fruit of the blossoming time, the Gothic period."[23] The point applies to polit-ical as well as artistic innovation: Morris praised the working-class demonstrations of 1887 (from which *News from Nowhere* dates the start of its social transformation) as much for their originality as for their efficacy, identifying "one of the signs of the genuineness" of the movement in the fact that "there is nothing in it of conscious and pedan-tic imitation of former changes—the French Revolution for instance."[24]

Nowhere may avoid the sterile inauthenticity of strict imitation, but the technological inertia of this idyllic future signals a covert persistence of the same threat. We have already seen that the Nowherians preserve some relics of the past, like the Houses of Parliament; they also keep many of the "ridiculous" old names, instead of rededicating their cities and streets to commemorate revolutionary milestones, on the theory that "it was nobody's business to alter [them], since the name of a dead folly doesn't bite" (78). This apparently toothless memorialization, however, functions as a kind of passive imitation; by conserving the old world, it obstructs the development of the new. In Morris's future, defined by the novel's subtitle as an "Epoch of Rest," everyone rests on the laurels of past accomplishments. "[T]his is not an age of inventions," Walter explains. "The last epoch did all that for us, and we are now content to use such of its inventions as we find handy" (192). This echo of *She*'s dangerously opportunistic recycling uncovers a materialist corollary to Morris's celebration of originality—the artifacts, as well as the example, of past epochs must be rejected; to progress is to discard.

As Sigfried Giedion has noted, nineteenth-century scientists practiced what Morris preached, yoking inventiveness to a regular program of destruction and disposal: "So firm was the assumption of progress, on the simplest material level, that many of the new devices and contrivances were destroyed as soon as superseded, with the result that historians now have inadequate records of the full range of mechanical invention during a period which in most other respects is amply documented."[25] Giedion's account testifies to a failure of the emerging institutional practices of Victorian science and museums to coordinate their dissonant goals. Further, Morris's model of technological quiescence hints that nineteenth-century scientists may not simply have jettisoned old "devices and contrivances" because they invented new ones, but may reciprocally have invented new devices under the impetus of a cultural mandate to dispose of the old. By contrast, the potentially disastrous effects of Nowhere's model of technological stagnation are registered in *The Time Machine*, where both the Morlocks' and the Eloi's embruting devolution results from passively relying on machinery made generations before (and where a well-stocked museum reveals an ethos of preservation that inhibits invention). In countless subsequent dystopias, a civilization that depends on a past epoch's technology collapses as soon as, in E. M. Forster's foreboding phrase, "The Machine Stops."[26]

With the exception of Morris's antitechnological bias, however, his Nowhere largely adheres to the joint principles of disposal and innovation. In fact, the genesis of this utopia, tellingly described as the Great Change, is not nearly so much about the new social structures established since the nineteenth century as about the destruction of the old. Anticipating Huxley's Kantian axiom that "every cosmic magma destined to evolve into a new world, has been the no less predestined end of a vanished predecessor,"[27] the Nowherians predicate the birth of their society on destruction. England has become "a pretty place . . . since the great clearing of the houses" (55), especially because "not an inch" of the East End was left standing in "The Clearing of Misery" (99); even those few buildings, like Westminster Abbey, that are preserved have been cleaned and subjected to a "great clearance . . . of the beastly monuments to fools and knaves, which once blocked [them] up" (69); and as for the factories, without undergoing anything so active as cleaning and clearing, they have simply "disappeared; only, since they were centres of nothing but 'manufacture,' and served no purpose but that of the gambling market, they have left less signs of their existence than London" (102). In Morris's account, the blueprint for creating a perfect society reproduces the formula for sculpture attributed to Michelangelo: find the angel in the marble and remove everything else. When Guest expresses surprise at the extent of the destruction during the Revolution—since he had assumed that the rebels and the reactionaries, both fighting for control of the nation's wealth, would be careful to preserve it—Hammond explains that for the revolutionaries this destruction was not collateral damage, but a fringe benefit: "It was perhaps rather a good than an evil thing that . . . there was so much destruction of wares, and instruments for making them as in this civil war. It was a common saying amongst them, Let the country be cleared . . . it was seen how little of any value there was in the old world" (157). This is the familiar rhetoric of destructive radicalism, which contemporary historians like James Anthony Froude had similarly defined as a matter of disposal: "The function of Radicalism in these days I conceive to be the burning up of rubbish."[28] Thus, *News from Nowhere*'s revolutionary social progress is essentially a clean-up project: "the new order of things had . . . [gotten] rid of the sprawling mess with which commercialism had littered the banks of the wide stream" (186).

Mess, litter, rubbish—all are famously subjective terms and, moreover, ones which, in the novel's view, the nineteenth century tended to confuse with their opposites. Guest first suspects that he has awoken to a new and different world when he discovers that "the soap-works with their smoke-vomiting chimneys were gone" (48): in the nineteenth century, even cleaning supplies are dirty.[29] Two hundred years later, Morris's utopia has mysteriously solved the problem of industrial pollution not by clarifying the distinctions between dirt and cleanliness, or the even trickier boundary between valuables and rubbish, but by further muddying them. When Guest arrives in the future, not yet aware of the Great Change, he tries to pay Dick for his services as a waterman. Dick's refusal initially reads as a fairly crude travesty of Victorian materialism: "As to your coins, they are curious, but not very old; they seem to be all of the reign of Victoria; you might give them to some scantily-furnished museum. Ours has enough of such coins, besides a fair number of earlier ones, many of which are beautiful, whereas these nineteenth-century ones are so beastly ugly, ain't they?" (50). Guest's coins are ugly in part because, like the ones in *After London*, they have changed from silver to a tarnished black, compounding the suggestion that money has become meaningless with the reminder (necessarily occluded in any currency-based economy) that coins, like other material things, are subject to natural decay as well as social devaluation.[30]

As in Ruskin, wealth has become "illth." But Dick does not decline payment only because the coins are simultaneously too new and too un-attractively aged—too common and too dirty—to have any value for the aesthetically inclined Nowherians. His real reason for refusing Guest's "gift" is a concern about the quantity, rather than the quality, of mate-rial things. It is explicitly a desire to avoid accumulation—not any worry about structural inequality or monopolistic exploitation—that motivates Nowhere's abjection of money: "you feel yourself bound to give me something which I am not to give to a neighbour, unless he has done something special for me . . . but . . . if one person gave me something, then another might, and another, and so on; and I hope you won't think me rude if I say that I shouldn't know where to stow away so many mementoes of friendship" (50). Rubbish is not just mat-ter out of place or out of time, but matter out of proportion. This bizarre misreading of the cash nexus imagines that currency is routinely hoarded rather than exchanged and that a wage laborer's main danger is accumulating too much money. Dick's refusal of payment thus fore-shadows the surprising central issue of the twenty-second-century econ-omy: how to keep supply from overtaking demand. In other words, *News from Nowhere* is not just engaged in a satiric reversal in which money has become valueless. Instead, it traces the more complex nego-tiations of an economic structure that is as concerned with how to get rid of goods—recall Dick's particular worry about the conditions under which he can give Guest's money away—as with how to produce or acquire them.[31]

Nowhere's answer to this disproportion of supply and demand—and its attendant threat of filling everyone's homes with useless clutter—is to create ways to take goods out of circulation. One of the few indus-tries described in this fantasy of unalienated labor is glassblowing, which Dick praises in typically perverse terms: "It makes a lot of pleasant work . . . for however much care you take of such goods, break they will, one day or another, so there is always plenty to do" (82). Jarring as it is to discover planned obsolescence in a communist utopia, Morris's radical-ism outdoes even Froude's forebodings, with an imaginary future not only set on discarding the accumulated rubbish of past societies but

238 ⌒ Natalka Freeland

structured so as to systematically produce goods designed to be thrown away. Going well beyond the anxieties about excessive material accumulation expressed in *She* or *After London*, *News from Nowhere* makes preemptive disposal an integral part of the economy rather than an incidental afterthought.

The Nowherians' fear that the conjunction of their high productive capacity and their comparatively low rate of consumption will result in a "work-famine" (128) is meant to sound outlandishly paradoxical to Victorian ears—the nineteenth century had both work and famine, but no precedent for Nowhere's extravagant love of labor. Yet the glut in production feared by Morris's communists is precisely the crisis that Marx described as *capitalism's* chief vulnerability:

> In these crises there breaks out an epidemic that, in all earlier epochs, would have seemed an absurdity—the epidemic of over-production. Society suddenly finds itself put back into a state of momentary barbarism; it appears as if a famine, a universal war of devastation had cut off the supply of every means of subsistence; industry and commerce seem to be destroyed; and why? Because there is too much civilization, too much means of subsistence, too much industry, too much commerce.

Morris's future earthly paradise replicates Marx's diagnosis of nineteenth-century ills. Marx identifies two solutions for this excess of unwanted goods: "And how does the bourgeoisie get over these crises? On the one hand by enforced destruction of a mass of productive forces; on the other, by the conquest of new markets."[32] We have already seen some evidence of the waste of productive forces in Nowhere's predilection for producing goods doomed to quick destruction. Conversely, Hammond disavows the more extroverted expedient in the strongest possible terms: "[before the Revolution] the countries within the ring of 'civilization' (that is, organized misery) were glutted with the abortions of the market, and force and fraud were used unsparingly to 'open up' countries *outside* that pale. This process of 'opening up' . . . shows us at its worst the great vice of the nineteenth century" (125).

This orthodox Marxist indictment of imperialism still leaves Nowhere with an oversupply of manufactured goods, and their destination is not hard to predict. Even after the fall of the empire and the end of the market economy, Morris postulates a clear cultural superiority and unidirectional flow of manufactures that was already a nostalgic nationalist fantasy by the late nineteenth century: "it is only in parts of Europe which are more advanced than the rest of the world that you will hear this talk of the fear of work-famine. Those lands that were once the colonies of Great Britain, for instance, and especially America—that part of it, above all, which was once the United States—are now and will be for a long while a great resource to us" (128). Hammond's description of using "very backward" countries like America as a dumping ground for Europe's overproduction defensively inverts the actual terms of this relationship; still reassuring Guest about the unlikelihood of a work-famine, Hammond explains "that for nearly one hundred years the people of the northern parts of America have been engaged in gradually making a dwelling place out of a stinking dust-heap; and there is still a great deal to do, especially as the country is so big" (128).

Like its Victorian counterpart, Nowhere also uses the "big" and imaginatively empty spaces of the globe as a receptacle for its stock of excess producers. When Guest wonders how densely populated twenty-second-century England can have been made over as a "garden," Dick provides an apologist's account of colonialism: "we have helped to populate other countries—where we were wanted and were called for" (106). Framing this relationship as voluntary, Dick defines it as a question of "wants," ambiguously conflating the mechanics of supply and demand with the more slippery dynamics of human desire. Since Hammond will later acknowledge that economic imperialism proceeds by creating false desires among the colonized peoples, Dick's benign rhetoric falls particularly flat. Of course, the plotting of innumerable Victorian novels confirms that this kind of compulsory emigration (of convicts, bigamists, bankrupts, and other troublemakers) is really a form of waste control. Wells's quasi-fictional *Anticipations* (1901), which ultimately advocates eugenics and forced sterilization to eliminate the unwanted population, is similarly less concerned with Marx's surplus production than with Malthus's surplus reproduction. Because the "vicious, helpless, and pauper masses" are "as inevitable in the social body as are waste matters and disintegrating cells in the body of an active and healthy man," the survival of the body politic clearly depends on the expulsion of "this bulky . . . excretion."[33] Meanwhile, scare-mongering narratives of reverse colonization and other utopias like Trollope's *The Fixed Period* had already begun to suggest that even the colonies could be expected to fill up sooner or later.[34] Set on an island off the coast of New Zealand—a typically Victorian projection of the end of the line—Trollope's novel imagines a surplus population with nowhere else to go instituting the only forms of waste management it has left: mandatory euthanasia and cremation.[35]

Under these circumstances, we might be excused for wondering how

Morris's response to material (and human) surpluses differs from that
of the capitalist system whose demolition he envisions. Both economies
are endangered by superabundance; both respond by developing self-
destructive modes of production and by exploiting the "underdeveloped"
areas of the globe. But *News from Nowhere* draws a crucial distinction.
Nowhere creates a system of wasteful production, manufacturing reli-
ably disposable goods like breakable glassware. By contrast, the nineteenth century responded to overproduction by manipulating patterns
of consumption: "they created in a never-ending series sham or artificial
necessaries, which became . . . of equal importance to them with the real
necessaries which supported life. . . . [They] 'created new wants,' to supply which . . . the hapless, helpless people had to sell themselves into the
slavery of hopeless toil so that they might have something wherewith
to purchase the nullities of 'civilization'" (124–26).[36] In other words, if
Marx identified "the conquest of new markets" as a key way for capitalist economies to offload their unwanted goods, Morris recognizes
that analogous marketing strategies hit much closer to home. Like Haggard's She, whose "empire is of the imagination" (175), capitalist economies effectively colonize the human psyche. Regenia Gagnier's account
of fin-de-siècle economic theory notes this shift from a discourse of
"needs" to one of "wants." Since needs are biologically and even culturally bounded, but desires are limitless, this changed emphasis justified
an ever-increasing pace of production.[37] The most radical premise of
Morris's utopia is its negation of this cultural mandate; Morris imagines a world in which all needs have been satisfied and, more importantly, all wants are satiable. In fact, desire in its most basic form is a
key metaphor for Nowhere's economy, giving concrete weight to the
fantasy of a natural love of labor: "The spirit of the new days . . . was
. . . intense and overweening love of the very skin and surface of the
earth on which man dwells, such as a lover has in the fair flesh of the
woman he loves" (158). Sexual desire then models the economically elusive goal of a perfect fit between supply and demand: "'Tis a good job
there are so many [women] that every Jack may have his Jill," Dick tells
Guest, "else I fear we should get fighting for them" (72).[38]

Even the simple mathematics of sexual reproduction—a Jill for every
Jack—turns out to be an unreliable guarantor of the compatibility of
supply and demand. All of the novel's main characters (except Hammond, who is presumably too old for this sort of thing) find themselves
with an oversupply of potential love objects. Meanwhile, in the economy itself, limited wants coupled with an unlimited work drive continue

to fuel the problem of productive excess. If the colonies are a reactionary solution to overproduction and breaking glassware an impractical one, Morris proposes a third alternative. Art, and in particular architectural ornament, is Nowhere's deceptively simple remedy for industrial society's old epidemic.[39] As Hammond explains, art, unlike more mechanical pursuits, becomes increasingly intricate and time-consuming as a culture develops; art is therefore "inexhaustible" (128). Similarly, Dick opines that "the energies of mankind are chiefly of use to them for [fine building]; for in that direction I can see no end to the work, while in many others a limit does seem possible" (70). The insatiability of human desires is replaced by the inexhaustibility of artistic demands, with the added benefit that disposing of surplus time, unlike surplus goods or populations, does not require a dustheap.[40] Art itself is wasteful almost by definition. Morris's famous imperative for happiness—"*Have nothing in your houses that you do not know to be useful, or believe to be beautiful*"[41]—implicitly pits (conjectural) aesthetics against (positive) utility, while *News from Nowhere* explicitly invokes beauty as a justification for squandering both natural resources and productive capacity. When Guest points out to Hammond, "You have spoken of wastes and forests. . . . Why do you keep such things in a garden [i.e., post-Revolutionary England]? and isn't it very wasteful to do so?" Hammond replies, strangely mustering artifice to justify nature:

> As to the land being a garden, I have heard that they used to have shrubberies and rockeries in gardens once; and though I might not like the artificial ones, I assure you that some of the natural rockeries of our garden are worth seeing. . . . Go and have a look at the sheep-walks . . . and tell me if you think we *waste* the land there by not covering it with factories for making things that nobody wants, which was the chief business of the nineteenth century. (106)

If beauty is beneficially wasteful, ugliness further represents the restrictive force of history. Before the Great Change, multisensory ugliness was universal: "even rich and powerful men . . . submitted to live amidst sights and sounds and smells which it is the very nature of man to abhor and flee from" (124). This ugliness was tolerated only through habit—history in its most visceral and local form: "You know that according to the old saw the beetle gets used to living in dung; and these people, whether they found the dung sweet or not, certainly lived in it" (125). This strange dichotomy between habit (or history) and art recalls Walter Pater's scandalous conclusion to *The Renaissance* (1873):

[O]ur failure is to form habits. . . . [O]ur one chance lies in expanding that interval [before death], in getting as many pulsations as possible into the given time. Great passions may give us this quickened sense of life. . . . Of such wisdom, the poetic passion, the desire of beauty, the love of art for its own sake, has most. For art comes to you proposing frankly to give nothing but the highest quality to your moments as they pass, and simply for those moments' sake.[42]

Like the other disposal systems to which *News from Nowhere* compares it, art is thus coded as a way of escaping the weight of precedent and history. Instead of accumulating time, art wastes it. Or, at least, good art does. Morris's utopia insists that bad art (specifically, the Victorian novel) functions, like capital, to sacrifice the present to the past. Thus Ellen, the "good fairy" (179) of the twenty-second century, reprimands her grandfather for his literary tastes:

"Books, books! always books, grandfather! When will you understand that after all it is the world which we live in that interests us; the world of which we are a part . . . ? Look!" she said, throwing open the casement [and pointing to the scenery] . . . "these are our books in these days!—and these," she said, stepping lightly up to the two lovers and laying a hand on each of their shoulders . . . "and even you, grandfather . . . with all your grumbling and wishing yourself back in the good old days." (175)[43]

Morris plays up this connection by making *News from Nowhere*'s one novelist a reactionary by temperament and a dustman by trade. Although the text never explains why, in this world in which the pleasure of labor is its only reward, anyone would choose to be a dustman, we are clearly meant to associate Henry Johnson's antiquarianism with his profession, and to see him as hopelessly mired in the detritus of the past. This impression is reinforced by the outward signs of his atavism: Henry literally wears his materialism on his sleeve, dressing so lavishly that he seems to be encased in golden armor. The combination of his clothes and his calling earns him the nickname Boffin, in jesting tribute to Dickens's famous "Golden Dustman." Since *Our Mutual Friend* (1865) is itself all about how the weight of the past—represented by a pile of garbage—threatens to crush its inheritors, Morris's allusion is more than a passing jibe.[44] Several decades before Morris wrote his utopia, Dickens earned backhanded praise when a Nonconformist minister announced to his congregation that two of the greatest forces for sanitary reform were Dickens and the cholera.[45] In *News from Nowhere*, which equates cholera and commerce (138), it is the reactionary pull of novels like Dickens's that needs to be consigned to the dustheap.

I began by noting that Wells's time traveller is so alert to generic norms that he discerns utopian fiction's need to explain its waste-disposal systems. But if Wells's novel violates this convention, it also calls attention to the wider stakes of utopian fiction's rejection of history. In *The Time Machine*, the eponymous invention is both a sign of future advances and a mechanism for anticipating a still more distant future—marking the distance the novel had traveled since Scott, neither the inventor nor his contemporaries ever seriously considers using the machine to explore the past. If *The Time Machine* foregoes the usual revolutionary pleasures of imaginatively discarding the accumulated debris of history, this is only to pave the way for the radical dissolution of all matter that forms the novel's eerie denouement. After leaving the world of the Eloi and Morlocks, the traveller proceeds even further forward, finally stopping only when he reaches the dark, silent, and lifeless future predicted by contemporary scientists as a consequence of the heat death of the sun. Balfour Stewart, professor of physics at Owens College, explained: "Universally diffused heat forms what we may call the great waste-heap of the universe, and this is growing larger year by year. . . . We are led to look to an end in which the whole universe will be one equally heated mass, and from which everything like life or motion or beauty will have utterly gone away."[46] By the turn of the century, the principle of the conservation of matter began to seem less urgent than the law of entropy, and utopian novelists began to worry less about the accumulation of centuries of history and rubbish than about the whimpering apocalypse of the final waste heap. As Stewart's comments reveal, even physicists questioned the future for beauty in this brave new world.

Notes

1. H. G. Wells, *The Time Machine* (Mineola, NY: Dover, 1995), 34–35. Subsequent references are included parenthetically in the body of the text.

2. See, for instance, Dickens's 1867 preface to *Oliver Twist*, where he insists that, despite the protestations of some skeptics, his portrayal of filthy and garbage-filled slums is literally accurate: "In the year one thousand eight hundred and fifty, it was publicly declared in London by an amazing Alderman, that Jacob's Island did not exist, and had never existed. Jacob's Island continues to exist (like an ill-bred place as it is) in the year one thousand eight hundred and sixty-seven." It is therefore "useless to discuss whether . . . [the unpleasant details of the narrative seem] natural or unnatural, probable or improbable,

right or wrong"; they are simply "TRUE" (Charles Dickens, preface, *The Adventures of Oliver Twist* [1837–38; Oxford: Oxford University Press, 1949], xvii).

3. H. Rider Haggard, *She* (Oxford: Oxford University Press, 1991), 214 n. Subsequent references are included parenthetically in the body of the text.

4. George Jennings, who was responsible for installing public "conveniences" in the Crystal Palace despite horrified opposition, maintained that "the Civilization of a people can be measured by their Domestic and Sanitary appliances" (quoted in Lawrence Wright, *Clean and Decent: The Fascinating History of the Bathroom and the WC* [London: Routledge and Kegan Paul, 1960], 200). Similarly, Dr. Southwood Smith concluded a description of an "offensive ditch, with exposed conveniences emptying into it," by rhetorically asking, "Can such a state of things exist in a country, that has made any progress in civilization!" (quoted in Hector Gavin, *The Unhealthiness of London* [1847] in *The Unhealthiness of London and The Habitations of the Industrial Classes* [New York: Garland, 1985], 23). Hector Gavin applied the same logic to arrive at a "disgraceful, and discreditable" comparison between Victorian England and ancient Rome, since the latter supplied a greater volume of water per capita through the aqueducts than the Victorians did through their pipe system (Gavin, 50).

5. See Edward Said, *Orientalism* (New York: Pantheon Books, 1978).

6. Ernest Renan, "What Is a Nation?" (1882), trans. Martin Thom, in *Nation and Narration*, ed. Homi Bhabha (New York: Routledge, 1990), 11.

7. William Morris, *News from Nowhere, or An Epoch of Rest,* in *News from Nowhere and Other Writings*, ed. Clive Wilmer (Harmondsworth, UK: Penguin, 1993), 69. Subsequent references are included parenthetically in the body of the text.

8. Mary Douglas, *Purity and Danger: An Analysis of the Concepts of Pollution and Taboo* (London: Routledge and Kegan Paul, 1966).

9. Richard Jefferies, *After London*, in *After London and Amaryllis at the Fair* (London: J. M. Dent and Sons, 1939), 3. Subsequent references are included parenthetically in the body of the text.

10. Michel de Certeau gives a suggestive account of this process, by which a repressed past resurfaces under the sign of pollution: "any autonomous order is founded upon what it eliminates; it produces a 'residue' condemned to be forgotten. But what was excluded re-infiltrates the place of its origin—now the present's clean [*propre*] place. It resurfaces, it troubles, it turns the present's feelings of being 'at home' into an illusion, it lurks—this 'wild,' this 'ob-scene,' this 'filth,' this 'resistance' of 'superstition'—within the walls of the residence, and, behind the back of the owner . . . it inscribes there the law of the other" (Michel de Certeau, *Heterologies: Discourse on the Other*, trans. Brian Massumi [Minneapolis: University of Minnesota Press, 1997], 3–4). As I argue below, in the utopian novels of the Victorian fin-de-siècle, this psychodynamic return of the repressed takes a distinctly economic turn.

11. Money is by definition a medium for the past to control the present: when I spend money I claim the right to goods or services now in return for

whatever I (or my legators) did to acquire the money in the past. This is why Marx and Engels insist that "In bourgeois society, living labour is but a means to increase accumulated labour. . . . In bourgeois society, therefore, the past dominates the present" (Karl Marx and Friedrich Engels, *The Communist Manifesto* [1848], trans. Samuel Moore [Harmondsworth, UK: Penguin, 1985], 97–98).

12. John Ruskin, *Unto This Last* (1862), in *Unto This Last and Other Writings*, ed. Clive Wilmer (Harmondsworth, UK: Penguin, 1985), 210–11.

13. John Sutherland, "Historical Fiction," in *The Stanford Companion to Victorian Fiction* (Stanford, CA: Stanford University Press, 1989), 297.

14. M. M. Bakhtin, *The Dialogic Imagination*, trans. Caryl Emerson and Michael Holquist (Austin: University of Texas Press, 1981); Jurij Lotman, *The Structure of the Artistic Text*, trans. R. Vroon (Ann Arbor: University of Michigan Press, 1977), 212–13.

15. Frank Kermode, *The Sense of an Ending: Studies in the Theory of Fiction* (Oxford: Oxford University Press, 1968), 5, 8.

16. Benjamin contends that it is "characteristic that not only a man's knowledge or wisdom, but above all his real life—and this is the stuff that stories are made of—first assumes transmissible form at the moment of his death" ("The Storyteller: Reflections on the Work of Nikolai Leskov," in *Illuminations*, trans. Harry Zohn [New York: Schocken Books, 1969], 94). Patrick Fairbarn, *Prophecy Viewed in Respect to Its Distinctive Nature* (Edinburgh and Philadelphia, 1856; 2nd ed., Edinburgh, 1865), 30; quoted in Mary Wilson Carpenter, *George Eliot and the Landscape of Time: Narrative Form and Protestant Apocalyptic History* (Chapel Hill: University of North Carolina Press, 1986), x.

17. Thomas Carlyle, "On History" (1830), in *Critical and Miscellaneous Essays,* 4 vols. (Chicago: Belford, Clarke and Co., n.d.), 3:157.

18. The increasing cultural prominence of the scientific version of this narrative pattern in the late nineteenth century helped to focus unprecedented attention on the future. As Wells observed, "In conjunction with the wide vistas opened by geological and astronomical discovery, the nineteenth century has indeed lost the very habit of thought from which the belief in a Fall arose. It is as if a hand had been put upon the head of the thoughtful man and had turned his eyes about from the past to the future" (*Anticipations of the Reaction of Mechanical and Scientific Progress upon Human Life and Thought* [1901; Mineola, NY: Dover, 1999], 163).

19. Morris's suggestion that heredity itself might be combated or at least mitigated is in turn part of a larger, radically anti-Darwinian pattern in the novel, in which plenty and cooperation replace scarcity and competition as the motive forces of personal and social progress. Of course, Darwin's Malthusian model of scarcity also provided the basis for almost all nineteenth-century political economy, making Morris's antievolutionary rhetoric a singularly appropriate vehicle for his critique of capitalist economics.

20. George Eliot, *Impressions of Theophrastus Such*, in *The Complete Works of George Eliot* (Boston: Colonial Press, n.d.), 8:16.

21. Fredric Jameson has suggested that this kind of imaginative escape from one's own historical situation is simply impossible—and that utopian novels do not even attempt it. Rather, he argues, utopias represent unbelievable futures to show that the future is literally inconceivable ("Progress Versus Utopia: or, Can We Imagine the Future?" *Science-Fiction Studies* 27 [July 1982]: 147–58).

22. Marx and Engels, *Communist Manifesto*, 106.

23. William Morris, *Collected Works*, 24 vols. (London: Longmans, Green, 1910–15), 23:203; May Morris, *William Morris: Artist, Writer, Socialist* (Oxford: Blackwell, 1936), 1:282; both quoted in A. Dwight Culler, *The Victorian Mirror of History* (New Haven, CT: Yale University Press, 1985), 238. Nothing could be further from Harold Bloom's agonistic model of Oedipal struggle: for Morris, the best art is created not by killing one's predecessors, but by proving that they are still alive. Morris's historicism more closely resembles Nietzsche's model of the monumental historian, who uses the past as a reminder "that greatness was in any event once *possible* and may thus be possible again" ("On the Uses and Disadvantages of History for Life" [1873] in *Untimely Meditations*, trans. Daniel Breazeale [Cambridge: Cambridge University Press, 1997], 69).

24. E. P. Thompson, *William Morris: Romantic to Revolutionary* (New York: Pantheon Books, 1977), 611; quoted in Culler, *Victorian Mirror*, 239.

25. Sigfried Giedion, *Space, Time, and Architecture* (Cambridge, MA: Harvard University Press, 1962), 9–10; quoted in Jerome Buckley, *The Triumph of Time: A Study of the Victorian Concepts of Time, History, Progress, and Decadence* (Cambridge, MA: Belknap Press, 1966), 37.

26. Forster used this portentous phrase as the title of a story in 1909.

27. Thomas H. Huxley, *Evolution and Ethics* (London: Macmillan, 1894), 8–9.

28. Waldo Hilary Dunn, *James Anthony Froude: A Biography* (Oxford: Oxford University Press, 1961), ii, 560.

29. Morris's equation of cleaning supplies and dirt is topical as well as ironic. As Anthony Wohl notes, soap works were defined as one of the "noxious trades" in the nascent antipollution legislation of the 1870s (see *Endangered Lives: Public Health in Victorian Britain* [Cambridge, MA: Harvard University Press, 1983], 205–32).

30. As Alfred Sohn-Rethel observes, "A coin has stamped upon its body that it is to serve as a means of exchange and not as an object of use. . . . Its physical matter has visibly become a mere carrier of its social function. A coin, therefore, is a thing which conforms to the postulates of the exchange abstraction and is supposed, among other things, to consist of an immutable substance, a substance over which time has no power, and which stands in authentic contrast to any matter found in nature" (*Intellectual and Manual Labour: A Critique of Epistemology* [1970], trans. Martin Sohn-Rethel [London: Macmillan, 1978], 59).

31. Georges Bataille's *The Accursed Share* provides a theoretical account of systemic expenditure, in which "energy, which constitutes wealth, must ultimately

be spent lavishly (without return) . . . [in] a series of profitable operations [that] has absolutely no other effect than the squandering of profits. . . . [I]t is necessary to dissipate a substantial portion of energy produced, sending it up in smoke" (*The Accursed Share: An Essay in General Economy*, vol. 1, *Consumption*, trans. Robert Hurley [New York: Zone Books, 1988], 22).

32. Marx and Engels, *Communist Manifesto*, 86.

33. Wells, *Anticipations*, 46–47. William Greenslade also discusses this "darker side to Wells's thinking"; see *Degeneration, Culture, and the Novel* (Cambridge: Cambridge University Press, 1994), 196. Greenslade's argument focuses on the fin-de-siècle discourses of degeneration and eugenics, tracing the middle-class attempts to stem the perceived "race-suicide" brought on by the higher birth rates among the lower orders.

34. Similarly, Ruskin noted both that emigration could not be a permanent solution to the problems of overpopulation and that untrammeled population growth (even granted expedients like emigration) sacrifices quality of life to mere survival: "Colonization [and] bringing in of waste lands . . . merely evade or delay the question. It will, indeed, be long before the world has been all colonized, and its deserts all brought under cultivation. But the radical question is, not how much habitable land is in the world, but how many human beings ought to be maintained on a given space of habitable land" ("Unto This Last," 224).

35. Elsewhere, Trollope generalizes the connection between disposal and progress: in a chapter of *Barchester Towers* entitled "The Rubbish Cart," Reverend Harding explains: "A man is sufficiently condemned if it can only be shown that either in politics or religion he does not belong to some new school established within the last score of years. He may then regard himself as rubbish and expect to be carted away" (Anthony Trollope, *Barchester Towers* [1857; Harmondsworth, UK: Penguin, 1987], 103).

36. This creation of false desires characterizes both the domestic and the global economies: the first part of the quotation refers to the creation of unnecessary necessities at home; the second part to the creation of new desires in the colonies.

37. Regenia Gagnier, *The Insatiability of Human Wants: Economics and Aesthetics in Market Society* (Chicago: University of Chicago Press, 2000). See in particular Gagnier's discussion of how nineteenth-century economic models could postulate an economy of scarcity rather than excess only "by excluding history from their analyses" (47).

38. Dick's easy assumption that love objects are undifferentiated enough to be fungible—that as long as the numbers match up, the desires will fall into line—betrays some distinctly capitalist ideological backsliding. Albert Hirschman notes that market economies collapse the range of human desires (passions like ambition, lust, and vanity) into a very small compass (the singular interest in money and what it can purchase). See *The Passions and the Interests: Political Arguments for Capitalism before Its Triumph* (Princeton, NJ:

Princeton University Press, 1977). As Dick admits, and as Nowhere's strong flavor of jealousy (leading to murder in one case and semivoluntary exile in another) demonstrates, the interplay between supply and desire is seldom so straightforward.

39. While *News from Nowhere* is structured as a journey to the countryside to show Guest the pleasure of agricultural work, its goal is endlessly deferred by visits to sites of less productive labor. In the last instance, Guest and his companions come upon the Obstinate Refusers, a group of builders and stone carvers who boycott the haymaking festival in favor of ornamenting a building. Bataille similarly pinpoints architectural decoration as a key method of expenditure, but for precapitalist economies: "The expression of intimacy in the church corresponds . . . to the needless consumption of labor: From the start the purpose of the edifice withdraws it from public utility, and this first movement is accentuated in a profusion of useless ornaments. For the construction of a church is not a profitable use of the available labor, but rather its consumption, the destruction of its utility" (*Accursed Share*, 1:132). Bataille argues that this form of transcendent wastefulness is no longer available in the bourgeois world, which can only overcome alienation by insisting on the radical independence of the material from the affective (135).

40. Morris's attempt to imagine a method of disposal that would not simply shift or delay the problem recalls earlier debates among Victorian sanitary reformers over sewage systems designed to *permanently* dispose of waste by flushing it out to sea. Advocates of recycling countered that this would mean losing a resource (nitrogen) that could otherwise be productively reused. As I discuss below, at the end of the century both scientists and novelists began again to consider whether the dangers of diffusion might outweigh the dangers of accumulation.

41. William Morris, "The Beauty of Life" (1880), in *The Collected Works of William Morris,* 24 vols. (New York: Russell and Russell, 1966), 22:76.

42. Walter Pater, *The Renaissance: Studies in Art and Poetry* (Oxford: Oxford University Press, 1986), 153. See also Frances Power Cobbe, "Backward Ho!" (*The New Quarterly Magazine,* January 1876, 231–62), which similarly faults antiquarianism, first and foremost, for its ugliness.

43. Morris may be protesting too much. His denunciation of "loathsome" (175) sentimental Victorian novels calls to mind *News from Nowhere*'s own focus on love plots and sentiment, at the expense of work and economics, in its final sections.

44. Morris's anxieties about the sterile accumulation of history, which would end in making art merely "a collection of the curiosities of the past," also took the form of a simultaneously scatological and eschatological allusion to *Our Mutual Friend*: "Was it all to end in a counting-house on the top of a cinder-heap, with Podsnap's drawing-room in the offing, and a Whig committee dealing out champagne to the rich and margarine to the poor in such convenient

proportions as would make all men contented together, though the pleasure of the eyes was gone from the world, and the place of Homer was to be taken by Huxley?" (Morris, *Collected Works*, 23:280; quoted in Culler, *Victorian Mirror*, 237).

45. Quoted in G. M. Young, *Victorian England* (Oxford: Oxford University Press, 1953), 55.

46. Balfour Stewart, *The Conservation of Energy* (London, 1873), 153; quoted in Buckley, *Triumph of Time*, 67.

Chapter 11

The Indian Subject of Colonial Hygiene

William Kupinse

Of all the writings on filth produced during the late nineteenth and early twentieth centuries, one of the most eclectic collections on the subject is the thirty-odd-year run of the journal *The Sanitary Record*. Published in London from 1874 to 1905, the *Record* usually fulfilled the promise of its subtitle, "A Monthly Journal of Public Health and the Progress of Sanitary Science," in a straightforward fashion. The *Record* offered lengthy discussions of "scavenging," plans for "refuse destructors," papers on the practice of the ocean disposal of "sewerage," and a fairly regular series of articles entitled "Soaps"; occasional pieces featured such enticing titles as "London Fogs and Public Health," "Arsenic in Beer," and "The Unsanitary Sausage."

In addition to these domestic concerns, however, the journal also reported frequently on the sanitary conditions of Britain's colonial possessions. Here, India was a favorite subject. An article titled "Indian Habits" (1882) observes, "The people of India seem to be in very much the condition of children. They must be made clean by compulsion until they arrive at that degree of moral education when dirt shall become hateful to them, and then they will keep themselves clean for their own sakes."[1] A later article, "A Sanitary Renaissance in India" (1903), takes a more reserved approach in forwarding its claim of Indians' innate resistance to sanitary progress; the article ascribes such resistance to the fact that "[s]anitary reform attacks the homes and the domestic life of the people" and "rides roughshod over some of their most cherished customs and traditions." That these traditions are revealed to be nothing more than superstition allows the author to outline a cultural scheme in which India is the less-evolved cousin of Britain, requiring the tutelage of its more advanced relative. "If the people of India only knew it, they are practising in their daily lives a most elaborate system of hygiene," the author argues. "The caste system is based on sanitary science as it was understood by the ancient Hindus."[2] Beyond its immediate condescension, "A Sanitary Renaissance" demonstrates an anthropological fascination with those cultural practices of India relating to social hygiene, even as it dismisses those practices as having outlived their usefulness. The respective positions assumed by the writers of "Indian Habits" and "A Sanitary Renaissance in India"—that of imperial denigration versus that of anthropological interest—characterize generally the body of sanitary commentary on India, which vacillates between derogatory and laudatory modes.

India is hardly alone in having served as the subject of a colonizer's hygienic gaze. Warwick Anderson describes the disciplinary role played by hygienic discourse in the more recent American administration of the Philippines, writing that "waste became the order of the day, the ordering principle of the colonial Philippines."[3] Anne McClintock explores how the nineteenth-century cult of domesticity employed racial tropes in its particular deployment of the hygienic commodity fetish, observing that in both England and its imperial territories—particularly British-administered regions of Africa—soap "persuasively mediate[d] the Victorian poetics of racial hygiene and imperial progress."[4] We might view these transcolonial practices described by Anderson and McClintock as a subset of the larger mechanism of empire's hegemonic description of its subjects. Aijaz Ahmad, contesting Fredric Jameson's claim to employ the term "third-world" as a neutral description, reminds us that "'Description' has been central in the colonial discourse. It was by assembling a monstrous machinery of descriptions . . . that the colonial discourse was able to classify and ideologically master the colonial subject, enabling itself to transform the descriptively verifiable multiplicity and difference into the ideologically felt hierarchy of value."[5]

What is unique about hygienic discourse on India, however, is the historical breadth of sanitary commentary on the former British colony, as well as the intensity of India's novelistic responses to this commentary; indeed, response to British hygienic discourse roughly coincides with the advent of the Indian novel in English. In an essay describing how garbage and disorder have been seen by colonizers, nationalists, and ethnosociologists alike as threats to Indian public character, Dipesh Chakrabarty gives a sense of the historical expanse of hygienic discourse on India, from Lord Wellesley's 1803 minute connecting Calcutta's sanitary conditions with the health and welfare of its citizens to V. S. Naipaul's repeated observation in *An Area of Darkness* (1964) that "Indians defecate everywhere."[6]

This essay considers three genres of colonial hygienic discourse spanning more than a century: early nineteenth-century British historiography on India, which echoed throughout the nineteenth century; early twentieth-century writings on rural reform; and early twentieth-century popular descriptions of Indian sages and fakirs. Culling selective examples from each category, I juxtapose each sanitary discourse with one of three Indian novels offering a significant response to the discourse: Lal Behari Day's *Govinda Samanta, or The History of a Bengal Raiyat* (1874), Mulk Raj Anand's *Coolie* (1936), and G. V. Desani's *All About H. Hatterr* (1948). My wish in each case is not, I should emphasize, to argue for the specific influence of a particular sanitary text on a given novel; rather, these hygienic discourses were so widespread that it is more useful to consider the literary texts as engaged with the social formation embodied in each sanitary example.

The Empire Bites Back: Colonizing Filth in *Govinda Samanta*

Lal Behari Day's *Govinda Samanta, or The History of a Bengal Raiyat* is among the earliest Indian novels written in English.[7] Submitted to a contest sponsored by a Bengali zamindar, an agricultural landholder, for "the best novel, to be written either in Bengali or in English, illustrating the 'Social and Domestic Life of the Rural Population and Working Classes of Bengal,'" *Govinda Samanta* was completed before early 1872, but was not published until the contest was belatedly judged in 1874.[8] Originally born Kala Goal De in Talpur, West Bengal, in 1824, Lal Behari Day converted to Christianity while a student at the missionary school run by Alexander Duff in Calcutta. Although Day, after his ordination, would break with Duff over his denial of membership in the mission council, Day served the Presbyterian church in India for several years, first as director of a Culna mission and later as pastor of an urban congregation in Calcutta. At the time he wrote *Govinda Samanta* in his late forties, Day had published little more than a religious tract, a short collection of essays, and a series of occasional pieces in the *Calcutta Review*.[9]

As its subtitle indicates, *Govinda Samanta* recounts the life of a raiyat, or contract farmer, in mid-nineteenth-century Bengal, though it devotes nearly equal time to telling the stories of Govinda's extended family. Interspersed with these familial accounts is a series of chapters detailing the domestic, religious, economic, and cultural practices of the rural Bengalis. Bearing titles such as "The Village Market," "Ladies' Parliament," and "All about Indigo," these chapters often seem disconnected from the main narrative of the Samanta family. K. S. Ramamurti, conceding to the view that these digressive chapters detract from *Govinda Samanta*'s novelistic form, nevertheless lauds them for their "authentic ethnographic information."[10]

Rather than detracting from its overall form, the ethnographic digressions of the novel in fact point to its interest in identifying and contesting British interpretations of Indian cultural practices—in particular, those relating to the hygienic practices of colonial subjects. Explanatory passages appear throughout Day's novel and are not confined to the "ethnographic" chapters. Chief among the interpretations *Govinda Samanta* works to contest are the derogatory readings of colonial hygiene. Indeed, Day's text demonstrates an obsession with sanitary discourse that would be difficult to account for otherwise. Few novels in English feature characters whose compulsion for bathing and hand washing is stronger than those in Day's text. During his lunch break in the fields, Badan Samanta, Govinda's father, "took hold of a little bamboo phial which was lying on the ground, poured from it on the palm of his hand a quantity of mustard oil, and besmeared with it every part of his body, the hair not excepted, not forgetting at the same time to push a little of the oil in the nostrils and in the ears." Lest the mustard oil bath prove insufficient, Badan and his oil-anointed brothers Gayaram and Kalmanik then bathe in a nearby pool (24–25). At the end of the day, the reader learns of Badan's further ablutions: "he washed his hands, feet, and face in the tank" (56). Badan and his brothers are not alone in this hygienic preoccupation. In the course of the novel, the reader further learns that each Hindu family, no matter how modest its means, has a personal barber; is presented with an oddly voyeuristic chapter describing the conversation in the women's public baths;[11] and is told, "Considering that Bengali Hindu peasants bathe every day throughout the year and every day wash their clothes in water, we have no hesitation saying that they are about the cleanest peasantry in the world" (141). Contra Naipaul, *Govinda Samanta* insists that Indians *bathe* everywhere.

While Day's response to hygienic and sanitary discourses is overdetermined by both the attitudes and texts prevalent at the time of its

composition, I would like briefly to explore one imperial work on colonial "filth" that embodies the kind of interpretative paradigm Day's
texts answer: James Mill's *History of British India*. First published in
three volumes in 1817, Mill's *History* had a considerable influence on
the British imagination of what was then still the administered territory
of the East India Company. Despite its early publication date, Mill's
History resonated in important ways throughout the nineteenth century. It was published in six volumes in 1820 and again in 1826, and
additional publications with varying sets of volumes continued to appear after Mill's death; 1840, 1845, 1848, and 1856 all saw volumes
of Mill's *History* published. The *History* played an institutional role that
extended beyond its public dissemination; the East India Company
adopted it as a textbook for the instruction of its administrators, and it
was largely on the basis of his book that Mill was hired by the East India
Company,[12] where he would rise to the position of assistant examiner.[13]
(He would later use his connections at the East India Company to secure
his son, John Stuart Mill, a clerkship in the company.)

That James Mill's *History* should have demonstrated such a lasting
influence—and conferred such professional benefits—is all the more
surprising given that, to quote Mill directly, "This writer, it will be
said, has never been in India."[14] This lack of direct experience does not
stop Mill from making some remarkable pronouncements on the cultural and religious practices of Indians, however; rather, he claims in the
introduction to his *History* that his never having visited India makes
him a more objective historian. Sharply contesting the sympathetic
stance of such Orientalist scholars as William Jones—whose discovery
of structural kinships between Sanskrit and Greek and Latin revealed
cultural affinities between East and West—Mill dismissed Indian practices as symbolically wasteful; for Mill, not only are Indian rituals of
pollution and purity often physically filthy, they are excessive in their
signifying efforts. "The causes of impurity among the Brahmens *[sic]* are
exceedingly numerous . . . [and] proportionally strange," Mill asserts,
adding later, "The rules of purification, which form a remarkable part
of this subject, are not less exorbitant in their number, or extravagant
in their forms." The tendency for rituals of pollution and purification
to fold into each other seems particularly disturbing to Mill. "All those
functions of the body, by which its offensive discharges are effected, or
its vital powers communicated, afford occasion for the ceremonies of
purification," he writes. Moreover, Indian purification rituals and sanitary practices strike Mill's Western eyes as polluting in themselves; as he
sarcastically observes, "Nor, in this enumeration, must the dung and

urine of the cow be forgotten; things so holy as to be of peculiar efficacy in the ceremonies of purification."[15]

As I have suggested, one aspect of Lal Behari Day's response to these attitudes is an excessive attention to detail when it comes to the hygienic practices of the Bengalis in his novel. But this response takes more complex forms as well, most notably in direct ethnographic explanations that contest the kind of assessments exemplified in Mill's *History*. In describing the Samanta women's morning household cleaning, Day turns an ethnographic eye to his defense of the process. His account is significant enough to merit quoting at length.

> [E]very inch of every floor of the room was besmeared by means of a piece of rag, with the said solution of cow-dung and water, and allowed to dry itself. The reader may think that this is a dirty business, and that the rooms must be the worst for being thus besmeared. But he is mistaken. He may take our word that the floor greatly improves by the process. It becomes smooth and glossy and no cracks are visible. And as for any disgusting smell, there is nothing of the sort—the smell, if anything, being positively pleasant. Hindu peasants besmear their cottages with a solution of cow-dung and water, because cow-dung is regarded ceremonially as a purifier; it is, however, a question why Hindu law-givers should have pitched upon cow-dung as a purifier. Has it any sanitary value? Has it any disinfecting property? From the universal practice of Hindus of Bengal, I should be inclined to think that cow-dung was a disinfectant; but I prefer to leave the matter in the hands of doctors and chemists. (66–67)

Asserting the connection between religious ritual and daily hygiene, Day challenges the British view of Indian practices as unhygienic. As evidence, he offers the kind of direct visual and olfactory testimony that a nonnative text such as Mill's *History* sorely lacks. Moreover, this passage suggests that the evolutionary success of an observance lends some credence to its efficacy; why would cleaning with cow-dung water be so widespread if there were no basis to its sanitary action? Day's final appeal to expert opinion—other scenes in the novel show him more than willing to accept the progress of "Western" science—calls for exactly the kind of expert analysis that summary judgments such as those found in Mill's *History* omit.

Such ethnographic rebuttals of British sanitary judgment pervade Day's novel. Of infant hygiene, Lal observes that "European doctors" would be shocked to learn that Bengali women lay their babies on boards and expose them naked—save for a coat of mustard oil—to the sun for hours. "Bengali peasant women know better," however, for this routine serves to acclimatize the infants. The "wild village pigs," claims Day, are far from filthy, as European eyes might deem, but rather serve as "great sanitary officers . . . who easily, instantaneously, and inexpensively remove all obnoxious matter from the neighborhood" (31). Even that mixture of hygienic, racial, and religious codes known as the caste system, which was among Indian practices second only to suttee in securing British opprobrium, is defended in Day's novel by means of ethnographic comparison. Unlike the British class system, the Indian caste system has at least some rationale, argues Day, because it is based upon vocation rather than wealth, and in that regard tends to be more flexible. While Day admits that neither system is ideal, he insists, "There is no country in the world where the spirit of caste is not to be found in some form or other" (353). Here Day turns the moralizing gaze of the social historian upon England itself—a remarkable move given the time in which he wrote.

If both *Govinda Samanta*'s structure and its thematic focus are inflected by its engagement with hygienic discourses, its style and tone evince a similar, though subtle, inflection. Day begins his novel with a prefatory note, warning the reader not to expect marvels, adventure, or love scenes—the latter, because Day wishes "not to pollute these pages with its description." Most important, Day insists that we should not expect "grandiloquent phraseology and gorgeous metaphors" but rather "a plain and unvarnished tale of a plain peasant, living in this plain country of Bengal . . . told in a plain manner." And, with a few exceptions such as a performative paragraph in which he disclaims "sesquipedalian" vocabulary (4), Day's diction is admirably concise. This precision, however, does not preclude moments of irony within his narration, irony that may go unremarked for the forthrightness with which it is delivered. Midway through the text, Day halts his narrative to explain "the reasons why the story has not as yet become interesting." Citing Johnson's pithy assertion that a reader would hang himself if he read Richardson for the story, Day offers the reader the following bargain: "[I]f, after reading some ten or twelve chapters more, you do not find the story increasing in interest, you will be at perfect liberty either to put a rope, or to tie a *kalasi* round your neck." The reader must turn to the novel's index of Bengali terms, however, to learn that a *kalasi* is a water pot and that Day has Indianized the menu of suicide options provided. Claiming the need to "wash his hands clean in [the] matter," Day attributes these violations of novelistic convention to his text's quest for realism, arguing that his aim is to depict not a *possible*, or even *probable*, but an *actual* raiyat (183–84).

This mixture of deadpan irony and an appeal to realism may seem a minor point, but it offers a more accurate accounting for the novel's style and tone, both of which might otherwise be assessed as naïve—as K. S. Ramamurti does when he writes that "*Govinda Samanta* is not a great novel, but a realistic story poignantly told . . . with no consciously developed form or plot"[16]—or unquestioningly imitative of English tradition, a charge Meenakshi Mukherjee rejects, claiming that the imitation present in Day's authorial framing is exploded in the course of the novel itself.[17] Indeed, what is most striking about Day's narrative method is the dissonant relationship he establishes between style and subject. Often this dissonance arises either during those moments when the narrator addresses his audience directly or when hygienic codes of native subject and colonizing reader come into contact. The description of a restless night spent by Kalamanik serves as an example of both these instances. Govinda's uncle, we are told, cannot sleep "on account of the bite of that little creature (the *Cimex lectularius*) which infests in shoals the dormitories of poorer people in Bengal as in England, but whose inodorous name in vernacular Anglo-Saxon we dare not mention in this history, in the event of some English lady honouring it with a perusal" (283). Here Day's suddenly inflated prose serves to inoculate his imagined feminine readership from the indelicacies of bedbugs, which, he helpfully observes, function more accurately as a marker of poverty than a signifier of colonial status. Hardly an example of "plain style," *Govinda Samanta* demonstrates a sophisticated response, both structurally and stylistically, to imperial discourses on colonial hygiene. Given its historical moment, this deadpan irony masquerading as "plain" style may have been a useful strategy. Written some three-quarters of a century before Independence—and coming just a decade and a half after the Sepoy mutiny—a subtle assertion of hygienic equality among colonizer and colonial subject could in itself be viewed as a politically efficacious move.[18] When it comes to bedbugs, Day's narrator wryly notes, we are all colonial subjects.

Filth as Fetish: Rural Reform and the Economics of Waste in Anand's *Coolie*

By the time he published *Coolie* in 1936, Mulk Raj Anand had to contend with the weight of more than a century of imperial discourse describing India's putatively inferior hygiene.[19] *Coolie* chronicles the brief life of Munoo, a young orphan who moves from house servant to pickle factory laborer to cotton millworker to rickshaw puller. In each of these moves, issues of waste and sanitation figure prominently. But Munoo's first move in the novel, from the rural Kanga hills to the suburban home of his first employer, an Indian subaccountant for the Imperial Bank, encourages a reading of the novel within a more immediate set of hygienic discourses than those expressed by James Mill in his *History of British India*, or even those general attitudes outlined in the *Sanitary Record*. Indeed, the publication of Anand's novel came in the midst of one of the most notable and sustained projects of hygienic missionary work—the sanitary reform of Frank Lugard Brayne. The nephew of Lord Lugard, the governor general of Nigeria, Brayne arrived in the Punjab in 1905 as an assistant commissioner in the Indian Civil Service, bringing with him the hygienic zeal—as Clive Dewey describes, the "soap habit"[20]—of his evangelical forbears. Brayne's best known project, the "Gurgaon Experiment" (1920–27), aimed to bring sanitary and agricultural reform to a rural region outside of Delhi, and Brayne went on to author more than a dozen books and pamphlets on the subject.[21]

Of particular concern to Brayne was the hygienic status of children, especially those in rural villages. In *Village Uplift in India* (1927), Brayne describes the upbringing of "the ordinary Gurgaon villager":

> His early youth was spent playing in the dust on the village muck heap and in what might best be described as the latrine-cum-rubbish-heap area. His eyes and nose were often running and flies settled in dozens on them and on his mouth. He was rarely if ever washed and never taught clean habits. He was much neglected.[22]

For Brayne, this filth and neglect served as a sign of moral failure—not of the children, but rather of their parents. Brayne describes the unsanitary status of children he has witnessed as "easily preventable, the result of slovenliness and ignorance."[23] What is most striking about the rhetoric of Brayne's moral failure argument, however, is that it does not rest—as we might expect from a missionary—on religious authority.[24] Instead, Brayne frames his argument in economic terms; as he would later summarize his position in *A Village ABC* in 1950, "Dirty children are dull and unhealthy. Dirty villages hate progress and are content to live in ignorance and poverty."[25] Or, as he more pithily addresses Indian parents in *Village Uplift*, "There is very little manure in the fields but plenty of filth in the village and on the children. Do you think that by manuring your children they will grow better?"[26]

In Anand's *Coolie*, however, the orphan Munoo bears the brunt of
the critique of his unhygienic status when he is sent to serve the middle-
class Mal family. When Munoo, following the rural custom of his
upbringing, urinates outside the family's home, he is berated by the
household's matriarch. "Vay, you shameless, vulgar, stupid hillboy!"
screams Bibiji. "We didn't know we were taking on an animal in our
employ, a shameless brute, a savage!"[27] Here Munoo's hygienic failure
serves as a marker of both geographical and class difference; moreover,
Bibiji's description of him as an "animal" taken into her "employ"
reveals the economic basis of his status within the family. Like Brayne's
ironic equation of children and "manured" agricultural products, Bibiji's
rant suggests Munoo's unfitness as an economic component of the suburban household. Indeed, what Bibiji worries about most is that Munoo's
filthy habits will make a negative impression upon her husband's British superiors, and thus thwart the family's chances for advancement.
But if Munoo suffers the opprobrium of suburban Indians, he fares
no better with the British sahibs. Shortly after, he is banished from the
subaccountant's home when he disrupts the visit of the bank manager,
a "Mr. England," who sees Munoo as a "dirtily clad urchin" and recalls his own superior's warning that "[a]ll the natives . . . were disease
ridden" (27–28).

No sooner is the dispossessed Munoo rescued by the kindly Prabh
Dyal, a former coolie who is now the owner of a pickle factory, than the
factory closes due to complaints that it is polluting the neighborhood.
Prabh Dyal remedies the situation by offering a gift to the complainants,
but the accusation of uncleanliness will come back to haunt him, transferred from the physical plant of the factory to the physical body of
Prabh Dyal himself. Politely questioning his unscrupulous partner Ganpat about the factory's inexplicably dismal finances, Prabh Dyal finds
himself confronted with a barrage of abuse of his coolie origins. "[G]o
and eat dung!" Ganpat tells him. "Your father was a coolie and you are
a coolie . . . you dirty swine" (96).

The animalized insults Ganpat hurls at Prabh Dyal—which are soon
seconded by a mob of the bankrupt factory's creditors—might strike
the reader as remarkable for their cruelty but unremarkable for their
logic, which would seem after all to be only the substitutional operation of metaphor. But the passage that immediately follows reveals that
in describing the position of the coolie, these epithets are closer to the
material adjacency of metonymy. Attempting to market his services to
earn money to help Prabh Dyal, Munoo faces the prospect of sleeping
in the open square of a grain market, where he hopes to find work in

the morning. The passage describing the square makes clear the abjection of both humans and animals, and echoes Brayne's economic reading of hygienic status:

> The square courtyard flanked on all sides by low mud shops . . . [was]
> crammed with snake-horned bullocks and stray rhinoceros-like bulls
> and skinny calves bespattered with their own dung, as they sat or
> stood, munching pieces of straw, snuffling their muzzles aimlessly,
> or masticating the grass which they had eaten some hours before,
> congested with the bodies of coolies, coloured like the earth on which
> they lay snoring, or crouching round a communal hubble-bubble, or
> shifting to explore a patch clear of puddles on which to rest. (106)

Here the coolies appear almost as an afterthought, on not quite the same level as the cattle whose space they share, their hookah a diversion similar to the cows' cud chewing, but their appearance of even less remark; they are simply "coloured like the earth." This commingling of humans and animals immediately melds into an image of their juxtaposed wastes: "The smell of stagnant drains, rotten grains, fresh cow-dung and urine, the foul savour of human and animal breath." This narrative focus on the grain market's by-products quickly shifts to reveal the product itself the next morning, when one of the merchants hires Munoo to haul sacks of wheat. Munoo understands the marking on the sacks—"FROM GOKAL CHAND, MOHAN LALL TO RALLI BROTHERS, EXPORTERS, KARACHI"—but he does not, the narrative observes, fathom "the laws of political economy, especially as they govern the export of wheat from India to England" (111).

A conventional Marxist reading of this passage would focus on the labor imbalance inherent in the exporting of the wheat. English pounds are exchanged for the bags of wheat, with the value of the wheat and currency representing a phantasmal presence of labor—really social relations between people and material relations between things, which appear to be "material relations between persons and social relationships between things"; for Marx, this displacement is what forms the commodity fetish.[28] In the case of the grain, we can imagine this objective relationship to value the labor of the grain carriers cheaply as compared to the labor of the British consumers. But the proximity of the account of the market square at night and the didactic narrative commentary about the political economy of exported wheat suggests that while a positive marker of production—namely, *value*—mediates between people, thus indicating a social relationship, this process of production necessarily creates a negative marker of value as well. If we understand "product" in its most expansive sense, as Raymond Williams has suggested, to include the whole of capitalism's material alterations, then industry's "by-products" are every bit as much its products as its goods: "the slag heap is as real a product as the coal, just as the river stinking with sewage and detergent is as much a product as the reservoir."[29] Returning to Marx, we can understand his statement that "Value . . . does not have its description branded on its forehead; it rather transforms every product of labour into a social hieroglyphic"[30] as suggesting that we read coolies' hygienic status as yet another character in this hieroglyphic. In the case of the coolies, this social hieroglyphic reveals a relationship of subservience to both the grain merchants and the market itself. To the extent that this marker maps excessive social meaning onto material conditions, we might usefully think of this process of mapping as the *fetishism of filth*. Although here filth fetishism carries a clearly undesirable significance, I will suggest later—in my reading of the final episode of *Coolie* and in my analysis of Desani's *All About H. Hatterr*—how filth fetishism can be equally productive of desire.

While the abject conditions the market-square coolies inhabit in Anand's novel reveal that the structural component of economic waste bears real and insistent material consequences, these consequences are inseparable from the symbolic abjection of the coolies within society. Shortly after the passage describing the market square at night, one of the merchants berates Munoo and the other coolies, describing them as swine, ironically reinforcing the metonymical equation of humans and animals in the earlier passage, while at the same time echoing the insults directed at Prabh Dyal.

The production of positive value (money) and the by-production of negative value (filth and waste) are not symmetrical, however. Commodities secure value through exchange, and thus reveal their social relations precisely at that moment of exchange. Filth receives its negative value through an observer encountering or remarking upon it, and expressing the sense of distaste, injustice, or revulsion to which he or she has been accustomed. As Mary Douglas observes, our notions of cleanliness and uncleanliness did not evolve primarily for their efficacy at preventing disease, but rather for their role in producing cultural meaning.[31] Despite this partial asymmetry, *filth as fetish* serves a similar structural role to the commodity fetish in that it depends upon physical objects mediating between people and carrying a concealed component of labor, but also bearing hidden traces of human suffering and environmental exploitation.

The passages I have quoted from *Coolie* reflect Anand's devotion to issues of social and economic justice, a devotion that manifested itself both in the 1930s and after. An avowed Marxist, Anand was strongly influenced by the 1935 Paris Conference in which writers such as Maxim Gorky, Thomas Mann, and E. M. Forster argued for a greater political engagement in the arts, and he helped to form the Progressive Writers Association, which arose in response to the Paris Conference.[32] Deeply invested in caste reform, labor organization, and Indian Independence, he was briefly jailed for his support of Gandhianism, and he was later consulted by Nehru. But it is precisely these political engagements that have led even sympathetic literary critics to view Anand's artistic achievement with suspicion, arguing that his political motivations often overshadow aesthetic considerations in his novels.[33]

In the case of *Coolie*, the charge that Anand sacrifices art for political propaganda often centers around the novel's final "Simla" section, in which Munoo is struck by an automobile carrying May Mainwaring, a one-quarter Indian, three-quarters British would-be socialite, who passes her days spending her absent husband's money. In this final section, in which Munoo slowly succumbs to tuberculosis, Anand devotes much of his attention to two characters who appear only in the novel's final thirty pages—Mrs. Mainwaring, who adopts Munoo as her servant, and Mohan, a socialist revolutionary. Predictably, much of the critical response to the Simla episode views these developments as narrative distractions. C. D. Narasimhaiah asserts that the section "isn't an organic part of the total pattern of the novel and exists apart, as it were, an after-thought, an accretion on so well-knit a work of art."[34] Saros Cowasjee similarly faults the chapter for Anand's "occasionally losing sight of his hero" and "devoting so much time and attention to portraying a minor character."[35]

I would like to insist, however, that the Simla episode—in particular Anand's rendering of May Mainwaring's interiority—is crucial to the structure of the novel as a whole, since it develops the focus on Munoo's hygienic status that has served as a major preoccupation of the novel. As in the case of the grain market coolies, the imperial fetishism of "native" filth is integral to both forms of subject construction. Unlike the earlier episodes in the novel, however—in which the fetishism of waste served a disciplinary role that produced the colonial subject as diseased, animalized, and abject—here Anand presents another variety of hygienic fetishism, a fetishism of markedly sexual nature. Indeed, May Mainwaring's designs upon the fifteen-year-old Munoo are unsettling. In a scene that follows shortly after Munoo is installed in her Simla summer home, his unhygienic status provides the occasion for an attempt at seduction. Calling Munoo over to examine his hands, "which she knew to be dirty from dusting," May Mainwaring addresses him as "[y]ou unclean boy," and insists on giving him a manicure, which she administers with a clearly erotic subtext, exposing her leg, "flutter[ing] her eyes," and pronouncing Munoo "Beautiful boy! Lovely boy!" (234). Munoo abruptly brings the seduction to a halt by falling at his memsahib's feet, but this does not minimize the fact that, for May Mainwaring, the attempted seduction represents a kind of sexualized slumming in which she desires a fetishized "other" whose differences of class, race, and colonial position she sees embodied in his unclean status.

That May Mainwaring's appreciation of Munoo as fetishized "other" both carries an economic component and inflects the formal qualities of the text is revealed in a passage describing her decision to keep him as her servant. "To Mrs. Mainwaring," we are told, Munoo was "a young boy with a lithe, supple body, with a small, delicate face, and with a pair of sensitive poet's eyes. . . . He was just the boy for her, just the right servant. She would be good to him, which was easy, because she was good-hearted" (227). Noteworthy in this passage is the slippage of narrative mode that occurs in rendering May Mainwaring's interiority. The novel's dominant mode thus far of evoking its characters' interiority has been that of ostensibly objective third-person narration—a convention frequently allied with critical or social realism—though tinged at times with the sort of authorial intrusiveness that works to support claims of Anand's propagandism. But here the language of May's reverie begins to seep without attribution into the narrative. "Sensitive poet's eyes" and "just the boy for her" belong to May, not the conventions of a realist narrative mode, and by the paragraph's concluding sentence, May's diction has replaced that of the established narrator.

The passing moment of free indirect discourse is hardly remarkable in a novel of the 1930s; what is significant, however, is that this glimpse into the interiority of a subject figured as colonizer in the text occurs precisely during the moment of May Mainwaring's fetishization of Munoo as "filthy" native. "Good-hearted," a congratulatory British self-description of imperial attitude, is clearly how Mrs. Mainwaring thinks of herself, and this kind of narrative slippage marks the representational fissure in an otherwise realist novel. Here prose style is inflected not simply by character, but by the implicit discourses of national identity that constitute May's subjecthood and allow her to fetishize Munoo based upon his perceived hygienic difference.

The varied ways in which characters read Munoo's hygienic status in *Coolie*—ranging from abject "vulgar hillboy" to eroticized "unclean boy"—suggest that a dichotomy lies at the root of filth fetishism. In his analysis of the stereotype as fetish, Homi Bhabha argues that because the colonial stereotype is predicated on the interplay between an imagined original unity and a recognition of difference, such an "ambivalence" is fundamental to the stereotype's structure: "The role of fetishistic identification, in the construction of discriminatory knowledges that depend upon the 'presence of difference,' is to provide a process of splitting and multiple/contradictory belief at the point of enunciation and subjectification."[36] One of Bhabha's significant contributions is to revise our understanding of fetishism as rooted solely in sexual difference by adding to this the productive elaboration of racial difference's role in the construction of the colonial stereotype as fetish.[37] I would like to complicate Bhabha's account further by pointing to the ways in which discourses of filth and hygiene form yet another layer of writing on this palimpsest. Indeed, whether as dirty hillboy or unclean boy with the "sensitive poet's eyes,"[38] Munoo cannot escape from processes of fetishization invoking sexual, racial, *and* hygienic difference, despite the divergent manifestation of these processes as stereotypes.

Performing Pollution in Desani's *All About H. Hatterr*

Bhabha's notion of the ambivalence rooted in the colonial stereotype offers a useful model for understanding another crucial Western-authored social formation of colonial filth: the willfully unhygienic body of the Indian truth-seeker. Accounts of Indian holy persons, gurus, sages, and supplicants figure prominently in writings on Indian religion and customs published for British readers in the first half of the twentieth century; common to these writings is a fascination with the corporeality and hygiene of the truth-seekers they describe. In *Living India* (1928), a popular account of Indian culture whose introduction is provided by the Irish theosophist and *Ulysses* personage "AE" (George Russell),[39] Savel Zimand observes that "[a]t numerous religious fairs and holy places ascetics dress in a coating of ash and sit in perpetual contemplation, their legs crossed under them, their eyes fixed vacantly upon nothing at all."[40] In *Popular Hinduism* (1935), L. S. S. O'Malley writes that the "Sadhu (a name which for our purposes may be taken as a general designation for different kinds of ascetics) . . . may wear saffron-coloured robes, or be content with a patchwork of rags, or go about in almost complete nudity. If he is a Sannyasi, his skin is covered with a fine powdery ash of greyish-blue colour . . . ; others again have long dishevelled locks or a dirty matted mop."[41] What is noteworthy about these accounts is how quickly their tone shifts from an anthropological fascination with the corporeality, dress, and hygiene of the ash-covered mystic as the embodiment of a non-Western spiritual transcendence to derision of the mystic's physical neglect and even suspicion of worldly motives. In *Hinduism* (1948), Alan Bouquet writes that "a morbid preoccupation with religion has reduced a good many [holy persons] to the level of pathological specimens, to wit the type described by Dr. John Wilson of the Free Church of Scotland, 'whose nails were grown into his cheeks, and who had a bird's nest upon his head.'"[42] The passage from Zimand further observes that while "some of [the mendicants] are no doubt genuine . . . many of them, under the cover of holiness, prey upon a hospitable people."[43] And Bouquet, responding to the claim that "an appreciable number of quasi-ascetics are fugitives from justice or escaped criminals," concurs that "[t]he saddhu's livery of ashes is a very convenient form of disguise, and indeed forms a kind of travelling sanctuary."[44]

Just as this fetishization of Indian hygiene vacillates between fascination with spiritual transcendence and condemnation of excessive fervor or charlatanism, so too does the anthropological rhetoric of these popular accounts waver between descriptions of ash-rubbing and asceticism as forms either of religious purification or of bodily and moral defilement. It is this ambivalence at the core of the Western gaze that will serve as the focal point of G. V. Desani's experimental novel, *All About H. Hatterr* (1948).[45] Borrowing the rhetoric of British accounts of Indian sages and purification rites, along with the tendency of these accounts to read physical markers as signs of interior pollution, Desani's novel refigures these stereotypes, revealing religious and anthropological truth claims to be performative, discursive constructions. At the same time, *All About H. Hatterr* complicates and questions the imperial gaze, since, as often as not, its polluting/purifying performances are conducted by hybrid subjects—even at times Westerners—for Indian eyes. Indeed, *All About H. Hatterr* affirms "pollution" as an enabling form of representation—an affirmation that the text embraces at the level of its own style, in which numerous regional dialects, class-based speech patterns, scientific terms, medical jargon, advertising appeals, and religious orthodoxies mutually infect each other, producing what Anthony Burgess terms a "gloriously impure" language.[46]

From the time of its publication in 1948, *All About H. Hatterr* has challenged critics with its defiance of generic categories. Consisting of seven episodes without a clearly defined plot, *Hatterr* begins with a "Warning" that describes the text as a "gesture," consenting it to be

266 ⌒ William Kupinse

termed a novel only to satisfy public demand. That this warning is followed by an author's note and yet another "Warning" only adds to the
generic confusion, as does the lengthy legal disclaimer by the protagonist's lawyer-*cum*-spiritual counsel, Sri. Y. Beliram, or Yati Rambeli as
he is known in his present incarnation, which itself includes appended
letters, poems, and questionable critical exegesis of Hatterr's "novel."
Indeed, one of the most telling remarks in Beliram's appendix, titled
"With Iron Hand, I Defend You, Mr. H. Hatterr, Gentleman!" is his
observation that dirt is "only matter, in the *wrong* place!" (293)—the
layers of generic insinuation and denial suggesting that the matter out
of place in the text is both the front and back matter.

To the extent that the text does possess a plot, its movement charts
the adventures of H. Hatterr, a half-Malaysian, half-European orphan
whose liminal position as half colonizer/half (post)colonial subject is
further complicated by his being raised by a Scotsman living in India.
Each of the seven episodes begins with a "Digest" introducing the questions the episode will address, followed by the "Instruction" of one of
seven Indian Sages, then a philosophical "Presumption," and finally the
"Life-Encounter" of Hatterr himself. Hatterr in turn prefaces each of
his "Life-Encounters" by relating a want or desire—for employment,
sexual gratification, religious enlightenment, social standing, wealth,
reconciliation with his wife, experience with nature—to his friend Banerrji, an Indian by birth but Anglophile by profession. Invariably, Hatterr's exploits require him to dirty his hands, or even his entire person,
frequently by assuming a religious identity, be it of supplicant or sage.
M. K. Naik has noted that Hatterr disrobes in every episode, but equally
important is the fact that the end of each episode most often finds Hatterr longing for a bath and proper clothing.[47] If, as I argue, Hatterr's
exploits in the seven sections work to uncover the fundamental ambivalence within the imperial stereotype of the unhygienic colonial
body—wavering between transcendence/purification and charlatanism/
pollution—his disrobing, self-sullying, and bathing reveal the possibility of performative manipulation inherent in the process of imperial
"readings" of colonial hygiene.

In the first episode, Hatterr, who has taken a newspaper post to earn
money after being blackmailed by his *dhobin* or washerwoman, receives
an assignment to interview the Sage of the Wilderness, author of a
learned commentary on Panini's Sanskrit grammar, for a "local colour"
piece. Upon meeting the Sage's disciple, Hatterr is impressed by his
remarkable stomach—"the largest, damme, I had yet seen!"—but he is
particularly struck by the figure's ritual application of ash. For Hatterr,

the disciple's ash-covered stomach becomes a fetish, a process partially enabled by Hatterr's consumption of the alcoholic beverage *todii*, but telling nonetheless:

> Thereon—as the Eastern religion has held there is no difference between flesh and *ash*—he had rubbed much of *ash*.
>
> Maybe because I was tired, maybe it was the todii effect telling on me, but as soon as I saw that man's stomach, a tremendous feeling of awe overpowered me.
>
> I wanted to go down on my knees, impromptu-like, salaam like hell, beat a tom-tom, and *worship* the feller's tummy, as if it were a demigod, unattached and independent of him! (50)

While Hatterr's fetishization of the ash-covered stomach suggests his desire for spiritual experience, Hatterr can only imagine this experience in the language of religious ritual, hence his desire to "salaam like hell, beat a tom-tom, and *worship* the feller's tummy." But this performative understanding of religious experience immediately allows for its commodification. Indeed, Hatterr's appeal to the Sage himself—whom he is delighted to find similarly covered with ash—makes clear the would-be reporter's economic interest in his subject. "Please, master, utter a few words of wisdom, and, through your humble [sic], comfort the reading classes. Earn merit from thy act of piety, O adorned with ash!" (50). In this episode, Hatterr conflates ritual purification and bodily hygiene by assuming that the marker of spiritual piety can be appropriated as a marketable signifier. In his encounter with the Sage of the Wilderness, however—as in each of the novel's episodes—Hatterr's attempt to exploit the corporeal markers of privileged Eastern religious knowledge for his material gain backfires. The Sage turns out to be more *faker* than *fakir*, a used clothing dealer whose ash rubbing is already pure performance, a performance that enables him to stock his wares with the discarded vestments of his visitors. Hatterr returns to the newspaper office ash covered and nearly nude, clothed only with a dirty, discarded towel.

This vacillation between ritual purification and bodily pollution is developed in an insistent fashion throughout the subsequent episodes through both Eastern *and* Western rituals; indeed, Hatterr's cultural hybridity does much to enable the episodes' various reversals. The second episode begins with an "Instruction" in which ash serves as the sign of defilement rather than purification as the Sage of Rangoon tells his disciple to "Extinguish the fires of passions through meditation!" The disciple responds by asserting the supremacy of claims of the flesh over self-willed asceticism: "Within the gaze-range of the velvet-black eyes of a desirable wench, thou knowest, the exigency of the vows of a he-nun are but a heap of ash, ash! mere residue of a corpse, a cadaver!" (62).[48] This admixture of pollution and purification will be repeated parodically in the "Life-Encounter" that follows, in which Hatterr professes his need for female companionship, what he refers to as "clean fun." His friend Banerrji, suspicious of Hatterr's motives, reminds him of his marriage, but finally relents and introduces him to Rosie Smythe, a Cockney woman who operates a circus with her husband, Bill. Holding out the promise of physical intimacy, she persuades Hatterr to accept a part in a lion-taming act. The act itself proves to be the ultimate performance of ritual pollution. The hybrid Hatterr is dressed as what the Smythes take to be a show Hindu, nude except for a bathing suit and a spotted handkerchief tied around his neck; a shiny top hat, their concession to his role as circus performer, provides the final touch. So attired, Hatterr's role is to lie on the ground and allow a lion to eat a steak off his bare chest, an unthinkable act for the Hindu he is supposed to represent, given that the steak is clearly a beefsteak, a "mooslab" as Hatterr calls it, as well as a bizarre choice of a circus act on the Smythes' part, considering the largely Hindu audience. During the first performance Hatterr does achieve a moment of transcendence by focusing his will according to the Sage's instruction, but his next performance finds Hatterr faced with an unusually tough steak on his chest, and thus an unusually long show. By the end of the performance, Hatterr manages to free himself from physical desire, but only by eliminating it through a performative defilement that leads him to imagine his own death. What is significant about the ritual, however, is the relationship of spectator and the defiled object that constitutes its gaze. Performed for an Indian audience, a sizable portion of which should see the ritual as pure abomination, the circus act inspires instead its admiration, if the hearty applause and Banerrji's commentary offer any indication. "As regards the last night's example, I must say, I have seen ideals lived before my eyes!" he tells Hatterr, adding, ". . . you are a true divine" (96). Not only in the humor of its outrageous circumstance, but more so through its odd relationship of spectator and spectacle, the episode reworks the notion of colonial mimicry, transposing the gaze from colonizer to colonized, and producing for Indian eyes a Western-authored performance (the circus, significantly, is billed as a London circus) of ritual pollution, in which physical defilement becomes the agent of spiritual purification.

While each of the four intervening episodes dramatizes Hatterr's maladroit negotiation of Indian purification and pollution rites, the seventh and final episode deserves special attention as it represents the text's only gesture toward the codes of pollution and purification inherent in the caste system. Here we find Hatterr visiting a *satsang*, an open air spiritual retreat, for recreation and moral uplift, which is led by an abusive guru named Punchum; Desani's description of the guru suggests he is of comparatively upper-caste status, if not a Brahmin. Hatterr witnesses one of the penitents at the *satsang*, upon confessing his misfortunes, inadvertently make a proscribed contact with Punchum: "Thereupon, the Master scrutinized a tear on his ash-coated foot. 'Thou . . .' he said to the young feller, pointing an index finger at his big toe, '. . . hast polluted an organ of this anatomy with the humidity of the eye'" (262). Their sympathy for the young penitent primed by the guru's abuse of his wayward tear, and by the hard-luck story of unrequited love the guru solicits from the penitent, the *satsang*-goers reach for their wallets.

The context of the guru's ire merits attention, for the tear is a more significant detail than it might appear. Mary Douglas observes that according to Hindu tradition, tears are not especially polluting, except insofar as they exert a relatively specific effect on social or caste status;[49] for this reason, the tears from the unworthy penitent can pollute the comparatively purer Master. Thus the *satsang*-goers' sympathy toward the penitent hints at a reaction against the rigidity of Indian caste structure and its concomitant pollution rules. Hatterr, who has reluctantly given to the penitent only as a result of *satsang* peer pressure, immediately perceives the pollution-abuse as a potential scam, one that he hopes to exploit by entering into partnership with the Master. Armed with a hard-luck story of his own, he arrives at the *satsang,* only to find that the ritual is even more performative than he had imagined; the guru already has a partner, the very same penitent from the previous evening.

If *All About H. Hatterr* presents the hygienic markers of spiritual status as fundamentally performative systems of signification—hence their vacillation between the rhetorics of purification and pollution—it demonstrates a similar understanding of literary style. Furthermore, just as the social significance of these hygienic markers is open to manipulation at the moment of the colonial encounter, so too are linguistic structures, and thus *Hatterr* adopts a style of linguistic contamination. Critics including D. M. Burjonjee and Molly Ramanujan have effectively dismantled Anthony Burgess's claim that the linguistic adulteration evidenced in Hatterr's own speech is a form of "Higher Babu"—that is, the inflatedly erudite misappropriation of English attributed to Indians seeking advancement under British administration. As Ramanujan observes, the novel does contain parodies of Babu English,[50] but these parodies are mouthed by secondary characters such as Banerrji, who misemploys Shakespearean quotation and legalese in an effort to assert authority. Hatterr himself, though he employs related strategies of stylistic impurity in the form of excess, incongruity, eclecticism, and accumulation, demonstrates linguistic mastery, not malapropism, and he seems less interested in asserting authority than in undermining it. The passage quoted earlier describing the ash rubbing in the Sage of the Wilderness episode offers an example of one of Hatterr's favorite strategies: beginning with an objective, anthropological account ("as the Eastern religion has held there is no difference between flesh and *ash*"), which merges into a kind of performative piety ("a tremendous feeling of awe overpowered me"), before devolving into colloquialism and materialism. As Hatterr thinks to himself in a subsequent passage: "Damme . . . I have heard stories of occult-clairvoyant sages making a penniless feller equal to Rockefeller in riches!" (52). This passage, like the rest of Desani's novel, demonstrates both the accretion and simultaneous distancing of various linguistic systems, but even more importantly refuses to privilege any particular system. An analogous strategy of contamination extends to the novel's generic allegiances, as well. M. K. Naik has noted the similarities between *Hatterr*'s structure and that of traditional Indian models of philosophical inquiry, conduct instruction, and religious teaching, including the Vedantins' *Nyaya* syllogism, the *Panchatantra*, the *Puranas*, and the *Upanishads*.[51] Yet at the same time critics have noted the presence of generic elements borrowed from such Western forms as the bildungsroman, modern surrealist prose, and picaresque novel.[52] This kind of overdetermined intertextuality has led to the critical dismissal of Desani as simply an imitator of Joyce, a charge Srinivas Aravumudan rejects, calling *Hatterr* an "affiliated" reworking of its intertextual models, which, like *Ulysses*, is committed to challenging "the ontological status of mastery."[53]

This notion of *Hatterr* as a challenge to mastery offers a useful way for considering the novel as a politically motivated text. Desani's own commentary on *Hatterr* makes a similar point:

> In my *All About H. Hatterr*, I have systematically concerned myself with the British (western) aims and means of achieving status and respectability. I have also, as definitely, dealt with the Indian (eastern) aims and means of achieving status and respectability, not forgetting the hereafter. My man, H. Hatterr, having consorted with both, ended by jeering at both and their sources.[54]

If linguistic register, literary genre, and a "means of achieving status and respectability" — whether Western or Eastern — are ideologically freighted categories, then contamination, overdetermination, and jeering might function as useful correctives. Far from simply engaging in politically disinterested language games, Desani's novel advances important cultural work. Subtitled "A Gesture" in its first edition, *All About H. Hatterr*'s prefatory "Warning" posits the gesture as its own form, and an overtly political one at that. "Melodramatic gestures against public security are a common form of self-expression in the East," the text wryly notes, citing the example of the Indian peasant who copes with misfortune by derailing a train. While this example might suggest that Desani's strategy is ultimately one of negation, I would like to propose that in post-Independence India, a gesture such as *Hatterr* could offer a useful check against the competing dangers of a nostalgic appeal to essential "national character" or a neocolonialism that replicates colonial economic and social inequities in a revised form. Indeed, if *All About H. Hatterr* resonates as a political text, this resonance arrives through the novel's challenge to essentialist renderings of nationhood at the moment of decolonization through its "gloriously impure" experimentation, in which not even the body of the text is above an affirmative sullying.

Conclusion: Textual Inf(l)ection

The representational strategies of these novels by Day, Anand, and Desani —which we might categorize respectively as realist, social-realist, and modern (or even postmodern)—are as historically situated as their political contexts: firmly Imperial, pre-Independence, and post-Independence. This division between the matter and manner of textual response is of course an artificial distinction, for the texts themselves demonstrate as keen an attention to tonal nuances within imperial discourses on colonial hygiene as they do to these discourses' ostensibly factual content. But even acknowledging this tonal keenness seems to me an insufficient answer to the larger questions about the relationship between hygienic response and literary technique raised by *Govinda Samanta*, *Coolie*, and *All About H. Hatterr*. Why should the moments in which one of the first Indian English novels manipulates its realistic representational mode coincide with its responses to British hygienic discourse? Similarly, why should one of the clearest examples of social realism of the 1930s disrupt its established narrative mode by exploring how a Westerner fetishizes the hygienic status of the novel's protagonist? And why should what might be described as the first postmodern Indian novel in English—a novel to which Rushdie has acknowledged a debt[55]—construct its spiritual simulacra, reveal the late-capitalist commodification of Indian culture, and explode a newly independent nation's *grands récits*, all with a handful of dust?

A partial answer to these questions is that as the English-language Indian novel reworks the genre according to the pressures of its colonial situation, the history of imperial description necessarily informs the imaginative responses of its authors. That these three significant texts in the genealogy of Indian writing in English should offer such a rich and emphatic response to British attitudes toward colonial hygiene suggests the central role these beliefs played within the social formations of the colonial, decolonizing, and postcolonial eras. For Day, providing an experientially grounded ethnography to remedy the speculative, secondhand ethnography of Mill's *History of British India* marks a crucial moment of nineteenth-century colonial self-authorization. Arriving at a middle point in this history, Anand's *Coolie* insists upon the economic roots of hygienic abjection, figuring this process from the perspectives of both Indian and British characters; its reversal in its final episodes to depict a hygienic fetishism produced by desire rather than dismissal suggests Anand's understanding of the vacillating quality of this particular construction of "otherness." By the time of the mock-anthropological *All About H. Hatterr*, the strategy Desani adopts is one of overt thematic and linguistic contamination, which seeks to undercut both imperial and neocolonial social formations. If we are surprised by the productiveness of these novelistic responses to sanitary and hygienic attitudes, then perhaps we can gain a better understanding of the perceived power of this imperial description, as well as the motive for these novels to inflect, and infect, themselves preemptively.

Notes

1. [Unsigned], "Indian Habits," *The Sanitary Record*, 15 August 1882, 61.

2. [Unsigned], "A Sanitary Renaissance in India," *The Sanitary Record*, 26 November 1903, 521.

3. Warwick Anderson, "Excremental Colonialism: Public Health and the Poetics of Pollution," *Critical Inquiry* 21 (Spring 1995): 645.

4. Anne McClintock, *Imperial Leather: Race, Gender, and Sexuality in the Colonial Contest* (New York: Routledge, 1995), 209.

5. Aijaz Ahmad, "Jameson's Rhetoric of Otherness and the 'National Allegory,'" *Social Text* 17 (1987): 6.

6. Dipesh Chakrabarty, "Open Space/Public Space: Garbage, Modernity, and India," *South Asia* 14, no. 1 (1991): 16, 17. V. S. Naipaul, *An Area of Darkness* (London: Andre Deutsch, 1964), 74.

7. *Govinda Samanta* is described most accurately as the second Indian novel written in English but the first successful foray in the genre. Bankim Chandra Chatterji's *Rajmohan's Wife*, serialized in 1864 but not published in book form until the twentieth century, holds the technical distinction of first Indian English novel, but most readers will agree with Salman Rushdie's assessment of it as "a dud," "a poor melodramatic thing" ("Introduction," in *Mirrorwork: 50 Years of Indian Writing*, ed. Salman Rushdie and Elizabeth West [New York: Henry Holt, 1997], xiv).

8. Lal Behari Day, *Govinda Samanta* (London: Macmillan, 1874), vii; subsequent references are to this edition and will be cited in the text.

9. Rajaiah D. Paul, *They Kept the Faith: Biographies of Gopeenath Nundi, Pyari Mohan Rudra, and Lal Behari Day* (Lucknow, India: Lucknow Publishing House, 1968), 88, 91, 105–6, 112–14.

10. K. S. Ramamurti, "Lal Behari Day: *Govinda Samanta*," *Literary Half-Yearly* 15 (1974) 65.

11. Remarking on the peril of discovery for a male visitor to the baths, Day's narrator conspires with the reader: "We must therefore get to the *ghat* some one or two hours before, and conceal ourselves among the thick foliage of a sacred *sriphal* tree (*Ægle Marmelos*) which stands just a little beyond the floor" (175).

12. William Thomas, "Editor's Introduction" to James Mill, *The History of British India,* abridged ed. (Chicago: University of Chicago Press, 1975), xii.

13. Martin Moir, "Introduction" to John Stuart Mill, *Writings on India*, in *The Collected Works of John Stuart Mill*, 33 vols., ed. John M. Robinson, Martin Moir, and Zawahir Moir (Toronto: University of Toronto Press, 1990), 30:xiii.

14. James Mill, *The History of British India,* 6 vols. (London: Baldwin, Cradock, and Joy, 1920), 1:ix.

15. Ibid., 344–45, 367.

16. Ramamurti, "Lal Behari Day: *Govinda Samanta*," 64.

17. Meenakshi Mukherjee, *The Perishable Empire* (New Delhi: Oxford, 2000), 57.

18. Mukherjee helpfully locates *Govinda Samanta*'s strategy of covert resistance within the context of the Dramatic Performance Control Act of 1876, which restricted dramatic critique of British Imperial presence within India (58).

19. Readers familiar with Anand's work may wonder at my choice of *Coolie* over Anand's novel *Untouchable* (London: Lawrence and Wishart, 1936), which traces a day in the life of Bakha, a dalit latrine sweeper. Though its emphasis on colonial hygiene and sanitation forms the focus of the text, its primary political investments lie in critiquing the caste system. It is thus less engaged in employing discourses of hygiene to explore the relational construction of imperial and colonial subjectivities, which is my interest in this essay.

20. Clive Dewey, *Anglo-Indian Attitudes: The Mind of the Indian Civil Service* (London: Hambledon Press, 1993), 34.

21. Dewey makes a convincing argument that Brayne's campaigns were

largely failures. For a contemporary account of the ineffectiveness of Brayne's project of sanitary reform, see Malcolm Darling, *Wisdom and Waste [in the Punjab Village]* (London: Oxford University Press, 1934).

22. Frank Lugard Brayne, *Village Uplift in India* (Allahabad, India: Pioneer Press, 1927), 117.

23. Ibid., 119.

24. Indeed, in *Rural Reconstruction in India* (1929), Brayne insists that in programs of Indian reform "religion must be severely left alone" (3).

25. Frank Lugard Brayne, *A Village ABC: 456 Brief Hints on Rural Reconstruction* (London: Oxford University Press, 1950), 34.

26. Brayne, *Village Uplift in India*, 29.

27. Mulk Raj Anand, *Coolie* (1936; Harmondsworth, UK: Penguin Books, 1945), 17; subsequent references are to this edition and will be cited in the text.

28. Karl Marx, *Capital: A Critique of Political Economy*, trans. Ben Fowkes (1867; New York: Vintage, 1977), 166, 163.

29. Raymond Williams, "Ideas of Nature," in *Problems in Materialism and Culture* (London: Verso, 1980), 83.

30. Marx, *Capital*, 167.

31. Mary Douglas, *Purity and Danger: An Analysis of the Concepts of Pollution and Taboo* (New York: Frederick A. Praeger, 1966), 29.

32. For a fuller account of Anand's socialism and its relationship to *Coolie*, see R. K. Dhawan, "The Thirties Movement and *Coolie*," in *The Novels of Mulk Raj Anand*, ed. R. K. Dhawan (New Delhi: Prestige Books, 1992): 54–65.

33. C. D. Narasimhaiah goes so far as to claim that Anand "seems to *share* the blame . . . with the critics for his own neglect," suggesting that Anand's well-publicized leftism negatively influenced critics and that the polemical overtones of his novels and short stories' *titles* detracted from readers' appreciation of his artistry. C. D. Narasimhaiah, *The Swan and the Eagle* (Shimla: Indian Institute of Advanced Study, 1968; rev. 1987), 110. For a useful summary of less sympathetic criticism that labeled Anand's work propaganda, see again Dhawan's "The Thirties Movement and *Coolie*."

34. Narasimhaiah, *The Swan and the Eagle*, 127.

35. Saros Cowasjee, "Coolie: An Appraisal," in *The Novels of Mulk Raj Anand*, ed. R. K. Dhawan (New Delhi: Prestige Books, 1992), 76.

36. Homi Bhabha, *The Location of Culture* (London: Routledge, 1994), 80.

37. In considering both racial and sexual notions of fetishim, however, Bhabha stresses that we must resist the tendency "to conflate, unproblematically, two forms of the marking." As he states later in the same chapter, "Within the apparatus of colonial power, the discourses of sexuality and of race relate in a process of *functional overdetermination* . . ." (67, 74; emphasis in original).

38. Race and hygiene are clearly linked in an epithet that appears early in the novel. Prem, one of the Mals' sons, jokingly imitates "the tone in which Englishmen talk to their native servants," telling Munoo to "[p]ut it down on the table, black man, you who relieve yourself on the ground!" (24).

39. Interestingly enough, Russell echoes Mill almost exactly in confessing, "I have never been to India . . ." George Russell ("AE"), "Introduction" to Savel Zimand, *Living India* (New York; London: Longmans, Green, and Co., 1928), ix.

40. Zimand, *Living India*, 69.

41. L. S. S. O'Malley, *Popular Hinduism: The Religion of the Masses* (Cambridge, UK: University Press, 1935), 207–8. Parenthetical commentary in original.

42. Alan Coates Bouquet, *Hinduism* (London: Hutchison's University Library, 1948), 148.

43. Zimand, *Living India*, 70.

44. Bouquet, *Hinduism*, 147n4.

45. Desani's novel was first published in London by Aldor in 1948 under the title *All About Mr. Hatterr*. I use the 1986 edition (New Paltz, NY: McPherson) on the grounds that it incorporates the author's final revisions; material additions to the 1948 text may be understood as reflecting the development of Desani's thought on India in the decades following Independence. Subsequent references are thus to the 1986 McPherson edition and will be cited within the text.

46. Anthony Burgess, "Introduction" to G. V. Desani, *All About H. Hatterr*, 10. Dated 1969, Burgess's "Introduction" first appears in the 1970 editions of *All About H. Hatterr* and is reprinted as the preface to the McPherson edition.

47. M. K. Naik, *Studies in Indian English Literature* (London: Oriental University Press, 1987), 11.

48. O'Malley cites a "credible account" of a North Indian sect who consume their cremated gurus' ashes; *Popular Hinduism*, 198.

49. Douglas, *Purity and Danger*, 125.

50. Desani, however, claims that *none* of the characters' language resembles Babu. In a talk republished in essay form, Desani writes that "the very personal language [Hatterr] uses, and other characters do, has nothing to do with the species of English called babu. Actually, babu is spoken by incompetent people and—apart from now and then amusing better speakers of English—it has little virtue as a means of expression." Desani's claims about his novel should probably be regarded with some skepticism, however, since in the same piece, after making an unlikely assertion about his text, he concludes, "If a professional book reviewer or aspiring critic cannot see this, he or she is deficient, as far as I am concerned, and he or she is not making a statement about H. Hatterr but about himself or herself" (G. V. Desani, "Difficulties of Communicating: An Oriental to a Western Audience," in *Awakened Conscience: Studies in Commonwealth Literature*, ed. C. D. Narasimhaiah [New Delhi: Sterling, 1978], 404, 403).

51. Naik, *Studies in Indian English Literature*, 23–24; Burgess, "Introduction" to *All About H. Hatterr*, 9; Naik, *Studies in Indian English Literature*, 27.

52. Burgess, "Introduction" to *All About H. Hatterr*, 9; Naik, *Studies in Indian English Literature*, 27; Srinivas Aravamudan, "Postcolonial Affiliations: *Ulysses* and *All About H. Hatterr*," in *Transcultural Joyce*, ed. Karen Lawrence (Cambridge: Cambridge University Press, 1998), 113.

53. Aravamudan, "Postcolonial Affiliations," 113.

54. G. V. Desani, "A Marginal Comment on the Problem of Medium in Bicultures," in *Individual and Community in Commonwealth Literature*, ed. Daniel Massa (Malta: Old University Press, 1979), 204.

55. Rushdie writes of Desani that "[m]y own writing . . . learned a trick or two from him." Salman Rushdie, "Introduction" to *Mirrorwork*, xvi. See also Rushdie, "Damme, This Is the Oriental Scene for You!," *New Yorker*, 23–30 June 1997, 50, 52, 54, 56–61.

Chapter 12

Abject Academy

Benjamin Lazier

> I do not want you to believe any of this because it is all crap, but it
> is the crap in which the piles of our pseudo-European culture are
> embedded, so you had better understand it because no one who
> does not understand the history and taxonomy of crap will ever
> come to know the difference between crap and pseudocrap
> and noncrap.
> —*Louis de Bernières*, Señor Vivo and the Coca Lord

What, strictly speaking, is a fart? Does the fart inhabit the realm of the spiritual or the sensual, the sacred or the profane, the ethereal or the base? How are the human sciences to contend with the recalcitrance of this unclassifiable spirit of the body? What are the conditions for the possibility of knowing flatulence? Or on a more prosaic note, how best to gauge the caliber of gas? By wind speed, volume, resonance, or tone? And what of the many grades of stink?

For twenty-nine weeks toward the end of 1938, these questions and others like them earned the attentions of a curious group of German intellectuals and professionals. Thirty-seven in all, their number included the illustrious zoologist Dr. Fladen, the ecologist Dr. Kaacke, Professor Kahrenforz the literary historian, as well as an eminent Germanist, a certain Professor Pissner.[1] Though the group variously labeled itself the *Academia Latina Cacata*, the Olet Academy, and the Order of Kakasophs, it settled finally on a name with a distinctively German pedigree, the *Neue Fruchtbringende Gesellschaft*. In this, the group harked back to the renowned seventeenth-century German literary society, which had as one of its primary goals the expulsion of foreign impurities from the German language. Whereas the original group hoped to isolate, abject, and suppress the filth in its midst, however, its latter-day incarnation embraced the abject, and more, celebrated it as the society's very *raison d'être*. What additionally distinguished this "New Fruitbringing Society" from its predecessor was the precise nature of the fruit of its labor: an eleven-hundred-page guide to the abject in all its forms. Its title: *Non Olet*—it does not stink.[2] Its libertarian vision of freedom: *scheiß, wohin du willst!* (608). Its motto, as we might imagine it: *je pête, donc je suis*.[3]

In truth, no such academy ever convened, at least not in the back room of a tavern in downtown Cologne as they claimed. They did in fact assemble, but only in the fecund imagination of a lone and driven individual, a resident and devotee of Cologne by the name of Josef Feinhals. Born in 1877, Feinhals trained first as an engineer before he transformed his father's tobacco firm into one of Germany's leading purveyors of quality cigars. His fortune made, Feinhals quickly became one of the key figures in Cologne's early twentieth-century cultural life. He supported the work of the German Werkbund, and served as patron to many artists whose work the Nazis would later commandeer as "degenerate." Contemporaries described him as impeccably neat and elegant, perhaps unsurprising for the author of an opus on filth. He was certainly erudite, with a sovereign command of Latin, Greek, French, and English, and the ability to render *leck mich*, short for "lick my ass," into no less than forty-seven languages.

Writing under the pseudonym Collofino, Feinhals had published several other iconoclastic volumes of intellectual humor, all under private auspices, before undertaking work on what would become his masterpiece, his true, if still unrecognized, bequest to Western culture.[4] Of the origins of the text itself, however, we know but the barest of details. Its place and date of publication, Nazi Germany on the eve of the Second World War, raise obvious questions about the history of its material production. For whatever else it may be, *Non Olet* is no Nazi text. If anything, the forms of community envisioned and practiced by the Oletarians worked specifically against Nazi aims: while the fascists sought to consolidate their hold on a purified *Blutgemeinschaft* or community of blood, the Oletarians busied themselves forging an elective community predicated on the filth common to all, a *Scheißgemeinschaft* at once highly particular but potentially universal in scope. As the Nazis developed rigorous programs for the identification, abjection, and disposal of waste from the German social body, the Oletarians embarked on nothing less than a religious crusade to preach the gospel of gas. As the process of *Gleichschaltung*, or ideological "coordination," transformed German universities into dogmatic cheerleaders, these *connoisseurs du cac* embarked on an ambitious and creative attempt to revive the human sciences under the proud banner of scatology. Perhaps most telling: as the Nazis insisted on the rigorous distinction between Aryan and Jew, the Oletarians collapsed racial boundaries, proclaiming the racial identity of Greek and Semite. It becomes all the more amazing that such resistance to the project of Nazi purity could take the material form that it did: 1102 pages in length, set in an elegant Garamond-Antiqua font by the Cologne art-book firm M. DuMont Schauberg, bound in marbled cloth with reinforced corners. The book's contents may have been abject. But the designation hardly applies to its form.

The abject has long (if not always) been the object of human contemplation. Such reflection has spanned a variety of discourses: medical, agricultural, ethnographic, and theological, to name the most prominent. Derived from the Latin *abjicere*, to throw away, the term denotes something once part of the body since expelled, but the term applies equally to any evacuation of the self or collective, whether understood in physical or psychological terms. In the period under consideration here, however, the abject arose to threaten the stability of disciplinary inquiry itself. The category proved especially disruptive to disciplines like ethnography and history grounded in hermeneutics. Construed as neither subject nor object, yet both, the abject understandably proved resistant to hermeneutic interpretation. Even as the abject returned as a disruptive force, however, it appeared at the same time embattled, fighting for a place in a world that for various reasons hoped to efface it. As such, the abject became figured as the suppressed "other" of the human sciences, as a category that required liberation from the yoke of disciplinary inquiry.

In the years between 1936 and 1939 the abject served as a lodestone for a peculiar academic activism. The members of these abject academies envisioned them as vanguard groups whose projects would provide communitarian alternatives to the atomism and apparent sterility of bourgeois life as well as to the totalizing form of community desired by fascism. In their most utopian moments, these Kakasophs believed their activities would usher in no less than a revolutionary transformation of everyday life. Dr. Ritzenfeger, for one, anticipated that the Oletarians would "finally come to discern the *causa movens* of the universe" (1015). Director Niedergesäss likewise insisted that the Olet-Akademie had "without doubt the potential to transform the entire world," for only they might establish a "new philosophy" whose ground would by definition "encompass all the peoples of the Earth" (162).

The Oletarians have little in common with today's defeatist discourse on the abject.[5] But their hopes for an abject academy endowed with a more positive, if still paradoxical, sense of community did have parallels in its own era. Many at the time—Musil, Kafka, Sartre among them—thematized the abject. But the Oletarian impulse took root between 1936 and 1939 most emphatically in the "College of Sociology" affiliated with Georges Bataille and in "Redemption through Sin," Gershom Scholem's monumental essay on Sabbatai Sevi, the seventeenth-century apostate messiah.[6] Bataille and the College seem an obvious case to include in a study of this sort. As Drs. Föttgenhauer and Ritzenfeger assembled in the smoky dark of their tavern, so their French counterparts convened in the back room of a Paris bookstore. Like the Olet Academy, the College had its antecedents in the communities first forged as children gathered covertly around the toilet, in "the consultations surrounded by bathroom stink."[7] As Michel Leiris recalled, it was there in the bathroom that "we felt most like accomplices, fomenting plots and developing a quasi-secret mythology" (CS, 25). So, too, did the members of the College express a desire for an integrated, activist science centered on notions of abjection and *dépense* (waste or expenditure); though for the College at least, abjection was thought to disintegrate lived communities and de-center scientific practice as much as to consolidate them. Finally, the College responded, as did the Oletarians, to the fascist challenge.[8]

Scholem appears incongruous in their company. By this time, after all, he had been in Palestine for more than a decade, far from the heady Parisian scene of which Bataille was a part. Nothing in Scholem's published oeuvre approached Bataille's exuberant invocation of the solar anus, of excrement, spittle, dejecta, and the like. Next to Bataille's Sadean rhetoric of excess, Scholem's careful and exacting philology appears staid and, at worst, as the very incarnation of the positivism that Bataille himself abjured. Yet there are compelling reasons for setting Scholem in comparison with Bataille, and with the Oletarians as well. For one, Scholem was not nearly as isolated from the Paris of the 1930s as his Jerusalem address might lead one to expect. He had links with the College through his closest friend, Walter Benjamin. Benjamin attended the College occasionally and had been scheduled to deliver a series of lectures there, a plan cut short, however, by the onset of war. After the war, Scholem would have dealings with the most important member of the College, Bataille, who sheltered Benjamin's papers after his flight from Paris.[9]

The same holds for Scholem's researches. Though at first glance tangential, his reading of Sevi's apostasy and of the apostate communities that sprang up in its wake raise the very questions of abjection and community that so vexed his contemporaries on the Continent. This is not to say that Scholem's work developed in conscious dialogue with the College, let alone with the Oletarians. A lack of mutual influence, however, only strengthens the case for understanding their parallel efforts as responses to a common historical precipitate: the specter of European fascism. Their responses coalesce. Their stories ought to be told as one.

Abject Communities

In his opening address to the College, in January 1938, Michel Leiris spoke of the antecedents of his interest in the *communitas* promised by the group. His most striking formulations privileged marginal spaces; only these could nourish the sacrality missing from modern life. Leiris reserved his most exalted rhetoric for the bathroom. There, he recalled, his brother sat perched "on the throne like an initiate of higher rank . . . I, the youngest, sat on an ordinary chamber pot that served as the neophyte's stool. The flushing mechanism and the hole were, in themselves, mysterious things, and even actually dangerous. . . . Had we been older and more erudite, we doubtless would not have hesitated to consider [them] directly in touch with the gods of the underworld." "Compared to the parlor," Leiris hypothesized, "the bathroom can be looked on as a cavern, a cave where one comes to be inspired by contacting the deepest, darkest subterranean powers. There, opposite the right-hand sacred of parental majesty, the sinister magic of a left-hand sacred took shape" (CS, 26). The exteriority of this abject realm of the left enabled those who dwelled within it to forge an interiority and communion of uncommon potency. As for the bathroom, then, it was there that Leiris and his elder brother "felt the most cut off, the most separate from everyone else, but also the closest to each other, the most shoulder to shoulder, the most in harmony, in this embryonic secret society that we two brothers formed" (CS, 26).

Other members of the College privileged similar spaces as forums for true community. Roger Caillois, for example, theorized festival as sacred counterpoint to an everyday world of work soaked in profanity. To the "dull continuity" of the latter, Caillois opposed the "intermittent explosions" of the former. "[D]aily repetition" against "frenzied elation," the "tranquil labors in which each one makes himself busy alone" against the "powerful inspiration of common ferment," "quiet toil" against the "fever of climactic moments": such are the distinctions by which Caillois marked out their respective domains (CS, 282). Caillois linked festival to the abject as well. Whereas the health of a human body "requires the regular evacuation of its impurities" such as urine, excrement,

282 🝔 Benjamin Lazier

and menstrual blood, so too must the cosmos abject its accumulated waste. It does so through festival; if retained, such waste would quickly transform into "the seeds of . . . annihilation" (*CS*, 284). Taken as a whole, Caillois defined festival as the "*paroxysm* of society, which it simultaneously purifies and renews" (*CS*, 301).

Given the absence of festival in the modern world, however, only a group akin to a secret society or religious order might induce a thoroughgoing transformation of everyday life. Such groups represent "the sole means for societies that have arrived at a real void, a static nonsense" (*CS*, 153). In a world "held in virtually complete servitude under the thumb of harsh necessity," in a world where "it has become inconceivable to contemplate doing anything other than the jobs, work, tasks that one *must* fulfill," the secret society bears the mark of "profound originality and . . . power," for it has the character of a totality that answers only to itself (*CS*, 155). Secret societies and religious orders attain such potency, as does festival, through a violent expenditure akin to abjection. For Caillois, these groups produce a sacred described as "a force within man and that spreads to the outside" (*CS*, 152). Bataille, likewise, described the affirmation of the will to exist, a will that distinguished such groups from their anemic contemporaries, as inseparable from "the will to expend, to burst forth" (*CS*, 155–56). Secret societies testify to the link between the abject and the antinomian, for they consist in "an outburst violating the rules of life," in a "sacred that expends" (*CS*, 156). The power of such groups derives from the self-loss of those who constitute it, from their capacity to abject. Bataille would forward similar ideas about pseudonymity and automutilation, as we will see shortly.

Similar themes not only figure in Scholem's work on "Redemption through Sin," but practically define it. To begin, Scholem understood Sabbatianism as a phenomenon akin to festival as theorized by the College. He described it as a transitional phase whose antinomian excess prepared the ground for a new, lawful regime. It paved the way, that is, for the *haskalah* or Jewish Enlightenment, a movement that would ironically come to suppress the memory of Sevi's anarchic messianism in the name of its assimilationist project. Scholem understood Sabbatianism — and here we would do well to recall Caillois — as a physical paroxysm also, as a series of "throes . . . towards a healthier national existence" (*RS*, 84–85). Like Bataille, Scholem privileged the limit-experience, or the experience of limits, as that which most truly reveals the authentic.

The trope of abjection governed Scholem's treatment of other movements in Jewish history also. Hasidism, for example, survived impulses similar to the Sabbatian only because it managed "to incorporate" its pneumatics "into its own collective body." "It was the genius of Hasidism," Scholem wrote, "that it knew where to set itself limits." Hasidism demarcated clearly between a useful, controlled, sublatable expenditure, and a useless expenditure of fatal excess. By contrast, the Sabbatians "aimlessly squandered" their energies and emotions. Sabbatianism took the form of an "eruption," of a "nihilistic conflagration." It gave vent to the "instincts of lawlessness and anarchy that lie deeply buried in every human soul," which now "burst forth more violently than ever." The Sabbatians "pressed on to the end, into the abyss of the mythical 'gates of impurity'" (RS, 91, 97, 109, 126). They reveal themselves, in Caillois's terms, as an abject group of the left-sacred, as the secret society par excellence.

Scholem by no means fabricated out of whole cloth the tight weave of Sabbatianism and the abject. Sabbatian theology also gives ample confirmation of the link. Sevi's apologists, for example, cast his descent into impurity as but a transitional phase, much like festival as Caillois described it. They charged the redeemer with entering the realm of the *kelipot* (the forces of evil, but literally "peel" or "shell") and enjoined him to gather back again to their source the divine sparks lost at the time of Adam's primordial sin. The descent into the *kelipah* and the journey of return they likened to administering "an emetic": as soon as such a man repents, he "spews forth all that was within him" (RS, 120). Other apologists understood Sevi's apostasy as an attempt to "quench the *kelipah* by giving it holiness to drink," also to induce a "spewing-forth" (RS, 119). In either case, vomit reigned.

The abject hero, also, plays a leading role in Scholem's reading of Sabbatianism, specifically in the person of Jacob Frank (1726–1791). A literary type with an ancient genealogy, the abject hero refers to figures monstrous in their depravity who nevertheless exert an irresistible power over those who find them otherwise despicable. A figure of "tremendous if satanic power," Frank represents both the culmination and total devolution of the Sabbatian impulse. With Frank, the world of Sabbatianism "has reached that ultimate stage of its development where it verges on self-annihilation" (RS, 128). Educated as a Sabbatian, Frank developed its theology in an earthy, exoteric direction that, in Scholem's estimation, left it utterly bereft of holiness or dignity. Frank advanced a notion of defeating evil from within, which entailed not an antinomianism calculated to bring the Devil to heel, but a thoroughgoing repudiation of all extant law and custom. This found ultimate license, Scholem tells us, in Frank's injunction to "cast oneself down into the abyss," to abase oneself voluntarily. Yet even Frank possessed qualities that commanded Scholem's admiration. For all his despotic nature, for all his "customary savagery," Frank still presided over a "hidden poetic impulse." For all the negativity of his teachings, "they nonetheless contained a genuine creed of life." Even his incoherencies and grotesqueries had in them a kernel of "vigor and imagination" (*RS*, 127, 128). In this, Scholem's treatment of Frank accords with the terms for the abject hero set out more generally by Julia Kristeva and Michael André Bernstein. In her exposition of Céline, Kristeva pronounced tolerable his noxious politics and hotheaded rage, given "the wild beauty of his style."[10] Like Scholem's Frank, Kristeva's Céline speaks the language of *délire*, a language of radical desublimation that moves from self-mastery to heteronomy, from transcendence to carnality. Though he may take Kristeva to task, Bernstein nevertheless resists the contrary impulse. He, too, refuses to declare Céline's anti Semitism the sine qua non for any reading that pretends to a modicum of ethics and responsibility. Despite Céline's egregious failures, Bernstein finds himself appreciative of the novelist's "stunning comic power and literary inventiveness," and duly notes the stylistic complexity of his work. In this, he replicates Scholem's stance on Frank.[11]

Headlessness

More than any other, the metaphor of headlessness united the work of Bataille, Scholem, and Feinhals. Put simply, headlessness (and pseudonymity, its literary counterpart) contested the coherence of masterful identities, whether individual or communal, even as it indexed the urge to transcend or supersede them. For Bataille, acephalic man reigned also as *surhomme*, whereas for Scholem, only he who courted headlessness might become the sort of "superjew" prophesied by the *Judenzarathustra*.[12] Headlessness for these figures did not assume the guise of punishment imposed from without, but of willing self-sacrifice, self-effacement, or automutilation. All of these were thematized as modes of abjection. Headlessness also aptly described the form taken by the abject community. Unlike the sort of community favored by the fascists, whose members shared a libidinal investment in an omnipotent leader, these acephalic communities lacked such a figurehead. Indeed, they gathered around the loss of one.

For Bataille, such sentiment found its most concrete expression in his secret society, *Acéphale*. This is not the place to recount the history of *Acéphale* and its complex, nuanced significance for Bataille, a task admirably carried out elsewhere.[13] Suffice it to say that automutilation was for Bataille the prerequisite for any literary project and, perhaps, for all creative undertakings. Van Gogh and a certain Gaston F., inspired by the former to bite off a finger at the sun's behest (with the hope that it might reinvigorate his career as a painter), thus serve as paradigmatic examples. The trope of abjection fully governs Bataille's thoughts on the phenomenon, described as "the rupture of personal homogeneity and the projection *outside the self* of a part of onself."[14] Hence, Bataille can argue that the severed finger or ear, the enucleated eye "do not appreciably differ from vomited food" (*VE,* 70). Automutilation, in other words, contests masterful identities by underscoring the porousness of the boundaries demarcating the self. It does so in the mode of the abject, which as neither subject nor object, yet both, points to a self that is always already decentered, but left, paradoxically perhaps, in a certain way intact. It grants to acephalic man a freedom unavailable to the man who has not lost his head. The automutilator finds beyond himself "not God, who is the prohibition against crime, but a being who is unaware of prohibition" (*VE,* 181). "The one who sacrifices is free," Bataille writes, "free to indulge in a similar disgorging, free, continuously identifying with the victim, to vomit his own being just as he has vomited a piece of himself or a bull, in other words free to throw himself suddenly *outside of himself*" (*VE,* 70).

Headlessness figures in Scholem's writings also. Here the crucial figure is the *Mauerrenner,* one who courts acephalicity by running headfirst into walls. In his diaries, Scholem deployed the term to describe the required affect of the committed Zionist, one unafraid to smash the boundaries of exile. Scholem attributed to Zion an incommensurability with Europe, a gap that ensured its purity. He therefore privileged modes of becoming that effaced the traces of exilic origins. The metaphor of the *Mauerrenner* operates in just such fashion; though the wallrunner may not lose his head, he does awake from the rubble afflicted with acute amnesia.[15] In "Redemption through Sin," Scholem wrote similarly of Jacob Frank and entourage. The one who mutilates or abases the self and so crosses over into the abyss "lead[s] a life of anarchic liberty as a freeman," unencumbered by the constraints of law, or the heteronomy of the past (*RS,* 131). He becomes paradoxically whole. As we have seen, Bataille wrote of acephalic man in virtually identical terms. Pierre Klossowski also made use of this lexicon when he referred to Sade as a "complete man," *l'homme integral,* given his "proud and glorious incapacity to serve," his refusal to be confined by limits (*CS,* 398). Taken in its entirety, this dynamic—expressed by Scholem as a young man, attributed by him to the Frankists and by Klossowski to Sade as established scholars—anticipates what Carolyn Dean would write much later of Bataille: that such a man's wholeness or manhood "is paradoxically linked to an experience of transgressing limits rather than of containment within boundaries that demarcate his being." And further: "the moment the self experiences itself as loss . . . is also the moment at which it is constituted as a self."[16]

Pseudonymity functions as the literary equivalent of automutilation and decapitation, and like them, is linked with the abject. Bataille published his novel *W.C.*, for example, under the name Henri Troppmann, the brother of a celebrated criminal decapitated in 1871.[17] If clean and proper texts need be authored by those with clean and proper names, it should come as no surprise that abject texts often find their origins, if not their very possibility, in pseudonymity.[18] Though a mode of self-restriction, pseudonymity opens possibilities unavailable to those with proper names. It is difficult to imagine an unadulterated celebration of shit, for example an abject text on the scale of *Non Olet*, written under anything but a pseudonym. On this count, John Gregory Bourke's work of 1891, *The Scatologic Rites of All Nations*, serves as a useful point of comparison.[19] Bourke could append his proper name only because his explicit disgust and ethnographic practice gave the pretense of a strict separation between subject and abject. By contrast, a pseudonym allows for the fusion of the sentiments of author with narrator, for the pseudonymous author need not speak in his own name. A fascination and overt love for the abject need not, as a consequence, be suppressed.

The absence of proper names figures in the workings of the abject community also. The Sabbatians, we recall, imposed an injunction against the impulse most obviously embodied in the use of proper names, the impulse to transparent self-representation, to appearing as one actually is. Against this impulse, they and their Marrano constituents privileged dissimulation and existential pseudonymity. Caillois, likewise, saw mimetic representation of the self as contrary to the ethos of the religious order. In a 1939 text on the sociology of the cleric, a text that explores (in allegorical form) the role of the intellectual in the popular front, Caillois set down a definition "according to which one cannot call a cleric anyone who speaks in his own name." "A cleric is first and foremost a member of a church," he continued, "and by that fact has given up the right to speak and even to think for himself, the right to say what he thinks."[20]

Non Olet presents an even more interesting case. Here we have a community composed of members whose names—Andrießen, Hinterding,

Pissarski, Popisser, Willfart—already testify to their abjection. They
need not adopt pseudonyms, as do members of most orders and secret
societies, for they enjoy the happy circumstance of names that mean
what they are. As a consequence, additions, alterations, or substitutions—
Popisser der Durchfällige, Drießen der Abortologe, Sentenze der Klug-
scheißer, Pupp der Fahrlässige, and Föttgenhauer der Steißtrommler are
a few Dr. Ritzenfeger considers and rejects—become at best superfluous.[21] Because they index processes of abjection, their names already
indicate the self-loss that would come with the adoption of a pseudonym. They *live* self-loss in a way, perhaps, that Bataille, Feinhals, or
Scholem cannot, because for the Oletarians, self-loss is not a matter of
voluntary self-abasement. Theirs is an existential condition, not an ideology actively pursued. They live, as paradoxical as it may sound, in a
postlapsarian state of grace.

Nor do they pine for a time before the Fall. This resistance to nostalgia has its sharpest articulation in a story recounted by Professor
Schissler, a creation story in which God grants bodily orifices to Adam
and Eve after their expulsion. Though their newfound capacity to abject
may have saved them from their bodily poisons, so the story goes, it
signaled also an end to their hopes for a return to paradise. Forester
Kramarsch responds, however, with hardly a trace of longing for a
prelapsarian state of grace. To be sure, he acknowledges the tragic consequence of their primordial transgression, the guilt that encumbers
man "in this earthly Dasein of his, so full of sorrow." "And yet," he
continues, "we nevertheless have reason enough to rejoice and laugh.
Let us remain for a while with the butt, this intrinsically lively and inexhaustible theme! Do you really believe that we would be gathered here,
that we would be discussing the philosophical problems associated with
the butt, in the event that we had no intestines, no hind-exit? I think
not. Perhaps we would have established a bowling-club, but that is all"
(58). Their names point to a valuation of the abject that diverges sharply
from that of Scholem or Bataille; the Oletarians value abjection not
because it reveals the limits of human experience, but because it reveals
human experience as the most everyday transgression of limits. The Oletarian community has a transgressive quality, but not, as with Scholem
and Bataille, an antinomian or criminal one.

Indeed, crime was for Bataille the sine qua non of the abject community, if not all human groups. In a lecture of February 1938, Bataille
elaborated a theory of power that placed crime at the "center of human
turmoil" since it generates "those sacred things that are of the left and
untouchable." This left-sacred in turn gives rise to "a fearful force," a

sacred of the "right and glorious." Once personified, however, this sacrality of the right stands at risk to the threat of further crime, "for the crime's recurrence is necessary to the intense movement . . . at the center of human groups" (CS, 135). To the confusion elicited by this cycle stand two possible responses, one tendered by tragedy, the other by Christianity. Whereas tragedy privileges identification with the criminal who kills the king, Christianity offers identification with the victim, the slain king. Unto his own day, Bataille argued, the Christian solution had prevailed, even if it came at the price of great hypocrisy. Christian theology, that is, deflects guilt for the sacrifice of God from the priest to the sins of the world. Though the Christian priest may style himself an ascetic "prudently avoiding any sin," he in fact wakes each morning to perform the work of the sinner: "he spills once more the blood of Christ" (CS, 144).

The case of Sabbatai Sevi conflates the two responses. Sevi not only slays himself (as Jew), but then makes his suicide (or apostasy) constitutive of his messianic kingship. His followers must then identify with both criminal and victim, for in Sevi's case, they are one and same. Confronted with his death, they experience it vicariously and in common, and find themselves bound through loss. They can hardly be said to have "fashioned" their community. Theirs hardly conforms to that notion of community elaborated in the contract theory of Hobbes and Locke, wherein individuals decide to commune out of common self-interest. Instead, they find that their community has simply come into being; it has happened as they confronted collectively the death of the other. In this, they better approximate the notion of community more recently theorized by Jean-Luc Nancy and Maurice Blanchot. Both evince deep hostility to any notion of community understood as the product of human intention, as a finished and stable work; both posit the death of the other as that which most powerfully binds.[22] The Sabbatians had to contend not only with that death but with the knowledge that only through that death and faith in the paradox of that death might the redemption come. As a consequence, they faced a profound dilemma: whether or not to join their messiah in the realm of the *kelipot*, whether or not to assist him in his struggle. The more ardent believer—the one dissatisfied with the "moderate Sabbatians" who saw it as the Messiah's fate, but not his own, to engage in acts of "strange holiness"—found himself "increasingly restive." As Scholem described it: "Was he to abandon the Messiah entirely just when the latter was engaged in the most bitter phase of his struggle with the power of evil? If the spark of the redemption had been experienced by all, why should not all do as the Redeemer? How could one refuse to go to his aid? And soon the cry was heard: Let us surrender ourselves as he did! Let us cram the maw of impurity with the power of holiness until it bursts from within" (*RS*, 109). The conversions that followed Sabbatai's apostasy indicate that some did just that. In this, the Sabbatian phenomenon might be likened to Jonestown, cited by Blanchot as one instance, if not the paradigmatic instance, in which "the community may lay itself open to its own communion."[23]

As Blanchot and Nancy have emphasized, Bataille excluded just such a "fusional fulfillment in some collective hypostasis." What counted for him was less a "state of ravishment where one forgets everything (oneself included)" than a sense of insufficiency and an inability to renounce it, "a movement that ruins immanence as well as the usual forms of transcendence."[24] That the Sabbatian phenomenon might be likened to collective suicide, but not equated with it, attains at this point decisive significance. Only on account of that gap might the radical Sabbatians be termed an unavowable community. Not literally dead, the radical Sabbatians nonetheless lived as metaphorical dead, for they chose in a way to live the death of their king. Their penchant for antinomian excess, understood now as a metonymic substitute for the foundational act of apostasy, reenacted that death time and again. Bound not by the collective affirmation of a covenant between God and man, nor purely by its negation, they found themselves implicated instead in an endless dialectic of the two.

Abject Discipline

By now, I hope, we might readily speak of a distinct mode of being-together, theorized or thematized in response to the exigencies posed by a specific moment in European history. Haunted by the specter of fascism, this moment had as one of its defining characteristics the attempt to abject and suppress all traces of unassimilable otherness, an impulse most obviously embodied by the Nazi program of racial cleansing. It should come, therefore, as little surprise that those invested in forms of community opposed to that of the fascists directed their energies toward the question of otherness and the abject as well. For the figures under consideration here, this question found its deepest resonance in the human sciences. All three sought to rehabilitate fields of knowledge and modes of investigation that had been abjected by the human sciences as normatively practiced. Their alternatives—intended either to supersede or supplement their conventional counterparts—posed their most thoroughgoing challenge in the form of an epistemology that took as its foundational problem the status of the abject as an object of knowledge.

A repudiation of the value-neutrality championed by the likes of Max Weber and for some time ascendant in the world of sociology formed the linchpin of their critique. Bataille, for example, decried the propensity of modern man to invest in science his hopes for the future, diagnosing it as one symptom among many indicating the general devirilization of modern life. "Deprived by fear of the need to be a man," modern man had, through his uncritical adulation of science, "renounced the *wholeness*" that remains his due, so long as he seeks "to live out his destiny." Though science should serve man in the pursuit of his destiny, Bataille argued, it had come instead to supplant it. Caillois held out similar hopes, the ambition that their abject academy would "exceed its initial plan, swing from a will for knowledge to a will for power, become the nucleus of a wider conspiracy." He engaged in such research with the "deliberate calculation" that this scholarly body "find a soul" (*CS*, 11, 14–15).

Their critique takes aim, then, less at method than at the moral devastations wrought by a science divorced from human destiny. A version of scientific practice in fact comprised the very possibility for the sort of revolution in everyday life Bataille and the College envisioned. Caillois, for example, insisted that only a peculiar kind of knowledge, that produced by the practice of "sacred sociology," might revivify a left-sacred that had atrophied with the advent of modernity (*CS*, 97). Bataille, meanwhile, argued for a science that would subvert itself. He seemed to favor a scientific version of defeating evil from within. He proposed to "enslave science through the use of weapons borrowed from it, by making itself produce the paralogisms that limit it" (*VE*, 81). He called not for the repudiation of science, nor for a departure or decoupling, but for a descent or immersion into its realm, and for a wild and ultimately self-destructive acceleration of its workings. Paralogism works on this view like the paroxysm induced by Sabbatai's descent into the *kelipot*, as a seizure that signals at once the apotheosis and paralysis of a regime. If, by virtue of his automutilation, acephalic man reigned also as *sur-homme*, we might say that abject discipline, likewise, functioned as a kind of *sur*-science.[25]

The same holds true for Scholem. In one of his most remarkable texts, a letter to the publisher Zalman Schocken, Scholem promised "a candid word" on the motives behind his decision, taken twenty years earlier, to embark on a study of the kabbalah. "In no way did I become a 'Kabbalist' inadvertently," he began. "I knew what I was doing." In the years immediately prior to his decision, years in which he withdrew from the study of mathematics and first donned the philologian's cap, he had been led "as much to the most rationalistic skepticism about [his] fields of study as to intuitive affirmation of mystical theses which walked the fine line between religion and nihilism." In particular, he saw it as his task to overturn several towering figures in the history of Jewish thought—Saadia Gaon, Maimonides, and Hermann Cohen. These had sought, for various reasons, "to construct antitheses to myth and pantheism, to refute them, although they should have concerned themselves with raising them to a higher level."[26]

Like Bataille, Scholem hoped not to revivify mythological thinking, but to engage in a form of science that would perform as myth. In a modern world bereft of myth's haunting ground, he thought, only the "magical mirror of philological criticism," a *wünderlicher Hohlspiegel*, might make visible once again that "mystical totality of the cosmos." Rendered more precisely as "concave mirror," the term *Hohlspiegel* implicitly contests an ideal of disinterested scientific inquiry that seeks a perfect reflection, a faithful duplication, or a mimetic representation of its object, an ideal best expressed by the metaphor of a flat mirror. By contrast, the concave mirror "incorporates" the object, envelops it, works on it, distorts it in consonance with its own design. With his metaphor, Scholem thus endorsed the scientific impulse, but redefined it as a form of magic, and one that held out the possibility for revelation, or for a "true communication from the mountain." Philology, as he conceived it, superseded both science and myth even as it preserved their traces, much like the "sacred sociology" offered up by the College.

Parody functioned as the Oletarian equivalent of the neo-Nietzschean *sur*-science practiced by Scholem and Bataille. If *sur*-science aims to replace its normative counterpart, however, the Oletarian parody of science retains its force only as long as its object survives more or less intact. Parody has a parasitic relation to its object. It depends on its object for its continued sustenance, and can replace it only at the cost of its own demise. The Oletarian version is perhaps best illustrated in the proposal of Dr. Niedergesäss to establish a university for the further development of their researches. This *Universitas litterarum scatologicarum*, as Dr. Ritzenfeger called it, was to consist of four faculties (like any other German university). The medical faculty, for instance, was to house an Institute for Pathological Physiology, where students would master the diagnosis and treatment of maladies like pathological flatulence, pneumatosis, and psychosomatic illnesses like *Vapeurs als*

292 ᧞ Benjamin Lazier

Modekrankheit, or flatulence as fad. The seminar in method and didactics was to be devoted to intensive study in the canonical works of *Olet: De flatibus* by Hippocrates, *De odore* by Plinius, the *De modo cacandi* by Rabelais. The philosophical faculty aspired to a similar mastery of its field, and encompassed the great thinkers from the time of the pre-Socratics through to Henri Bergson and Nicolai Hartmann. Its more practical offerings included a three-tiered course on the *Ars honeste farzandi in societate*, or the art of farting politely in public, divided into beginner's exercises, exercises in style (for advanced students), and a daily practicum. With the assent of the others, Dr. Niedergesäss insisted that their university would for future generations "attain a worldwide importance." "It stands beyond doubt," he continued, "that our researches are in a position to transform the entire world" (162).

But the Oletarians did not stop there; they pushed on to the end in their quest for an exhaustive treatment of the subject. It included, first, an extensive discussion on how best to evaluate the fart. Professor Kahrenforz, for example, took issue with those who would advocate measuring wind speed, *Windstärke*, and proposed instead to measure by volume or *Tonstärke*. Kahrenforz illustrated his thesis with the story of a certain Bernardo, a middling Renaissance artist whose masterfart, or *Meisterfurz*, unleashed in the center of cinquecento Florence, was definitively registered in San Miniato, a full three kilometers away (38–39). They debated passionately over the source of the first fart in historical writing: "Not for nothing is Herodotus known as the father of history," claimed Professor Andriessen, "for with him begins also the history of the fart." Professor Schissler countered, however, with the observation that Homer, not Herodotus, had first inserted the fart into world literature. Both, however, seemed content with the reservation that they spoke only of the first recorded fart, "and not the first fart over all. For the fart has been since the very beginning and is older than mankind itself" (923–24). They compiled a bibliography devoted exclusively to French-language treatises on the fart, including such favorites as *Éloge du Pet*, a revolutionary tract penned *An VII de la Liberté*. All this came to a head in a total elaboration of the fart as a platonic idea, or in what Professor Kahrenforz called a *Gesamtbetrachtung des Furzes in der platonischen Idee*. He insisted it thematize no less than the following: the fart as natural occurrence, as declaration of war in ancient times, and as a means of commerce with paupers; the fart in its import for those hard of hearing, in its relation to the cosmos, in medicine, in hysteria, in etymology, in the mores of all peoples, in the plastic and rhetorical arts, in music, politics, history, and the anecdote; the fart as a universal language; and last but certainly not least, the fart and the Church fathers (102).

But what are the implications of approaching the fart in this way? What does it presume about the status of the fart, or of the abject more generally, as an object of knowledge? To treat of the abject as a platonic idea means first to distinguish between any physical instantiation of the abject—a pile of crap, or a puddle of vomit—and the immutable, spaceless, immaterial Form of which it is but an imperfect replica. The distinction presupposes an epistemological correlate. The Oletarians distinguish, that is, between physical abjects—which might be known through the senses but cannot be the object of true knowledge precisely on that account—and their Form. This latter Abject might be known by the elect, but as a Form it resists human appropriation, helps to ensure worldly harmony, and provides a template by which to define and classify its lesser copies. To cast the Oletarian approach to the abject as platonic makes intelligible a good deal of what might otherwise be dismissed as fantasy. Take, for example, their insistence on the timelessness of the fart. In their estimation, as we have seen, the fart has simply always been, independent of human cognition, anterior to humankind altogether. In this instance they seem to speak less of the fart than they do of its form, the Fart. It also makes intelligible the delight taken in the visual scrutiny of their excrement. Such inspection provides "a not inconsiderable aesthetic pleasure," as Dr. Ritzenfeger put it, because only in so doing might the metaphysicians of stink advance upon the idea of Olet. It should come, then, as little surprise that Ritzenfeger would register dismay with a newer line of toilets unequipped with the viewing platform so critical to his philosophical pursuits. If the contemplation of the Forms, prompted by the visual encounter with their copies, defines the good life for the platonist philosopher, then the pursuit of the Abject, inspired by a similar engagement with actual abjects, must be said to define the Oletarian equivalent.

The distinction between abject and Abject raises questions that lead us back to Bataille. As Form, the Abject lacks that gross, unsublatable excess sometimes attributed to its lesser cousin. On the other hand, the distinction can stress the converse: any actual abject, material to its core, resists every effort to idealize it. Jacques Derrida, for example, once discerned precisely this quality in vomit.[27] To be sure, vomit might inspire the studied contemplation of Vomit, but could never be confused or mistaken for it. Though hardly a platonist, Bataille came to think of the abject in a way that replicated (even as it inverted) the Oletarian distinction. He elaborated a theory of "base matter" that preserved the dualism, but shifted its orientation: it indexed not the good, but evil (*VE*, 47–51).

Bataille's notion of "base matter" had its ground in his name for abject discipline: heterology. Heterology presupposed the incommensurability of the abject, its resistance to cognition and sublation. As Denis Hollier has put it, heterology styled itself as the "theory of that which theory expels" (*CS*, xix). Elsewhere Bataille defined heterology more specifically as "the science of what is completely other" (*VE*, 102). As such, heterology might approach its object (or abject) only via a series of statements about what it is not. Heterology dare not produce an idea *of* the abject, for that would defeat its purpose, but it might well develop second-order ideas *about* the abject, about the way in which an unknowable abject works (or unworks) in a broader universe of meaning. Bataille opposed those who claimed to assimilate base matter in the name of productivity, just as he and Caillois felt uneasy about the ease with which lawful regimes co-opted the antinomian excess of festival. He hoped to disrupt through the practice of heterology those economies predicated on a seamless circulation of the abject, those economies for whom excretion was understood as "simply a middle term between two appropriations" (*VE*, 99). Bataille wished to put the abject to use, but he wanted to do so in a way that preserved and harnessed its negativity for the purposes of cultural and political critique.

Bataille's position found a pointed repudiation in the notion, championed by the Oletarians, of a worldwide *Exkrementbilanz*. Like Bataille, the Order of Kakasophs denigrated those economies based on the international flow of cash or gold or other arbitrary currencies. In their stead, and against Bataille, they held up an economic theory based on the import and export of shit. For as Ritzenfeger insisted, only this latter resource carries with it the true measure of a nation's productivity. An account of the rise of Rome offered historical confirmation. As the Roman empire incorporated ever greater amounts of land, so the story goes, it gorged itself on the granaries of the nations within its domain. "Rome became richer and richer" as all "this nourishment hauled in from foreign lands fertilized the Italian earth in the form of excrement." The cultural brilliance of the Renaissance, Ritzenfeger argued, had the conditions of its possibility not least in the enrichment of the Roman earth twelve centuries before. With the collective assent of the Oletarians, Ritzenfeger drew the logical conclusion: "We should tear down our toll-booths and open our borders. We should allow everything that is edible to stream unchecked into our land." Germany would thereby enrich itself, and could expect to reap a physical and spiritual harvest on par with the Renaissance (1035). Whereas Bataille sought to reserve an autonomy for excretion, the Oletarians understood it as one phase in a holistic process of which it was always a subordinate part. They valued excrement not for its capacity to disrupt meaning but for its fecundity. Just as excrement posed for them little threat of toxicity, so, too, did the abject as an object of knowledge pose little threat of hermeneutic disruption. Shit, after all, lacked for the Oletarians any quality to distinguish it epistemologically from other objects. That their distinction between abject and Abject preserved base matter as in fact base did so not at the expense of normative science, but precisely in its name.

If fecal matter stood apart for Bataille in its otherness, it stood apart also in its sacrality. For heterology, Bataille proposed the term *agiology* as a surrogate, with the reservation that "one would have to catch the double meaning of *agio* (analogous to the double meaning of *sacer*), *soiled* as well as *holy*." "But it is above all the term *scatology*," Bataille continued, "that retains in the present circumstances . . . an incontestable expressive value as the doublet of an abstract term such as *heterology*." Scatology performs this semantic work only insofar as it points to the holiness of the base. As an object of knowledge, then, God and the abject pose for Bataille similar hermeneutic problems. Both resist cognition; both get set up as objects of knowledge—categorized, classified, understood—at the expense of how they *work* to produce or disrupt meaning (what they *are* remains unknowable). Such thinking, Bataille insisted, ought to come as no shock to those "familiar with the problems posed by the history of religions," for the cadaver—here a metonymic substitute for the abject generally—"is not much more repugnant than shit, and the specter that projects its horror is sacred even in the eyes of modern theologians" (*VE,* 102). In Bataille's conception, then, heterology functioned as negative theology. The two were isomorphic, insofar as "the specific character of fecal matter or of the specter can only be the object of a series of negations" (*VE,* 98). Together, the sacrality and filth Bataille attributed to the abject led him to characterize it as an incommensurable alterity, a difference that resists circulation and sublation. Matter, he insisted, can in fact "only be defined as the *nonlogical difference* that represents in relation to the *economy* of the universe what *crime* represents in relation to the law" (*VE,* 129).

Abject discipline, then, functioned for Bataille as antinomian discipline. This equation surfaced in Scholem's work as well, even if Scholem drew from it adversarial conclusions. Toward the beginning of his

investigation into the Sabbatian phenomenon, Scholem openly acknowledged the transferential sympathies that linked him to his object of
study. Without fail, he claimed, his predecessors willfully misunderstood
Sabbatianism, preferring instead to suppress the memory of its anarchic
messianism and desire for total liberation. They did so because such
irrational, particularist, and lawless exuberance posed a grave threat to
their own hopes for a liberal, assimilationist solution to the problem of
Jewish emancipation. Or to redescribe this impulse in the lexicon of
the abject: the exponents of normative Jewish historiography sought to
make themselves—and by extension, the Jewish community—palatable,
digestible, clean, and proper by abjecting and suppressing the filth in its
past. Rid of toxin, become rational, they might then more easily assimilate into a "universalist" German social body understood in similarly
rationalist terms. As a result of this impulse, Scholem found himself confronted with a strict limit, situated "before a blank wall, not only of
misunderstanding, but often of an actual refusal to understand" (RS,
78). Implicitly, then, Scholem linked the failure to appreciate the Sabbatian phenomenon to the erection of unporous boundaries—a blank
wall—between subject and object. The *Mauerrenner*, it seems, must
perform his work once again, this time not merely as a Zionist intent
on effacing the traces of his exilic past, but as a philologist and historian determined to blur those boundaries between subject and abject
artificially erected by his predecessors. Scholem declared himself ready
to take up this mantle, to uncover "beneath the surface of lawlessness,
antinomianism, and catastrophic negation" the "powerful constructive
impulses at work" (RS, 84). He wished not only to recover the abject,
but to do so in a way that Bataille would have found anathema.

The metaphor of the wall figured in Scholem's letter to Schocken
also. There he wrote of the obstacles that hindered an appreciation of
the kabbalah's true historical role, of a "realm of associations which
had to touch our own most human experiences." Scholem at first felt
inclined to describe that lack of access in terms of a missing key, lost by
those Jewish scholars operating with "the obtuse standard of Enlightenment." But he went on to revise his initial reaction: "perhaps it wasn't
so much the key that was missing, but courage: courage to venture
out into an abyss, which one day could end up in us ourselves, courage
also to penetrate through the symbolic plane and through the wall of
history." In terms reminiscent of Bataille, Scholem described a process
of transgressing limits that threatened, even presupposed, the risk of
self-loss, the risk that the space once filled by a self would come instead
to be emptied. This emptiness, it is crucial to note, takes place not

within the boundaries demarcated by a solitary self, but as an abyss "in us ourselves." Scholem's formulation moves subtly—and against grammatical convention—from the solitary transgressor to the abyssal community. Wittingly or not, Scholem thus implied what Bataille openly asserted: a logic that links transgression, self-loss, and a distinct form of community. In Scholem's case, as in Bataille's, this logic played itself out in the human sciences. Failure to fulfill the task he had set for himself, to penetrate "the misty wall of history," Scholem likened to suffering *den Tod in der Professur*, death in the professor's chair. This death he likened further to self-sacrifice. "The necessity of historical criticism and critical history cannot be replaced by anything else," Scholem continued, even if such pursuits "demand a sacrificial victim."[28] The "sacred sociologist" or the philologian cum kabbalist must first incur the risk, but both Scholem and Bataille imagined this gesture as one that would inaugurate new forms of community well beyond the confines of the academy, if not a new age altogether.

Abject Legacies

It is this optimism that most distinguishes the sensibilities of Scholem, Bataille, and the Oletarians from the discourse of the abject in today's academy. Their expectations set them off most sharply, of course, from the denigration of the abject, cast as a symptom either of regressive escapism or of bourgeois self-loathing. Even when the abject earns a more positive valuation in contemporary discussions, its accolades come with heavy caveats. Theorists like Kristeva might appreciate the heady style of an abject hero like Céline, but feel compelled nevertheless to acknowledge the toxicity of his discourse. Others, preeminently those on the Foucauldian left, may invoke the abject in the service of resistance, but with at best guarded hopes for success. By contrast, Scholem, Bataille, and Feinhals all discerned in the abject something well worth attending to, whether a vital force suppressed from Jewish historical consciousness, an unknowable center of energy that might wreak havoc with academic discipline and invigorate a society gone flaccid, or a legitimate object of inquiry too long ignored by the human sciences.

They also discovered in the abject a repressed truth about what it means to be human. In different ways, they each declared that at base, we are base, that the boundaries of our selves are themselves porous, that a community worth living comes not at the expense of our abject condition but on account of it—even as they drew from these insights pointedly dissimilar conclusions. For Scholem, they underwrote an attempt to harness the darker, subterranean powers coursing through Jewish history. For Bataille and the College they sanctioned a similar effort, calculated not so much to channel the base and anarchic impulses of human being as to unleash them. For Feinhals, they authorized a crusade at once farcical and serious, whose universalist ethos took inspiration from the filth common to us all. Their efforts should not be dismissed as dangerous fantasy or frivolous perversion, tempting as that may be given the more chastened times in which we live. They deserve, rather, to be understood as legitimate—if occasionally outrageous— attempts to come to terms with the historical challenge to community and selfhood posed by the rise of European fascism.

This *historical* component of their legacy has not yet attained the recognition it deserves. A number of reasons, in fact, make plausible an interpretation that finds in the discourse uniting them origins of notions now of great moment in postmodernist and poststructuralist thought. For one, we find instantiated the beginnings of what has come to be known as an "unworkable" or "unavowable" community. Most genealogies cast the thought of Nancy and Blanchot on community as meditations inspired largely by the writings of one man, Georges Bataille. Though this emplotment is in essence correct, it remains insufficient. The story of the abject academies offers a supplementary perspective. It finds the origins of the unavowable or unworkable community not merely in the extension of one person's thought (Bataille's); rather, it discerns them in a much broader cultural mood, marked by a formal coherence at times startling in its consistency. From this perspective, poststructuralist work on community has its origins in an identifiable discursive response to a historical precipitate, the rise of fascism in Europe. That this precipitate managed to cast together figures otherwise historically and temperamentally opposed, that it compelled thinkers as diverse as Bataille and Popisser, Caillois and Kramarsch, Leiris and Lekarsch, Scholem, Schissler, Ritzenfeger, and Willfart to speak an identifiable, if internally fractured, language—all this only testifies to its power. If poststructuralism is understood historically as a rarefied philosophical response to fascism and its attendant horrors, as a wide-ranging recuperative move, then the discourse of the abject examined here must be seen to have set, in part, its foundational terms.

The abject academies endure not only in recent thinking on the notion of community, but in the questions they raise about disciplinarity and transgression as well. On the one hand, these questions thematize transgression between and among disciplines. Most notably, the College and the Oletarians posed a challenge to the institutional frame within which academic investigation might be conducted. But perhaps more importantly, they challenged normative science by explicitly thematizing transgression as a mode of scientific practice. Scholem, for example, transposed into the practice of philology an antinomian ethos once confined to the religious sphere. Bataille and the College, meanwhile, hoped to revivify, in the practice of heterology, the kinds of energies once flowing through gnostic dualism or primitive festival. Only the Oletarians refused to engage in an antinomian practice; their repudiation of normative science, however, manifested itself no less in their parody of method and in their very field of inquiry.

Despite their favorable disposition toward transgression, the abject academies tell us something important about its limits as well. It is a basic truth that the antinomian, even as he transgresses the law, finds in the law the conditions of his possibility. Even the most dedicated transgressor cannot cross boundaries where none are to be found. For this reason, perhaps, the abject academies shied from a total fusion with the abject, or in psychoanalytic terms, from a language of total desublimation, and instead chose to identify human being and being-together with the *process* of abjection. They thought of being and community as an incessant crossing of limits, whether those limits were to be found at the margins of human experience, or, in the case of the Oletarians, in the most quotidian of practices. They did not erase boundaries so much as cross them; they did not dissolve limits so much as render them porous. From this perspective, transgression inevitably has about it a conservative moment, for it dialectically preserves the law even as it defies it, notwithstanding the blithe talk of revolution from its more ardent—and wishful—proponents. For similar reasons, the story of these abject academies will perhaps provide a frame for more recent talk of transgression between disciplines. They may well comprise the historical origins of such a discourse, abject origins that have since been suppressed or forgotten, consigned to the outhouse, banished from sight.

Notes

Thanks to David Biale, Tony Bliss, Carla Hesse, Martin Jay, Thomas Laqueur, Samuel Moyn, Jonathan Sheehan, and Randolf Starn for their suggestions, and, for their enthusiasm and advice, to my colleagues in the Olet Studies Working Group: William A. Cohen, Ryan Johnson, Max Leva, Jan Plamper, Norman Sissman, and Gillian Weiss.

 1. *Fladen* (cowpie), etc.

 2. *Non Olet, oder die heiteren Tischgespräche des Collofino über den Orbis Cacatus nebst den neuesten erkenntnistheoretischen Betrachtungen über das*

Leben in seiner phantastischen Wirklichkeit erzählt von ihm selbst. ORBIS CACA-
TUS, *das ißt Umständlicher Bericht über* DIE BESCHISSENE WELT *mit schönen
Kupfern geziert, für die Gebildeten aller Stände wie auch für den Gebrauch in
Familien hergerichtet, aus heiteren Tischgesprächen mit Fleiß gesammelt und
erstmals in solchem Umfang ans Licht gestellt von* COLLOFINO *Mitglied der
Neuen Fruchtbringenden Gesellschaft.* [It does not stink, or the lively conversations of Collofino on the Orbis Cacatus alongside the newest epistemic-
theoretical observations on life in its fantastic reality as told by him himself.
ORBIS CACATUS, that is, a comprehensive report on THE SHIT-UPON WORLD,
adorned with beautiful engravings, suitable for the educated of all classes of
society as for use in the family, industriously gathered from lively conversations
and brought to light for the first time to such an extent by COLLOFINO, member of the New Fruitbringing Society] (Köln: Privatdruck, 1939). Hereafter cited
in the text. All translations, unless otherwise noted, are by the author.

3. "Shit whither you wish!"; "I fart, therefore I am."

4. *Die Geschichten des Collofino* (Köln: Privatdruck, 1918).

5. Most prominently, Michael Bernstein, *Bitter Carnival: Ressentiment and
the Abject Hero* (Princeton, NJ: Princeton University Press, 1992).

6. Gershom Scholem, "*Mitzvah ha-ba'ah ba-avera,*" *Knesset* 2 (1936/37):
347–92, translated in *The Messianic Idea in Judaism and Other Essays on Jewish Spirituality* (New York: Schocken, 1955), hereafter abbreviated *RS*.

7. Michel Leiris, "The Sacred in Everyday Life," in Denis Hollier, ed., *The
College of Sociology (1937–1939)*, trans. Betsy Wing (Minneapolis: University
of Minnesota Press, 1988), 31. Hereafter abbreviated *CS*.

8. Maurice Blanchot, *The Unavowable Community*, trans. Pierre Joris
(Barrytown, NY: Station Hill Press, 1988), 4.

9. Steven M. Wasserstrom, "Defeating Evil from Within," *Journal of Jewish Thought and Philosophy* 6 (1997): 44–48.

10. Julia Kristeva, *Powers of Horror: An Essay on Abjection*, trans. Leon S.
Roudiez (New York: Columbia University Press, 1982), 174.

11. Bernstein, *Bitter Carnival*, 122.

12. On Bataille, see Allan Stoekl, *Agonies of the Intellectual: Commitment,
Subjectivity, and the Performative in the Twentieth-Century French Tradition*
(Lincoln: University of Nebraska Press, 1992), 268. On Scholem, see Benjamin
Lazier, "Writing the *Judenzarathustra*: Gershom Scholem's Response to Moder-
nity, 1913–1917," *New German Critique* 85 (2002): 33–67.

13. Carolyn J. Dean, *The Self and Its Pleasures: Bataille, Lacan, and the History of the Decentered Subject* (Ithaca, NY: Cornell University Press, 1992),
201–45; Stoekl, *Agonies*, chapter 10; Stoekl, *Politics, Writing, Mutilation* (Minneapolis: University of Minnesota Press, 1985).

14. Georges Bataille, *Visions of Excess: Selected Writings, 1927–1939*, ed.
and trans. Allan Stoekl (Minneapolis: University of Minnesota Press, 1985), 67.
Hereafter abbreviated *VE*.

15. Lazier, "Writing the *Judenzarathustra*," 60.

16. Dean, *The Self and Its Pleasures,* 244–45.

17. Ibid., 232.

18. Denis Hollier, *Against Architecture* (Cambridge, MA: MIT Press, 1989), 154.

19. John Gregory Bourke, *Scatologic Rites of All Nations. A Dissertation upon the Employment of Excrementitious Remedial Agents in Religion, Therapeutics, Divination, Witchcraft, Love-Philters, etc., in all Parts of the Globe. Based upon Original Notes and Personal Observation, and upon Compilation from Over One Thousand Authorities. Not for General Perusal.* (Washington, DC: W. H. Lowdermilk, 1891). Bourke's work appeared in a German translation, *Der Unrat in Sitte, Brauch, Glauben und Gewohnheitrecht der Völker* (Leipzig: Ethnologischer Verlag, 1913), graced with a signed photo of the intrepid proktosoph and with a foreword by Sigmund Freud.

20. Cited in Denis Hollier, "Mimesis and Castration, 1937," *October* 31 (Winter 1984): 10.

21. Popisser der Durchfällige (Butpisser the Diarrheac), Drießen der Abortologe (Drizzler the Water Closetologist), Pupp der Fahrlässige (Fart the Windletter), etc.

22. See Nancy, *The Inoperative Community,* trans. Peter Connor, Lisa Garbus, Michael Holland, and Simona Sawhney (Minneapolis: University of Minnesota Press, 1991), and Blanchot's "response," *The Unavowable Community.*

23. Blanchot, *Unavowable Community,* 7.

24. Ibid.

25. This formulation resonates also with *surfascisme,* a term that expressed both Bataille's attraction to the fascist project and his repudiation of it.

26. David Biale, *Gershom Scholem* (Cambridge, MA: Harvard University Press, 1982), 31–32. Translations from this book are my own.

27. Martin Jay, *Cultural Semantics* (Amherst: University of Massachusetts Press, 1998), 148.

28. Biale, *Gershom Scholem,* 74–76.

Contributors

David S. Barnes is associate professor in the Department of the History and Sociology of Science at the University of Pennsylvania. He is author of *The Making of a Social Disease: Tuberculosis in Nineteenth-Century France* and is writing a book about germs and disgust in late-nineteenth-century public health.

Neil Blackadder is author of *Performing Opposition: Modern Theater and the Scandalized Audience.* He is associate professor of theater at Knox College, where he teaches dramatic literature and dramaturgy and directs student productions. His work has appeared in *New Theatre Quarterly, Theatre History Studies,* and *American Theatre.*

Joseph Bristow is professor of English at the University of California, Los Angeles. He has recently edited *The Cambridge Companion to Victorian Poetry, Wilde Writings: Contextual Conditions,* and the Oxford English Texts edition of Oscar Wilde's *The Picture of Dorian Gray.* He is completing a book-length study of sexual desire in Victorian poetry.

Joseph W. Childers teaches English at the University of California, Riverside. He is author of *Novel Possibilities: Fiction and the Formation of Early Victorian Culture.* He is completing a study on the presence of the ethnic other in England in the nineteenth century.

Eileen Cleere is assistant professor of English at Southwestern University and is author of *Avuncularism: Capitalism, Patriarchy, and Nineteenth-Century English Culture*. Her essays on Victorian literature and culture have appeared in *Novel, Genders,* and *Representations*. She is working on a book about Victorian art and sanitation reform.

William A. Cohen is associate professor of English at the University of Maryland. He is author of *Sex Scandal: The Private Parts of Victorian Fiction*, and his essays have appeared in *Nineteenth-Century Literature, ELH,* and *Novel*.

Natalka Freeland is assistant professor of English at the University of California, Irvine. She has published on Elizabeth Gaskell, Wilkie Collins, Ann Radcliffe, and Edgar Allan Poe, and is completing a book on rubbish, value, and progress in the Victorian novel.

Pamela K. Gilbert is associate professor of English at the University of Florida and editor of the series Studies in the Long Nineteenth Century. She is author of *Disease, Desire, and the Body in Victorian Women's Popular Novels* and *Mapping the Victorian Social Body*. She is editor of *Imagined Londons* and coeditor (with Marlene Tromp and Aeron Haynie) of *Beyond Sensation: Mary Elizabeth Braddon in Context*. Her work has appeared in *Nineteenth-Century Studies, Women and Performance, English,* and *LIT: Literature/Interpretation/Theory*.

Christopher Hamlin is professor in the Department of History and the Program in the History and Philosophy of Science at the University of Notre Dame and honorary professor of Public Health and Policy at the London School of Hygiene and Tropical Medicine. He is author of *A Science of Impurity* and *Public Health and Social Justice in the Age of Chadwick,* and coauthor (with Philip T. Shepard) of *Deep Disagreement in U.S. Agriculture: Making Sense of Policy Conflict*. His current work concerns the prehistory of ecology and environmentalism, examining how natural processes, from population stability to decomposition, were understood within the framework of Anglican natural theology.

Ryan Johnson is completing a Ph.D. in the Department of English at Stanford University, where his dissertation examined the literary and cultural effects of nineteenth-century British philology. He has served as general editor of the *Stanford Humanities Review*.

William Kupinse is assistant professor of English at the University of Puget Sound. He has published essays on waste in the work of H. G. Wells and trash fiction in James Joyce. He is working on a book tentatively titled *The Remains of Empire: Waste, Nation, and Modernism.*

Benjamin Lazier teaches modern European intellectual history at the University of Chicago. He is working on a book called *Redemption through Sin: Judaism and Heresy in Interwar Europe,* which addresses the problem of secularization in twentieth-century philosophy and theology.

David L. Pike is associate professor of literature and film at American University. He is author of *Passage through Hell: Modernist Descents, Medieval Underworlds* and *Subterranean Cities: Subways, Cemeteries, Sewers, and the Culture of Paris and London* and is coeditor of the *Longman Anthology of World Literature.* He has published widely on medieval literature and on nineteenth- and twentieth-century urban literature and film.

David Trotter is King Edward VII Professor of English Literature at the University of Cambridge. His most recent books are *Cooking with Mud: The Idea of Mess in Nineteenth-Century Art and Literature* and *Paranoid Modernism: Literary Experiment, Psychosis, and the Professionalization of English Society.*

Index

Lightning Source UK Ltd.
Milton Keynes UK
UKHW020252260221
379369UK00009B/248